COMPLETE GUIDE TO
FLORIDA WILDFLOWERS

COMPLETE GUIDE TO
FLORIDA
WILDFLOWERS

Over 600 Wildflowers of the Sunshine State including
National Parks, Forests, Preserves, and More than 160 State Parks

ROGER L. HAMMER

GUILFORD, CONNECTICUT
HELENA, MONTANA

FALCONGUIDES®

An imprint of Globe Pequot
Falcon, FalconGuides, and Make Adventure Your Story are registered trademarks of Rowman & Littlefield.

Distributed by NATIONAL BOOK NETWORK

Copyright © 2018 Rowman & Littlefield

Map © Rowman & Littlefield
All interior photographs by Roger L. Hammer unless otherwise noted

British Library Cataloguing-in-Publication Information available

Library of Congress Cataloging in Publication Data available
ISBN 978-1-4930-3093-4 (paperback)
ISBN 978-1-4930-3094-1 (e-book)

∞™ The paper used in this publication meets the minimum requirements of American National Standard for Information Sciences—Permanence of Paper for Printed Library Materials, ANSI/NISO Z39.48-1992.

Printed in the United States of America

The author and Globe Pequot assume no liability for accidents happening to, or injuries sustained by, readers who engage in the activities described in this book. Neither the author nor the publisher in any way endorses the consumption or other uses of wild plants that are mentioned in this book, and they assume no liability for personal accident, illness, or death related to these activities

FOR THE WILD AND WONDERFUL
FLORIDA I KNEW AS A CHILD,
AND TO MY WIFE, MICHELLE.
YOU ARE MY WILD FLOWER.

The Tropic of Cracker has no boundaries. In Florida it simply occurs, as unbidden as sand-spurs or wildflowers, rooting in the minds of Floridians who have links to their past and kinship to their native heritage. Without forgetting practicality, it lifts spirits and fires imaginations.

Wildflowers splashing a simple trail of color across a drab field can induce it. Individual sensitivities determine it. Whatever brings to the mind a confirming identification with native Florida, whatever reassures that there can be natural beauty and treasured culture among common folk and in common places can conjure up the Tropic of Cracker.

—Al Burt, *The Tropic of Cracker*, 1999

CONTENTS

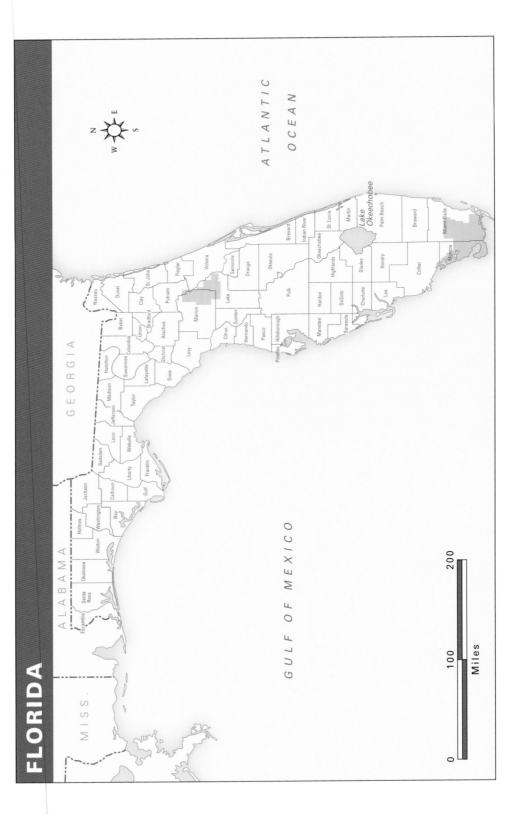

ACKNOWLEDGMENTS

Delving into a project of this magnitude involved knowing exceptional people willing to give of themselves more than I should ever deserve. Most of all, it took the heartening support of my wife, Michelle, and her father, Ed Briois, who tended to our menagerie of pets and kept birdseed and peanuts out for the wild birds and squirrels in my absence.

Long days in the field, often solo, searching for common and rare wildflowers in every conceivable habitat, combined with lonely nights in Florida's small-town motels, or sleeping in my truck, are only part of what it took to complete this undertaking.

Among the extra-special people who went far beyond the call of duty to help locate wildflowers in the panhandle was Virginia Craig of Tallahassee, who offered lists of plants and their blooming seasons, plus provided spirited companionship in the field along with our friend, Floyd Griffith. Virginia and Floyd won't quit looking for wildflowers until it gets too dark to see, and the many days spent with them, often joined by Bill and Marcia Boothe and the esteemed Loran Anderson, were just plain fun. I also benefited from the friendship of Billy Bailey at Florida Caverns State Park, who knows where to find rare plants in the park better than anyone. Plus, many wildflowers in Central Florida would have been impossible to find without the cherished companionship of my good friend Kris DeLaney from Avon Park.

Those who deserve much more than just an honorable mention include Julie Applegate, Adam Arendell, Wilson Baker, Donna Bollenbach, Keith Bradley, Edwin Bridges, James Cheak, Brandon Corbet, Alan Cressler, Scott Davis, Shirley Denton, Eleanor Dietrich, Jim Draper, Chris Evans, Donna Andersen Glann-Smyth, David Hall, John Hays, Jake Heaton, Craig Huegel, Jake Ingram, Michael Jenkins, Pete Johnson, Susan Kolterman, Liz Langston, Carol Lippincott, Chuck McCartney, Travis and Karen MacClendon, Wayne Matchett, Wendy Mazuk, Richard Moyroud, Gil Nelson, Guy Nesom, Jeff Norcini, Mike Owen, Lisa Roberts, Tom and Helen Roth, Annie Schmidt, Michael Stanfield, Sally Steinauer, Walter Taylor, Alan Weakley, George Wilder, Wally Wilder, Chuck Wilson, and Daniel Young.

Infinite thanks also go to Richard Wunderlin, Bruce Hansen, and Alan Franck, all from the University of South Florida, for answering my countless e-mails regarding obscure botanical name derivations and supplying redacted herbarium label data to help locate critically imperiled wildflowers.

I also felt the spiritual presence of my mother, Martha (1924–2014), who always let me run free in the outdoors when I was a youngster. Thanks, Mom.

Lastly, this guide would not be in your hands without the talented staff who create FalconGuides. They deserve a standing ovation.

INTRODUCTION

My older brother, Russell, and I enjoyed an idyllic childhood growing up in a beach-front home in 1950s and 1960s Cocoa Beach, Florida. In those days, coastal dune plants stretched uninterrupted as far as one could see, and there were many days when not a single human footprint on miles of beach sand could be seen except ours. Hardy dune wild-flowers were abundant, as were gopher tortoises, six-lined racerunners, and beach crabs. Shorebirds galore graced the beach, while mullet by the millions migrated through the surf, providing a bounty of food for bottlenose dolphins, predatory fish, and brown pelicans. It was wild Florida at its best.

Remnants of wild, natural Florida still exist within our state parks, national parks and preserves, state and federal conservation areas, and sanctuaries managed by organizations like National Audubon Society and The Nature Conservancy. Then there are city, county, and private natural areas that play a vital role in connecting larger preserves with natural corridors, providing places of refuge for native plants and wildlife, and offering rest stops for migrating birds to refuel on their way to and from their nesting grounds.

Today there are turnpikes and airliners bringing tens of millions of tourists to the Sunshine State each year. Many come for the fantasyland of Walt Disney World or to sunbathe on Florida's world-famous beaches. Others come for the exemplary inshore and offshore sportfishing, or to hop aboard a cruise ship for a Caribbean vacation. Florida's current population is a whopping 20 million, and an estimated 1,000 people a day move to the Sunshine State to find their place in the sun, placing mounting pressure on Flori-da's natural areas.

If you desire a future where Florida still offers wild natural beauty, then please help support Florida's national, state, and regional parks. They are all that is left.

Some comforting news is that Old Florida can be more a state of mind than a place, and remnants of its charm in the form of wildflowers are still there to be discovered. I still love finding them and hope you will too, because it is my sincere hope that this wildflower guide helps rejuvenate your soul and reconnects you with nature. It is something worth sharing.

How to Use This Guide

According to the *Florida Plant Atlas* there are currently 3,285 native plants recorded in Florida, including 242 Florida endemics that are found nowhere else on Earth, represent-ing 7.3 percent of the total native flora. Of these, 49 Florida native plants are now on the federal endangered list, 11 are on the federal threatened list, 445 are state-listed endangered species, and 115 are state-listed threatened species. They are the collateral damage caused by rampant development, agribusiness, and phosphate strip mines; habitat degradation from improper management; and invasive exotic plants and animals, including destructive feral hogs.

This guide features 686 native wildflowers, including 101 Florida endemics, representing 103 plant families. Due to space limitations, naturalized exotics were excluded in order to showcase Florida's native wildflowers. Woody shrubs were also limited in favor of herbaceous species because Florida is rich in herbaceous wildflowers, and they are what most people envision when they hear the word "wildflower." Many species are so common they can be seen along roadsides, while others require considerable effort to track down. Still others are so rare that to find them takes plain luck, pure coincidence, much diligence, or the help of those who know their whereabouts. If you encounter a rare species, cherish the moment—future generations may not have the same opportunity.

Like other wildflower FalconGuides, this book is arranged in six color groups based on the most prominent color of the flower, or inflorescence. Within these color groups the plants are first arranged alphabetically by the botanical name of the plant family, followed by the genus, species, and sometimes subspecies or variety. Many Florida wildflowers range into Canada, the neotropics, or even Africa and Asia, so common names can change from one region to the next, or from one language to another. Botanical names may also change on occasion, but synonyms are provided if another name has been in recent use.

In this guide, the range for each species includes only Florida, and it is noted if a species is endemic to the state and found nowhere else. It is not always possible to include leaves in flower photographs, so a brief description of the plant, leaf shape, and size is provided. The etymology of the botanical name is offered for each species, along with such facts as edibility, medicinal uses, poisonous aspects, pollinators, uses in home gardens to attract birds or butterflies, or people associated with the plant.

Habitats

Florida habitats vary greatly, and changes in elevation by only a few inches can not only determine the habitat type but also the types of wildflowers you will find. There are also microhabitats within specific habitats, such as solution holes in tropical hardwood hammocks, depression marshes and bogs surrounded by pine flatwoods, seepage slopes, and deep sloughs inside forested swamps. The habitats mentioned in this guide are, in a very broad sense, the habitat types one would expect to encounter in Florida's parks and preserves.

Upland Deciduous Hardwood Forests, Bottomland Forests, and River Forests

These temperate forests are composed of evergreen and deciduous hardwoods or a mix of hardwoods and cypress. They may be dry (xeric), moist (mesic), or even flooded (hydric), so the plant species that make up these forests are extremely diverse. Some of Florida's prettiest rivers flow through these forests, including the fabled Suwannee River.

River Forest

Pine Flatwoods and High Pine

Pine flatwoods are floristically rich, sparsely stocked with pines (*Pinus* spp.) and with patches of saw palmetto (*Serenoa repens*). Fire plays an important role in maintaining pine flatwoods, so to see a riot of wildflowers, check this plant community within a few weeks or months following fire. Look also for saucer-shaped depression marshes within this habitat for an entirely different pallet of wildflowers, including carnivorous species like pitcher-plants, bladderworts, sundews, and butterworts. High pine habitat is dry, with an overstory of pines and an understory dominated by grasses.

High Pine

Pine Rocklands

Pine rocklands occur in southern Florida, especially on the Miami Rock Ridge in southern Miami-Dade County, Long Pine Key in Everglades National Park, and Big Pine Key in the Florida Keys. Pine rocklands are characterized by outcroppings of bare, jagged, oolitic limestone, often with numerous solution holes that make travel by foot difficult and painful. The overstory tree is the slash pine (*Pinus elliottii*) with a rich understory of mostly tropical shrubs (or trees that are kept shrubby by fire) interspersed with grasses, forbs, and palms.

Tropical Hammocks

Hammocks in southernmost Florida are dominated by hardwood trees of tropical origin. These tropical trees arrived here by seeds transported across the Straits of Florida and the Gulf of Mexico in the bellies of migratory songbirds, as well as by tropical storms and ocean currents. There is very little understory in mature tropical hammocks, and most have deep solution holes carved into the limestone that hold water during the rainy season.

Pine Rockland

Tropical Hammock

Mangrove Forest   Saltmarsh Habitat

Mangroves

Mangrove forests are the least floristically diverse plant community in Florida, yet they are a critically important nursery ground for countless fish and marine organisms, and they provide essential roosting and nesting sites for herons, egrets, cormorants, pelicans, and many other birds. The tree that typically dominates this plant community is the red mangrove (*Rhizophora mangle*) that produces a maze of arching prop roots. Mangroves are protected because of their crucial role in buffering Florida's shorelines from storm surges.

Salt Marshes

Like mangroves, salt marshes are floristically challenged because they are inundated during parts of the year with salt water. The dominant plant in salt marshes is saltwort (*Batis maritima*), but all plants that make up this habitat must be able to tolerate extremely harsh conditions.

Cypress Swamps and Mixed Hardwood Swamps

Cypress swamps are dominated by either bald cypress (*Taxodium distichum*) or pond cypress (*Taxodium ascendens*). Some are dome shaped, with taller trees in the deeper center, graduating to smaller trees toward the outer fringe. Cypress domes form in depressions and are commonly seen in Big Cypress National Preserve and Everglades National Park. Three of the most famous swamps in Florida are Fakahatchee and Corkscrew Swamps in southwest Florida and the famed Okefenokee Swamp in southeastern Georgia, which crosses into northeastern Florida, forming the headwaters of the Suwannee River. Swamps may be flooded all year or dry in late winter.

Linear swamps are called strands and may be intermixed with cypress and broad-leaved hardwoods. Strands are basically shallow, forested rivers. Deeper drainage areas in swamps are called sloughs.

Dry Prairies

The Kissimmee Prairie encompasses tens of thousands of acres of dry prairie, and much of it is protected within Kissimmee Prairie Preserve State Park and the adjacent Avon Park Air Force Range north and west of Lake Okeechobee. Here you will find vast, open, essentially treeless grasslands interrupted by patches of saw palmetto (*Serenoa repens*) and dwarf live oak (*Quercus minima*) that are kept low and shrubby by frequent fires. Dry prairies can be flooded at times, although the duration is short due to the sandy substrate that drains quickly.

Cypress Swamp

Dry Prairie

Wet Prairie

Wet Prairies

Wet prairies are scattered about mainland Florida, and good examples can be seen at Paynes Prairie in northern Florida as well as Big Cypress National Preserve and Everglades National Park in southern Florida. They can be categorized as short-hydroperiod or long-hydroperiod, depending on how long they are flooded during the year. Short-hydroperiod glades are flooded only during the rainy season, from summer into fall. Wet prairies are dependent on flooding and fire, and they are rich in wildflowers.

Beach Dunes

A prerequisite for beach dune vegetation is the ability to tolerate dry, nutrient-deficient sand along with salt spray and occasional inundation by salt water from tides and storm surges. Beach dune plants must also be able to survive the full fury of hurricanes. They are a hardy bunch of plants, and many species play a vital role in stabilizing beach sand from erosion by wind and tides.

Beach Dunes

Scrub and Sandhills

Scrub

These plant communities are combined because both are relict beach dunes created when sea levels were much higher than they are today. Scrub habitat on the Lake Wales Ridge, which runs down the center of peninsular Florida from Lake County to Highlands County, has the highest percentage of endemic plant species in the state because it was once an isolated island when the Florida Plateau was submerged. Some important portions of the Lake Wales Ridge are protected within Archbold Biological Station, Lake Wales Ridge National Wildlife Refuge, and Tiger Creek Preserve.

Sandhills are typically characterized by low, rolling hills sparsely populated by pines. Coastal sandhills are often referred to as scrubby flatwoods.

Outdoor Ethics

Wildflowers help support entire ecosystems by offering food for wildlife, in the form of nectar and pollen for bees, butterflies, and other pollinators, as well as for nectar-seeking and insect-eating birds like hummingbirds, warblers, flycatchers, and vireos. They also provide important forage for deer, rabbits, and wild turkeys. Pollinated flowers produce fruits and seeds that are consumed by countless birds and mammals, all the way up the food chain to the Florida black bear. The leaves of many wildflowers offer larval food for butterflies and moths, and they are fed on by a host of other insects. Some spiders are pollinator predators, hanging out around flowers to nab a meal when small insects stop for a visit.

We all have childhood memories of picking wildflowers, but a better lesson to teach children is the role wildflowers play in nature and that it is fun seeing them in the wild and leaving them where they belong.

BLUE AND PURPLE FLOWERS

Stokesia laevis

This section includes flowers ranging from pale blue to deep indigo and from lavender to violet. Since lavender flowers grade into pink, you should check the Pink section if you do not find the flower you are looking for here.

PINELAND TWINFLOWER
Dyschoriste angusta (A. Gray) Small
Acanthus family (Acanthaceae)

Description: The 4"–8" stems bear opposite, nearly sessile, linear to linear-elliptic, hairy leaves that average ⅜" long. The funnel-shaped flowers have 5 lobes with darker purple dots on the lower lobe. The flowers are in the upper leaf axils and measure about ⅜" long and ¼" wide.

Bloom Season: All year

Habitat/Range: Pinelands in Wakulla, Hernando, Polk, and Highlands Counties and from Lee and Martin Counties south into the Florida Keys

Comments: *Dyschoriste* means "poorly" and "split," in apparent reference to the slightly lobed stigma, but some sources say it means "difficult to separate," alluding to the valves of the capsule. The name *angusta* means "narrow" and relates to the leaf shape. Some species are used in the Caribbean to cure "pains in the waistline" and to "relieve women's tiredness." It is a larval host plant of the common buckeye butterfly.

SWAMP SNAKEHERB
Dyschoriste humistrata (Michx.) Kuntze
Acanthus family (Acanthaceae)

Description: The ovate to obovate leaves measure ½"–2½" long and half as wide. Flowers are axillary, typically paired, and are about ⅜" long and wide, marked with dark purple lines in the throat.

Bloom Season: All year

Habitat/Range: Floodplain forests from Gadsden, Liberty, and Franklin Counties east and south to Sarasota, DeSoto, and Volusia Counties

Comments: The name *humistrata* relates to the species' low-growing habit. It was first described as *Ruellia humistrata* by French botanist André Michaux (1746–1802), but the name wasn't published until 1803, the year after his untimely death in Madagascar. It was revised to *Dyschoriste humistrata* in 1891 by German botanist Carl Ernst Otto Kuntze (1843–1907). The name snakeherb relates to its medicinal use as a poultice to treat snakebite by Native Americans and early colonists. It is dormant in winter, resprouting in spring.

OBLONGLEAF TWINFLOWER
Dyschoriste oblongifolia (Michx.) Kuntze
Acanthus family (Acanthaceae)

Description: This species is 2"–10" tall with opposite, sessile, coarsely hairy leaves. The oblong-
elliptic leaves are ½"–1⅛" long and ⅜"–¾" wide.
The axillary, 5-lobed flowers measure ⅝"–¾" long
and ⅜"–½" wide, often in pairs in the leaf axils.

Bloom Season: March to October

Habitat/Range: Flatwoods and sandhills of Florida
south to Collier County

Comments: The name *oblongifolia* refers to the
oblong leaves. The flowers are much larger than
those of the previous 2 species. Fire plays an
important role in the species' survival, and it will
disappear from areas that have not been subjected
to periodic burns, or in times of prolonged drought.
Butterfly gardeners sometimes grow this species
as a larval host plant for the common buckeye butterfly. Due to its larger flowers, it can be mistaken
for a species of *Ruellia* and was once even placed
in that genus.

PINELAND WATERWILLOW
Justicia angusta (Chapm.) Small
Acanthus family (Acanthaceae)

Description: Pineland waterwillow is often emer-
gent in shallow water and has small, opposite,
linear leaves that are sessile or with short petioles. The pale purple to violet flowers are usually
solitary on long stems and measure ⅜"–½" wide,
with a 2-lobed upper lip and a 3-lobed lower lip.
The upper lip is strongly curled.

Bloom Season: All year

Habitat/Range: Freshwater wetlands of mainland
Florida

Comments: *Justicia* honors Scottish attorney and
gardening enthusiast James Justice (1698–1763),
who wrote books about gardening in Scotland. The
name *angusta* alludes to the narrow leaves. This
species was thought to be endemic to Florida until
its recent discovery in Georgia. The Miccosukee
believed it had the ability to "restore the virility
to a man sixty to a hundred years old" when
combined with a secret song that was considered
dangerous to sing.

THICKLEAF WATERWILLOW

Justicia crassifolia (Chapm.) Chapm. ex Small
Acanthus family (Acanthaceae)

Description: Stems reach 8"–16" tall, with narrowly linear, opposite leaves (spatulate near the base) to 6" long. Bright purple flowers are about 1" long.

Bloom Season: Principally May to June but sporadic all year

Habitat/Range: Endemic to wet flatwoods, bogs, and cypress swamps of Gulf and Franklin Counties in Florida's lower central panhandle

Comments: The name *crassifolia* refers to the thick leaves of this state-listed endangered species. Botanist Alvan Wentworth Chapman (1809–1899) first described this species in 1860 as *Dianthera crassifolia*. Chapman moved from New England to Florida in 1835; he published his *Flora of the Southern United States* in 1883 and died at his home in Apalachicola, Florida, at the age of 90. Members of this genus often grow in standing water, but this species may be found growing in soils that are seasonally wet.

CAROLINA WILD PETUNIA

Ruellia caroliniensis (J.F. Gmel.) Steud.
Acanthus family (Acanthaceae)

Description: This erect perennial reaches 16" tall, with opposite, hairy, elliptic leaves that average 1½"–2" long and ¾"–1" wide. Flowers are about 1¼"–1½" wide. The capsules are pubescent.

Bloom Season: All year

Habitat/Range: Sandhills and wet flatwoods through much of mainland Florida

Comments: *Ruellia* honors French herbalist Jean de la Ruelle (1474–1537), who latinized his name to Johannes Ruellius. The name *caroliniensis* refers to South Carolina. German botanist Johann Friedrich Gmelin (1748–1804) described this species in 1792 as *Pattersonia caroliniensis*, but it was relegated to the genus *Ruellia* in 1841 by German botanist Ernst Gottlieb von Steudel (1783–1856). It is cultivated by gardeners and is a larval host of the common buckeye butterfly. The invasive exotic Mexican bluebell (*Ruellia simplex*) has similar flowers and reaches 4' tall.

PINELAND WILD PETUNIA
Ruellia succulenta Small
Acanthus family (Acanthaceae)

Description: The decumbent or ascending, succulent stems reach 4"–8" tall, with somewhat fleshy, hairy leaves that measure 1½"–2" long and ¾"–1" wide. The leaves are sometimes reddish purple. The trumpet-shaped, 1½" flowers range from violet to pink. The capsules are glabrous.

Bloom Season: All year

Habitat/Range: Endemic to rocky and sandy pinelands of Charlotte, Lee, Collier, Miami-Dade, and Monroe Counties, including the Florida Keys

Comments: The name *succulenta* refers to the succulent stems. It was once regarded as a subspecies and variety of *Ruellia caroliniensis*. Botanist John Kunkel Small (1869–1938) first described it as *Ruellia succulenta* in 1905 from plants collected in 1903 with his botanist friend, Joel Jackson Carter (1843–1912), between Coconut Grove and Cutler in Miami-Dade County. It is a larval host of the malachite and common buckeye butterflies.

RATTLESNAKE MASTER
Eryngium aquaticum L.
Carrot family (Apiaceae)

Description: The toothed, basal leaves of this species are grasslike, up to 6" long and ⅜" wide, often emerging from standing water. Flowering stems reach about 24"–36" tall, branching near the top. Round, attractive heads of blue flowers measure ½" wide.

Bloom Season: May to September

Habitat/Range: Marshes, ditches, and swamps south through Florida to Manatee, Polk, Osceola, and Indian River Counties

Comments: *Eryngium* is from *eryngion*, the Greek name for *Eryngium campestre*. The name *aquaticum* refers to its wetland habitat. This species may form extensive colonies in flooded roadside ditches, and the flowers will likely be covered with skippers and other small butterflies seeking nectar. For this reason, it merits horticultural attention. The common name is for its use as a wishful antidote for rattlesnake venom, especially among the Alabama, Cherokee, and Delaware tribes.

FRAGRANT ERYNGO
Eryngium aromaticum Baldwin
Carrot family (Apiaceae)

Description: The thick, ovate, basal leaves average 1"–2½" long and are irregularly toothed. The main stem is erect, but the lower branches typically spread horizontally across the ground. The whorled stem leaves are deeply divided into 3 pointed lobes; the pale blue flowers are in globose, ½" bristly heads.

Bloom Season: September to January

Habitat/Range: Sandy habitats of Franklin and Liberty Counties in the Florida panhandle and throughout the peninsula

Comments: The name *aromaticum* refers to the aromatic leaves that smell strongly of carrots when crushed. Members of this genus serve as larval host plants for the black swallowtail butterfly. Pennsylvania physician and botanist William Baldwin (1779–1819) first described this species in 1817. Baldwin made major contributions to the herbaria of many notable botanists of his time. There are 9 species in this genus in Florida.

EASTERN BLUESTAR
Amsonia tabernaemontana Walter
Dogbane family (Apocynaceae)

Description: This perennial reaches 3' tall, with smooth stems and lanceolate to elliptic leaves 3"–4" long and ¾"–1" wide (the uppermost leaves are sessile). Pale blue, ¾" star-shaped flowers are in terminal clusters.

Bloom Season: March to August

Habitat/Range: Floodplain forests of the Florida panhandle east to Columbia, Alachua, and Levy Counties

Comments: *Amsonia* commemorates English physician John Amson (1698–1763), who moved to Virginia and was mayor of Williamsburg from 1750 to 1751. The name *tabernaemontana* honors Jacob Theodor von Bergzabern (1520–1590), who changed his name to Jacobus Theodorus Tabernaemontanus (literally "tavern in the mountains"). This species is sometimes cultivated and excels when planted in moist, loamy soils in sunny or partly shaded locations. Fringed bluestar (*Amsonia ciliata*) has short-petiolate upper leaves.

FLORIDA MILKVINE
Matelea floridana (Vail) Woodson
Dogbane family (Apocynaceae)

Description: This twining milkweed has milky sap and cordate leaves measuring up to 4" long and 1¾" wide. The axillary flowers measure about ⅝" wide. The elongated pod is spiny.

Bloom Season: April to August

Habitat/Range: Hardwood forests of Florida south to Hillsborough and Polk Counties; also Miami-Dade County

Comments: *Matelea* was named by French botanist Jean Baptiste Christophore Fusée Aublet (1720–1778) and is believed to be a French Guiana aboriginal name. The name *floridana* relates to Florida, where this species was first collected and then described in 1899 as *Vincetoxicum floridanum* by botanist Anna Murray Vail (1863–1955). *Vincetoxicum means* "poison beater" and alludes to its perceived antidotal properties for venomous snake bites. It is a state-listed endangered species and a larval host for queen and monarch butterflies.

VIRGINIA SNAKEROOT
Aristolochia serpentaria L.
Birthwort family (Aristolochiaceae)

Description: The stems are erect or decumbent to 24" long, with alternate, lanceolate to ovate leaves, cordate at the base, and measuring up to 6" long and 2" wide. The flowers are about ⅜" long.

Bloom Season: April to October

Habitat/Range: Mesic forests and sandhills through the panhandle south to DeSoto and Highlands Counties

Comments: *Aristolochia* means "best delivery," for the ancient use to aid childbirth. The name *serpentaria* relates to its reputed power to render venomous snakebites harmless. The rhizome smells like turpentine or menthol and was made into a popular herbal tonic as a gastric stimulant when taken in small quantities, but in large doses it may lead to violent gastric distress and respiratory paralysis. The voracious larvae of pipevine and polydamas swallowtail butterflies may eat the plant down to the ground, stems and all.

FLORIDA KEYS WHITEWEED

Ageratum maritimum Kunth
Aster family (Asteraceae)

Description: The stems of this multibranched herb average 8"–12" tall, forming rhizomatous colonies. The coarsely toothed leaves are deltate-ovate to oblong and measure ¾"–1⅜" long and ⅜"–½" wide. Pale blue or white flower heads are about ¼" wide.

Bloom Season: All year

Habitat/Range: Hammocks and dunes of the Florida Keys

Comments: *Ageratum* translates to "not old age" and relates to the long-lasting flowers. The name *maritimum* alludes to the species' coastal (maritime) habitat. In Florida, this state-listed endangered species is restricted to the Florida Keys, but it has become somewhat popular in the Florida native-plant nursery trade, especially for butterfly gardeners. It is also called Cape Sable whiteweed, even though it does not occur on Cape Sable. Blue mink (*Ageratum houstonianum*) is naturalized in central and southern Florida and has similar flowers.

CAROLINA ASTER OR CLIMBING ASTER

Ampelaster carolinianus (Walter) G.L. Nesom
(Also *Symphyotrichum carolinianum* [Walter] Wunderlin & B.F. Hansen)
Aster family (Asteraceae)

Description: The elliptic to lanceolate leaves of this vining species range from ¾"–2⅜" long, with stem leaves that clasp nearly around the stem. The ray flowers vary from rosy purple to pale pink, and the flower heads measure 1"–1½" wide. Seeds are wind dispersed.

Bloom Season: October to May

Habitat/Range: Freshwater wetlands from the central panhandle south through mainland Florida

Comments: *Ampelaster* translates to "vining aster." The name *carolinianus* in this case refers to South Carolina, where it was first discovered in 1788. It is sometimes cultivated for its attractive flowers that are visited by bees and butterflies, but it must be grown in reliably moist conditions and can climb 15' or more into trees and over shrubs. This genus represents the only vining aster in Florida.

FLORIDA PAINTBRUSH

Carphephorus corymbosus (Nutt.) Torr. & A. Gray
Aster family (Asteraceae)

Description: An erect, leafy stem to 3' tall or more arises from a basal rosette and is topped by tightly bunched ⅜" heads of disk flowers. The stem leaves are much smaller than the basal leaves. Fruits are 10-angled, cone-shaped achenes.

Bloom Season: June to November

Habitat/Range: Sandy habitats of mainland Florida

Comments: *Carphephorus* translates to "chaff-bearing," in reference to the dry, scaly floral bracts. The name *corymbosus* refers to the flowers being arranged in a corymb. The common name alludes to the paintbrush-like hairs on the seeding heads. Leaf extracts are combined with horseradish to treat urinary infections, and the leaves of some species in this genus are used to flavor cigarettes. Recent DNA-based research may move this species back to the genus *Liatris*. It is a top-notch butterfly attractor and is sometimes cultivated by Florida gardeners.

BRISTLELEAF CHAFFHEAD

Carphephorus pseudoliatris Cass.
Aster family (Asteraceae)

Description: The coarsely hairy basal leaves are narrowly linear, mostly 4"–10" long, reducing in size up the stem. The leaves are gland-dotted on the upper surface. Flower heads are in terminal corymbs on hairy stems (peduncles).

Bloom Season: July to December

Habitat/Range: Wet savannas, pine barrens, and seepage bogs of Escambia County east to Gadsden, Liberty, and Wakulla Counties in the Florida panhandle

Comments: The name *pseudoliatris* translates to "false liatris" and alludes to this species' close alliance to the genus *Liatris*. It was first described in 1816 by French botanist Alexandre Henri Gabriel de Cassini (1781–1832). A synonym of this species is *Liatris squamosa*, named by botanist Thomas Nuttall (1786–1859) in 1834. This is the type species of the genus and, following taxonomic revisions, may end up being the only member of *Carphephorus* in Florida.

CAPE SABLE THOROUGHWORT
Chromolaena frustrata (B.L. Rob.) R.M. King & H. Rob.
Aster family (Asteraceae)

Description: The stems have short, scattered hairs and 3-nerved, shallowly toothed, elliptic-lanceolate leaves from ½"–1" long and ⅜"–½" wide. Flower heads are in clusters of 2–6, with pale blue to lavender florets.

Bloom Season: All year

Habitat/Range: Edges of coastal hammocks and mangroves of Miami-Dade and Monroe Counties (mainland and Florida Keys)

Comments: *Chromolaena* alludes to the colored involucral bracts of the type species. The name *frustrata* relates to botanist Benjamin Lincoln Robinson (1864–1935) becoming frustrated while attempting to describe this species in 1911 due to its resemblance to a Jamaican species. It does not occur on Cape Sable, but the entire area from Flamingo to the southwest tip of Florida was once referred to as Cape Sable. It is a state and federal endangered species.

BLUE MISTFLOWER
Conoclinium coelestinum (L.) DC.
Aster family (Asteraceae)

Description: The stems are usually erect to about 12" tall with serrated, triangular to ovate leaves ranging from 1"–2½" long and half as wide. The flower heads are blue to blue-violet, each measuring about ⅜" wide.

Bloom Season: All year

Habitat/Range: Coastal and inland habitats throughout Florida

Comments: *Conoclinium* alludes to the conical receptacles. The name *coelestinum* refers to the celestial-blue flowers. Blue mistflower attracts a dazzling assortment of butterflies and is sometimes cultivated by Florida gardeners. It is the only member of the genus in Florida. Bluemink (*Ageratum houstonianum*), naturalized along roadsides of Florida, has very similar flowers but is not rhizomatous. Pussyfoot (*Praxelis clematidea*) is naturalized in Central Florida and has very similar flowers but hairy leaves that smell like cat urine when crushed.

ELEPHANTSFOOT
Elephantopus elatus Bertol.
Aster family (Asteraceae)

Description: The ground-hugging basal leaves of this species reach up to 10" long and 3" wide. The leaves are elliptic in shape and scalloped or toothed along the margins. The flowering stem is covered with spreading hairs and can reach 24"–48" tall. It is topped with small, violet flowers and 3 triangular, leaflike bracts.

Bloom Season: April to November

Habitat/Range: Sandhills and flatwoods throughout mainland Florida

Comments: *Elephantopus* means "elephant foot" and is believed to be an aboriginal name of a species in India. The name *elatus* means "tall." Italian botanist Antonio Bertoloni (1775–1869) named this species in 1850. Some species are used medicinally to treat asthma and other respiratory ailments. Carolina elephantsfoot (*Elephantopus carolinianus*) has a leafy stem and is usually without basal leaves when flowering.

FLAXLEAF ASTER
Ionactis linariifolia (L.) Greene
Aster family (Asteraceae)

Description: Herbaceous to semi-woody stems average 10"–20" tall with numerous, alternate, stiff, narrowly linear stem leaves ranging from ½"–1½" long and up to ¼" wide. The flower heads are single or in loose, flat-topped arrays, each about 1"–1¼" wide. The ray florets range from lavender to blue-violet.

Bloom Season: September to December

Habitat/Range: Sandhills from Escambia County east across the panhandle to Jackson, Liberty, and Wakulla Counties (also Nassau County)

Comments: *Ionactis* means "violet ray" and is descriptive of the violet ray flowers. The name *linariifolia* relates to the narrowly linear leaves. It can be distinguished from other asters by the combination of short and long tufted hairs on the achenes, a trait that enables the seeds to be easily dispersed by wind. Botanist Edward Lee Greene (1843–1915) established the genus in 1897.

PRAIRIE BLAZING-STAR
Liatris aspera Michx.
Aster family (Asteraceae)

Description: Short, stiff hairs cover the stems with hairy, narrowly lanceolate or linear leaves that become smaller up the stem, appearing whorled at the base. The lowermost leaves can measure up to 12" long and 1" wide. Flowers are arranged in dense, ½"–1" clusters, opening at the top of the stalk first. The seeds are attached to long, stiff hairs that allow them to be dispersed by wind.

Bloom Season: August to November

Habitat/Range: Dry prairies and xeric woodlands of Jackson, Leon, Wakulla, Columbia, and Alachua Counties

Comments: *Liatris* may have come from the Gaelic *liatrus* ("spoon-shaped") and refer to the shape of the tuberous roots on some species. The name *aspera* refers to the rough texture of the stems and leaves. The species ranges across the eastern half of North America and was first described in 1803 from plants collected in Illinois. Bees and butterflies are effective pollinators.

CHAPMAN'S BLAZING-STAR
Liatris chapmanii Torr. & A. Gray
Aster family (Asteraceae)

Description: Needlelike leaves are congested along an erect, unbranched stem that reaches 36"–48" tall, with the leaves becoming shorter up the stem. Flowers are in terminal spikes, with buds that open from the top downward. Each flower is star shaped and measures about ¼" wide.

Bloom Season: March to November but principally August to September

Habitat/Range: Scrub and sandhills through most of mainland Florida

Comments: The name *chapmanii* honors renowned botanist Alvan Wentworth Chapman (1809–1899), who moved to the Florida panhandle in 1835 and died at the age of 90 in his Apalachicola home. He is buried beside his wife at Chestnut Cemetery near the mouth of the Apalachicola River. The spikes of flowers are real showstoppers along nature trails and are magnets for a wide variety of butterflies. Another common name is Chapman's gayfeather.

ELEGANT BLAZING-STAR
Liatris elegans (Walter) Michx.
Aster family (Asteraceae)

Description: The stems average 12"–24" tall and are covered with short, soft hairs. Narrowly oblanceolate basal leaves measure 2½"–8" long and up to about ⅜" wide, usually withering before flowering. The white, star-shaped, ⅜"–½" flowers are subtended by pink, lavender, or white bracts (phyllaries).

Bloom Season: August to October

Habitat/Range: Sandhills, wet savannas, and streambanks across most of northern Florida south to Flagler, Marion, Sumter, and Pasco Counties

Comments: The name *elegans* is for the elegance of this species when blooming. Some Native American tribes rubbed their horses with a tea made from *Liatris* leaves in the belief that it increased their speed and endurance. It was first described as *Staehelina elegans* in 1788 by British-American botanist Thomas Walter (1740–1789) in his *Flora Caroliniana*. Another name is pinkscale gayfeather. Plants with white floral bracts are referred to as var. *kralii*.

GHOLSON'S BLAZING-STAR
Liatris gholsonii L.C. Anderson
Aster family (Asteraceae)

Description: Flowering plants average 24"–30" tall but may reach 48" in height. The stems are finely pubescent, with mostly basal, elliptic to lanceolate-elliptic leaves 6"–8" long and ½"–¾" wide. The star-shaped, ¼" flowers are typically crowded along the stems but may be in loose arrays.

Bloom Season: August to November

Habitat/Range: Endemic to xeric woodlands of Gadsden and Liberty Counties

Comments: The name *gholsonii* commemorates legendary Florida botanist Angus Gholson (1921–2014), who was regarded as a great storyteller, conservationist, and Southern gentleman. Noted botanist Loran Crittendon Anderson (1936–), professor emeritus at Florida State University, described this species in 2002 from plants collected in Liberty County. It is closely allied to *Liatris gracilis*, and attempts have been made to relegate it as a variety of that species.

SCRUB BLAZING-STAR

Liatris ohlingerae (S.F. Blake) B.L. Rob.
Aster family (Asteraceae)

Description: The erect flowering stems of scrub blazing-star may reach 36" tall. Basal leaves reach 6" long, and the narrow stem leaves are 1"–3" long and alternately spiral up the stem. Each flower is about ⅜" wide, forming heads about 1" wide.

Bloom Season: June to October

Habitat/Range: Endemic to rosemary and sand pine–oak scrub on the Lake Wales Ridge in Polk and Highlands Counties

Comments: The name *ohlingerae* honors Sophronia Carson Ohlinger (1872–1940), a student and staff member at Rollins College in Orange County from 1920 to 1922, moving to Polk County in 1930. Scrub blazing-star is a state and federal endangered species. It was moved from *Lacinaria* to the genus *Liatris* in 1934 by American botanist Benjamin Lincoln Robinson (1864–1935). Reports of it occurring in DeSoto County are because present-day Highlands County was a part of DeSoto County prior to 1921. It is also called sand-torch.

SCALY BLAZING-STAR

Liatris squarrosa (L.) Michx.
Aster family (Asteraceae)

Description: The glabrous to hairy stems reach 12"–24" tall, with alternate, linear, glabrous or hairy, 4"–6" leaves that become much smaller up the stem. Each stem terminates in a flat-topped flower head consisting of pink, tubular disk florets subtended by a series of scaly floral bracts. The flower heads may be strongly recurved.

Bloom Season: July to August

Habitat/Range: Sandhills and pinelands of Escambia, Santa Rosa, Washington, Jackson, and Gadsden Counties

Comments: The name *squarrosa* means "rough" and alludes to the scaly floral bracts (phyllaries). These floral bracts help distinguish it from all other *Liatris* species in Florida. Look for it in Three Rivers State Park. Larvae of the blazing-star flower moth (*Schinia sanguinea*) feed on the flowers and immature seeds, and larvae of the blazing-star borer moth (*Papaipema beeriana*) tunnel through the roots.

NARROWLEAF BLAZING-STAR

Liatris tenuifolia Nutt. var. *quadriflora* Chapm.
Aster family (Asteraceae)

Description: The linear basal leaves are some-what grasslike and measure 4"–12" long and up to ¼" wide. Flowering stems reach 16"–60" tall and are lined along the upper half with clusters of star-shaped flowers that open from the top of the stem downward.

Bloom Season: August to October

Habitat/Range: Sand ridges, scrub, and pinelands through much of peninsula Florida and in Escambia, Bay, Franklin, and Taylor Counties

Comments: The name *tenuifolia* means "slender leaved"; *quadriflora* refers to the florets often being arranged 4 to a head. When members of this genus bloom, they attract a riot of nectar-seeking butterflies. This species was first discovered in 1883 growing along the Caloosahatchee River in Lee County. Check leaf characteristics; there are 17 other species in Florida, and many have similar flowers.

PINELAND CHAFFHEAD OR PRAIRIE STARS

Litrisa carnosa Small
(Also *Carphephorus carnosus* [Small] C.W. James)
Aster family (Asteraceae)

Description: The linear to lanceolate basal leaves reach 3" long and form a ground-hugging rosette. The tall, hairy flowering stems are topped by an array of purple disk flowers.

Bloom Season: June to November

Habitat/Range: Endemic to prairies and low pinelands from Volusia, Orange, and Polk Counties south to Lee, Highlands, Okeechobee, and Martin Counties

Comments: *Litrisa* is an anagram of *Liatris*. The name *carnosa* alludes to the fleshy, thick, soft-textured leaves. The species was first described in 1924 by botanist John Kunkel Small (1869–1938) from plants collected in 1922 from Highlands County with John B. DeWinkeler (1886–1963). It was moved to *Carphephorus* in 1958 by Charles William James (1929–) but returned to *Litrisa* on the basis of molecular DNA, which also suggests it is originally of hybrid origin.

STOKES' ASTER
Stokesia laevis (Hill) Greene
Aster family (Asteraceae)

Description: The narrowly winged petioles measure 2"–4" long; the leaf blades reach 3"–6" long and ¾"–2" wide. The stem (cauline) leaves are sessile and clasping. Very showy blue (rarely white) flower heads reach 2½" wide.

Bloom Season: May to September

Habitat/Range: Wet pinelands, savannas, and openings in woodlands discontinuously across the Florida panhandle and in Nassau and Flagler Counties

Comments: *Stokesia* honors physician and botanist Jonathan Stokes (1755–1831), who was one of the first physicians to run clinical tests on the use of digitalis to treat heart disease. The name *laevis* means "smooth," referring to the glabrous leaves. The species was first described in 1768 as *Carthamus laevis* but was moved to the genus *Stokesia* in 1893. It is native to the southeastern United States, and there are several named cultivars in the nursery trade.

SCALELEAF ASTER
Symphyotrichum adnatum (Nutt.) G.L. Nesom
Aster family (Asteraceae)

Description: The upper leaves of this species are appressed tightly to the brittle, wirelike stems, somewhat resembling scales. Flowering stems reach 2' tall, and the 1½"–2" basal leaves are alternate and rough to the touch. The flower heads are about ¾" wide.

Bloom Season: All year

Habitat/Range: Sandhills and flatwoods, mostly through the Florida panhandle and from Citrus, Sumter, and Polk Counties south into the Florida Keys; also Columbia and Nassau Counties

Comments: *Symphyotrichum* is Greek for "junction" and "hair," perhaps alluding to the bristles on the European cultivar used to describe the genus. *Symphyotrichum* replaces *Aster* in the New World. The name *adnatum* is Latin for "joined to" and refers to the clasping upper leaves. Small butterflies, especially crescents, blues, and hairstreaks, visit the disk flowers for nectar.

SAVANNAH ASTER
Symphyotrichum chapmanii (Torr. & A. Gray)
Semple & Brouillet
Aster family (Asteraceae)

Description: The linear-lanceolate basal leaves have long petioles and are present when flowering, with linear, clasping to subclasping stem (cauline) leaves, often with revolute margins. Stem leaves measure 1½"–4" long. The flower heads reach 1½"–1¾" wide.

Bloom Season: September to December

Habitat/Range: Wet pine savannas from Santa Rosa County east to Jackson, Liberty, and Wakulla Counties in the Florida panhandle; also Alachua and St. Lucie Counties

Comments: The name *chapmanii* honors botanist Alvan Wentworth Chapman (1809–1899), who settled in Marianna, Quincy, and Apalachicola, Florida. He is buried in Apalachicola beside his wife at Chestnut Cemetery. This species is exceptionally pretty and, with its large heads of flowers, blue rays, and yellow disks, could easily win a *Symphyotrichum* beauty contest in Florida.

EASTERN SILVER ASTER
Symphyotrichum concolor (L.) G.L. Nesom
Aster family (Asteraceae)

Description: The common name came from the silvery hairs that cover both sides of the leaves. The leaves are elliptic-lanceolate, usually canted up the stem, and measure up to 2" long and ½" wide. The basal leaves wither away before flowering. The flowering stems are topped by stalked heads of flowers with 8–16 blue rays and average 12"–24" tall.

Bloom Season: All year

Habitat/Range: Sandhills and flatwoods across the Florida panhandle and discontinuously south to the Florida Keys (Monroe County)

Comments: The name *concolor* means "one-colored," referring to the ray flowers. This species will be most noticeable in areas that have burned recently. Small butterflies visit the disk flowers (especially hairstreaks, crescents, and skippers). This is one of the most distinctive members of the genus and will likely not be confused with any other species.

ELLIOTT'S ASTER
Symphyotrichum elliottii (Torr. & A. Gray)
G.L. Nesom
Aster family (Asteraceae)

Description: Elliott's aster has long rhizomes that create large colonies. The stems are mostly smooth, sometimes purplish pink, and can reach 5' tall. The toothed elliptic leaves measure 2"–9" long and ⅜"–2" wide. The flower heads measure about 1" wide, with rays that range from lavender to pinkish or white.

Bloom Season: August to December

Habitat/Range: Wet flatwoods, marshes, bogs, and roadside ditches from Bay and Calhoun Counties across to Taylor, Bradford, and Duval Counties south to Collier and Miami-Dade Counties

Comments: The name *elliottii* honors American botanist Stephen Elliott (1771–1830). Native-plant enthusiasts sometimes cultivate this species, but it is difficult to keep within its bounds because it spreads aggressively from rhizomes. Autumn is the best time to look for it flowering in wet roadside ditches, where it produces masses of flowers.

VANILLALEAF
Trilisa odoratissima (J.F. Gmel.) Cass.
(Also *Carphephorus odoratissimus* [J.F. Gmel.] H. Herbert)
Aster family (Asteraceae)

Description: Tall, glabrous stems arise from a basal rosette of obovate leaves measuring up to 6" long and 2" wide. There are 7–10 fragrant florets in each head.

Bloom Season: August to December

Habitat/Range: Pine flatwoods and sandhills across the Florida panhandle south in the peninsula to Citrus, Sumter, Lake, Osceola, and Brevard Counties

Comments: *Trilisa* is an anagram of *Liatris*. The name *odoratissima* relates to the strong odor of vanilla from dried leaves, which were once used to flavor pipe tobacco. This species was moved to the genus *Trilisa* in 1828 by botanist Alexander Henri Gabriel de Cassini (1791–1832) and reinstated from *Carphephorus* in 2011. Some taxonomists believe it properly belongs in the genus *Liatris*. The similar var. *subtropicanus* occurs from Central Florida southward and lacks the vanilla scent.

HAIRY CHAFFHEAD

Trilisa paniculata (Walt.) Cass.
(Also *Carphephorus paniculatus* [J.F. Gmel.]
H.J.-C. Hebert)
Aster family (Asteraceae)

Description: The reddish-purple stems of this species are densely hairy and average 20"–30" tall. The narrowly elliptic basal leaves are 1"–10" long, with much smaller stem leaves. The ³⁄₁₆" flowers are in a columnar array.

Bloom Season: August to January

Habitat/Range: Wet flatwoods and bogs south in Florida to Palm Beach and Collier Counties

Comments: The name *paniculata* relates to the panicles of flowers. It is also called deertongue due to the shape of the large basal leaves. German botanist Johann Friedrich Gmelin (1748–1804) first described this species as *Chrysocoma paniculata* in 1792, but it was then placed in the genus *Trilisa* in 1828, moved to *Carphephorus* in 1968, and returned to *Trilisa* in 2011 based on a combination of molecular and morphological data. Butterflies are common sights around the flowers.

TALL IRONWEED

Vernonia angustifolia Michx.
Aster family (Asteraceae)

Description: The mid-stem leaves are linear-lanceolate to filiform and measure 2"–4½" long and less than ⅛" wide. Flower heads are in corymbs or panicles covering the top of the plant, with 12–20 flowers in each head.

Bloom Season: June to October

Habitat/Range: Sandhills and pinelands across the Florida panhandle and northern peninsula south to Pasco, Polk, Highlands, and Brevard Counties

Comments: *Vernonia* honors British botanist William Vernon (1666–1711), who came to the United States in 1698 to collect plants, animals, fossils, and shells for Cambridge University. The name *angustifolia* relates to the narrow leaves. Members of this genus are involved in folklore to treat "the bite of serpents" and "women's problems" and to promote sweating in children. Giant ironweed (*Vernonia gigantea*) has similar flower heads but is much taller, with large, toothed leaves.

FLORIDA IRONWEED
Vernonia blodgettii Small
Aster family (Asteraceae)

Description: The smooth, 6"–12" stems bear alternate, sessile, linear or narrowly lanceolate leaves that range from 2"–4" long and up to ½" wide. The heads of flowers are bright pinkish lavender.

Bloom Season: All year

Habitat/Range: Pineland and prairie margins in Orange and Indian River Counties and from Sarasota, DeSoto, Hendry, and Martin Counties south through the Florida Keys (Monroe County)

Comments: The name *blodgettii* commemorates one of the most important figures in southern Florida's early botanical history, John Loomis Blodgett (1809–1853). Another prominent Florida botanist, John Kunkel Small (1869–1938), named this species in honor of Blodgett's contributions to the field of botany. It was recently dethroned as a Florida endemic by its discovery on Andros Island, Bahamas. This species flowers in profusion following fire in its habitat.

CLASPING WAREA
Warea amplexifolia (Nutt.) Nutt.
Mustard family (Brassicaceae)

Description: This annual has alternate, heart-shaped, ½"–1¼" leaves that appear to encircle the stem. It may reach 40" tall, with rounded clusters of violet or white flowers with spoon-shaped petals.

Bloom Season: August to October

Habitat/Range: Endemic to sandhills of Lake, Marion, Orange, Osceola, and Polk Counties, typically where longleaf pine and wiregrass occur

Comments: *Warea* honors South Carolina teacher and plant collector Nathaniel Alcock Ware (1789–1854), who first collected this species in Florida. Ware died of yellow fever in Galveston, Texas, at the age of 65. The name *amplexifolia* is descriptive of the clasping leaves. This federal endangered species is threatened by habitat loss and fire suppression. It was extirpated in Orange County due to wholesale demolition of its habitat by developers but was reintroduced in a sandhill preserve in 2014.

SESSILELEAF PINELANDCRESS
Warea sessilifolia Nash
Mustard family (Brassicaceae)

Description: This annual reaches 24"–36" tall, with sessile, ovate to lanceolate stem leaves to 1" long and up to about ⅜" wide. The flowers are purple or pink, with broadly obovate petals.

Bloom Season: August to October

Habitat/Range: Sandhills of Escambia County east to Leon and Wakulla Counties in the Florida panhandle

Comments: The name *sessilifolia* refers to the sessile (stemless) leaves. This species was described in 1890 by New York Botanical Garden botanist George Valentine Nash (1864–1921) from plants collected in Leon County. It is locally common in the Florida panhandle and is also known from Georgia and Alabama. It is not a listed species but is considered to be of conservation concern. Butterflies visit the flowers along with bees and bee flies. Carolina pinelandcress (*Warea cuneifolia*) has pale flowers and is found in Jackson, Gadsden, and Liberty Counties.

NODDING NIXIE
Apteria aphylla (Nutt.) Barnhart ex Small
Burmannia family (Burmanniaceae)

Description: Frail, purple stems stand 1"–10" tall, either leafless or with minuscule, scalelike, purplish stem leaves. Flowers may be purple or white with purple markings and measure about ⅜" long.

Bloom Season: All year

Habitat/Range: Bay swamps and mesic forests scattered throughout much of mainland Florida

Comments: *Apteria* means "without wing," for the wingless flowers that separate it from species of *Burmannia*. The name *aphylla* means "leafless." This is the only species in the genus, but botanist Thomas Nuttall (1786–1859) first described it in 1822 as *Lobelia aphylla*. The common name relates to the nodding flowers and to a mythical shapeshifting water spirit called a nixie. It does not photosynthesize but derives nutrients by parasitizing soil fungi, a habit of this family, referred to as "mycorrhizal cheaters."

31

AMERICAN BELLFLOWER
Campanula americana L.
Bellflower family (Campanulaceae)

Description: This annual or biennial reaches
2'–6' tall, with alternate, elliptic to ovate, toothed
leaves that measure 3"–6" long and up to 2" wide,
tapering to a point. The 5-lobed flowers are satiny
and measure about 1" across. Flowers are axillary
along the hairy stems and also form clusters at the
top of the central stem.

Bloom Season: June to November

Habitat/Range: Floodplain forests and bluffs
in Gadsden, Liberty, and Jackson Counties in
Florida's central panhandle

Comments: *Campanula* means "a bell" and refers
to the flower shape of some members of the
genus. The name *americana* relates to it being
from America. One unusual trait of this species is
that seeds germinating in the fall become annuals,
while those germinating in springtime are biennial.
Bumblebees and butterflies visit the flowers for
nectar and are effective pollinators.

FLORIDA BELLFLOWER
Campanula floridana S. Watson ex A. Gray
Bellflower family (Campanulaceae)

Description: The leaves of this species are linear-
lanceolate, ½"–1½" long and ¹⁄₁₆"–¼" wide, with
entire or obscurely toothed margins. The flowers
are ½"–⅝" wide with 5 narrow, widely spreading
lobes subtended by green sepals.

Bloom Season: All year

Habitat/Range: Endemic to pond margins and
freshwater marshes of the central panhandle south
to Collier County

Comments: The name *floridana* means "of
Florida." Of our 3 native species, this is one of 2
endemics and the only species that is widespread
in Florida. Its botanical name was originally
published by American botanist Sereno Watson
(1826–1892) but was invalid in accordance with
the International Code of Botanical Nomenclature.
The name was resubmitted by American botanist
Asa Gray (1810–1888) and then accepted. It occurs
along roadsides and trails that bisect its habitat.

APALACHICOLA LOBELIA

Lobelia apalachicolensis D.D. Spaulding,
T.W. Barger & H.E. Horne
Bellflower family (Campanulaceae)

Description: The broadly elliptic-ovate leaves, toothed calyx lobes, yellow sap, and densely pubescent underside of the lower lip are diagnostic for this new species. The narrow stem leaves have glandular teeth and reach 2½" long and 1¼" wide. The showy flowers are about 1" long. Flowering plants may reach 5' tall.

Bloom Season: September to November

Habitat/Range: Endemic to wet pine flatwoods of Franklin, Leon, Liberty, and Wakulla Counties

Comments: *Lobelia* honors Flemish herbalist Matthias de l'Obel (1538–1616). The name *apalachicolensis* is for the Apalachicola region of the Florida panhandle. Botanist Robert K. Godfrey (1911–2000) first collected this species in Liberty County in 1954, but it wasn't described until 2016. It is a good example of an undescribed species hiding in plain sight along roadsides.

BOYKIN'S LOBELIA

Lobelia boykinii Torr. & A. Gray ex A. DC.
Bellflower family (Campanulaceae)

Description: This frail herb spreads by underground rhizomes. Needlelike leaves from ⅜"–1" long are spaced widely apart on mostly unbranched stems that average 12"–24" tall. The ⅜"–½" pale blue flowers are axillary or terminal.

Bloom Season: May to July

Habitat/Range: Wet flatwoods and pond margins of Gadsden, Jackson, Okaloosa, and Santa Rosa Counties

Comments: The name *boykinii* honors Georgia field botanist Samuel Boykin (1786–1846), who was also commemorated with the genus *Boykinia* (Saxifragaceae) and *Polygala boykinii* (Polygalaceae). Threats to this state-listed endangered species are fire suppression and loss of pollinators (bees and bee flies). It was photographed at Blackwater River State Park near Holt, Florida, in Santa Rosa County, where it was occasional in the pineland understory, hidden among grasses. Look for it in early summer.

SHORTLEAF LOBELIA
Lobelia brevifolia Nutt. ex A. DC.
Bellflower family (Campanulaceae)

Description: The consistently short leaves of this species are diagnostic. The stems are unbranched, with numerous linear-oblong stem leaves, typically about ¼"–⅜" long. The ½" flowers range from azure to nearly purple.

Bloom Season: July to December

Habitat/Range: Wet pine flatwoods and seepage slopes from Escambia County east across the panhandle to Franklin, Liberty, and Leon Counties

Comments: The name *brevifolia* is descriptive of the short leaves. Lobelia identification can sometimes be tricky, but this species always has very short leaves and, in Florida, only occurs in the panhandle. Bees, bee flies, and butterflies visit the flowers and are effective pollinators. Native Americans used lobelias medicinally to induce vomiting, and some species were even referred to as pukeweed. The plants contain lobeline and may be fatal if eaten in quantity.

BAY LOBELIA
Lobelia feayana A. Gray
Bellflower family (Campanulaceae)

Description: The basal leaves are ¼"–⅝" long and broadly ovate or kidney shaped. The upper leaves are elliptic, sometimes with scalloped margins. The flowers are about 5⁄16" wide and range from pale blue to pinkish violet.

Bloom Season: All year

Habitat/Range: Endemic to moist habitats from the eastern Florida panhandle south through the peninsula

Comments: The name *feayana* honors physician and botanist William T. Féay (1803–1879). Native Americans used *Lobelia siphilitica* to treat syphilis, a sexually transmitted disease believed to have been carried to Europe in 1493 by crewmen aboard ships captained by Christopher Columbus (1451–1506). Studies conducted by European doctors later found the plant to be ineffective as a cure. The small flowers of bay lobelia can turn roadsides blue.

GLADES LOBELIA
Lobelia glandulosa Walter
Bellflower family (Campanulaceae)

Description: The 2'–3' stems of glades lobelia bear linear or lanceolate, alternate leaves that typically have small, gland-tipped teeth along the margins. The ½" flowers have 2 lips, the upper one strongly curled with 2 lobes, the bottom one divided into 3 lobes.

Bloom Season: All year

Habitat/Range: Freshwater wetlands throughout Florida

Comments: The name *glandulosa* refers to the gland-tipped teeth on the leaves. Lobelia leaves contain toxic alkaloids, and their consumption can cause nausea, pupil dilation, salivation, convulsions, coma, and death. The tropane alkaloid lobeline has been used to expel mucus, induce vomiting, and treat venereal diseases, but its adverse effects and toxicity have limited many of its medicinal uses. Hummingbirds visit the flowers for nectar.

DOWNY LOBELIA
Lobelia puberula Michx.
Bellflower family (Campanulaceae)

Description: The toothed, softly hairy (puberulent) leaves are elliptic, ovate, or obovate and average 2"–4" long and ½"–1½" wide. The blue to pinkish-violet flowers are about ½" wide, typically with 2 parallel white lines on the lip.

Bloom Season: April to November

Habitat/Range: Forests, swamps, and roadsides south in Florida to Brevard, Hernando, and Lake Counties

Comments: The name *puberula* refers to the soft, downy hairs on the stems and leaves. Like several Florida native plants described by French botanist André Michaux (1746–1802), the name of this species wasn't published until 1803, a year after he succumbed to a tropical fever in Madagascar. There are more than 400 lobelia species worldwide, with a sub-cosmopolitan distribution in tropical and warm temperate regions. Some tropical species were smoked in Mayan cultures for their narcotic effects.

VENUS' LOOKING-GLASS
Triodanis perfoliata (L.) Nieuwl.
Bellflower family (Campanulaceae)

Description: This annual has ribbed stems and ovate to elliptic, alternate, clasping leaves averaging ⅜"–¾" long. The axillary, sessile flowers measure about ⅜" across.

Bloom Season: February to May

Habitat/Range: Disturbed sites of northern and central peninsular Florida and the panhandle

Comments: *Triodanis* means "three-toothed" and possibly relates to the 3 calyx lobes on some flowers or the pores on the capsule. The name *perfoliata* refers to the stems that seemingly perforate the leaves. Belgium-born botanist and Reverend Julius Arthur Nieuwland (1878–1936) placed it in the genus *Triodanis* in 1914. The common name relates to the shiny seeds that resemble a looking glass, or tiny mirrors. Bees and small butterflies visit the flowers; buntings, goldfinches, and sparrows eat the seeds. Native Americans made a tea of the roots to relieve indigestion.

WHITEMOUTH DAYFLOWER
Commelina erecta L.
Spiderwort family (Commelinaceae)

Description: The clasping, alternate, linear leaves measure 1"–6" long and ⅛"–½" wide. Each flower is about 1" wide, with 2 large blue (rarely white) petals and a much smaller white petal.

Bloom Season: All year

Habitat/Range: Dry, open woodlands throughout Florida

Comments: *Commelina* honors Dutch botanists Jan (1629–1692) and his nephew Caspar (1667–1732) Commelin. A story holds that a third Commelin never accomplished much in the field of botany, represented in the flowers by the 2 prominent petals and a third inconspicuous petal. The name *erecta* refers to the species' erect growth habit. Dayflower relates to the ephemeral flowers that open once and congeal by midday. There are six nonnative *Commelina* species naturalized in Florida. Virginia dayflower (*Commelina virginica*), with pale blue flowers, is native to the panhandle and the northern peninsula.

BLUEJACKET

Tradescantia ohiensis Raf.
Spiderwort family (Commelinaceae)

Description: Long, sheathing, swordlike, succulent leaves average 5"–9" long and ⅜"–¾" wide. Flowers are in clusters atop succulent stems, each bearing 3 deep blue to rose (rarely white) petals with a tuft of bearded filaments.

Bloom Season: February to September

Habitat/Range: Wet to dry disturbed sites of Florida south to Lake Okeechobee

Comments: *Tradescantia* honors English naturalists and gardeners John Tradescant (1570–1638) and his son John (1608–1662). The elder Tradescant designed many famous British gardens, including the garden at St. Augustine's Abbey in Kent, England. The name *ohiensis* relates to Ohio, where this species was first collected in 1814. Bluejacket is widely cultivated for its showy flowers and ease of care. It is commonly seen along roadsides within its Florida range and will readily hybridize with the following species.

LONGLEAF SPIDERWORT

Tradescantia roseolens Small
Spiderwort family (Commelinaceae)

Description: The long, linear leaves are spirally arranged and measure 4"–16" long and ¼"–⅝" wide. Flowers are about ¾"–⅞" wide and range in color from deep or pale blue to pink, with blue or pink bearded filaments. Different color forms can be found growing together within the same population.

Bloom Season: February to August

Habitat/Range: Oak-palmetto scrub, pinelands, sandhills, and roadsides mostly in the center of the state from Duval County south to Highlands County

Comments: The name *roseolens* refers to the rose-scented flowers. Botanist John Kunkel Small (1869–1938) collected the type specimen in 1921 south of Avon Park, right where the plant photographed was found growing along roadsides. Honeybees and bumblebees are the principal pollinators. Members of this genus were once used as a treatment for spider bites, hence the name spiderwort.

FLORIDA LADY'S NIGHTCAP
Bonamia grandiflora (A. Gray) Hallier f.
Morning-Glory family (Convolvulaceae)

Description: The prostrate stems of this trailing species reach 36" long and spread across open sand. The ovate leaves average ¾"–1½" long and ⅜"–¾" wide, with silky hairs. The flowers measure 2½"–3" across.

Bloom Season: April to August

Habitat/Range: Endemic to sand pine scrub in Charlotte, Hardee, Highlands, Hillsborough, Lake, Manatee, Marion, Orange, Osceola, and Polk Counties

Comments: *Bonamia* commemorates French botanist and physician François Bonamy (1710–1786) and was named by renowned French botanist Louis-Marie Aubert du Petit-Thouars (1758–1831). The name *grandiflora* alludes to the grand size of the flowers compared to other members of the genus. It is a state-listed endangered species and was added to the federal registry in 1987 as threatened, mostly due to habitat loss on the Lake Wales Ridge for citrus groves.

SLENDER DWARF MORNING-GLORY
Evolvulus alsinoides (L.) L.
Morning-Glory family (Convolvulaceae)

Description: This spreading species has vinelike branches that radiate outward from the central stem, with lanceolate, alternate, hairy leaves that average ⅜"–¾" long and ⅜" wide. The flowers are about ⅜" wide on long, axillary stems.

Bloom Season: All year

Habitat/Range: Coastal rock barrens and shell middens of Lee, Broward, and Miami-Dade Counties through the Florida Keys (Monroe County)

Comments: *Evolvulus* translates to "lacking" and "twining," referring to the non-twining stems. The name *alsinoides* relates to its resemblance to a member of the genus *Alsine* (Caryophyllaceae). It has a wide global range and is used medicinally to promote hair growth and to treat fever, colds, venereal diseases, bronchitis, depression, and dementia. The 3 other native members of this genus in Florida all have white flowers of similar size.

TIEVINE

Ipomoea cordatotriloba Dennst.
Morning-Glory family (Convolvulaceae)

Description: The leaves of this twining vine are cordate and often 3-lobed, averaging about 3"–3½" long and 2"–2½" wide. The funnel-shaped flowers are about 2"–2½" wide and range from lavender to light pink, always with a darker throat. The calyx is covered with long hairs.

Bloom Season: April to November

Habitat/Range: Disturbed sites throughout Florida

Comments: *Ipomoea* means "wormlike" and alludes to the twining habit of some species. The name *cordatotriloba* refers to the cordate, often tri-lobed leaves. It was described in 1810 by botanist August Wilhelm Dennstedt (1776–1826). This vine can be so rampant and aggressive it can entirely engulf nearby shrubbery, but gardeners looking beyond its misbehavior will enjoy a continuous swarm of butterflies around flowering specimens. This species is common along roadsides and fencerows. Another name is purple bindweed.

RAILROAD VINE

Ipomoea pes-caprae (L.) R. Br. ssp. *brasiliensis* (L.) Ooststr.
Morning-Glory family (Convolvulaceae)

Description: This trailing vine has rounded or oblong, 2"–4" leaves with notched tips. The stems reach 20' or more, and the funnel-shaped flowers are typically solitary, each 2"–3" wide, with rose-purple nectar guides radiating into the throat.

Bloom Season: All year

Habitat/Range: Beach dunes along Florida's coastlines, including the Florida Keys

Comments: The name *pes-caprae* refers to the goat foot–shaped leaves; *brasiliensis* means "of Brazil," where this subspecies was first collected. In ancient Hawaii, the flowers were used as a soothing sheath after circumcision, and the stems were used to smite the ocean to bring rough waves for enemies at sea. It is an important dune stabilizer, with stems that often run parallel down the dunes, like railroad tracks. Another name within its range is creeper-on-the-Earth-by-the-sea.

SALTMARSH MORNING-GLORY
Ipomoea sagittata Poir.
Morning-Glory family (Convolvulaceae)

Description: The leaves of this twining vine are very narrowly arrow-shaped and range from 1½"–4" long and ½"–¾" wide. Funnel-shaped flowers are axillary and measure 2½"–3" wide, ranging from rose purple to lavender with a darker throat.

Bloom Season: All year

Habitat/Range: Brackish and freshwater marshes discontinuously across the Florida panhandle through much of the peninsula to the Florida Keys

Comments: The name *sagittata* describes the arrowhead-shaped (sagittate) leaves, which separate it from any other native species. It is quite common, and flower production is best in wet years. Despite the common name, this morning-glory is commonly found in freshwater habitats as well as along canal banks. Oceanblue morning-glory (*Ipomoea indica*) is also very common and has similar flowers, but wide, heart-shaped or lobed leaves.

SKYBLUE CLUSTERVINE
Jacquemontia pentanthos (Jacq.) G. Don
Morning-Glory family (Convolvulaceae)

Description: This perennial twiner has alternate, cordate to ovate leaves to 2" long and 1¼"–2" wide. The flowers average ¾" wide.

Bloom Season: All year

Habitat/Range: Coastal strand and disturbed sites from Broward and Collier Counties south through the Florida Keys (Monroe County)

Comments: *Jacquemontia* honors botanist Victor Vincelas Jacquemont (1801–1832), who traveled to India in 1828 to collect plant and animal specimens but died of cholera in Bombay at the age of 31. The name *pentanthos* refers to the 5 stamens. The species was moved from *Convolvulus* to *Jacquemontia* in 1837 by botanist George Don (1798–1856). Native-plant enthusiasts cultivate this state-listed endangered species for its cheerful, butterfly-attracting blossoms, which are often produced in profusion. It is more commonly encountered in the Florida Keys than on the mainland.

GROUNDNUT
Apios americana Medik.
Pea family (Fabaceae)

Description: This vine climbs by twining counter-clockwise with leaves divided into 5–7 pointed leaflets from 3"–5" long and ¾"–1¼" wide. The brownish-purple, ½" flowers have an explosive tripping mechanism that slings pollen onto visiting insects. The roots are lined with brown-skinned, white-fleshed tubers.

Bloom Season: May to December

Habitat/Range: Floodplain forests and roadside ditches throughout much of mainland Florida

Comments: *Apios* means "a pear" and relates to the shape of the tubers. The name *americana* means "of America." The underground tubers of this plant were recorded many times in early litera-ture as an important, nutritious food for indigenous people of the Americas and European colonists. The seeds were also boiled and eaten. German botanist Friedrich Kasimir Medikus (1736–1808) first named it in 1787. Other names are Indian potato and hopniss.

FLORIDA BUTTERFLY PEA
Centrosema arenicola (Small) F.J. Herm.
Pea family (Fabaceae)

Description: The twining stems reach 10' long, with leaves separated into 3 oval or lanceolate leaflets measuring up to 2" long and ½"–¾" wide. The flowers average about 1¼"–1½" wide.

Bloom Season: May to October

Habitat/Range: Endemic to sandhills from Dixie, Columbia, and Duval Counties south to Brevard, Osceola, Highlands, and Hillsborough Counties

Comments: *Centrosema* is Greek for "spur" and "standard," referring to the short spur behind the standard. The name *arenicola* relates to growing in sand. This state-listed endangered species was first collected in Lake County near Eustis in 1894 by George Valentine Nash (1864–1921) and described in 1903 as *Centrosema floridana* by John Kunkel Small (1869–1938). Its range overlaps with the following species, but the wider leaflets and longer petioles are diagnostic features that help separate them.

SPURRED BUTTERFLY PEA
Centrosema virginianum (L.) Benth.
Pea family (Fabaceae)

Description: This is a petite, perennial vine with trailing or twining stems. The compound leaves are alternate and divided into 3 narrow leaflets, each about 1"–1⅜" long and ¼"–⅜" wide. The ¾"–1¼" flowers are solitary or in pairs and range from purplish lavender to pale violet.

Bloom Season: All year

Habitat/Range: Pinelands, hammock margins, and coastal strand throughout Florida

Comments: The name *virginianum* means "of Virginia," where this species was first collected in the 1830s. The common name alludes to the butterfly-shaped flowers, but the long-tailed skipper uses the plant as larval food. This species responds quickly after fire, showing off its flowers as it trails across the charred ground. It is surprisingly seldom cultivated. The calyx lobes are equal to or exceed the length of the tube, which separates the genus from *Clitoria*, with its shorter calyx lobes.

SWEET-SCENTED PIGEONWINGS
Clitoria fragrans Small
Pea family (Fabaceae)

Description: The leaves of this upright herb are divided into 3 linear or linear-elliptic leaflets that measure up to 2" long and ⅜" wide. The sweetly fragrant, violet or pink flowers reach 2" long.

Bloom Season: May to July

Habitat/Range: Endemic to sandhills and scrub on the Lake Wales Ridge in Lake, Orange, Polk, and Highlands Counties

Comments: *Clitoria* alludes to the similarity of the keel to a clitoris on female genitalia. When the genus was first named by Carolus Linnaeus (1707–1778), he received sharp criticism from other botanists. The name *fragrans* means "fragrant." This is a state-listed endangered species and is on the federal registry as threatened. It was described in 1926 by botanist John Kunkel Small (1869–1938) from plants collected in Highlands County. Some species have been used as sexual stimulants for humans and to ensure fertility in domestic animals.

ATLANTIC PIGEONWINGS
Clitoria mariana L.
Pea family (Fabaceae)

Description: The upper leaves of this species have 3 ovate to ovate-lanceolate leaflets that reach up to 2½" long and ¾" wide. The flowers are similar to the previous species, but with a long corolla tube.

Bloom Season: March to October

Habitat/Range: Sandhills, scrub, and forest margins through much of mainland Florida

Comments: The name *mariana* relates to plants with mottled leaves, or species from Maryland. Atlantic pigeonwings is more common and widespread in Florida than the previous endemic species, and both are larval host plants of the long-tailed skipper, hoary edge, and southern cloudywing butterflies. Other members of the genus occur in Asia and Madagascar, and some have flowers that are used to dye rice blue; others are dipped in batter and fried. *Clitoria ternatea* is naturalized from Ternate Island in eastern Indonesia and has dark blue flowers.

SKYBLUE LUPINE
Lupinus cumulicola Small
Pea family (Fabaceae)

Description: The stems are usually erect, with gray-green, silky pubescent, elliptic leaves that average 2"–3" long and 1"–1½" wide. Flowers are about ⅜" tall. The pods have a curved beak.

Bloom Season: January to May

Habitat/Range: Endemic to Lake Wales Ridge scrub in Highlands, Lake, Osceola, and Polk Counties

Comments: *Lupinus* is from *lupus* ("wolf") and alludes to the belief that these plants consumed soil fertility. The name *cumulicola* means "dweller on a heap or mound," in this case, sand. It comes from the same root word for cumulus clouds, which form billowing mounds in the sky. Some botanists consider this a synonym of *Lupinus diffusus*, but it differs by its habitat, range, prostrate to decumbent stems, orbicular-reniform standard, and a nearly straight beak on the pods. The seeds of some species were used in ancient Greece to psychoactively prepare people to commune with the dead.

AMERICAN WISTERIA
Wisteria frutescens (L.) Poir.
Pea family (Fabaceae)

Description: American wisteria is a vining species with clockwise twining stems and compound leaves with 9–15 oblong leaflets that measure ¾"–2½" long. Densely clustered, fragrant flowers are on pendent racemes to 6" long. The seeds are poisonous to eat.

Bloom Season: April to June

Habitat/Range: Riverbanks, wet forests, and lakesides south in Florida to Orange County

Comments: *Wisteria* commemorates American physician and anatomist Caspar Wistar (1761–1818), with his surname misspelled in the naming of the genus. The name *frutescens* refers to the species' shrubby growth habit. Long-tailed skipper, silver-spotted skipper, and zarucco duskywing butterflies use the leaves as larval food. Chinese wisteria (*Wisteria sinensis*), with blue or white flowers, is naturalized throughout the Florida panhandle into central Florida and is a popular garden subject.

SEASIDE GENTIAN
Eustoma exaltatum (L.) Salisb. ex G. Don
Gentian family (Gentianaceae)

Description: The opposite, gray-green leaves of this annual clasp the stem and measure ¾"–2½" long and half as wide. Flowers resemble small tulips, with petals that may be bluish purple or white but always with dark purple bases. Each flower is about ¾" wide.

Bloom Season: December to August

Habitat/Range: Shoreline habitats and moist prairies through Florida's coastal counties

Comments: *Eustoma* means "beautiful mouth" and relates to the attractiveness of the cupped flowers that resemble small tulips. The name *exaltatum* means "very tall," alluding to its growth habit. White and purple color forms often grow together in the same populations. Selected cultivars of this and another species (*Eustoma russellianum*) are popular in the cut-flower trade. Some people acquire a skin rash from contact with the sap. It is also called catchfly prairie-gentian.

HARVESTBELLS
Gentiana saponaria L.
Gentian family (Gentianaceae)

Description: Plants range from 6"–24" tall, with narrowly ovate or elliptic, sessile leaves that reach 3½" long and 1½" wide. The 1½"–2" flowers are often closed (or nearly so) at the top.

Bloom Season: October to November

Habitat/Range: Creek swamps of Gadsden and Wakulla Counties

Comments: *Gentiana* is for King Gentius of Illyria, who ruled the Ardiaean State (present-day western Balkans) from 181 to 168 BC, and who discovered the medicinal virtues of Mediterranean gentians. The name *saponaria* means "soap-like," but in this case it relates to the leaves resembling those of *Saponaria* (Caryophyllaceae). Another name is soapwort gentian. The roots were used by Native Americans as a tonic or worn to give one strength. Bumblebees force their way into the flower buds and are effective pollinators. The common name relates to the bell-shaped flowers signaling the fall harvest season.

SKYFLOWER
Hydrolea corymbosa J. Macbr. ex Elliott
False Fiddleleaf family (Hydroleaceae)

Description: Skyflower may reach 2' tall, with spirally arranged leaves on smooth stems. The leaves are elliptic to lanceolate, mostly 1"–2" long and half as wide. Bright blue flowers, each about ¾"–1" wide, are produced in flat-topped clusters.

Bloom Season: May to November

Habitat/Range: Freshwater wetlands, pond margins, and flooded roadside ditches from Leon and Wakulla Counties south through mainland Florida

Comments: *Hydrolea* translates to "water loving," and the name *corymbosa* refers to the corymb of flowers. A corymb is a flat-topped cluster of flowers that progressively open from the outside inward. Members of this genus are autogamous, meaning their own pollen fertilizes the flowers. There is hardly a richer blue on any other wildflower, but skyflower is not widely cultivated because it requires shallow water or permanently wet soil to be grown successfully.

BARTRAM'S IXIA

Calydorea caelestina (W. Bartram) Goldblatt & Henrich
Iris family (Iridaceae)

Description: There are usually just 2 narrowly lanceolate or linear basal leaves that are only about 1/16" wide with 1–2 stem (cauline) leaves. The flowers measure about 2¼" wide.

Bloom Season: May to October

Habitat/Range: Endemic to grassy flatwoods of northeastern Florida in Baker, Duval, Union, Bradford, Clay, St. Johns, and Putnam Counties

Comments: *Calydorea* is Greek for "sheathed spear" and is believed to allude to the spear-shaped flower buds. The name *caelestina* relates to the celestial blue flower color. The flowers of this state-listed endangered species open at dawn and last about 3 hours. Famed naturalist William Bartram (1739–1823) first described this species as *Ixia caelestina* in his 1791 book, *Travels*. Although the species epithet should be *coelestina*, the errant spelling takes precedence because that is how Bartram published the name.

PRAIRIE BLUEFLAG

Iris savannarum Small
(Also *Iris hexagona* Walter; *Iris hexagona* Walter var. *savannarum* [Small] R.C. Foster)
Iris family (Iridaceae)

Description: The flat, linear, swordlike leaves reach 4' long and 1" wide, spreading in 1 plane like a fan. The showy flowers reach 4"–5" across.

Bloom Season: March to June

Habitat/Range: Endemic to freshwater wetlands across most of mainland Florida

Comments: *Iris* was named for the Greek goddess Iris, who appeared as a rainbow and sent messages to the gods. The name *savannarum* relates to it growing in savannas. Some botanists relegate this species as a synonym of *Iris hexagona*, while botanists with the *Flora of North America* regard that species as extremely rare and only known from two Florida counties (Dixie and Taylor), with a single, disjunct population in South Carolina. They cite capsule shape, leaf color, bloom season, winter dormancy, and floral differences to separate the 2 species.

CELESTIAL LILY
Nemastylis floridana Small
Iris family (Iridaceae)

Description: Thin, grasslike leaves arise from an underground bulb and average 10"–20" long. The celestial blue flowers have 3 petals and 3 sepals (combined as tepals), with each flower measuring 1½"–1¾" across. Buds turn blue the day they will be opening, and they spring open instantly.

Bloom Season: August to October

Habitat/Range: Endemic to wet flatwoods and freshwater marshes from St. Johns and Putnam Counties to Pasco, Polk, Osceola, and Okeechobee Counties south into Broward County

Comments: *Nemastylis* translates to "thread" and "pillar," alluding to the style (a structure in female flower parts) that bears threadlike appendages. The name *floridana* relates to Florida. This species was described in 1931 by botanist John Kunkel Small (1869–1938) from plants he collected west of New Smyrna (Volusia County). The ephemeral flowers are open between 4 and 6 p.m., so "happy hour flower" would be a good name. It is a state-listed endangered species and is most commonly found growing in the St. Johns River drainage from Duval to Brevard and Osceola Counties. The photograph was taken in the Tosohatchee Wildlife Management Area in eastern Orange County.

NARROWLEAF BLUE-EYED-GRASS
Sisyrinchium angustifolium Mill.
Iris family (Iridaceae)

Description: The leaves of this iris relative are in a fanlike arrangement, growing in tufts from rhizomes and resembling a grass when not in flower. The leaves are narrowly linear and average 8"–14" long and ¹⁄₁₆"–⅛" wide. The starlike flowers are about ½" wide.

Bloom Season: All year

Habitat/Range: Wet soils throughout Florida

Comments: *Sisyrinchium* is a name used by Greek philosopher Theophrastus (372–287 BC) for a related plant. The name *angustifolium* means "narrow leaved." This species can be abundant along roadsides that bisect its habitat. It has a long list of botanical synonyms, and the Flora of Florida currently recognizes four native species in Florida, but John Kunkel Small (1869–1938) listed 16 species for the state in his 1933 publication, *Manual of the Southeastern Flora.*

JEWELED BLUE-EYED-GRASS
Sisyrinchium xerophyllum Greene
Iris family (Iridaceae)

Description: This species spreads by rhizomes and has narrowly linear, scabrous leaves that reach ¼" wide and formed in robust tufts. The ½" flowers are pale blue to bluish violet, with yellow centers and dark blue nectar guides (lines that guide insects to aid in pollination).

Bloom Season: All year

Habitat/Range: Sandy soil in open woodlands from Walton County to Leon and Wakulla Counties, with scattered populations throughout peninsular Florida

Comments: The name *xerophyllum* is Greek for "dry leaf." American botanist Edward Lee Greene (1843–1915) described this species in 1899 from plants collected by botanist George Valentine Nash (1864–1921) in Lake County, Florida. Nash's blue-eyed-grass (*Sisyrinchium nashii*) is similar but has narrower leaves in smaller tufts. Annual blue-eyed-grass (*Sisyrinchium rosulatum*) is naturalized from South America and has small, yellow to pale violet flowers.

ETONIA FALSE ROSEMARY
Conradina etonia Kral & McCartney
Mint family (Lamiceae)

Description: This species reaches 2'–4' tall, with leaves that are curled under (revolute) along the margins. The leaves average ½"–1" long and ¼" wide, dotted with glands on the upper surface and hairy on both surfaces. The flowers are ¾"–1" long with a sharply bent floral tube.

Bloom Season: October to November

Habitat/Range: Endemic to white sand scrub in Putnam County

Comments: *Conradina* honors the Philadelphia Academy of Natural Sciences librarian and botanist Solomon White Conrad (1779–1831). The name *etonia* is taken from *etoniah,* a Timucuan word meaning "tribal town," and refers to an area in present-day Putnam County, Florida, where the Timucuan Agua Dulce tribe settled in the sixteenth century. Others say it comes from a Creek word for "go elsewhere." It is a federal endangered species. Another false rosemary in Putnam County was recently described as *Conradina cygniflora.*

APALACHICOLA FALSE ROSEMARY
Conradina glabra Shinners
Mint family (Lamiaceae)

Description: This species forms a densely branched mound of stems to 30" tall with needle-like leaves that are smooth above and minutely hairy below. The ½" flowers are typically in pairs or groups of 3.

Bloom Season: Mostly March to June

Habitat/Range: Endemic to white sand scrub and sandhills in Liberty County

Comments: The name *glabra* refers to the glabrous upper surface of the leaves. American botanist Lloyd Herbert Shinners (1918–1971) named it in 1962 from plants collected in Liberty County in 1952. This is a federal endangered species, and most of the currently known populations occur in pine plantations and along road swales and fencerows. This rare species is threatened by habitat loss, but some populations are protected within Torreya State Park. Glabrous plants in Santa Rosa County that were originally thought to be *Conradina canescens* may prove to be a new species.

EASTERN FLORIDA FALSE ROSEMARY

Conradina grandiflora Small
Mint family (Lamiaceae)

Description: The dark green, needlelike leaves of this 2'–4' shrubby species are about ¾" long and line the brittle stems. The lip on the hairy, pale purplish flowers is covered with purple dots, and each flower measures about ¾" long and ½" wide.

Bloom Season: All year, peaking in early summer

Habitat/Range: Endemic to coastal scrub of the easternmost counties of peninsular Florida, from Volusia County to Osceola County (historically Miami-Dade County)

Comments: The name *grandiflora* relates to the large flowers of this species compared to other members of the genus. Intrepid botanist John Kunkel Small (1869–1938) first collected this species near Sebastian, Florida (Indian River County), on April 19, 1924, and is exactly where the photograph was taken for this guide. It is a state-listed threatened species. See also *Conradina brevifolia* in the White section.

APALACHICOLA FALSE DRAGONHEAD

Physostegia godfreyi P.D. Cantino
Mint family (Lamiaceae)

Description: This rhizomatous species reaches 12"–18" tall, with narrow elliptic leaves from 1"–2½" long. The pale rose or white flowers are ¾" long, with purple venation on the 3-lobed lip. All or parts of the nutlets are warty (all other Florida species have smooth nutlets).

Bloom Season: May to December

Habitat/Range: Endemic to moist pine savannas in Walton, Bay, Calhoun, Gulf, Franklin, Liberty, and Wakulla Counties

Comments: *Physostegia* is Greek for "bladder" and "covering," alluding to the inflated calyx covering the fruits. The name *godfreyi* honors Florida State University botany professor Robert Kenneth Godfrey (1911–2000). It was described in 1979 by Ohio University botany professor Philip D. Cantino (1948–). Populations of this state-listed threatened species are mostly centered in the Apalachicola National Forest, where it can be locally common.

EASTERN FALSE DRAGONHEAD
Physostegia purpurea (Walter) S.F. Blake
Mint family (Lamiaceae)

Description: The leaf margins may be scalloped or have pointed teeth, and the upper leaves are greatly reduced in size compared to the basal leaves. Flowering plants range from 1'–3' tall and are topped with flowers spaced opposite each other along the stem. The flowers are 1⅜"–2" long, with deeply lobed lips and purple dots in the throat.

Bloom Season: April to November

Habitat/Range: Wet habitats and roadsides throughout much of the Florida peninsula into the central panhandle

Comments: The name *purpurea* refers to the purple flowers, although they range from rose purple to light pink. Butterfly gardeners occasionally cultivate it, and it is sometimes used in the cut-flower trade. It was once placed in the genus *Dracocephalum,* meaning "dragon head." Obedient plant (*Physostegia virginiana*) has larger flowers and is naturalized in northern and central Florida.

WILD PENNYROYAL
Piloblephis rigida (W. Bartram ex Benth.) Raf.
Mint family (Lamiaceae)

Description: The hairy, ascending stems of this brittle species form mounds 6"–24" tall. The needlelike leaves measure ⅜" long and are highly aromatic when crushed. Small, lavender flowers are in compact, cone-like spikes at the branch tips. The upper lip is 3-lobed; the lower lip is 2-lobed.

Bloom Season: All year

Habitat/Range: Sandy habitats throughout much of peninsular Florida

Comments: *Piloblephis* means "hairy eyelid" and relates to the hairlike pubescence on the sepals. The name *rigida* means "stiff," alluding to the leaves. The minty leaves are used to flavor soups and stews and to brew a refreshing tea. It also had numerous medicinal uses, especially for fevers. Old World pennyroyal (*Mentha pulegium*) was commonly used as a flea deterrent. Middle Age herbalists called it *pulioll-royall*, which would later give way to the name pennyroyal.

AZURE BLUE SAGE
Salvia azurea Michx. ex Lam.
Mint family (Lamiaceae)

Description: Azure blue sage averages 2'–4' tall, with spikes of blue or white, ¾" flowers terminating each stem. Two parallel white stripes may be present on the lip. Grayish-green leaves are narrowly lanceolate, with serrations toward the tip, and average 2"–4" long and ⅜"–½" wide.

Bloom Season: August to November

Habitat/Range: Flatwoods and sandhills south in Florida to Hillsborough and Orange Counties (vouchered also in Broward County)

Comments: *Salvia* is Latin for "safe" or "well" and alludes to the long history of medicinal use of this genus. The name *azurea* refers to the azure blue color of the flowers. French botanist André Michaux (1746–1802) first described this species invalidly, but French naturalist Jean-Baptiste Lamarck (1744–1829) successfully published the name in 1792. The flowers attract butterflies and hummingbirds.

LYRELEAF SAGE
Salvia lyrata L.
Mint family (Lamiaceae)

Description: The wavy, spatulate or oval basal leaves with a broad, rounded tip range from 2"–6" long and are divided partway to the midrib. The hairy flower spike is 6"–24" tall, and each flower is about ⅜" long and ³⁄₁₆" wide.

Bloom Season: February to November

Habitat/Range: Pinelands and roadsides south in Florida to Collier, Highlands, and Martin Counties

Comments: The name *lyrata* alludes to the lyre-shaped leaves. Many members of this genus are favorites of butterfly and hummingbird gardeners and have a long history of herbal and medicinal uses dating back to Pliny (AD 23–79) and Greek physician Pedanius Dioscorides (AD 40–90). In sixteenth-century America, extracts of this plant were unsuccessfully used to treat cancer. This is an exceptionally common wildflower along moist roadsides through much of Florida. Flower colors vary widely from purple to pinkish violet. This genus is popular in the nursery trade.

FLORIDA SCRUB SKULLCAP
Scutellaria arenicola Small
Mint family (Lamiaceae)

Description: This near endemic species produces a basal rosette of toothed, broadly ovate to deltoid leaves that become smaller and narrower up the stem. Flowering plants reach 8"–12" tall, with hairy flowers that measure ½"–⅝" wide. The flowers range from lavender-blue to pale violet.

Bloom Season: May to November

Habitat/Range: Scrub and sandhills south in Florida to Highlands and Collier Counties

Comments: *Scutellaria* means "small dish" and alludes to the saucer-like protuberance on the calyx. The name *arenicola* refers to its growing in sand. The name skullcap is based on the resemblance of the flowers to a type of military helmet worn by American colonists. Botanist John Kunkel Small (1869–1938) described this species in 1898 from plants collected in 1894 by botanist and horticulturist George Valentine Nash (1864–1921) near Eustis, Florida (Lake County).

HAVANA SKULLCAP
Scutellaria havanensis Jacq.
Mint family (Lamiaceae)

Description: The opposite, softly hairy leaves are ovate and measure ⅜"–⅝" long with entire or slightly toothed margins. The delicate ½" flowers emerge from the upper leaf axils. Plants typically reach 4"–6" tall.

Bloom Season: All year

Habitat/Range: Pine rocklands of Miami-Dade County and the Florida Keys (Monroe County)

Comments: The name *havanensis* refers to Havana, Cuba, where the type specimen was collected and described in 1760 by botanist Nikolaus Joseph von Jacquin (1766–1839). Cubans use this plant to treat infections, swelling of the feet, and psoriasis. In parts of its range, the seeds are ground and used to treat sarcoptic mange in dogs. There are 12 native members of this genus in Florida, and this is the only species that occurs in Miami-Dade and Monroe Counties. Butterflies sometimes visit the flowers, and it is occasionally cultivated by native-plant enthusiasts.

HOARY SKULLCAP
Scutellaria incana Biehler
Mint family (Lamiaceae)

Description: The pubescent stems of this perennial reach 2'–3' tall, with ovate, mostly glabrous,
toothed leaves that measure 1½"–3" long and
¾"–1" wide. The ½"–⅝" flowers are in terminal
racemes.

Bloom Season: September to October

Habitat/Range: Pinelands and deciduous woods
from Escambia County eastward to Jefferson and
Wakulla Counties in the Florida panhandle

Comments: The name *incana* loosely translates
to "hoary-white," referring to the fine pubescence
that gives the stems and flowers the appearance of being covered with hoarfrost. It was first
described in 1807 by German botanist Johann
Friedrich Theodor Biehler (1785–1850). Bumblebees are the principal pollinator, but the flowers
are also visited by butterflies and bee flies seeking
nectar. The similar helmet skullcap (*Scutellaria
integrifolia*) is common in Florida and has entire
leaves above the middle of the stem.

FORKED BLUECURLS
Trichostema dichotomum L.
Mint family (Lamiaceae)

Description: Forked bluecurls reaches 2' tall and
has square stems covered by minute, glandular
hairs. The oblong to ovate leaves are opposite,
about 2" long and ¾" wide, with entire margins.
Flowers are in 3- to 7-flowered axillary clusters
with curled stamens.

Bloom Season: April to November

Habitat/Range: Sandy soils of beaches and dry
woodlands throughout mainland Florida

Comments: *Trichostema* is Greek for "hair" and
"stamen," referring to the slender stalks of the
anthers. The name *dichotomum* means "forked,"
alluding to the forked inflorescence. Some
members of this genus are allelopathic, capable of
limiting competition by chemically inhibiting the
growth of other plants growing nearby. Narrowleaf
bluecurls (*Trichostema setaceum*) is rare in central
and northern Florida. Taxonomic studies are under-
way to determine if some *Trichostema* populations
in Florida represent undescribed species.

BLUE BUTTERWORT
Pinguicula caerulea Walter
Bladderwort family (Lentibulariaceae)

Description: The leaves are widest near the base and overlap to form a rosette, each leaf measuring ⅝"–1¼" long. Flowers are ¾"–1" wide and held on erect stems from 4"–12" tall.

Bloom Season: January to May

Habitat/Range: Low pinelands and bogs throughout most of peninsular Florida and west in the panhandle to Franklin and Liberty Counties

Comments: *Pinguicula* alludes to the greasy texture of the leaf surface. The name *caerulea* means "blue" and describes the typical flower color. Butterworts are carnivorous and trap small insects on the viscid leaves, where they are digested by enzyme secretions. When small insects become stuck to the mucilage coating on the leaf surface, the margins slowly curl over but never completely close. The leaf margins unfurl after the insect has been dissolved. The leaves were once used to curdle milk, hence the name butterwort.

VIOLET BUTTERWORT
Pinguicula ionantha R.K. Godfrey
Bladderwort family (Lentibulariaceae)

Description: Rosettes of overlapping, light green, oblong leaves average 2½"–4" across. The leaves are essentially flat, with the edges rolled upward. The scape may reach 6" tall and is topped by a single violet or white flower that measures ¾"–1" wide.

Bloom Season: January to April

Habitat/Range: Endemic to wet flatwoods and bogs of Bay, Gulf, Liberty, Franklin, and Wakulla Counties in the Florida panhandle

Comments: The name *ionantha* refers to the violet color of the flowers, although white-flowered forms are common. It is a state-listed endangered species and registered as a federal threatened species. It was first described in 1961 by Florida State University botanist Robert Kenneth Godfrey (1911–2000) from plants he collected near Sumatra in the Apalachicola National Forest (Franklin County) in 1960. It is also called panhandle butterwort.

SOUTHERN BUTTERWORT
Pinguicula primuliflora C.E. Wood & R.K. Godfrey
Bladderwort family (Lentibulariaceae)

Description: An erect flower spike arises from a yellowish green, 2"–4" rosette of leaves and is topped by a single, pale blue or 2-toned flower that measures about 1" wide.

Bloom Season: February to June

Habitat/Range: Bogs and edges of ponds and spring runs from Escambia County east to Holmes, Washington, and Bay Counties; also Wakulla County in the Florida panhandle

Comments: The name *primuliflora* relates to the flowers resembling a *Primula*, or primrose. This state-listed endangered species is also called primrose butterwort and can be locally common in the proper habitat. It was described in 1957 by botanists Carroll E. Wood Jr. (1921–2009) and Robert Kenneth Godfrey (1911–2000) from plants collected at Cluster Springs in Walton County on March 4, 1956. It is native to the southeastern United States.

SMALL BUTTERWORT
Pinguicula pumila Michx.
Bladderwort family (Lentibulariaceae)

Description: This petite species has a tiny basal rosette of leaves that are viscid to the touch. The leaves are elliptic to ovate and average ¼"–⅜" long. Solitary flowers are on erect stems that may reach 8" tall. An erect stem is topped by a flower that measures about ⅜" wide, varying from white, violet, or pale rose (rarely yellow) and marked with purple or yellow.

Bloom Season: All year

Habitat/Range: Damp habitats from Walton County east and south into the Florida Keys

Comments: The name *pumila* means "little," referring to its tiny rosette of leaves. Like other species in this genus, the leaves entrap and digest small insects. It prefers damp soils but can sometimes be found rooted in limestone crevices. It often shares its habitat with other carnivorous species such as sundews (*Drosera*) and pitcherplants (*Sarracenia*) but can be difficult to find when not blooming.

PURPLE BLADDERWORT
Utricularia purpurea Walter
Bladderwort family (Lentibulariaceae)

Description: Like other members of the genus, this aquatic, carnivorous species has filament-like leaves that branch into threadlike segments. There is usually a bladderlike trap at the end of the segments. Flower spikes can reach 6" tall, each topped by 1–4 light purple or violet, ⅜" flowers.

Bloom Season: All year

Habitat/Range: Wetlands, ponds, and lakes throughout mainland Florida

Comments: *Utricularia* is Latin for "small bag," referring to the traps on the leaves. When a tiny aquatic organism triggers a trap, it is sucked inside and the trap closes. Once captured, enzymes digest nutrients from the prey. The name *purpurea* refers to the purple flowers. This species may be floating in water or stranded in mud and is the most common of the 4 species in Florida with purple or violet flowers. There are 10 Florida native species in this genus with yellow flowers.

SAVANNAH FALSE PIMPERNEL
Lindernia grandiflora Nutt.
Lindernia family (Linderniaceae)

Description: This species has prostrate or ascending stems with opposite, clasping, ovate leaves measuring up to ⅜" long and ½" wide. The slender flower stems are axillary and topped by a single flower. The flowers are about ¼" wide, with a purple-spotted lip.

Bloom Season: All year

Habitat/Range: Freshwater wetlands throughout much of mainland Florida west in the panhandle to Leon and Franklin Counties

Comments: *Lindernia* honors German botanist Franz Balthazar von Lindern (1682–1755). The name *grandiflora* relates to its large flowers compared to those of the other species in the genus. Also called angel's tears or blue moneywort, it frequents shady trails that traverse mesic flatwoods. The naturalized exotic *Lindernia crustacea* differs by having a purple line across the lower lip. This genus has been previously placed in the Plantain (Plantaginaceae) and Figwort (Scrophulariaceae) families.

FLORIDA LOOSESTRIFE

Lythrum flagellare Shuttlew. ex Chapm.
Loosestrife family (Lythraceae)

Description: The slender stems of this species are usually trailing across the ground with opposite, oval to ovate leaves that are mostly ¼"–½" long and half as wide. The flowers are pinkish lavender and measure about ⅜" wide.

Bloom Season: February to June

Habitat/Range: Endemic to wet prairies and moist roadsides from Hernando and Orange Counties south to Collier County, mostly north and west of Lake Okeechobee

Comments: *Lythrum* means "blood" and relates to the color of the flowers of *Lythrum salicaria* and for its medicinal use to stop bleeding. The name *flagellare* alludes to the long, supple stems of this species. It was first collected in Sarasota County in 1883 and is under review for federal listing. Winged loosestrife (*Lythrum alatum* var. *lanceolatum*) and wand loosestrife (*Lythrum lineare*) are shrubby and have similar flowers.

STREAM BOGMOSS

Mayaca fluviatilis Aubl.
Bogmoss family (Mayacaceae)

Description: This species has narrowly linear leaves that spiral along narrow, succulent stems. The ⅝" flowers each have 3 violet or pinkish petals with a white center.

Bloom Season: All year

Habitat/Range: In wet soils along seepage slopes or aquatic in streams, spring runs, and rivers across the panhandle and discontinuously south to Highlands County

Comments: *Mayaca* is a name used by Spanish explorers for a Native American tribe with settlements along the upper St. Johns River at Hontoon Island in present-day Volusia County. The Mayacans were encountered in 1566 by Pedro Menéndez (1519–1574) when he attempted to sail up the St. Johns River and was met with hostility. The name *fluviatilis* means "growing in rivers." Some taxonomists acknowledge *Mayaca aubletii* as a separate species in Florida, but the slight variation used to separate them may be due to a function of habitat.

TROPICAL ROYALBLUE WATERLILY
Nymphaea elegans Hook.
Waterlily family (Nymphaeaceae)

Description: The leaves of this species are rounded and deeply notched at the base, ranging from 4"–8" in diameter (green above, purple below). The petals of the fragrant, solitary flowers are usually tinged with violet to some degree but may appear white. The flowers are held 4"–6" above the water surface and range from 2½"–4" wide.

Bloom Season: April to November

Habitat/Range: Lakes, ponds, and shallow canals of Nassau County and along Florida's west coast from Levy County south to Collier County

Comments: *Nymphaea* relates to water nymphs in Greek mythology, depicted as young, beautiful girls, or naiads, identified with rivers, ponds, lakes, and springs. The name *elegans* means "elegant." Gallinules, moorhens, green herons, and rails often walk on the leaves of water lilies to hunt aquatic snails and other prey. Beetles and bumblebees are likely pollinators.

VIOLET ORCHID
Ionopsis utricularioides (Sw.) Lindl.
Orchid family (Orchidaceae)

Description: This epiphytic species has 1–5 thick, prominently ribbed leaves that average 2"–4" long and ½"–⅝" wide. The pale violet flowers are produced in an airy panicle, with small sepals and petals above the much larger, broadly spreading, 2-lobed lip. The lip is typically about ⅜" wide.

Bloom Season: December to June

Habitat/Range: Hardwood swamps of Palm Beach, Collier, and mainland Monroe County

Comments: *Ionopsis* alludes to the flowers resembling those of a violet (Violaceae); *utricularioides* relates to the flowers resembling those of a *Utricularia* (Lentibulariaceae), the bladderworts. This imperiled, state-listed endangered species prefers small branches of the host tree and is sometimes found dangling by only a few thin roots. Its stronghold in Florida is in the Fakahatchee Swamp, where it often grows on Coastal Plain willow (*Salix caroliniana*).

TALL TWAYBLADE

Liparis nervosa (Thunb.) Lindl.
(Also *Liparis elata* Lindl.)
Orchid Family (Orchidaceae)

Description: This terrestrial or semi-epiphytic orchid has large, longitudinally-pleated leaves that reach 10" long and 5" wide. The 6"–8" erect flower spike bears ⅜"–½" flowers.

Bloom Season: Mostly August–September

Habitat/Range: Terrestrial or on mossy, decomposing stumps and fallen logs in hardwood swamps of Hernando, Hillsborough, Collier, and Miami-Dade Counties

Comments: *Liparis* means "glossy" and refers to the glossy luster of the leaves. The name *nervosa* relates to the prominent veins on the leaves. The populations of this endangered orchid are mostly centered in the deep swamps of Collier County. It has a wide global range and was first described as *Ophrys nervosa* in 1784 by Swedish naturalist Carl Peter Thunberg (1743–1828) from plants collected in Japan. In swamps it is often found growing on fallen tree trunks in association with mosses and ferns.

SOUTHERN TWAYBLADE

Listera australis Lindl.
(Also *Neottia bifolia* [Raf.] Baumbach)
Orchid family (Orchidaceae)

Description: A pair of dark green, ovate to elliptic leaves range from ½"–1½" long and ¼"–¾" wide, with purplish green stems that typically stand 6"–10" tall. From 5–25 reddish purple flowers have a linear and deeply forked lip. Flower length is ½" or less.

Bloom Season: January to March

Habitat/Range: Humus of moist woods, with scattered populations from Escambia to Duval County south to Sarasota, Manatee, and Polk Counties

Comments: *Listera* honors English physician and naturalist Martin Lister (1638–1711). The name *australis* means "southern" and relates to the species' range. A recent taxonomic study suggests *Neottia* has priority over *Listera*, but many renowned orchid taxonomists find the argument unconvincing. This species ranks as one of the most difficult orchids to see when flowering because it blends in so well with the leaf litter.

CLAMSHELL ORCHID

Prosthechea cochleata (L.) W.E. Higgins
(Also *Encyclia cochleata* [L.] Dressler)
Orchid family (Orchidaceae)

Description: The leaves of this epiphyte are linear-lanceolate, average 4"–8" long and ½"–1" wide, and are attached to a hard pseudobulb. The purple lip is uppermost, with narrow, yellowish, twisted sepals and petals protruding downward.

Bloom Season: October to May

Habitat/Range: Hammocks and wooded swamps of Lee, Collier, Monroe (mainland), and Miami-Dade Counties

Comments: *Prosthechea* means "appendix" and refers to the appendage on the back of the column. The name *cochleata* means "shell shaped" and alludes to the clamshell-shaped lip. This state-listed endangered species was first discovered in Florida in 1877 by botanist Abram Paschal Garber (1838–1881). It was moved to the genus *Prosthechea* in 1998 by American botanist Wesley Ervin Higgins (1949–). It ranges into the tropical Americas and is widely cultivated.

AMERICAN BLUEHEARTS

Buchnera americana L.
Broomrape family (Orobanchaceae)

Description: The frail stems of bluehearts average 8"–12" tall, with narrow, opposite leaves that reduce in size up the stem. The lower leaves range from 1"–2" long and ¼"–⅜" wide. Violet or white 5-lobed flowers top the slender flowering stem. The flowers are about ⅜" wide with 1 to several open at a time.

Bloom Season: All year

Habitat/Range: Pinelands, marshes, and roadsides throughout Florida

Comments: *Buchnera* honors German botanist Johann Gottfried Büchner (1695–1749), who wrote books in Latin. The name *americana* means "of America." White-flowered forms have been referred to as a distinct species (*Buchnera floridana*). It can gain sustenance from other plants as a hemiparasite and is a larval host of the common buckeye butterfly. It was recently moved from the Figwort family (Scrophulariaceae).

MAYPOP OR APRICOT VINE
Passiflora incarnata L.
Passionflower family (Passifloraceae)

Description: Maypop is a high-climbing vine with 3-lobed, serrate leaves to 3"–4" wide. The showy, fragrant flowers are 2½"–3¼" wide with pink to pale purple sepals and petals. The ovoid, yellowish-green fruits are 2"–2½" wide.

Bloom Season: March to October

Habitat/Range: A variety of habitats throughout mainland Florida

Comments: *Passiflora* is Latin for "passion flower" and relates to the crucifixion of Jesus. The name *incarnata* means "flesh colored," alluding to the pinkish flowers on some plants. The name maypop refers to the hollow fruits that begin ripening in May and pop loudly when crushed. The Cherokee gave it the name *ocoee*, translating to "apricot place," and is the name source of the Ocoee River in Tennessee and the town of Ocoee, Florida. It is a larval host of heliconian butterflies and the ple-beian sphinx moth. The plant spreads aggressively in cultivation.

BLUE WATER HYSSOP
Bacopa caroliniana (Walter) B.L. Rob.
Plantain family (Plantaginaceae)

Description: The mat-forming succulent stems and leaves of this species smell like lemon when crushed. The stems are typically about 6" tall, with opposite, sessile, softly hairy leaves that alternate in direction on the stem. The leaves are ovate to about ⅝" long and ¼"–½" wide. The ⅜", 5-lobed, bright blue flowers are solitary in the upper leaf axils.

Bloom Season: May to November

Habitat/Range: Freshwater wetlands throughout mainland Florida

Comments: *Bacopa* is an aboriginal name among indigenous people of French Guiana. The name *caroliniana* means "of the Carolinas." It is sometimes called lemon bacopa because of the pungent, lemon-like odor emitted from crushed leaves. The name hyssop relates to the garden herb anise (*Hyssopus officinalis*). This and other members of the Figwort family (Scrophularia-ceae) were recently moved to the Plantain family (Plantaginaceae).

BLUE TOADFLAX
Linaria canadensis (L.) Chaz.
Plantain family (Plantaginaceae)

Description: This biennial reaches 8"–24" tall, with narrowly linear, alternate leaves measuring ⅜"–1" long. Smaller but wider leaves on the prostrate stems are opposite or whorled. The flowers measure about ⁵⁄₁₆" long and nearly as wide.

Bloom Season: February to May

Habitat/Range: Fields and roadsides throughout mainland Florida

Comments: *Linaria* alludes to the leaves of *Linaria vulgaris*, which resemble a species of *Linum* (Linaceae). The name *canadensis* means "of Canada." The Iroquois used leaves of a related species as an anti-love elixir. The name toadflax is said to have come from the flowers resembling small toads, but it is also said that the word "toad" in Old English means "false," relating to the resemblance of the leaves to a species of flax (Linaceae). It is a larval host plant of the common buckeye butterfly.

CAROLINA SEA LAVENDER
Limonium carolinianum (Walter) Britton
Leadwort family (Plumbaginaceae)

Description: The spatulate or obovate leaves form a basal rosette and measure 2"–6" long and ⅝"–1½" wide. The flowers are in open, airy panicles, with each lavender flower measuring about ⅛" wide.

Bloom Season: June to December

Habitat/Range: Brackish marshes and salt flats along the Atlantic and Gulf coasts of Florida, including the Florida Keys

Comments: *Limonium* means "meadow" and alludes to the frequency of some species to inhabit coastal prairies. The name *carolinianum* relates to South Carolina, where this species was first collected by botanist Thomas Walter (1740–1789) and described in 1788 as *Statice caroliniana*. A significant threat to this species in the United States is wholesale harvesting of flowering stems for dried floral arrangements. It is also called statice and marsh rosemary.

WILD BLUE PHLOX
Phlox divaricata L.
Phlox family (Polemoniaceae)

Description: This phlox reaches 20" tall, with hairy, sessile, ovate-lanceolate leaves that measure 1"–2" long and ⅜"–½" wide. The flowers are pleasantly fragrant and measure ¾"–1" wide.

Bloom Season: February to May

Habitat/Range: Calcareous mesic forests of Gadsden, Liberty, Jackson, and Washington Counties in the Florida panhandle

Comments: *Phlox* is Greek for "flame" and relates to the flaming pink flowers of some species. The name *divaricata* means "wide spreading" and relates to the plant's spreading growth habit. This species ranges across eastern North America and is widely cultivated, with numerous pastel color forms in the nursery trade. Popular cultivars are Blue Moon, Clouds of Perfume, Fuller's White, and Chattahoochee. Long-tongued insects like butterflies, moths, and large bees are effective cross-pollinators. Some species are used in roadside beautification projects.

DOWNY PHLOX
Phlox pilosa L.
Phlox family (Polemoniaceae)

Description: The narrowly linear, spreading leaves of downy phlox average 1½"–3½" long and ⅛"–¼" wide (the upper leaves are noticeably longer than the bracts). The 5-lobed flowers are typically ¾"–1" wide and produced in terminal clusters.

Bloom Season: March to June

Habitat/Range: Dry, open woods and sandhills through the panhandle and northern Florida south to Pinellas, Hillsborough, and Polk Counties

Comments: The name *pilosa* means "hairy" and alludes to the sticky hairs covering the stems, leaves, and calyx. There are 67 species of *Phlox* worldwide, and many are popular garden subjects, adding splashes of bright color in sunny locations. Two species of sphinx moths, the trumpet vine sphinx and hummingbird clearwing, visit the flowers of *Phlox* in Florida and serve as pollinators. This is the most commonly encountered of the 6 Florida native species and has the widest Florida range.

CHAPMAN'S MILKWORT
Polygala chapmanii Torr. & A. Gray
Milkwort family (Polygalaceae)

Description: This frail species reaches 12"–24" tall, with few, tiny grasslike leaves. The ⅛" flowers are in terminal racemes and range from light violet to pale pink.

Bloom Season: May to November

Habitat/Range: Wet flatwoods and bogs in the Florida panhandle from Liberty and Franklin Counties west to Escambia County

Comments: *Polygala* means "much milk," in the fanciful belief that milkworts could increase lactation. The name *chapmanii* honors American physician and pioneering botanist Alvan Wentworth Chapman (1809–1899), who graduated from Amherst College in Massachusetts then moved to Georgia, where he took an interest in botany, and later settled in Marianna, Quincy, and Apalachicola, Florida. He is buried in Apalachicola beside his wife at Chestnut Cemetery. Chapman's milkwort is found from Georgia across the southeastern states to Louisiana.

RACEMED MILKWORT
Polygala polygama Walter
Milkwort family (Polygalaceae)

Description: Erect or spreading, usually unbranched, angular stems are lined with alternate, narrowly oblong-oblanceolate, spine-tipped, sessile leaves that average ⅝"–1½" long and ⅛"–¼" wide. A raceme of small, purple to pinkish violet flowers top the stems, and each flower measures about ¼" across. Cleistogamous flowers are sometimes produced underground or at the base of the plant.

Bloom Season: February to August.

Habitat/Range: Sandhills and flatwoods of the eastern United States.

Comments: The name *polygama* combines "many" or "several" and "marriage" (as in polygamy). In this case, it relates to the normal flowers and the self-pollinating (cleistogamous) flowers produced on the same plant. Hairs on the seeds attract ants, which in turn disperse the seeds. It is similar to Lewton's milkwort (*Polygala lewtonii*), which has leaves with rounded tips.

PICKERELWEED
Pontederia cordata L.
Pickerelweed family (Pontederiaceae)

Description: Pickerelweed is an aquatic plant with fleshy, heart-shaped or lanceolate leaves. Plants usually emerge from standing water, reaching 3' tall, with leaf blades measuring 4"–8" long and 1"–4" wide. The erect flower spike is densely covered with blue (rarely white), 2-lipped flowers that measure about ¼" wide.

Bloom Season: All year

Habitat/Range: Freshwater wetlands and roadside ditches throughout Florida

Comments: *Pontederia* honors Italian botanist and professor Guilo Pontedera (1688–1757). The name *cordata* relates to the heart-shaped (cordate) leaf blades. The common name refers to the pickerel, a fish that often uses this plant for cover, especially when young. The flowers attract bees and a multitude of butterflies. It is related to the invasive water-hyacinth (*Eichhornia crassipes*) that clogs waterways throughout Florida.

ROUNDLOBED LIVERLEAF
Anemone americana (DC.) H. Hara
Buttercup family (Ranunculaceae)

Description: The hairy, round-lobed leaves are green or liver-colored, often purplish beneath, and measure ½"–2½" long and 1"–3½" wide. The blue, solitary flowers are about ⅜" wide. Hairy, aerial shoots are horizontal or ascending and sprout from rhizomes.

Bloom Season: February to May

Habitat/Range: Wooded slopes and streambanks in Jackson and Gadsden Counties

Comments: *Anemone* is from the Greek *anemos* ("wind"). In Greek mythology, young and handsome Adonis, who was born from a myrrh tree, was gored by a wild boar sent by the jealous goddess Artemis. Adonis died in Aphrodite's arms, who so loved him that she sprinkled nectar on his blood and out sprang the blood-red *Anemone coronaria*, with petals that blow off easily in the wind. The name *americana* refers to America. This state-listed endangered species ranges across much of eastern North America.

PINE-HYACINTH
Clematis baldwinii Torr. & A. Gray
Buttercup family (Ranunculaceae)

Description: Pine-hyacinth reaches 8"–24" tall, with linear or broadly lanceolate leaves that average 1"–4" long and are often deeply divided into 5 segments. The nodding flowers are 1"–2" long with curled, frilly, pinkish purple or white sepals.

Bloom Season: February to November

Habitat/Range: Endemic to flatwoods and pine-lands from Levy, Marion, and St. Johns Counties south through mainland Florida

Comments: *Clematis* was a name used by Greek physician Pedanius Dioscorides (AD 40–90) for a climbing plant with long, flexible branches. The name *baldwinii* honors Pennsylvania physician and botanist William Baldwin (1779–1819). Botanists John Torrey (1796–1873) and Asa Gray (1810–1888) described it in 1838. The name *hyacinth* relates to Hyacinthus, a boy in Greek mythology who is said to have died accidentally from a discus thrown by Apollo, who then created a flower from the boy's blood.

SWAMP LEATHER-FLOWER OR FAIRY HATS
Clematis crispa L.
Buttercup family (Ranunculaceae)

Description: The stems of this species trail close to the ground but may reach 6' tall or more with support. The compound leaves typically bear 4–10 lanceolate to ovate leaflets measuring 1¼"–4" long and ⅜"–1½" wide. Mildly fragrant, bell-shaped flowers average about 1" long and hang downward. The plant climbs by tendrils.

Bloom Season: March to August

Habitat/Range: Floodplain forests and riverbanks south in Florida to Lake Okeechobee

Comments: The name *crispa* alludes to the wavy sepal margins. It is commonly cultivated within its native range in the United States and makes a pretty garden subject that blooms throughout the summer, with flowers in blue, lavender, or pink. There are 6 native members of the genus in Florida, including the previous endemic species. The name fairy hats came from Florida botanist Craig Huegel's granddaughter, Caroline.

AMERICAN BELLS
Clematis glaucophylla Small
Buttercup family (Ranunculaceae)

Description: The stems of this vine reach 15' long, with leaves divided into 4–10 lobed or unlobed leaflets and a tendril-like terminal leaflet. The bell-shaped, purplish-red to deep rose-red flowers are pendent and measure about 1" long. The seeds are attached to plume-like filaments that aid in wind dispersal.

Bloom Season: May to September

Habitat/Range: Wet forests from Washington County to Leon County in the Florida panhandle; also Levy County

Comments: The name *glaucophylla* relates to the white or grayish (glaucous) lower surface of the leaves. It was first described by American botanist John Kunkel Small (1869–1938) in 1897 from plants collected in Georgia in July 1893. Other common names are whiteleaf leather-flower and panhandler. It is also found in Georgia, Alabama, Mississippi, and Oklahoma. The long, flexible stems are often used to make wreaths.

NETLEAF LEATHER-FLOWER
Clematis reticulata Walter
Buttercup family (Ranunculaceae)

Description: This climber has angled stems that reach 10' in length, with compound leaves and opposite, ovate leaflets that have netlike venation. The bell-shaped flowers are pendent, measuring about 1"–1¼" long. The mature fruits have fuzzy, feathery tails.

Bloom Season: April to August

Habitat/Range: Open woods and thickets through much of the Florida panhandle south in the peninsula to Sarasota, DeSoto, Highlands, Osceola, and Brevard Counties

Comments: The name *reticulata* describes the intricate network of veins on the leaf blades (reticulate). It is also called netleaf virgin's-bower. Bumblebees are frequent visitors to the flowers, and a variety of songbirds feed on the seeds. Soldier beetles, known as "Spanish flies," are attracted to the plant, and these have been regarded as an aphrodisiac since the 1500s. Plant juices may cause blistering of the skin.

CAROLINA LARKSPUR
Delphinium carolinianum Walter
Buttercup family (Ranunculaceae)

Description: Unbranched stems reach 24"–36" tall, with interesting spurred, blue flowers lining a narrow, terminal spike. Each flower is about ¾" tall. Basal leaves reach 4" long and wide and are palmately divided into narrow segments.

Bloom Season: April to July

Habitat/Range: Openings in woodlands of Gadsden County

Comments: *Delphinium* was derived from the Greek word *delphinion* ("dolphin"), for the shape of the flower on the species used to describe the genus. The name *carolinianum* relates to South Carolina, where this species was first collected and described in 1788 by British-American botanist Thomas Walter (1740–1789). It is a state-listed endangered species due to its limited range in Florida, but it also ranges across much of the eastern and midwestern United States. The plant can be fatal if eaten, but the seeds have been ground and mixed with alcohol to kill head lice.

CHATTAHOOCHEE RIVER WAKEROBIN
Trillium decipiens J.D. Freeman
Wakerobin family (Trilliaceae)

Description: This species may reach 12" tall, with spreading, strongly mottled, lanceolate leaves held on top of the stem well above the ground. The lanceolate flower petals range from maroon to greenish brown, turning brown with age.

Bloom Season: February to April

Habitat/Range: Floodplain forests and riverbanks of Walton, Washington, and Jackson Counties

Comments: *Trillium* means "triple," alluding to the flower parts arranged in 3s. The name *decipiens* means "deceiving" or "misleading" and alludes to its resemblance to the much shorter *Trillium underwoodii.* This species sometimes grows in mixed populations with other species, and the common name relates to its propensity to grow along the Chattahoochee River, which forms part of the Georgia-Alabama border and also part of the Florida-Georgia border in the central panhandle.

LANCELEAF WAKEROBIN
Trillium lancifolium Raf.
Wakerobin family (Trilliaceae)

Description: Lanceleaf wakerobin reaches 8"–18", tall with narrowly lanceolate-elliptic, mottled leaves that tend to droop. The 1"–2", purplish-green flower petals are narrowly linear and crinkled and have the texture of crepe paper.

Bloom Season: February to May

Habitat/Range: Floodplain forests and riverbanks of Jackson, Gadsden, and Liberty Counties

Comments: The name *lancifolium* refers to the lanceolate (lance-shaped) leaves. The narrowness of the leaves and flower petals makes it easy to tell apart from the other Florida species. The name wakerobin relates to being a symbol of spring, like the American robin. This and the previous species can be found growing along the banks of the Chattahoochee River and its tributaries. For added adventure, look for them while paddling a canoe down the river in Jackson County from early February into March.

SPOTTED WAKEROBIN
Trillium maculatum Raf.
Wakerobin family (Trilliaceae)

Description: Plants of this species reach 12"–20" tall, with broadly elliptic leaves that can be strongly mottled with bronze-green blotches underlain with maroon. The stiffly erect flower petals are spatulate, broadest above the middle, and range from maroon to dark garnet red.

Bloom Season: January to April

Habitat/Range: Floodplain forests of Jackson, Leon, Jefferson, Suwannee, Columbia, and Alachua Counties

Comments: The name *maculatum* means "spotted" or "blotched" and alludes to the colorful mottling on the leaves. This species ranges south into Florida from South Carolina, Georgia, and Alabama, but it is quite cold hardy and survives in cultivation as far north as Canada. *Trillium* species are noted garden subjects in England and have received the Award of Garden Merit from the Royal Horticultural Society. They are considered harbingers of spring.

LONGBRACT WAKEROBIN OR TOADSHADE

Trillium underwoodii Small
Wakerobin family (Trilliaceae)

Description: This rhizomatous species reaches 10" tall, with leaves blotched light and dark green, often with the leaf tips drooping to the ground. The erect, foul-smelling flowers have 2"–3" deep maroon or purplish-red petals.

Bloom Season: January to March

Habitat/Range: Rich deciduous forests from Jackson, Bay, and Liberty Counties east across the northern border counties to Columbia County

Comments: The name *underwoodii* is for American botanist, professor, and New York Botanical Garden staff member Lucien Marcus Underwood (1853–1907). After losing his life savings during the New York Stock Exchange crisis of 1907, Underwood became despondent and attempted to stab his wife and daughter at their Connecticut home before stabbing himself to death after they escaped. The name toadshade relates to toads, which like to hide beneath the leaves, like an umbrella.

BLUE PORTERWEED

Stachytarpheta jamaicensis (L.) Vahl
Verbena family (Verbenaceae)

Description: This species usually produces stems that spread horizontally and is typically only about 10" tall. The coarsely toothed leaves range from 1"–4" long and ¾"–1¾" wide. The green, quill-like spikes produce 1 to several flowers at a time, each about ⅜" wide.

Bloom Season: All year

Habitat/Range: Pinelands and disturbed sites of Wakulla, Hillsborough, Osceola, Brevard, and Indian River Counties and from Martin and Lee Counties south through the Florida Keys

Comments: *Stachytarpheta* means "thick spike" and alludes to the flower spike. The name *jamaicensis* relates to Jamaica. This species hybridizes with the naturalized *Stachytarpheta cayennensis* (to 6' tall) and forms *Stachytarpheta* x *intercedens*, with an upright growth habit. Individual flowers last a single day and attract nectar-seeking butterflies. The leaves are larval food of the tropical buckeye butterfly.

EARLY BLUE VIOLET
Viola palmata L.
Violet family (Violaceae)

Description: This early-blooming species has 2–3 ovate to elliptic, glabrous or pubescent, mid-season leaves with 3–9 lobes. The flowers are about ¾", with dense, white hairs near the throat. The seeds are explosively dehiscent, sometimes ejected several feet from the parent plant.

Bloom Season: December to April

Habitat/Range: Mesic woodlands, flatwoods, and seepage slopes through the Florida panhandle and south in the peninsula to Palm Beach and Lee Counties

Comments: *Viola* is the classical Latin name for a violet. The name *palmata* refers to the palmately lobed leaves. Violet perfume comes from sweet acacia (*Vachellia farnesiana*), a member of the pea family, and is cultivated in France for perfume production. Violet flowers are fragrant, but they contain chemicals that can briefly turn off the ability of the human nose to detect the scent consecutively, which is not a very good trait for a perfume.

SOUTHERN COASTAL VIOLET
Viola septemloba LeConte
Violet family (Violaceae)

Description: The 5–6 mid-season leaves are usually glabrous, with 7–9 lobes and a broadly cordate base. The lobes are narrowly elliptic, lanceolate, or spatulate. The flowers are about ¾" and range from light to dark blue-violet.

Bloom Season: February to May

Habitat/Range: Mesic deciduous forests from Santa Rosa County discontinuously east across northern Florida to Nassau and Duval Counties south in the peninsula to Manatee and DeSoto Counties

Comments: The name *septemloba* refers to the 7 lobes on the leaves of the plant that American naturalist John Eatton LeConte (1784–1860) used to describe this species in 1828. This species may not be distinct from *Viola palmata* but is kept separate in the *Flora of North America*. The genus requires taxonomic scrutiny, because a 1997 study showed that some plants referred to as *Viola palmata,* with lobed and unlobed leaves, are hybrids.

COMMON BLUE VIOLET
Viola sororia Willd.
Violet family (Violaceae)

Description: The nearly orbicular, toothed leaves form a rosette measuring up to 3" across. The flowers reach ¾" wide and range from pale to rich blue (rarely white). It is not stoloniferous.

Bloom Season: January to July

Habitat/Range: Mesic forests through much of mainland Florida

Comments: The name *sororia* means "sisterly," alluding to its similarity to other violets. It is the state wildflower of Wisconsin, Rhode Island, Illinois, and New Jersey. Hover flies seek nectar from the flowers and are effective pollinators. Violets were once called "lesbian flowers," because in the early 1900s lesbians would offer the flowers to women when they were wooing. This was called "Sapphic desire" because the Greek poet Sappho (ca. 630–570 BC), from the Greek island of Lesbos, wrote a love poem about her partner wearing a garland of violet flowers. Even today, violets remain a symbol for lesbians.

APPALACHIAN BLUE VIOLET
Viola walteri House
Violet family (Violaceae)

Description: This stoloniferous violet has trailing stems with rounded leaves to 1¼" wide; the stems root at the nodes to produce spreading colonies in shady, deciduous forests. The flowers are about ¾" wide and stand about 1" above the foliage.

Bloom Season: January to April

Habitat/Range: Mesic hardwood forests from Jackson and Calhoun Counties east to Jefferson County; also Columbia, Gilchrist, Alachua, and Citrus Counties

Comments: The name *Viola walteri* was published in 1906 by botanist Homer Doliver House (1878–1949) to honor British-American botanist Thomas Walter (1740–1789). This species is also called prostrate blue violet and Walter's violet. It ranges from Virginia and Ohio through the southeastern states to Arkansas and Texas. The cultivar Silver Gem is common in the nursery trade.

PINK FLOWERS

Coreopsis nudata

This section includes flowers ranging from pale pink to deep magenta. You may also need to check the Blue and Purple and the Red and Orange sections of this book if the flower you are looking for is not found here.

SWEET SHAGGYTUFT OR PINELAND PINKLET
Stenandrium dulce (Cav.) Nees
Acanthus family (Acanthaceae)

Description: The dark green, ovate, ground-hugging leaves form a rosette, with each leaf measuring ¾"–1¼" long and half as wide. Young leaves have long, coarse marginal hairs. The scape stands 2"–4" tall with several sweetly fragrant, pink, ½" flowers.

Bloom Season: All year

Habitat/Range: Wet pinelands and prairies from Citrus and Lake Counties south through the peninsula

Comments: *Stenandrium* is Greek for "tight anthers." The name *dulce* means "sweet" and refers to the sweet-scented flowers. Another common name is rattlesnake flower, alluding to its misconceived use as a remedy for rattlesnake bites. The Miccosukee are said to have placed leaves near sleeping babies to keep them from dreaming about scary animals. In some habitats, it tolerates flooding in the rainy season but eventually requires fire to thin out competition.

SEAPURSLANE
Sesuvium portulacastrum (L.) L.
Mesembryanthemum family (Aizoaceae)

Description: The smooth, fleshy stems of this species may be up to 36" long and sometimes mound up to 12" tall. The succulent leaves are linear to lanceolate and measure ½"–2" long and ¼"–⅜" wide. Star-shaped flowers are about ½" wide.

Bloom Season: All year

Habitat/Range: Coastal shorelines nearly throughout Florida

Comments: *Sesuvium* alludes to Sesuvii, one of the Gallic maritime states mentioned by Roman politician, dictator, and military general Julius Caesar (100–44 BC). The name *portulacastrum* refers to its resemblance to a *Portulaca* (Portulacaceae), the purslanes. The leaves are high in vitamin C and could have saved many shipwrecked sailors from dying of scurvy. It has a global distribution in tropical and warm-temperate regions and is sold as a vegetable in Asian markets. In the Caribbean, the pulverized leaves are used to soothe puncture wounds from venomous fish.

DESERT HORSEPURSLANE

Trianthema portulacastrum L.
Mesembryanthemum family (Aizoaceae)

Description: The prostrate or decumbent, reddish, succulent stems of this species are usually glabrous and diffusely branched. The fleshy, elliptic to orbicular leaves measure ¾"–1½" long, with long petioles. Axillary, 5-lobed flowers measure about ½" wide.

Bloom Season: All year

Habitat/Range: Open coastal habitats and disturbed sites of Flagler, Seminole, Hillsborough, Manatee, Palm Beach, Miami-Dade, and Monroe Counties, including the Florida Keys

Comments: *Trianthema* relates to the 3 flowers on the type species described by botanist Carolus Linnaeus (1707–1778) in 1753. The name *portulacastrum* refers to its resemblance to a *Portulaca* (Portulacaceae), the purslanes. It is naturalized in India, where it is commonly used medicinally as a cathartic (purgative), but it is toxic if taken in quantity. Its common name relates to its growing in moist areas in deserts.

MEADOW GARLIC

Allium canadense L. var. *mobilense* (Regel) Ownbey
Amaryllis family (Amaryllidaceae)

Description: The leaves range from 6"–12" long and about ⅛" wide or less, with a distinct odor of garlic when crushed. The pinkish, fragrant flowers are in terminal clusters and reach about ⅜" wide.

Bloom Season: April to May

Habitat/Range: Pine savannas and open disturbed sites through the Florida panhandle and in Alachua County

Comments: *Allium* is a classical name for garlic. The name *canadense* means "of Canada"; *mobilense* relates to Mobile, Alabama, where the type specimen of this variety was collected. This variety does not produce bulblets, unlike *Allium canadense* var. *canadense*, which is frequent in northern and central Florida. The flowers are visited by bees and small butterflies. It is related to some well-known garden subjects, such as chives, onions, garlic, shallots, and scallions.

CLASPING MILKWEED
Asclepias amplexicaulis Sm.
Dogbane family (Apocynaceae)

Description: Oval to broadly oblong, opposite leaves are sessile and measure 1½"–5" long and 1"–2½" wide, with wavy margins. The 12"–36" stems are topped by rounded clusters of pink flowers often tinged with green.

Bloom Season: April to June

Habitat/Range: Open, sandy fields, savannas, and roadsides across the Florida panhandle and from Lafayette, Columbia, Baker, and Duval Counties discontinuously south to Hernando and Polk Counties

Comments: *Asclepias* was named for Aesculapius, Greek god of medicine. The name *amplexicaulis* means "clasping stems" but in this case refers to the leaves that clasp the stems. It was first described in 1797 by botanist James Edward Smith (1759–1828) from plants collected in Georgia. It is one of the showiest native milkweeds in Florida and is sometimes cultivated by gardeners for its beauty and butterfly-attracting attributes.

CAROLINA MILKWEED
Asclepias cinerea Walter
Dogbane family (Apocynaceae)

Description: This is a wiry species with very few, narrowly linear, widely spaced leaves that reach about 2"–3" long. The mostly drooping flowers are in loose clusters on long stalks (pedicels), each flower measuring about ½" wide with pinkish gray undertones.

Bloom Season: June to September

Habitat/Range: Sandhills and flatwoods through the panhandle to Levy, Putnam, Marion, and St. Johns Counties

Comments: The name *cinerea* means "ash colored" and relates to the grayish cast of the flowers. When growing among grasses, this species is exceptionally difficult to find. It was first described in 1788 by British-American botanist Thomas Walter (1740–1789) from plants collected in South Carolina. Walter is best known for his work cataloging the flowering plants of South Carolina.

ROSE MILKWEED
Asclepias incarnata L.
Dogbane family (Apocynaceae)

Description: This erect, usually multi-stemmed species reaches 2'–4' tall, with opposite, lanceolate leaves that reach 6" long and 1½" wide. Small pink to mauve flowers are in very attractive, compact arrangements. Seeds are attached to tufts of white fiber and are dispersed by wind.

Bloom Season: June to August

Habitat/Range: Freshwater wetlands through the panhandle to Levy, Putnam, Marion, and St. Johns Counties

Comments: The name *incarnata* means "flesh colored" and alludes to the pink flower color. The flowers emit a pleasant fragrance reminiscent of cinnamon. Pollination relies on a visiting insect slipping on the horn so that one of its legs enters a slit between the nectar cups. Pollen stuck to its legs may be transferred to another flower in the same manner. Some insects get their legs trapped in the slits and perish, all for the want of nectar. Gardeners frequently grow this species to attract monarch and queen butterflies.

MICHAUX'S MILKWEED
Asclepias michauxii Decne.
Dogbane family (Apocynaceae)

Description: The long, narrowly linear leaves of this milkweed are mostly opposite along weakly branched stems that are typically no taller than 12"–16". Topping the main stem is a cluster of pinkish flowers forming an umbel.

Bloom Season: April to June

Habitat/Range: Sandhills, flatwoods, and pine savannas through much of the panhandle and the northeastern peninsula

Comments: The name *michauxii* commemorates famed French botanist and explorer André Michaux (1746–1802), who died of yellow fever in Madagascar. French botanist and agronomist Joseph Decaisne (1807–1882) first described this species as *Asclepias michauxii* in 1844. Decaisne collaborated with Asa Gray (1810–1888), widely regarded as the most important botanist of the nineteenth century. Like other milkweeds, this species is a larval host plant for queen and monarch butterflies, but it is seldom cultivated.

PINK BOG MILKWEED
Asclepias rubra L.
Dogbane family (Apocynaceae)

Description: Stems of this handsome species reach 4' tall, often branching near the top. Leaves are opposite, narrowly lanceolate, and reach 7" long and 1¼" wide. The flowers are in terminal or axillary clusters and range in color from pale to rich pink.

Bloom Season: June to July

Habitat/Range: Bogs and streambanks in Bay, Walton, Okaloosa, Santa Rosa, and Escambia Counties in the western panhandle

Comments: The name *rubra* means "red" and relates to the flower color in parts of its native range, although in Florida the flowers are in various shades of pink. The plant photographed was in the Blackwater River State Forest in Santa Rosa County. It ranks among the prettiest milkweeds in Florida but is not widely cultivated, even among faithful butterfly gardeners. A chemical extracted from milkweed seeds is currently being tested as a potential pesticide for nematodes. Another name is red silkweed.

FLYR'S NEMESIS
Brickellia cordifolia Elliott
Aster family (Asteraceae)

Description: The toothed, cordate leaves of this 3'–4' perennial average 2"–3" long and 1"–2" wide. Heads of pink to white disk flowers are clustered at the top of the stems.

Bloom Season: August to November

Habitat/Range: Open, sandy woodlands of Jackson, Gadsden, Leon, Wakulla, Jefferson, and Alachua Counties

Comments: *Brickellia* honors Irish-born physician and naturalist John Brickell (1748–1809), who lived in Georgia. The name *cordifolia* refers to the cordate (heart-shaped) leaves. It was first described in 1823 by Texas botanist Stephen Elliott (1771–1830) from plants collected in Georgia. The common name is for botanist Lowell David Flyr (1937–1971), who studied this genus. Flyr took his own life while admitted to a Texas hospital for bipolar depression. It has been falsely reported that he died in a car wreck while searching for this species in Georgia.

BULL THISTLE

Cirsium horridulum Michx.
Aster family (Asteraceae)

Description: The wickedly spiny, lobed or deeply incised leaves of this biennial reach 12" long and 2" wide, forming a basal rosette. The leaves on flowering stems are clasping, smaller, and not as deeply cut. Flower heads range from 2"–3" in diameter and vary from pink, rosy purple, lavender, or yellow to white.

Bloom Season: All year

Habitat/Range: Pinelands, prairies, and roadsides throughout Florida

Comments: *Cirsium* means "swollen vein," alluding to the medicinal use of thistles to treat varicose veins. The name *horridulum* means "prickly." Bull thistle, often seen along roadsides and in pasturelands throughout Florida, is a larval host plant of little metalmark and painted lady butterflies. In Greek mythology, thistles appeared on Earth to grieve the loss of Daphnis, a shepherd said to be the creator of pastoral poetry. This species is also listed in the Yellow section of this guide.

NUTTALL'S THISTLE

Cirsium nuttallii DC.
Aster family (Asteraceae)

Description: This very spiny biennial reaches 10' tall, often branching near the top, with strongly ribbed stems. Leaves are sessile, 4"–10" long and 1"–4" wide, with sharp spines on the tips of the lobes. Heads of pink to lavender disk flowers are ⅝"–1" wide and shaped like a shaving brush.

Bloom Season: April to August

Habitat/Range: Wet pine savannas, flatwoods, and roadsides in the western panhandle and throughout most of the peninsula

Comments: The name *nuttallii* honors English botanist Thomas Nuttall (1786–1859), who traveled in Florida in 1830. Six other Florida native plants also honor Nuttall. Many insects visit the flowers, including a variety of butterflies. This plant is often found in pastures, where it escapes grazing by livestock due to of its abundant sharp spines. Green lynx spiders often hide on the flowers to grab an easy meal when an insect stops for nectar.

GEORGIA TICKSEED
Coreopsis nudata Nutt.
Aster family (Asteraceae)

Description: This species is easy to identify because it is Florida's only *Coreopsis* with pink ray florets. It is typically 1'–2' tall but may reach 4' in height, with glabrous (smooth), slender stems and narrowly linear lower leaves.

Bloom Season: April to June

Habitat/Range: Wet prairies, flatwoods, bogs, and wet roadsides across the Florida panhandle and in five counties of northeast Florida.

Comments: *Coreopsis* means "tick-like," alluding to the seeds, which resemble ticks. The name *nudata* means "naked" or "bare" and relates to the mostly leafless upper stems. English botanist Thomas Nuttall (1786–1859) traveled around Florida and described this species in 1818 from plants collected in Nassau County. Butterflies visit the yellow disk flowers along with bees and nectar-seeking wasps. All native species of *Coreopsis* are Florida's official state wildflower.

THISTLELEAF ASTER
Eurybia eryngiifolia (Torr. & A. Gray) G.L. Nesom
Aster family (Asteraceae)

Description: The erect stems reach 12"–24" tall and are covered with long, soft hairs (villous). Linear, grasslike, leathery leaves occur basally and along the stems, either entire or remotely serrate, 2"–4" long and up to ¼" wide. Flower heads are about 1"–1¼" wide.

Bloom Season: April to November

Habitat/Range: Pine flatwoods, pine savannas, bogs, and moist, sandy roadsides in the central panhandle from Walton County east to Leon and Wakulla Counties

Comments: *Eurybia* is Greek for "wide" and "few" and is believed to allude to the few, wide-spreading ray florets. The name *eryngiifolia* relates to the leaves resembling those of an *Eryngium* (Apiaceae). It was first described as *Prionopsis chapmanii* in 1842 by botanists John Torrey (1796–1873) and Asa Gray (1810–1888). Another name is coyote-thistle aster. It also ranges into Georgia and Alabama.

ROSE-RUSH
Lygodesmia aphylla (Nutt.) DC.
Aster family (Asteraceae)

Description: The erect, rush-like, 12"–32" tall stems of rose-rush sometimes fork near the top, with leaves that are represented by either narrow scales or a few elongated, linear blades near the base. Basal leaves are often absent during flowering. Flower heads are light rose lavender to about 1⅜" wide, with ray flowers that are toothed at the tip. There are no disk florets.

Bloom Season: March to August

Habitat/Range: Sandy flatwoods and scrub from Jackson, Calhoun, and Bay Counties down the peninsula to Collier and Broward Counties

Comments: *Lygodesmia* is from the Greek *lygos*, "a pliant twig," and *desme*, "a bundle," referring to the clustered, rush-like stems. The name *aphylla* means "without leaves," referring to the plant's bare stems. The flowers open by midmorning, closing by late afternoon. The sap of some species turns blue when chewed like gum.

GRASSLEAF BARBARA'S BUTTONS
Marshallia graminifolia (Walter) Small
Aster family (Asteraceae)

Description: The oblanceolate basal leaves range from 1½"–10" long and ⅛"–½" wide with linear, ascending, grasslike stem leaves. Pinkish lavender flowers are in ¾"–1⅛" heads, opening in concentric circles and fading to white with age.

Bloom Season: July to October

Habitat/Range: Bogs and wet pinelands across the panhandle, in northeastern Florida, and from Pasco, Orange, and Brevard Counties to Highlands and Palm Beach Counties

Comments: *Marshallia* honors American botanist Moses Marshall (1758–1813), cousin of famed naturalist John Bartram (1699–1777). The name *graminifolia* relates to the grasslike leaves of this species. The common name derivation is obscure, but the first use of "Barbara's buttons" was by botanist John Kunkel Small in his *Flora of the Southeastern United States*, published in 1933. There are 2 other species in north Florida.

COASTAL PLAIN PALAFOX

Palafoxia integrifolia (Nutt.) Torr. & A. Gray
Aster family (Asteraceae)

Description: This palafox averages 2'–4' tall, with alternate, glossy, lanceolate to linear leaves 1"–3" long and ⅛"–½" wide. The pink or white flowers are in terminal clusters with 5 spreading corolla lobes.

Bloom Season: August to November

Habitat/Range: Scrub, sandhills, and pinelands from Jackson, Liberty, and Franklin Counties east and south throughout mainland Florida

Comments: *Palafoxia* honors Spanish patriot José Rebolledo de Palafox y Melci (1776–1847), Duke of Saragossa, who fought against Napoleon's armies. The name *integrifolia* means "with entire or uncut leaves." This species was first described by English botanist Thomas Nuttall (1786–1859) in 1818 as *Polypteris integrifolia* from collections he made in Georgia along the banks of the Altamaha River. Some taxonomists believe this species should be separated from the genus *Palafoxia*.

ROSY CAMPHORWEED

Pluchea baccharis (Mill.) Pruski
(Also *Pluchea rosea* R.K. Godfrey)
Aster family (Asteraceae)

Description: The leaves of this species smell like camphor when crushed and are covered with copious soft hairs. It typically grows less than 12" tall, with alternate sessile leaves that measure ¾"–2¾" long and ¼"–1" wide. Rose-pink disk flowers are in compact heads.

Bloom Season: All year

Habitat/Range: Freshwater wetlands throughout Florida

Comments: *Pluchea* honors French abbot and naturalist Noël-Antoine Pluche (1688–1761). The name *baccharis* may come from the Greek *bakcharis*, used by Greek physician Pedanius Dioscorides (AD 40–90). Settlers in the South placed the aromatic leaves in their bedding to deter fleas, giving rise to another common name, marsh fleabane. It was first described in 1768 as *Conyza baccharis* by botanist Phillip Miller (1691–1771) from collections made in Mexico.

SALTMARSH FLEABANE OR SWEETSCENT

Pluchea odorata (L.) Cass.
Aster family (Asteraceae)

Description: This shrubby species reaches about 4' tall with hairy, toothed, ovate to lanceolate leaves ranging from 2"–5" long and 1½"–2½" wide. The scented flower heads are numerous in dense, flat-topped clusters.

Bloom Season: All year

Habitat/Range: Coastal and inland marshes from Walton County west and south into the Florida Keys

Comments: The name *odorata* relates to the fragrant leaves and flowers. This species was first described in 1759 as *Conyza odorata* by Swedish botanist Carolus Linnaeus (1707–1778) but was relegated to the genus *Pluchea* in 1826 by French botanist Alexandre Henri Gabriel de Cassini (1781–1832). Although butterflies swarm on the flowers, the plant is surprisingly seldom cultivated. In the Caribbean, the leaves are used in a tea to treat colds, night sweats, menstrual difficulties, and stomach disorders.

EASTERN FRINGED CATCHFLY OR FRINGED CAMPION

Silene catesbaei Walter
(Also *Silene polypetala* [Walter] Fernald & B.G. Schub.)
Pink family (Caryophyllaceae)

Description: This species forms rhizomatous colonies with rosettes of spatulate leaves that measure ¾"–3½" long and ⅜"–1" wide. The flowers are typically in 3-flowered cymes, each measuring 2"–3" wide with 5 frilly petals.

Bloom Season: March to May

Habitat/Range: Deciduous forests and wooded bluffs of Jackson and Gadsden Counties in the central panhandle

Comments: *Silene* is derived from Silenus, a folkloric man of the forest sometimes depicted as a drunk covered in foam, which relates to the many species in this group that are coated with a sticky secretion that traps flies. The name *catesbaei* honors English naturalist Mark Catesby (1682–1749), who collected plants in Virginia and the Carolinas. This is a federal endangered species in its limited natural range in Florida and Georgia.

FLORIDA SCRUB ROSELING
Cuthbertia ornata Small
(Also *Callisia ornata* [Small] G.C. Tucker)
Spiderwort family (Commelinaceae)

Description: The narrowly linear leaves are ascending and average 4"–6" long and ⅛" wide or less. The 3-petaled flowers are about ¾" wide and range in color from pale pink to rich rose pink (rarely white). The petal margins are crenate.

Bloom Season: March to September

Habitat/Range: Endemic to scrub and sandhills in Gulf, Franklin, and Wakulla Counties, and from Alachua County continuously south to Collier and Broward Counties

Comments: *Cuthbertia* honors Alfred Cuthbert (1857–1932), a keen naturalist who lived in Manatee County and collected plants in Florida, Georgia, and South Carolina. The name *ornata* relates to the ornate flowers. Botanist John Kunkel Small (1869–1938) described this species in 1933 from plants collected in sandhill habitat between Avon Park and Sebring (Highlands County) in 1919.

PINK SUNDEW
Drosera capillaris Poir.
Sundew family (Droseraceae)

Description: The spoon-shaped leaves form a 1½"–2" rosette, and the leaf blades are covered with gland-tipped tentacles (glandular trichomes) that exude a glimmering, sticky secretion. The flowers are about ⅜" wide.

Bloom Season: April to July

Habitat/Range: Wet, acidic soils of flatwoods and bogs throughout mainland Florida

Comments: *Drosera* means "dewy" and relates to the dewlike leaf secretions. The name *capillaris* means "of hair" and refers to the hairlike tentacles on the leaves. Secretions from leaf glands trap and dissolve small insects for nutrients. The leaf secretions have been used to treat warts and corns and were once thought to be a powerful aphrodisiac. In Greek mythology, Drosera was a female spirit (naiad or nymph) presiding over streams, rivers, and lakes. Dwarf sundew (*Drosera brevifolia*) is similar but produces a much smaller rosette of leaves.

TRACY'S SUNDEW
Drosera tracyi (Diels) Macfarl.
Sundew family (Droseraceae)

Description: The stems unfurl like a fern fiddlehead and reach 12"–20" long. The thread-like leaves lack red pigment and are covered with gland-tipped hairs that capture and dissolve soft-bodied insects. The pink (rarely white) flowers are ¾"–1" wide.

Bloom Season: April to June

Habitat/Range: Bogs and wet flatwoods from Leon and Wakulla Counties westward through most of the Florida panhandle

Comments: The name *tracyi* honors American botanist Samuel Mills Tracy (1847–1920), who became a botany professor at the University of Missouri. This is the only sundew that is restricted to the United States, and most of its populations are in the Florida panhandle. It was once regarded as a variety of the similar *Drosera filiformis* but was given species rank by botanist John Muirhead Macfarlane (1855–1943) in 1914. Members of this genus are found on every continent except Antarctica.

WICKY
Kalmia hirsuta Walter
Heath family (Ericaceae)

Description: Wicky is a small, trailing species often hidden by other vegetation. The leaves average ⅜" long and ⅛" wide, with coarse hairs along the margins. The ½" cupped flowers are lobed, light pink, and marked irregularly with small red dots.

Bloom Season: April to November

Habitat/Range: Flatwoods and scrub south in Florida to Hernando, Lake, and Flagler Counties

Comments: *Kalmia* honors Finnish botanist Pehr Kalm (1716–1779), a student of famed Swedish botanist Carolus Linnaeus (1707–1778). The name *hirsuta* refers to the stiff, coarse hairs on the leaves. The name wicky is believed to have come from an Algonquian name in Quebec for sheep laurel (*Kalmia angustifolia*). The leaves of this and other species are toxic to livestock and humans, plus the flowers will produce bitter-tasting, toxic honey. Another common name for this species is hairy mountain laurel.

BAY BEAN
Canavalia rosea (Sw.) DC.
Pea family (Fabaceae)

Description: This trailing vine has leathery leaves that are divided into 3 large leaflets. The leaflets are almost circular in outline and measure 2½"–4" long and 2"–3" wide. Flowers are in axillary racemes, with 2–3 rosy, ¾" flowers produced at each node. The pods are 5"–6" long and 1"–1½" wide.

Bloom Season: All year

Habitat/Range: Beach dunes from Dixie and Volusia Counties south along both coasts into the Florida Keys

Comments: *Canavalia* is derived from *kavavali,* or "forest climber" in the Indo-Aryan languages spoken in India. The name *rosea* refers to the rose-pink flowers. Swiss botanist Augustin Pyramus de Candolle (1778–1841) published the name *Canavalia rosea* in 1825. The seeds are toxic to ingest and may cause unpleasant hallucinations, but the leaves are eaten as a vegetable in Asia. Ocean currents transport the buoyant seeds around the world. Bay bean helps stabilize dunes by trapping sand with its long stems.

PINK PRAIRIECLOVER
Dalea carnea (Michx.) Poir.
Pea family (Fabaceae)

Description: This bushy species can reach about 24" tall but is often only about 1' in height, with low, widely spreading branches. The compound leaves have very narrow segments. Attractive pink flowers surround an oblong head produced atop long stems.

Bloom Season: May to October

Habitat/Range: Pine flatwoods and meadows through much of mainland Florida from Taylor, Baker, and Nassau Counties south

Comments: *Dalea* commemorates English physician and botanist Samuel Dale (1659–1739). The name *carnea* is Latin for "flesh pink." Two varieties of this species in Florida (var. *albida* and var. *gracilis*) produce white flowers and are called whitetassels. See also summer farewell (*Dalea pinnata*) in the White section of this guide. When in flower, members of this genus are very attractive to bees and butterflies, but none are widely cultivated in Florida.

FÉAY'S PRAIRIECLOVER

Dalea feayi (Chapm.) Barneby
Pea family (Fabaceae)

Description: Plants of this species reach 18"–24" tall, with a rounded growth habit. The leaves are deeply dissected, with narrowly linear divisions. The leaves average ¾"–1" long. The heads of flowers measure about ¾"–⅞" across.

Bloom Season: March to December

Habitat/Range: Scrub and sandhills in scattered populations in Franklin and Wakulla Counties and from Marion, Putnam, and Volusia Counties south

Comments: The name *feayi* commemorates American physician William T. Féay (1803–1879), who became interested in botany as an avocation. Féay fled Georgia during the Civil War and took refuge in Florida, where he collected plants. There are 3 other Florida native plants that honor Féay. This species is most common in Florida, but there are several populations in southern Georgia, where it is considered rare. A flowering plant will likely be surrounded by a host of butterflies.

FLORIDA TICKTREFOIL

Desmodium floridanum Chapm.
Pea family (Fabaceae)

Description: The lowermost leaves of this 2'–3' species have 1 leaflet, and the upper leaves have 3 leaflets measuring 1½"–3" long and ½"–1¼" wide. The rhomboid terminal leaflet is the largest. Flowers are in loose, terminal panicles, each measuring about ½" long and ¼" wide.

Bloom Season: April to November

Habitat/Range: Sandhills, scrubby flatwoods, and forest margins throughout much of mainland Florida

Comments: *Desmodium* means "chain" and "to resemble," referring to the jointed pods. The name *floridanum* relates to Florida, where this species was first collected in 1860 by botanist Alvan Wentworth Chapman (1809–1899). Like all species in this genus, the pods are connected to form chains that stick to clothing, hair, and feathers as a means of dispersal. There are 19 native species in Florida and 5 weedy, naturalized exotics.

PINE ROCKLAND MILKPEA
Galactia pinetorum Small
Pea family (Fabaceae)

Description: The 3 narrowly oblong leaflets are typically about ⅜" wide or less but may reach ½" wide, with raised venation on both surfaces. The flowers range from ⅝"–1" long. Stems do not twine.

Bloom Season: All year

Habitat/Range: Endemic to pine rocklands of Miami-Dade County

Comments: *Galactia* means "milky," a name first used in 1756 to describe a species that had milky sap, but our *Galactia* species lack milky sap. The name *pinetorum* refers to its pineland habitat. This imperiled, state-listed endangered species is restricted to remnant pine rockland parcels from about SW 34 Street south to the Navy Wells Pineland Preserve at SW 360 Street, and on Long Pine Key in Everglades National Park. Some taxonomists include this species with the common *Galactia volubilis*, with wider leaflets and twining stems. The endemic *Galactia smallii* of southern Miami-Dade County has narrower leaflets.

FLORIDA HAMMOCK MILKPEA
Galactia striata (Jacq.) Urb.
Pea family (Fabaceae)

Description: The leaves of this twining legume are divided into 3 ovate-elliptic leaflets, each measuring about 1½"–2½" long and ¾"–1" wide. The ⅜" flowers differ from other species by the thin white lines on the standard.

Bloom Season: All year

Habitat Range: Coastal hammocks from Manatee County south along the Gulf Coast to Miami-Dade County and through the Florida Keys

Comments: The name *striata* relates to the striations on the standard. This is a larval host plant of the zestos skipper, which has recently disappeared from Florida. It was last reported from Key West but has not been seen since January 2004. Aerial spraying for mosquito control and the spread of imported fire ants that attack butterfly eggs and larvae are believed to have contributed to the butterfly's demise. There are no other milkpeas in Florida with striations on the standard, making this species easy to identify.

NAKEDFLOWER TICKTREFOIL
Hylodesmum nudiflorum (L.) H. Ohashi & R.R. Mill
Pea family (Fabaceae)

Description: This erect perennial may reach about 24" tall, with foliar stems bearing 3 ovate leaflets from 1⅝"–3⅜" long and 1"–2" wide. Flowering stems are typically leafless. The flowers are about ⅜" wide.

Bloom Season: June to October

Habitat/Range: Mesic forests from Okaloosa County discontinuously east in the Florida panhandle to Jefferson County and disjunct in Alachua County

Comments: *Hylodesmum* refers to being an abbreviated form of *Desmodium* (Fabaceae). The name *nudiflorum* references the leafless or nearly leafless flowering stem. This species has a wide range, from Quebec to Ontario south into Florida. It was moved from the Linnaean genus *Hedysarum* to *Hylodesmum* in 2000 by botanists Hiroyoshi Ohashi (1936–) and Robert Reid Mill (1950–). Two other native members of the genus in Florida are restricted to the panhandle.

SCRUB LUPINE
Lupinus aridorum McFarlin ex Beckner
(Also *Lupinus westianus* Small var. *aridorum*
[McFarlin ex Beckner] Isely)
Pea family (Fabaceae)

Description: Flowering plants typically reach about 12"–16" tall, with 1"–3" oval leaves that are covered with silky silver hairs. The ½" flowers are pinkish to nearly white, with black and maroon on the standard.

Bloom Season: March to April

Habitat/Range: Endemic to sand pine scrub of Orange, Osceola, and Polk Counties

Comments: *Lupinus* is Latin for "wolf" and alludes to the mistaken belief that these plants consumed soil fertility. The name *aridorum* refers to growing in arid places. This federal endangered species was first discovered in 1900 but wasn't named until 1982. It is trying to survive in a precarious place—that part of central Florida that has been overrun by development and agribusiness. The population in Orange County lies between the City of Orlando and the sprawl of Walt Disney World.

SUNDIAL LUPINE
Lupinus perennis L.
Pea family (Fabaceae)

Description: This lupine reaches 12"–24" tall and has a compact branching habit. Alternate leaves are palmate, with 7–11 oblanceolate leaflets arranged in a whorl. Narrow racemes of ¾" flowers reach 10" long and range from violet to blue.

Bloom Season: March to July

Habitat/Range: Sandhills and dry, open woods across the panhandle and the northern peninsula from Escambia County east to Clay, Baker, and Nassau Counties

Comments: The name *perennis* relates to being a perennial. The larvae of several species of butterflies and moths feed on the leaves, and the flowers are visited and pollinated by long-tongued bees. The whorled leaflets of this species make identification easy, and they can move from horizontal to vertical as the day progresses, hence the name sundial lupine. Some species are poisonous to livestock, particularly sheep. Sundial lupine is the larval host plant of the frosted elfin butterfly in northern Florida.

LADY LUPINE
Lupinus villosus Willd.
Pea family (Fabaceae)

Description: This short-lived perennial reaches about 18" tall in flower, with softly hairy (villose) leaves held slightly erect. The leaves have long petioles and average 4"–6" long and ¾"–1" wide. Flowers are pink with a dark maroon spot on the standard.

Bloom Season: March to May

Habitat/Range: Sandhills and dry, open woodlands south in Florida to Citrus and Polk Counties

Comments: The name *villosus* refers to the softly hairy (villose) leaves. The name lupine is pronounced "loo-pin" and is sometimes shortened in gardening books to lupin. Lupines are popular garden subjects in parts of North America and Europe, but Florida species have strict soil requirements that make them nearly impossible to cultivate. This species was named in 1802 by German botanist Carl Ludwig von Willdenow (1765–1812). The seeds of some species are eaten in Europe and the Middle East.

FLORIDA SENSITIVE BRIER
Mimosa quadrivalvis L. var. *angustata*
(Torr. & A. Gray) Barneby
Pea family (Fabaceae)

Description: The thorny stems are ribbed and may trail 6' or more, scrambling across low vegetation. The bipinnately compound leaves have numerous fine leaflets with evident lateral venation on the lower surface. The flowers are in round, ½"-wide clusters.

Bloom Season: May to November

Habitat/Range: Scrub and sandhills throughout much of mainland Florida

Comments: *Mimosa* means "mimic" and refers to the leaflets on some species that close when touched. The name *quadrivalvis* means "4 valves," referring to the 4 valves of the pods. The name *angustata* means "narrowed." The small, recurved thorns can make walking through patches of this vining species a very painful experience. Another variety found in central Florida (var. *floridana*) is characterized by having only the central vein evident on the lower surface of the leaflets.

SUNSHINE MIMOSA
Mimosa strigillosa Torr. & A. Gray
Pea family (Fabaceae)

Description: This thornless, hairy, mat-forming species spreads by rhizomes and bears alternate, bipinnate leaves that are divided into as many as 21 pairs of small, linear leaflets. The leaflets are sensitive and close when touched. The flower heads consist mostly of pink stamens.

Bloom Season: March to September

Habitat/Range: Sandy habitats and roadsides from Calhoun, Leon, and Nassau Counties south through mainland Florida

Comments: The name *strigillosa* refers to the tiny, straight, appressed (strigose) hairs. This plant is a popular ground cover because it spreads rapidly by rhizomes that crisscross to form a dense, ground-hugging mat. It is sometimes used in parking lot islands because it can tolerate light foot traffic and drought. The flowers attract bees, and the leaves serve as larval food for a sulphur butterfly called the little yellow. Another name is powderpuff.

SANDHILL BEAN
Phaseolus sinuatus Torr. & A. Gray
Pea family (Fabaceae)

Description: This twining vine has compound leaves with 3 diagnostic 3-lobed, broadly ovate leaflets measuring ½"–3" long and up to 2" wide, often with white mottling. The raceme of flowers may be branched at the base, with each flower measuring about ½" long.

Bloom Season: July to November

Habitat/Range: Sandhills and sandy pinelands, with populations scattered through mainland Florida from Okaloosa County to Miami-Dade County

Comments: *Phaseolus* means "little boat" and alludes to the shape of the seeds of the type species. The name *sinuatus* means "with a wavy margin" (sinuate). It was first described in 1838 and is closely related to such New World edible crops as string, wax, kidney, and lima beans. It was once regarded as a variety of *Phaseolus polystachios*, which has unlobed leaflets and light pink flowers. It was photographed at Silver Springs State Park (Marion County).

PINK FUZZYBEAN
Strophostyles umbellata (Muhl. ex Willd.) Britton
Pea family (Fabaceae)

Description: This trailing or climbing vine has 3 lanceolate to elliptic-oblong leaflets that average 1½"–2" long and ⅝"–1" wide. Long axillary stems bear 3–4 flowers, each measuring about 1" across. The pods are hairy.

Bloom Season: July to November

Habitat/Range: Open woodlands from Escambia County discontinuously east to Nassau County and south to Volusia, Pasco, Pinellas, and DeSoto Counties

Comments: *Strophostyles* is Greek for "turning" and "pillar," in apparent reference to the spiraling style. The name *umbellata* means "umbrella-like" and alludes to the inflorescence. This species ranges from New York to Oklahoma south into Texas and Florida. Various Native American tribes used members of this genus medicinally to treat typhoid fever and topically to treat poison ivy rash. It was photographed at Florida Caverns State Park (Jackson County).

CORAL HOARYPEA
Tephrosia corallicola (Small) León
(Also *Tephrosia angustissima* Shuttlew. ex Chapm.
var. *corallicola* [Small] Isley)
Pea family (Fabaceae)

Description: This species has stems that spread outward from a taproot with hairy, compound leaves from 2"–2½" long and leaflets ranging from ⅜"–½" long and ¼"–⅜" wide. The flowers average ⅜" wide.

Bloom Season: March to October

Habitat/Range: Pinelands of Miami-Dade and Collier Counties (reported from Hillsborough County)

Comments: *Tephrosia* means "ash-colored" and relates to the grayish pubescence on the leaves of some species. The name *corallicola* relates to growing on coral (actually, oolitic limestone). Botanist John Kunkel Small (1869–1938) first discovered this species near Coconut Grove (Miami-Dade County) in 1904. It is a state-listed endangered species currently known only from Everglades National Park, Big Cypress National Preserve, and Ludlam Pineland Preserve (also Isla de la Juventud, Cuba).

RUGEL'S HOARYPEA
Tephrosia rugelii Shuttlew. ex B.L. Rob.
Pea family (Fabaceae)

Description: Rugel's hoarypea has a prostrate or weakly ascendant growth habit with minute, bronze hairs covering the stems and leaves. The compound leaves have obovate leaflets from ¾" long and ⅜" wide, and the petiole is equal to or shorter than the length of the lowest leaflet. Red flower buds turn yellow then open white and fade to pink in a single day. Flowers are about ⅝" wide.

Bloom Season: April to November

Habitat/Range: Endemic to scrubby flatwoods of peninsular Florida

Comments: The name *rugelii* honors German-born botanist Ferdinand Ignatius Xavier Rugel (1806–1879), who collected in Florida, Cuba, and southern Appalachia. Florida hoarypea (*Tephrosia floridana*) is similar but with petioles 2–4 times longer than the length of the lowest leaflet. Some species are used medicinally to treat depression, dementia, diabetes, hemorrhoids, and malaria.

GOAT'S RUE
Tephrosia virginiana (L.) Pers.
Pea family (Fabaceae)

Description: This legume reaches 12"–24" tall, with hairy stems and alternate leaves divided into opposite, pubescent, elliptic-lanceolate leaflets that measure ½"–1" long and ¼"–⅜" wide. The ¾" flowers have reddish-pink wings surrounding the keel and a white or creamy yellow standard that becomes pink as the day progresses.

Bloom Season: April to May

Habitat/Range: Sandy soils of savannas; open, dry woodlands and adjacent roadsides through much of the panhandle and in Duval, Clay, Putnam, Marion, Lake, Orange, Citrus, and Hernando Counties

Comments: The name *virginiana* relates to Virginia, where it was first collected. Bees visit the flowers for pollen and nectar, and the leaves serve as larval food for the southern cloudywing butterfly. The common name literally means "goat's regret," for the bitter tasting leaves. The roots contain rotenone and have been used to poison fish and insects.

COASTAL ROSEGENTIAN
Sabatia calycina (Lam.) A. Heller
Gentian family (Gentianaceae)

Description: The upper stem leaves are slightly larger than those lower on the stem and are mostly elliptic, averaging ½"–¾" long and ⅛"–¼" wide. There can be 5, 6, or 7 corolla lobes, ranging from pink to white, with wide calyx lobes visible behind the corolla. The center of the flowers may be green or yellow, sometimes surrounded by an irregular reddish circle. The flowers average ⅝"–¾" wide.

Bloom Season: April to October

Habitat/Range: Floodplain forests and flatwoods throughout much of mainland Florida

Comments: *Sabatia* honors Italian botanist Liberato Sabbati (1714–1779), who was the keeper of the Roman Botanic Garden. The name *calycina* refers to the conspicuous calyx lobes. It often grows in the company of other members of the genus, especially *Sabatia stellaris*. The common name is misleading, because this species can be found in inland habitats as well as coastal.

BARTRAM'S ROSEGENTIAN

Sabatia decandra (Walter) R.M. Harper
(Also *Sabatia bartramii* Wilbur)
Gentian family (Gentianaceae)

Description: The succulent lower leaves are spatulate or narrowly oblong, 1½"–3½" long and ⅜"–⅝" wide, forming a rosette. The upper stem leaves are equal to or narrower than the stem. The 2"–2¾" flowers have 10–14 corolla lobes that range from rich rosy magenta to pale pink or white.

Bloom Season: May to September

Habitat/Range: Freshwater wetlands throughout most of mainland Florida

Comments: The name *decandra* refers to 10 stamens. The common name commemorates John Bartram (1699–1777) and his renowned naturalist son William Bartram (1739–1823). The chief of the Alachua Seminole tribe of northern Florida, Ahaya the Cowkeeper, referred to William as *puc-puggee* ("flower hunter"). This spectacular wildflower often flowers in shallow water during the dreadful heat of summer, when mosquitoes are as thick as the humidity.

MARSH ROSEGENTIAN

Sabatia dodecandra (L.) Britton, Sterns & Poggenb.
Gentian family (Gentianaceae)

Description: Key differences between this and the previous species are that the upper stem leaves of this species are thin (not succulent), lanceolate, and much wider than the stem. The flowers are very similar, although this species may have more stamens.

Bloom Season: Mostly June to September

Habitat/Range: Wet prairies and cypress pond margins in Escambia, Santa Rosa, and Washington Counties and from Gadsden and Franklin Counties east to Madison and Lafayette Counties; also Nassau County

Comments: The name *dodecandra* refers to 12 stamens but this is not a reliable characteristic. The range of this and the previous species overlap in the northernmost Florida counties, but this species becomes more widespread north of Florida. It was moved from the genus *Chironia* to *Sabatia* in 1888. It frequents habitats where other members of the genus occur.

SWAMP PINK ROSEGENTIAN
Sabatia foliosa Fernald
(Also *Sabatia dodecandra* [L.] Britton, Sterns &
Poggenb. var. *foliosa* [Fern.] Wilbur)
Gentian family (Gentianaceae)

Description: The upper leaves of this stoloniferous, 10"–14" bushy species are narrowly
lanceolate to broadly linear and measure ¾"–1½"
long. Each flower measures 2"–2½" across and
can range from rich rose pink to 2-toned pink and
white.

Bloom Season: June to September

Habitat/Range: Cypress ponds and openings along
blackwater rivers from Escambia discontinuously
east to Madison, Lafayette, and Taylor Counties,
plus Nassau County

Comments: The name *foliosa* relates to the plant's
leafy appearance. Some taxonomists insist that
this is a distinct species separated from *Sabatia
dodecandra* by having internodes usually equaled
in length by the leaves and with stolons commonly present. Others relegate it as a variety (var.
foliosa) of *Sabatia dodecandra*. Choose whichever
name you like better.

PINEWOODS ROSEGENTIAN
Sabatia gentianoides Elliott
Gentian family (Gentianaceae)

Description: The stems of this species reach
12"–18" tall, and it is the only pink-flowered
member of the genus in our flora that produces
clusters of flowers. Narrowly linear bracts extend
beyond the petals, and each flower measures up
to 2" across.

Bloom Season: June to August

Habitat/Range: Pine flatwoods and bogs from
Escambia County east to Jackson, Liberty, and
Franklin Counties, plus the northeastern peninsula
and disjunct in Indian River County

Comments: The name *gentianoides* relates to the
flowers being produced in clusters like those of a
gentian (Gentianaceae). The genus was named to
honor Italian botanist Liberato Sabbati, so it is pronounced "sa-BAT-ee-uh," not "sa-BAY-she-uh," as
is often heard. American botanist Stephen Elliott
(1771–1830) first described this species in 1817 in
his work *A Sketch of the Botany of South-Carolina
and Georgia*.

LARGEFLOWER ROSEGENTIAN
Sabatia grandiflora (A. Gray) Small
Gentian family (Gentianaceae)

Description: The uppermost leaves of this annual are thick, wrinkled, and not as wide as the stem, which helps differentiate it from the following species. The lower leaves measure ¾"–1½" long to ¼" wide. The flowers may reach 1¾" wide and vary in color from deep rose to pale pink (rarely white).

Bloom Season: All year

Habitat/Range: Wet flatwoods and marshes throughout most of Florida, but absent in parts of the panhandle

Comments: The name *grandiflora* refers to this species' large flowers, but there are other species with much larger flowers. The Seminole used this and the following species to treat "sun sickness" and to make a bitter tonic as a substitute for quinine. It was also taken to treat indigestion. Other species were used to treat yellow fever and to promote appetite and digestion. It was first collected in Florida along the Indian River in Brevard County in 1874.

ROSE-OF-PLYMOUTH
Sabatia stellaris Pursh
Gentian family (Gentianaceae)

Description: The prominently veined uppermost leaves of this species are thin, smooth, and equal to or wider than the stem. The lower leaves are ½"–1¼" long and ³⁄₁₆" wide. The 1"–1½" flowers have 5 (rarely 6) lobes that vary from deep rose, pale pink, or white to 2-toned pink and white. A red, jagged line encircles the base of the corolla lobes.

Bloom Season: All year

Habitat/Range: Flatwoods of mostly coastal counties of Florida into the Florida Keys

Comments: The name *stellaris* refers to the star-like flowers. This is the most frequently encountered of the 12 members of the genus that occur in Florida. It was named in 1814 by German-American botanist Frederick Traugott Pursh (1774–1820). The common name came from seventeenth-century Pilgrims of Plymouth, Massachusetts, who thought *Sabatia* referred to the Sabbath, when it really referred to Italian botanist Liberato Sabbati (1714–1779).

CAROLINA CRANESBILL
Geranium carolinianum L.
Geranium family (Geraniaceae)

Description: The finely pubescent, palmate leaves average 1"–2" wide and are deeply dissected with secondary lobes. The flowers are pink to nearly white and measure about ⁵⁄₁₆" wide. The fruits are divided into 5 segments with a narrow, ½" long, erect beak.

Bloom Season: January to June

Habitat/Range: Moist, shady trails and disturbed sites throughout most of mainland Florida

Comments: *Geranium* means "a crane," alluding to the long beak on the fruits that Linnaeus thought resembled a crane's bill. The name *carolinianum* refers to the Carolinas. The plant has been used medicinally to treat such ills as dysentery, skin rash, diarrhea, wounds, and cancer. Small bees and hoverflies visit the blossoms for nectar. It is a frequent weed in residential lawns throughout Florida, especially in shady, moist areas. Ground doves and mourning doves feed on the seeds.

ASHE'S CALAMINT
Calamintha ashei (Weath.) Shinners
(Also *Clinopodium ashei* [Weath.] Shinners)
Mint family (Lamiaceae)

Description: The shiny, aromatic, ¼"–½" leaves are strongly revolute (curled under along the margins). It reaches about 20" tall with an abundance of ½" flowers. Crushed leaves smell like basil.

Bloom Season: January to May

Habitat/Range: Pine scrub habitat of Florida's xeric central highlands from Marion and Volusia Counties to Glades County

Comments: *Calamintha* means "beautiful mint." The name *ashei* honors botanist William Willard Ashe (1872–1932), who described hundreds of new species in the southeastern United States. This species chemically inhibits the growth and seed germination of nearby plants (allelopathy). Because of this, it is typically found growing where there are few other competing plants nearby. It is a state-listed threatened species.

FLORIDA CALAMINT

Calamintha dentata Chapm.
(Also *Clinopodium dentatum* [Chapm.] Kuntze)
Mint family (Lamiaceae)

Description: This densely branched shrubby species reaches 30" tall, with ovate, opposite, pubescent leaves in clusters along the stems. The apex of the leaf blade is toothed (dentate). The 2-lipped, pinkish, ⅝" flowers are dotted with purple.

Bloom Season: April to December

Habitat/Range: Sandhills and dry bluff forests from Walton County east to Gadsden and Wakulla Counties in the central panhandle

Comments: The name *dentata* refers to the dentate (outward pointing) teeth on the leaf margins. The leaves have a musky-minty aroma when crushed. This species has also been recorded from a single county in Georgia, where it may no longer be present. If that is true, this species is now endemic to Florida. Although it is a state-listed threatened species, it has weedy tendencies and sometimes colonizes sandy roadsides that bisect its habitat.

LAKE WALES BALM

Dicerandra christmanii Huck & Judd
Mint family (Lamiaceae)

Description: Lake Wales balm is a small, shrubby species to 20" tall, with spreading or ascending branches. Some branches are persistently leafy; others flower then die back after fruiting. The narrow leaves are opposite and range from ⅜"–½" long and up to ⅛" wide. Crushed leaves smell like eucalyptus oil. The cream ½" flowers have magenta spots and 2 pairs of stamens with yellow anthers.

Bloom Season: August to September

Habitat/Range: Endemic to yellow-sand scrub and sandhills on the Lake Wales Ridge in Polk County

Comments: *Dicerandra* refers to the 2 hornlike spurs on the anthers that characterize the genus. The name *christmanii* honors botanist Steven P. Christman (1945–), who first realized this was a distinct species and was named as such in 1989, the same year it was registered as a federal endangered species. It is highly vulnerable to extinction.

LONGSPUR BALM
Dicerandra cornutissima Huck
Mint family (Lamiaceae)

Description: This species reaches about 18" tall, with herbaceous branches developed from a woody base. The thin needlelike leaves reach about ½" long and have a strong minty odor. The ½" flowers are pinkish coral with darker dots and white, spurred anthers.

Bloom Season: September

Habitat/Range: Endemic to scrub habitat in Marion and Sumter Counties

Comments: The name *cornutissima* relates to the prominent spur on the anthers. Longspur balm is currently known from only 15 populations. Other populations within its limited range have already been lost to development, which remains a threat to its habitat. It was placed on the federal registry as an endangered species in November 1985 due to its rarity and vulnerability to human and natural threats. Wildflower enthusiasts should look for it in September along the Cross Florida Greenway in Marion County.

FLORIDA BALM
Dicerandra densiflora Benth.
Mint family (Lamiaceae)

Description: Florida balm is an annual but may persist a second year. It is typically unbranched or with a few ascending branches above the non-woody base. The narrowly lanceolate leaves are pungently aromatic and measure up to 1" long and ³⁄₁₆" wide. The ½" flowers are crowded in the leaf axils, forming whorls around the stem. The anthers are white.

Bloom Season: June to October

Habitat/Range: Endemic to sandhills of northern peninsular Florida south to Levy and Volusia Counties

Comments: The name *densiflora* is descriptive of the crowded flowers in the leaf axils. Flowering specimens are literally balls of pink and can be seen from car windows while driving through remnant patches of its habitat within its natural range. English botanist George Bentham (1800–1884) described this species in 1848. Thirteen years later he became president of the Linnaean Society of London.

SCRUB BALM
Dicerandra frutescens Shinners
Mint family (Lamiaceae)

Description: Scrub balm is a subshrub to 20"
tall with spreading or prostrate branches. Some
branches are persistently leafy; others die back
after fruiting. The leaves smell of peppermint and
are narrowly oblong-elliptic to linear-oblanceolate
and measure ½"–1" long and up to ⅛" wide. The
½" flowers are white or blushed pink with vivid
pink spots.

Bloom Season: August to September

Habitat/Range: Endemic to yellow-sand scrub
and sandhills on the southern portion of the Lake
Wales Ridge in Highlands County

Comments: The name *frutescens* refers to the
shrubby growth habit. Scrub balm can be found
at the Archbold Biological Station in Highlands
County, where the populations are closely moni-
tored by research botanists. It was named in 1962
by botanist Lloyd Herbert Shinners (1918–1971)
and was listed as a federal endangered species in
November 1985. It is also called Lloyd's mint.

SMOKY BALM
Dicerandra fumella Huck
Mint family (Lamiaceae)

Description: Smoky balm reaches about 8"–12" in
height, with opposite branches arising from a taproot. Linear leaves are opposite along the stems,
with white to pale pink flowers that are dotted
with purple. The anthers are yellow.

Bloom Season: September to November

Habitat/Range: Xeric sandhills of the westernmost
Florida panhandle from Escambia County east to
Washington County

Comments: The name *fumella* means "smoky"
and relates to the smoky hue of the flowers. It
was first described in 2010 from plants collected
in Okaloosa County and was previously identified as *Dicerandra linearifolia*. The leaves smell
strongly of peppermint when crushed. It has a
very restricted range in Florida and is listed as
imperiled (S2 ranking) in Alabama. It hybridizes
with *Dicerandra linearifolia* var. *robustior* to form a
plant that produces bright pink flowers with yellow
anthers.

LAKELA'S BALM
Dicerandra immaculata Lakela
Mint family (Lamiaceae)

Description: This is the only species of *Dicerandra* in the southeastern United States that typically does not have spots on the flowers. It reaches about 14" tall with an upright growth habit. The narrowly oval to rhombic leaves average 1" long and ⅛"–⅜" wide. The ⅜" purplish-pink (rarely white) flowers bear purple anthers.

Bloom Season: Principally September to November

Habitat/Range: Endemic to sand pine scrub of Indian River and St. Lucie Counties

Comments: The name *immaculata* alludes to the lack of spots on the flowers. It was described in 1963 by botanist Olga Lakela (1890–1980), curator of the University of South Florida herbarium from 1960 to 1973, and added to the federal registry as endangered in July 1984 due to its rarity and threats to its habitat. It is known from a single population in nine unprotected sites. A white-flowered form was named forma *nivea* by Olga Lakela.

SAVANNAS MINT
Dicerandra immaculata Lakela var. *savannarum* Huck
Mint family (Lamiaceae)

Description: Savannas mint has a sprawling growth habit, with stems that root at the nodes when they touch the ground. The diamond-shaped (rhombic) leaves average about 1" long and ⅛"–⅜" wide. Flowers measure about ⅜", with 2–3 flowers per axil, and usually lack spots. The anthers are brownish.

Bloom Season: September to October

Habitat/Range: Endemic to coastal scrub savannas and sand ridges of St. Lucie County

Comments: The name *savannarum* refers to the species' growing in savannas in Savannas Preserve State Park. Botanists Keith Bradley (1971–) and George Gann (1961–) first discovered savannas mint in 1995 along a St. Lucie County railway and on private property. The railway population was relocated to Bok Tower Gardens in 2005 to propagate for reintroduction into protected preserves. It differs from the typical variety in growth habit, anther color, and scent.

COASTAL PLAIN BALM

Dicerandra linearifolia (Elliott) Benth.
var. *robustior* Huck
Mint family (Lamiaceae)

Description: Coastal Plain balm is an annual that reaches about 12"–14" in height, with obovate to rhombic leaves ½"–1" long and up to ⅜" wide. The ½" flowers are 3–7 per axil with reddish-brown anthers.

Bloom Season: September to November

Habitat/Range: Sandy and sandy clay habitats through the central and eastern panhandle; also Duval, Alachua, and Citrus Counties

Comments: The name *linearifolia* relates to the linear leaves. The name *robustior* describes its robust habit compared to the typical variety (var. *linearifolia*) in northwest Georgia. Taxonomic studies are under way to possibly relegate var. *robustior* as a distinct species. The plant photographed was among thousands growing in a pine plantation in Calhoun County that created a pink ground cover. It is one of 2 members of the genus in Florida that is not endemic.

BLUSHING SCRUB BALM

Dicerandra modesta (Huck) Huck
Mint family (Lamiaceae)

Description: This bushy species reaches 12" tall, with oblong to oblanceolate leaves averaging ½"–¾" long and about ⅛" wide. The leaves smell minty. White to purplish-pink, ½" flowers have vivid reddish-pink dots. The anthers are white to reddish brown.

Bloom Season: August to October

Habitat/Range: Endemic to scrub habitat in Polk County

Comments: The name *modesta* means "modest" and alludes to the flowers turning darker pink with age, as though blushing. This federal endangered species occurs along the eastern edge of the Lake Wales Ridge, where native-plant enthusiasts Nancy Bissett (1945–) and Steve Riefler (1952–) first discovered it while searching for a rare *Rhododendron* in Polk County. Botanist Kris DeLaney (1951–) later found additional populations. It is on the threshold of extinction and will be lost forever without sustained intervention.

TITUSVILLE BALM
Dicerandra thinicola H.A. Mill.
Mint family (Lamiaceae)

Description: This bushy perennial reaches 12"–30" tall, with many ascending stems. The narrowly linear leaves measure ¼"–¾" long and ⅛" or less wide and have a wintergreen odor. Flowers measure about ⅜" and are in whorls of 3–7 along the top third of the stems. The anthers are purple.

Bloom Season: October to December

Habitat/Range: Endemic to relict yellow-sand dunes near Titusville in Brevard County

Comments: The name *thinicola* means "sand dweller," alluding to the relict dunes it inhabits. This critically imperiled state-listed endangered species has an extremely restricted range, and very few plants are located within preserves. It was described in 1993 by botanist Harvey Alfred Miller (1928–). Attempts have been made to relegate this and other species as varieties of *Dicerandra frutescens*; others believe it is a hybrid, even though it is the only *Dicerandra* in Brevard County.

MOCK PENNYROYAL
Stachydeoma graveolens (Chapm. ex A. Gray) Small
(Also *Hedeoma graveolens* Chapm. ex A. Gray)
Mint family (Lamiaceae)

Description: The stems of this species reach about 12" tall. The fragrant, elliptic leaves are about ½" long, with reflexed margins lined with long, shaggy glandular hairs. The ½" flowers have a 3-lobed lower lip.

Bloom Season: May to September

Habitat/Range: Endemic to xeric pine flatwoods and sandhills of the central panhandle from Bay County east to Leon and Wakulla Counties

Comments: *Stachydeoma* combines *stachys* ("spike") and the genus *Hedeoma*, meaning "scent" and "mint." The name *graveolens* translates to "heavily scented," alluding to the plant's fragrant leaves. This state-listed endangered species is known from only 7 central panhandle counties, where it is mostly found in sandy upland habitats. Members of this genus contain essential oils that create the fragrance but can be lethal if ingested in quantity.

FLORIDA BETONY

Stachys floridana Shuttlw. ex Benth.
Mint family (Lamiaceae)

Description: This square-stemmed perennial herb spreads by rhizomes and tubers, often forming dense roadside colonies. The hairy, somewhat heart-shaped, opposite leaves range from 1"–2" long and ⅜"–¾" wide. The ⅜" flowers are in whorls along an erect spike.

Bloom Season: March to November

Habitat/Range: Flatwoods and roadsides throughout mainland Florida

Comments: *Stachys* refers to the spiked inflorescence. The name *floridana* relates to Florida, where it was first collected near Tallahassee in 1843. It is also called woundwort, for its uses to treat wounds, and rattlesnake weed, in reference to the segmented tubers that resemble a rattlesnake's rattle. The tubers are edible raw or cooked and resemble radishes in flavor. It is aggressive in cultivation, quickly spreading out of bounds by underground rhizomes, and is difficult to control.

WOOD SAGE

Teucrium canadense L.
Mint family (Lamiaceae)

Description: This cold-tolerant species produces erect, 1'–3' square stems. The opposite leaves are hairy and range from narrowly lanceolate to elliptic, 2"–4½" long and ⅜"–2" wide, with scalloped margins. Pale pink to lavender, wide-lipped, ⅜"–½" flowers are held on upright stems. The plant spreads by rhizomes and can form extensive colonies.

Bloom Season: April to November

Habitat/Range: Freshwater wetlands throughout mainland Florida

Comments: *Teucrium* honors Teucer, king of Troy, who fought alongside his half-brother Ajax in the Trojan War. The name *canadense* means "of Canada." Some species in this genus are used as a catnip substitute and to brew a medicinal tea to treat fascial muscle twitching caused by St. Vitus' dance (Sydenham's chorea), a motor nerve disorder once believed to be cured only by a pilgrimage to the shrine of Saint Vitus.

LAVENDER BLADDERWORT

Utricularia resupinata B.D. Greene ex Bigelow
Bladderwort family (Lentibulariaceae)

Description: The slender, filament-like, 3-parted leaves of this carnivorous species reach 1¼" long and bear small bladders (traps). The ¼" pink to lavender flowers are borne singly on erect stems held above the water.

Bloom Season: March to November

Habitat/Range: Wet flatwoods and pond margins scattered throughout much of mainland Florida

Comments: *Utricularia* is Latin for "little bag," alluding to the small, bag-like traps on the leaves of all species. The name *resupinata* refers to having the flowers twisted one-half turn on the axis to face upward (resupinate). This diminutive species is widespread in Florida but will be nearly impossible to recognize if not in flower. Like all species in this genus, it possesses small traps that catch and digest small aquatic organisms. The type specimen was collected in Massachusetts by botanist Benjamin Daniel Greene (1793–1862) in 1840.

WOODLAND POPPYMALLOW

Callirhoe papaver (Cav.) A. Gray
Mallow family (Malvaceae)

Description: The spreading stems of this species sometimes ascend to about 12" tall but may trail across the ground to 6' or more from a deep taproot. The lobed leaves are divided into 3–5 linear to elliptic segments. The 5-petaled flowers are rosy pink with a white base and reach about 2"–2½" wide.

Bloom Season: April to June

Habitat/Range: Dry woodlands of Gadsden, Jackson, Leon, and Alachua Counties

Comments: *Callirhoe* honors the naiad Callirrhoe, daughter of the river god Achelous, who was often depicted as a bearded man with a serpent body and horned head. Achelous offered Callirrhoe in marriage to Alcmaeon if he would retrieve the clothes and jewelry his mother was wearing when she sent her husband to his death in battle. The name *papaver* relates to the resemblance of the flowers to a *Papaver* (Papaveraceae). It is a state-listed endangered species.

LINDENLEAF ROSEMALLOW
Hibiscus furcellatus Desr.
Mallow family (Malvaceae)

Description: The softly hairy leaves of this 5'–6' shrubby species are typically deeply 3-lobed and average 2½"–4½" long. Showy, somewhat nodding flowers are about 3"–4" wide with uniformly pink petals, darker near the base.

Bloom Season: All year

Habitat/Range: Freshwater swamps, marshes, flatwoods, and roadside ditches along Florida's east coast from Brevard to Broward County, and in Highlands and Lee Counties

Comments: *Hibiscus* is said to come from the Greek *ibiscos,* for living in marshes with ibis. The name *furcellatus* refers to the notched apex on the involucral bracts. It is also called sleepy hibiscus, because the flower petals do not spread open like other members of the genus. It usually dies back in winter but may persist in warm winters. Hummingbirds visit the flowers, but it is seldom cultivated by Florida gardeners. Its range extends into the neotropics.

SWAMP ROSEMALLOW
Hibiscus grandiflorus Michx.
Mallow family (Malvaceae)

Description: Swamp rosemallow reaches 6'–10' tall, with softly hairy leaves and long petioles. The leaves are mostly 3-lobed with irregular teeth along the margins and measure 4"–7" long and up to 6" wide. The 4"–5" flowers appear in the leaf axils and range from pink to white.

Bloom Season: May to September

Habitat/Range: Freshwater wetlands and roadside ditches throughout much of mainland Florida

Comments: The name *grandiflorus* refers to the large flowers. Water garden enthusiasts sometimes cultivate this species for its captivating flowers. The stems die back in winter then resprout vigorously in early spring. Orioles and hummingbirds sip nectar from the flowers, and bees are frequently seen gathering the pollen. Swamp rosemallow can form extensive colonies along roadside ditches, but the flowers close around midday, so you only have the morning hours to admire them.

VIRGINIA SALTMARSH MALLOW
Kosteletzkya pentacarpos (L.) Ledeb.
(Also *Kosteletzkya virginica* [L.] Presl.)
Mallow family (Malvaceae)

Description: This pretty 2'–4' mallow has hairs covering the leaves and stems. The 1"–3" leaves may be triangular or lobed, with irregular teeth along the margins. The flowers are about 2" wide and open for 1 day.

Bloom Season: Mostly June to September

Habitat/Range: Brackish and freshwater wetlands throughout much of mainland Florida

Comments: *Kosteletzkya* honors Czechoslovakian botanist Vincenz Franz Kosteletzky (1801–1887). The name *pentacarpos* refers to the 5 carpels that make up the ovule-bearing part of the flower. This species has recently gained attention as a source of biodiesel fuel. The leaves can be cooked as a potherb or used to thicken soups, and the cooking water can be whipped into meringue. White fenrose (*Kosteletzkya depressa*) has smaller white flowers and is found in mainland Miami-Dade and Monroe Counties.

BRETONICA PELUDA
Melochia spicata (L.) Fryxell
Mallow family (Malvaceae)

Description: The softly pubescent, ovate-oblong leaves range from ¾"–1½" long. Pink to violet ½" axillary flowers have thin, dark pink irregular lines on the petals.

Bloom Season: All year

Habitat/Range: Sandhills and flatwoods in Suwannee County; also Pinellas, Sumter, and Polk Counties south to Collier and Miami-Dade Counties

Comments: *Melochia* is from *melóchich,* an Arabic name for a related *Corchorus* species but used for this group of plants in 1753 by botanist Carolus Linnaeus (1707–1778). The name *spicata* refers to flowers arranged in a spike. It was originally named *Malva spicata* in 1759 but was moved to the genus *Melochia* in 1988 by botanist Paul Arnold Fryxell (1927–2011). This genus has been previously placed in Byttneriaceae and Sterculiaceae. The common name translates from Spanish to "hairy bretonica." Bees and butterflies visit the flowers.

SAVANNAH MEADOWBEAUTY
Rhexia alifanus Walter
Melastome family (Melastomataceae)

Description: This species is recognized by its smooth stems and opposite, narrowly lanceolate, bluish-green leaves with 3 conspicuous longitudinal veins. The flowers are among the showiest of the genus and measure about 2"–2¼" across.

Bloom Season: May to August

Habitat/Range: Savannas, flatwoods, and bogs across the Florida panhandle through the northeastern counties and south to Orange County

Comments: *Rhexia* is a name used by Roman scholar Pliny (AD 23–79) for a plant useful in treating ruptures. The name *alifanus* refers to the urn-shaped fruits that resemble special glasses made in Alife, Italy, and used for drinking wine. It was described in 1788 by British-American botanist Thomas Walter (1740–1789). Like other species in this genus, its pollen is self-incompatible, requiring pollen to be carried from one plant to another by bees and other insects.

MARYLAND MEADOWBEAUTY
Rhexia mariana L.
Melastome family (Melastomataceae)

Description: This species may reach 30" tall, with narrow, linear, toothed leaves that range from ½"–3" long and ⅛"–¼" wide. The rounded petals measure ¾"–1" long and about ½" wide.

Bloom Season: February to November

Habitat/Range: Flatwoods, pond margins, and roadside ditches through the Florida panhandle and peninsula south to Martin, Hendry, and Collier Counties

Comments: The name *mariana* relates to Maryland, where it was first collected in 1700. This species very closely resembles West Indian meadowbeauty (*Rhexia cubensis*) but differs mostly by having a hypanthium shorter than ⅖". A hypanthium is the cuplike or tubular enlargement of the receptacle of the flower, surrounding or united with the carpels. The color of the petals ranges from rich rose pink to pale pink to pure white. Another common name is pale meadowbeauty. Correctly identifying species in this genus can be perplexing.

111

NUTTALL'S MEADOWBEAUTY
Rhexia nuttallii C.W. James
Melastome family (Melastomataceae)

Description: This small species typically reaches 3"–6" tall, with ovate leaves that measure ½"–¾" long and ⅜"–½" wide with blunt teeth and short hairs along the margins. Flowers measure about ⅝"–¾" wide, with glandular hairs on the seed capsules.

Bloom Season: March to September

Habitat/Range: Flatwoods and savannas from Walton County east and south to Collier and Palm Beach Counties

Comments: The name *nuttallii* honors English botanist Thomas Nuttall (1786–1859), who traveled around Florida in 1830. It was named *Rhexia serrulata* by Nuttall in 1813 but renamed *Rhexia nuttallii* by botanist Charles William James (1929–) in 1956. You must be in the field in the morning, because the flowers begin to close at midday. Barely touching the petals will cause them to fall off, which is a frustrating trait for wildflower photographers. It is similar to the following species.

FRINGED MEADOWBEAUTY
Rhexia petiolata Walter
Melastome family (Melastomataceae)

Description: The stems of this meadowbeauty may reach 24" tall but are usually less than half that height. The oval leaves have long hairs along the margins, and the blades have short petioles. The 4-petaled flowers are about 1" wide.

Bloom Season: June to November

Habitat/Range: Savannas, coastal prairies, bogs, and flatwoods through mainland Florida south to Indian River and Collier Counties

Comments: The name *petiolata* relates to the leaves having petioles (not sessile), and the common name alludes to the fringe of long hairs on the leaf margins. It was first described in 1788 by British-American botanist Thomas Walter (1740–1789) in his *Flora Caroliniana*, but he died an untimely death at the age of 49 soon after its publication. The flowers of this species may be very slightly larger than the previous species, and it lacks the glandular hairs on the seed capsules.

BURROWING FOUR-O'CLOCK

Okenia hypogaea Schltdl. & Cham.
Four-O'Clock family (Nyctaginaceae)

Description: The leaves of this annual are oppo-site, densely pubescent, and range from 1"–1½" long and ¾"–1" wide. The 5-lobed, rosy pink to magenta 1¼" flowers are solitary in the leaf axils. The flowers bend down after fertilization, pushing the developing fruits underground to ripen and preventing them from washing away by tides.

Bloom Season: March to November

Habitat/Range: Beach dunes from St. Lucie County south along the coast to Key Biscayne in Miami-Dade County

Comments: *Okenia* honors German botanist Lorenz Oken (1779–1851), who is best known for dividing animals into 5 classes. The name *hypogaea* means "underground," referring to the fruits that develop beneath the sand. Another name is beach peanut. This state-listed endangered species is one of the most attractive dune plants in Florida, but it is threatened by coastal development.

SOUTHERN BEEBLOSSOM

Oenothera simulans (Small) W.L. Wagner & Hoch
(Also *Gaura angustifolia* Michx.)
Evening Primrose family (Onagraceae)

Description: Southern beeblossom is a tall, wispy plant with leaves 1½"–5" long, narrowly oblong or lanceolate, with toothed margins. Tubular flowers, each about 1" wide, open white at sunset and then fade to pink the next day.

Bloom Season: February to November

Habitat/Range: Pinelands, dunes, and roadsides throughout Florida

Comments: One translation of *Oenothera* is that it was taken from *oinos* ("wine") and *thera* ("imbibing"), relating to its use in making wine "to make the heart merry." The name *simulans* means "resembling," for its resemblance to a species of *Gaura*. Bees visit the flowers, and the leaves are larval food for the beautiful clouded crimson moth and a hummingbird-like hawkmoth called the proud, or gaura, sphinx, with larvae that can defoliate the plant. The botanical name is a recent revision.

PINE-PINK
Bletia purpurea (Lam.) DC.
Orchid family (Orchidaceae)

Description: The palmlike leaves of this state-listed threatened orchid arise from ovoid pseudo-bulbs. The leaves are linear-lanceolate, pleated longitudinally, and reach 6"–18" long and 1"–2" wide. A 2'–5' flower spike emerges from the base of the pseudobulb and is branched near the top. Flowers are ½"–¾" wide.

Bloom Season: January to June

Habitat/Range: Pinelands and swamps of Polk County and from Lee and Martin Counties south into the Florida Keys

Comments: *Bletia* honors eighteenth-century botanist Don Luis Blet. The name *purpurea* means "purple," but the flowers are pink (rarely white). Some populations become pollinated in bud (cleistogamous) and never fully open. The endangered *Bletia patula* has larger flowers and occurs only in a single location in Everglades National Park. The Caribbean *Bletia florida*, with dark pinkish-purple flowers, has escaped cultivation in Miami-Dade County.

BEARDED GRASSPINK
Calopogon barbatus (Walter) Ames
Orchid family (Orchidaceae)

Description: The 3"–10" linear leaves are appressed to the flower stem, with up to 12 flowers crowded at the top. The bright magenta to pale pink (rarely white) ¾" flowers typically open simultaneously to create an attractive display. The odorless flowers have petals that are widest below the middle.

Bloom Season: December to May

Habitat/Range: Wet flatwoods and bogs across the eastern panhandle through most of the peninsula to Palm Beach and Collier Counties

Comments: *Calopogon* means "beautiful beard," alluding to the bristles on the lip. The name *barbatus* means "bearded." Members of this genus offer no pollinator reward, but bees mistake the bristles on the lip for a tuft of stamens, and the weight of the bee causes the lip to bend downward, pressing the hapless insect onto the sticky pollinia. The attached pollinia will be transferred to the next flower the bee visits.

MANYFLOWERED GRASSPINK
Calopogon multiflorus Lindl.
Orchid family (Orchidaceae)

Description: Characteristics of this species are its strong floral perfume and purple flower stem that turns green after flowering. The narrowly linear leaves reach 6" long. The flowers are about ¾" and may number up to 15, mostly open at the same time. The petals are widest above the middle.

Bloom Season: Principally April to May

Habitat/Range: Wet flatwoods and damp meadows across the eastern panhandle through most of the peninsula to Miami-Dade and Collier Counties

Comments: The name *multiflorus* refers to the many flowers produced by this species. It is highly dependent on fire to trigger flowering and may skip flowering for years until its habitat burns again. It flowers in profusion following winter or early spring fires or may be entirely absent in the same habitat in the absence of fire. Of the 5 species of *Calopogon*, 4 occur in Florida.

PALE GRASSPINK
Calopogon pallidus Chapm.
Orchid family (Orchidaceae)

Description: There are 1–2 narrowly linear ribbed leaves that measure 4"–8" long and up to ³⁄₁₆" wide that are about half as tall as the flowering stem. The 2 lateral sepals are distinctly upturned and are a key identifying characteristic. The faintly fragrant, widely spaced pale pink (rarely magenta or white) flowers measure ¾"–⅝" wide and open sequentially up the stem over a long period.

Bloom Season: December to June

Habitat/Range: Bogs, wet flatwoods, and savannas through most of the panhandle and peninsula south to Broward and Collier Counties

Comments: The name *pallidus* relates to the typically pallid (pale) flowers. This species often grows in association with other members of the genus, but the upturned lateral sepals make the pale grasspink easy to identify. Natural hybrids of this and other species are known from Florida. This species is found in scattered locations throughout central Florida.

TUBEROUS GRASSPINK

Calopogon tuberosus (L.) BSP
Orchid family (Orchidaceae)

Description: From 1–5 erect, linear, lanceolate leaves arise from an underground corm with leaves ranging from 12"–16" long and ⅜"–½" wide. Flower colors range from rosy pink or pale pink to white, with petals that are ¾" long or less.

Bloom Season: March to July.

Habitat/Range: Marshes and wet flatwoods through the panhandle and south in the peninsula to Broward, Highlands, and Manatee Counties

Comments: The name *tuberosus* refers to this species' tuberous corms. It is replaced in the southern counties by the more robust var. *simpsonii,* with petals that exceed ¾" long. In 1888 botanists Nathaniel Lord Britton (1859–1934), Emerson Ellick Sterns (1846–1926), and Justus Ferdinand Poggenburg (1840–1893) collaborated in the naming of this species. Carpenter bees are deceived by the stamen-mimicking bristles on the lip of the flowers and gain nothing for their pollinating services.

COASTAL PLAIN ROSEBUD ORCHID

Cleistesiopsis oricamporum P.M. Brown
Orchid family (Orchidaceae)

Description: When flowering, this terrestrial orchid reaches 14" tall, with leaves measuring 1½"–5½" long and ¼"–⅝" wide. One flower (rarely 2) tops each stem. The lip is 1" long, with 3 recurved sepals. The flowers emit a sweet vanilla fragrance.

Bloom Season: April to June

Habitat/Range: Wet flatwoods and bogs across the panhandle and the northern peninsula south to Lake and Marion Counties

Comments: *Cleistesiopsis* relates to the resemblance to the South American orchid genus *Cleistes*. The name *oricamporum* translates to "coast" and "plain." There is much disagreement regarding the taxonomy of this species, with some favoring the name *Cleistesiopsis divaricata* for the plants in Florida; others use *Cleistesiopsis bifaria*. Some even place it in the genus *Pogonia*. When a bee enters the flower, a hinged anther deposits pollinia on the bee's thorax.

TINY ORCHID
Lepanthopsis melanantha (Rchb. f.) Ames
Orchid family (Orchidaceae)

Description: This minuscule orchid forms small clusters that stand only 1½"–1¾" tall, with thin, sheathed stems topped by a single leaf blade that averages 1⅛" long and ½" wide. Purplish-pink flowers are in a single rank and barely reach ⅛" long.

Bloom Season: Sporadically all year

Habitat/Range: Epiphytic in the Fakahatchee Swamp (Collier County)

Comments: *Lepanthopsis* relates to similarities to the orchid genus *Lepanthes*. The name *melanantha* translates to "black flower" and alludes to the flowers' turning black when dried. This critically imperiled orchid is so rare in Florida that very few people have seen it in the wild. It inhabits very remote, nearly inaccessible sloughs deep in the Fakahatchee Swamp in Collier County. The author has encountered only 7 plants in more than 30 years of exploring the Fakahatchee Swamp, with never more than a single plant on the host tree.

ROSE POGONIA
Pogonia ophioglossoides (L.) Ker Gawl.
Orchid family (Orchidaceae)

Description: This quaint native orchid averages 5"–10" tall and has a solitary, elliptic to ovate, fleshy leaf to 4" long and ¾" wide. The ¾" flowers are in shades of pink with a frilly, darker lip.

Bloom Season: March to May

Habitat/Range: Wet meadows, flatwoods, and bogs throughout most of Florida south to Lee and Palm Beach Counties

Comments: *Pogonia* means "beard" and refers to the bearded crest of the lip. The name *ophioglossoides* relates to the resemblance of the plant to an adder's-tongue fern in the genus *Ophioglossum*, which translates to "resembling the tongue of a snake." This state-listed threatened species was described by Carolus Linnaeus (1707–1778) as *Arethusa ophioglossoides* but was moved into the genus *Pogonia* in 1816 by English botanist John Bellenden Ker Gawler (1764–1842). It can form extensive colonies.

PINELAND FALSE FOXGLOVE
Agalinis divaricata (Chapm.) Pennell
Broomrape family (Orobanchaceae)

Description: The thin stems of this species have an open, wiry, branching habit with horizontal, narrowly linear leaves. The typically paired flowers have marginal hairs and are about 1⅛" wide, with the corolla lobes flattened over the stamens.

Bloom Season: September to October

Habitat/Range: Dry, longleaf pine forests and savannas from Santa Rosa County east in the panhandle to Leon and Wakulla Counties and in Levy, Alachua, Marion, Citrus, and Hernando Counties

Comments: Greek polymath Constantine Samuel Rafinesque (1783–1840) gave this group of plants the name *Agalinis* because he thought some species resembled flax, in the genus *Linum*. The name *divaricata* means "wide spreading" or "straggling" (divaricate), alluding to the growth habit. Members of this genus are larval host plants of the common buckeye butterfly in Florida.

BEACH FALSE FOXGLOVE
Agalinis fasciculata (Elliott) Raf.
Broomrape family (Orobanchaceae)

Description: This loosely branched annual reaches 3' tall, with narrowly linear leaves measuring ¾"–1½" long. The flowers are ⅝"–1" wide with 2 parallel, cream stripes in the throat surrounded by dark pink dots.

Bloom Season: May to September

Habitat/Range: Beaches, sandhills, and flatwoods throughout mainland Florida

Comments: The name *fasciculata* relates to the bundled stems and leaves of this species. American botanist Stephen Elliott (1771–1830) first described this species in 1822 as *Gerardia fasciculata* from plants collected in South Carolina. *Agalinis* had been previously placed in the Figwort family (Scrophulariaceae), but molecular DNA testing showed the genus was more closely allied to the broomrape family. All members of this family are capable of parasitizing other plants (hemiparasitic), and some are host specific.

JACKSON FALSE FOXGLOVE
Agalinis filicaulis (Benth.) Pennell
Broomrape family (Orobanchaceae)

Description: The spindly, wiry stems are relatively few-branched, with opposite, scalelike leaves that are barely discernible without a hand lens. The 5/16" flowers are few, mostly single or in pairs, and lack spots.

Bloom Season: September to December

Habitat/Range: Pine flatwoods, seepage slopes, and savannas from Escambia County east across the panhandle to Jackson, Liberty, and Wakulla Counties; also Columbia, St. Johns, Flagler, Pasco, and Osceola Counties in the peninsula

Comments: The name *filicaulis* relates to the species' very slender stems. The flowers of this species are small and often hidden among grasses. When not blooming, it would be nearly impossible to find. *Agalinis aphylla* has alternate scalelike leaves, and the flowers are larger, more numerous, and with yellow lines and darker spots in the throat. The common name is for Jackson Parish, Louisiana.

FLAXLEAF FALSE FOXGLOVE
Agalinis linifolia (Nutt.) Britton
Broomrape family (Orobanchaceae)

Description: The sparsely branched stems of this rhizomatous species reach 3' tall, with very narrow, linear leaves 3/4"–2" long. The 5/8"–1" hairy flowers are somewhat bell shaped, and the throat is adorned with dark pink spots.

Bloom Season: June to November

Habitat/Range: Freshwater wetlands throughout most of mainland Florida

Comments: The name *linifolia* refers to the resemblance of the leaves to flax in the genus *Linum* (Linaceae). Members of this genus are hemiparasites, capable of deriving nutrients from other plants. There are 19 members of the genus in Florida, with about 70 species native to the Americas. Flaxleaf false foxglove is the only perennial species native to the United States. Botanist Francis Whittier Pennell (1886–1952) was the first to study this genus and published his first work on North American species in 1913. Bees are the pollinators.

HERB-OF-GRACE
Bacopa monnieri (L.) Pennell
Plantain family (Plantaginaceae)

Description: The opposite, spatulate leaves of this succulent, mat-forming herb range from ¼"–⅜" long. The 5-lobed, pale pink to nearly white flowers appear from the leaf axils and are ⅜"–½" wide.

Bloom Season: All year

Habitat/Range: Freshwater and brackish wetlands throughout most of Florida except some of the northernmost counties

Comments: *Bacopa* is an aboriginal name among indigenous people of French Guiana. The name *monnieri* honors Louis Guillaume le Monnier (1717–1799), a French scientist who studied electricity but received such ridicule he became a botanist. Bacopa is sold in capsule form as a nutritional supplement to promote brain health, memory, and emotional comfort. It is a preferred larval host plant of the white peacock butterfly but is seldom purposely cultivated. It was formerly placed in the Figwort family (Scrophulariaceae).

EUSTIS LAKE BEARDTONGUE
Penstemon australis Small
Plantain family (Plantaginaceae)

Description: Flowering plants reach 10"–30" tall or more, with opposite, clasping, toothed leaves averaging 2"–3½" long and ⅜"–½" wide, tapering to a point. The oblanceolate basal leaves are larger. Tubular pink flowers are about ⅝"–1" long and ¼"–⅜" wide, with a strip of yellow bristles on the lip.

Bloom Season: April to July

Habitat/Range: Sandhills, flatwoods, and upland woods through the panhandle and northern Florida south to Hernando and Polk Counties

Comments: *Penstemon* means "five" and "stamen," referring to the 4 fertile stamens and 1 sterile stamen on the type species of the genus. The name *australis* means "southern" and alludes to the southern range of this species. The common name relates to Lake Eustis (Lake County), near where the type specimen was collected in 1895. The flowers attract bees and hummingbirds, but Florida gardeners seldom cultivate this species.

EASTERN SMOOTH BEARDTONGUE
Penstemon laevigatus Aiton
Plantain family (Plantaginaceae)

Description: This species reaches 2'–3' tall when flowering, with lanceolate, opposite stem leaves that average 2"–3" long and ⅜"–1" wide (widest near the base). The ¾"–1" long flowers are pink to nearly white with prominent yellow bristles in the throat. The axis of the inflorescence is smooth, and the buds and calyx are covered with glandular hairs.

Bloom Season: April to July

Habitat/Range: Sandhills and flatwoods of Gadsden and Jackson Counties in the Florida panhandle

Comments: The name *laevigatus* means "smooth" and refers to the stems. Butterflies and ruby-throated hummingbirds are fond of the flowers, but it is only sparingly cultivated in the Florida native-plant nursery trade, perhaps because of a limited source of seeds. This species barely makes it into Florida from adjacent Georgia, so it is by far the least common member of this genus in our flora.

FLORIDA PHLOX
Phlox floridana Benth.
Phlox family (Polemoniaceae)

Description: The ascending, linear to broadly lanceolate upper leaves of this species are opposite, or nearly so, and grade into the bracts. The pale or rich pink (rarely white), showy flowers are about ¾" wide.

Bloom Season: April to November

Habitat/Range: Sandhills, flatwoods, and open forests from Okaloosa County west to Jefferson, Gilchrist, and Dixie Counties; also Clay and Hernando Counties

Comments: *Phlox* is Greek for "flame" and relates to the flaming pink and red flowers of some species. The name *floridana* relates to Florida, but the species also occurs in neighboring Georgia and Alabama. The plant photographed was along the Big Pine Trail in the Chinsegut Wildlife and Environmental Area near Brooksville (Hernando County). The most commonly seen species is *Phlox drummondii*, naturalized from Texas and used for roadside beautification projects in Florida.

SHOWY MILKWORT

Asemeia grandiflora (Walter) Small
(Also *Asemeia violacea* [Aubl.] J.F.B. Pastore
& J.R. Abbott; *Polygala grandiflora* Walter.)
Milkwort family (Polygalaceae)

Description: The stems of this species are 6"–16" tall, with narrow, lanceolate, alternate leaves that average ½"–1½" long and ¼"–⅜" wide. Flowers are on terminal spikes and have 2 winglike, pinkish-violet (rarely white) sepals that measure ³⁄₁₆"–⁵⁄₁₆" long.

Bloom Season: All year

Habitat/Range: Pinelands and prairies throughout Florida, including the Florida Keys

Comments: *Asemeia* is believed to be a corruption of *assideo*, "to resemble," alluding to its resemblance to the better-known genus *Polygala*. The genus *Asemeia* was separated from *Polygala* in 2012 on the basis of molecular DNA. The name *grandiflora* refers to the large flowers compared with related species. This group of milkworts is a taxonomic mess, so more detailed phylogenetic and taxonomic studies are needed.

DRUMHEADS

Polygala cruciata L.
Milkwort family (Polygalaceae)

Description: Drumheads reaches 3"–12" tall, with whorled, linear or linear-elliptic leaves with the lower leaves smaller than those above. The leaves average ⅜"–1½" long. The raceme is dense, mostly oblong in outline, with a compact arrangement of flowers that open progressively from the bottom upward. Two of the sepals are formed into petal-like wings and are colored like the petals. These are white when fresh but become pinkish violet with age.

Bloom Season: March to September

Habitat/Range: Flatwoods and wet meadows throughout most of mainland Florida south to Broward and Collier Counties

Comments: *Polygala* means "much milk," in the fanciful belief that milkworts could increase lactation. The word *gala* ("milk") also makes up the word "galaxy," as in the Milky Way. The name *cruciata* means "forming a cross," alluding to the flower shape. It is often found growing among other milkworts.

PROCESSION FLOWER

Polygala incarnata L.
Milkwort family (Polygalaceae)

Description: The leaves are linear, often with their bases appressed to the stem, and measure ¼"–½" long. The tubular flowers are about ³⁄₁₆" long. The flowers are twice as long as the wings and have 3 pinkish-rose (rarely white) petals that unite into a tube, flaring into 6 lobes.

Bloom Season: All year

Habitat/Range: Sandy soil in open, sunny habitats throughout mainland Florida

Comments: The name *incarnata* means "flesh colored," referring to the pink flower color. Milkworts once received unwarranted attention as a cure for snakebite. Ants harvest the nutritious arils of this species and unwittingly plant the seeds when they transport them underground in their nests. The common name relates to the flowers' opening in a procession up the inflorescence, or to garlands and nosegays made of the flowers for maidens who walk in religious processions celebrating the fifth Sunday after Easter.

SAND SWEETHEARTS

Polygala lewtonii Small
Milkwort family (Polygalaceae)

Description: Lewton's milkwort reaches 8" tall, with several angled stems lined with ascending, narrowly linear leaves to ½" long. The ⅜" dark pink to violet flowers have 2 spreading, winglike sepals. In addition to the showy flowers, inconspicuous cleistogamous (self-pollinating) flowers occur on the lower stems and belowground.

Bloom Season: February to April

Habitat/Range: Endemic to sandhills and oak-pine barrens in Marion, Lake, Brevard, Osceola, Polk, and Highlands Counties

Comments: The name *lewtonii* is for botanist Frederick Lewis Lewton (1874–1959), who received an honorary Doctor of Science degree from Rollins College in Winter Park. The name sand sweethearts was coined by Florida biologist Linda Duever because the species grows in sandy areas and always flowers on Valentine's Day. This federal endangered species is also called Lewton's milkwort.

SANDHILL WIREWEED

Polygonella robusta (Small) G.L. Nesom
& V.M. Bates
Buckwheat family (Polygonaceae)

Description: The multibranched stems of this species range from 12"–36" tall and often branch horizontally. The striated, linear leaves range from ¾"–3" long and no more than ⅛" wide. The small flowers create showy 2"–3" racemes that range from white to pink as the flowers age, then drying orange.

Bloom Season: April to December

Habitat/Range: Endemic to sandhills and scrub from Bay, Franklin, and Wakulla Counties through much of the peninsula to Charlotte, Glades, and Palm Beach Counties

Comments: *Polygonella* is a diminutive of *Polygonum* and refers to the many swollen nodes on the stem. Another common name is sandhill jointweed. The name *robusta* refers to the robust growth habit compared with other members of the genus. Botanist John Kunkel Small (1869–1938) named it *Thysanella robusta* in 1909 from plants collected in Manatee County in 1901.

KISS-ME-QUICK

Portulaca pilosa L.
Purslane family (Portulacaceae)

Description: The prostrate, succulent stems have shaggy, white hairs in the leaf axils. The narrow, succulent leaves measure about ½" long and less than ⅛" wide. The ⅜" flowers are clustered at the branch tips and are surrounded by hairs.

Bloom Season: All year

Habitat/Range: Sandy habitats throughout most of mainland Florida

Comments: *Portulaca* means "little door" and refers to the lid of the capsule. The name *pilosa* means "with long soft hairs." Kiss-me-quick is a name given to short-lived flowers but also refers to various things that are attractive, including kiss-me-quick bonnets worn by fashionable women in the 1800s, with ribbons that were tied under the chin on one side with "kissing strings" and a short lock of hair curled in front of each ear. The naturalized Paraguayan purslane (*Portulaca amilis*) has dark pink flowers and much wider leaves.

BEACH CREEPER
Ernodea littoralis Sw.
Madder family (Rubiaceae)

Description: The glossy, opposite leaves of this mounding plant are lanceolate and range from ¾"–1½" long and up to ½" wide, with 3–5 longitudinal veins. The tubular flowers have 4 tightly curled terminal lobes and measure ½"–⅝" long. Oval, ¼" fruits are golden yellow.

Bloom Season: All year

Habitat/Range: Coastal dunes from Volusia, Pinellas, and Hillsborough Counties south along both coasts into the Florida Keys

Comments: *Ernodea* is Greek for "offshoot," alluding to the many leafy branches along the stem. The name *littoralis* refers to the species' coastal habitat, the littoral zone. It is also called golden creeper and coughbush. Use this species as a drought- and salt-tolerant ground cover and for border plantings. Coker's golden creeper (*Ernodea cokeri*) is similar but has narrower leaves with a single vein and inhabits pine rocklands of Miami-Dade County and the Florida Keys.

POVERTY WEED
Hexasepalum teres (Walter) J.H. Kirkbr.
(Also *Diodia teres* Walter)
Madder family (Rubiaceae)

Description: This annual is typically upright to 4"–8" tall, with opposite, linear-lanceolate leaves from ½"–1¼" long and ⅛"–¼" wide. The 4-lobed, axillary flowers are pinkish violet and measure about ¼" wide. The capsules are cylindrical.

Bloom Season: April to November

Habitat/Range: Sandhills, dunes, and flatwoods throughout most of mainland Florida

Comments: *Hexasepalum* refers to the 6 sepals of the type species. The name *teres* means "cylindrical" and alludes to the capsules. The species was moved from the genus *Diodia* in 2014 by botanist Joseph Harold Kirkbride (1943–). The common name relates to the impoverished soil this weedy species often inhabits. Caterpillars of the tersa sphinx moth feed on the leaves, and the seeds are a favored food of quail. The plants are grown in pastures as fodder for livestock, and this species has spread far out of its natural range.

GULF PITCHERPLANT
Sarracenia rosea Naczi et al.
Pitcherplant family (Sarraceniaceae)

Description: The pitchers of this species are decumbent or ascending in basal rosettes and with a hood extending above the lip. Pitchers average 4"–8" long (to 11") and 1"–2" wide. Showy, nodding flowers are pale pink to rich rosy pink and reach 3" wide.

Bloom Season: March to April

Habitat/Range: Swamps, seepage bogs, savannas, and wet roadsides from Escambia County east to Gadsden, Liberty, and Franklin Counties in the Florida panhandle

Comments: *Sarracenia* honors French surgeon and botanist Michel Sarrazin (1659–1734), who immigrated to Canada in 1684 and was the first to state that this group of plants caught insects, a claim that was ridiculed until naturalist Charles Darwin (1809–1882) wrote about it in 1875. The name *rosea* alludes to the rosy pink flowers. This state-listed threatened species occurs along the Gulf Coastal Plain from Georgia to Mississippi.

BEACH VERBENA
Glandularia maritima (Small) Small
Verbena family (Verbenaceae)

Description: The opposite leaves may be variously lobed, toothed, or deeply incised and average about 1½" long and 1" wide. The pinkish to rose-purple, ⅜"–½" flowers have glands on the calyx.

Bloom Season: All year

Habitat/Range: Endemic to dunes and sandy pinelands from St. Johns County south along the Atlantic coast to the Florida Keys; also Levy, Hendry, and Collier Counties

Comments: *Glandularia* relates to the glandular appearance around the stigma. The name *maritima* is a reference to "maritime" or "growing by the sea." This state-listed endangered species is cultivated by butterfly gardeners in Florida and is nearly identical to the endemic Tampa mock vervain (*Glandularia tampensis*), which differs mostly by its hairy, non-glandular calyx and its wider range along Florida's west coast. *Glandularia canadensis* has rosy pink flowers and occurs in northern Florida.

RED AND ORANGE FLOWERS

Platanthera ciliaris

This section includes flowers ranging from pale orange to dark red. Many flowers will turn orange, red, or burgundy as they age, so you may need to check other color sections.

SIXANGLE FOLDWING
Dicliptera sexangularis (L.) Juss.
Acanthus family (Acanthaceae)

Description: The 6-angled stems of this bushy herb can reach 4' tall. The opposite leaves are ovate and average 1½"–2" long and ¾"–1¼" wide. Red, hairy, tubular flowers are curved and flattened vertically, ranging from ¾"–1" long.

Bloom Season: All year

Habitat/Range: Coastal strand, salt marshes, hammock margins, and mangroves scattered through Florida, mostly from Levy and Volusia Counties south; also Calhoun County

Comments: *Dicliptera* is Greek for "folding" and "wing," referring to the 2 winglike divisions of the seed capsule. The name *sexangularis* means "6-angled," alluding to the stems. This species is weedy in cultivation, but butterflies and hummingbirds visit the flowers. In coastal habitats it serves as a larval host plant for the Cuban crescent butterfly. Branched foldwing (*Dicliptera brachiata*) has nearly straight pink or purple blossoms.

FOUR-PETAL PAWPAW
Asimina tetramera Small
Custard-Apple family (Annonaceae)

Description: The fetid flowers of this shrubby species have creamy white outer petals when young, becoming peach colored with maroon streaks. Leaves are narrowly oblong from 2"–4" long and ⅜"–¾" wide. The ripe, yellowish-green fruits have an odor of bananas.

Bloom Season: April to July

Habitat/Range: Endemic to coastal sand pine scrub of Palm Beach, Martin, and St. Lucie Counties

Comments: *Asimina* is taken from *assimin,* a Native American word for pawpaw. The name *tetramera* means "four-merous" for the number of flower parts. This federal endangered species is threatened by habitat loss, fire suppression, and the killing of pollinators by spraying pesticides for mosquito control. It was first discovered in 1924 near Rio, Florida (Martin County). More flowers appear on plants that have been burned the previous season. The similar *Asimina pygmea* occurs in pinelands north of the range of this species.

PRAIRIE MILKWEED
Asclepias lanceolata Walter
Dogbane family (Apocynaceae)

Description: The linear or narrowly lanceolate leaves of this wetland species are 4"–8" long and ⅛"–½" wide. Individual flowers are about ¼" wide and are in few-flowered, terminal clusters. The corolla lobes are reflexed and arch downward beneath the 5-lobed calyx. The flowers are generally 2-toned red and reddish orange. Like other members of the genus, the seeds are wind dispersed.

Bloom Season: All year

Habitat/Range: Wet prairies throughout most of mainland Florida

Comments: *Asclepias* was named for Aesculapius, Greek god of medicine. The name *lanceolata* refers to the species' lance-shaped leaves. The small clusters of flowers typically stand well above competing vegetation in wet prairies and are hard to miss. Although the leaves are larval food for monarch and queen butterflies, the plant requires permanently wet soil to be successfully cultivated.

BUTTERFLY MILKWEED
Asclepias tuberosa L.
Dogbane family (Apocynaceae)

Description: The coarsely hairy leaves average 2"–4" long and ½"–1" wide and do not exude milky sap when broken. The flowers measure ¼"–⅜" and are uniformly light to dark reddish orange.

Bloom Season: All year

Habitat/Range: Dry, sandy soils through much of mainland Florida

Comments: The name *tuberosa* refers to the species' tuberous roots. It is a popular garden plant for its attractive blossoms, drought tolerance, and butterfly-attracting attributes. Tender young leaves, flowers, and the immature pods are larval food for monarch and queen butterflies. Native Americans brewed a tea from the leaves to induce vomiting during rituals, but the plant is toxic if eaten in quantity. Its medicinal use to treat pleurisy gave rise to the name pleurisy root. Swedish-Finnish botanist Pehr Kalm (1716–1779) wrote that it cured women's "hysteric passion," described as a convulsive illness with a fear of dying.

GRASSLEAF CONEFLOWER
Rudbeckia graminifolia (Torr. & A. Gray)
C.L. Boynton & Beadle
Aster family (Asteraceae)

Description: Flowering stems reach about 16"–24" tall, with narrow basal leaves to about 8"–12" long and ¼" wide or less. A single flower head tops an elongated, nearly naked stem with reddish-maroon ray florets and a concentric ring of tiny yellow disk florets.

Bloom Season: April to October

Habitat/Range: Wet pinelands, bogs, and cypress swamps of Bay, Calhoun, Gulf, Liberty, Franklin, and Leon Counties in the Florida panhandle

Comments: *Rudbeckia* honors botany professor Olaus Rudbeck (1660–1740), whose most famous student was Carl Linneaus (1707–1778), who latinized his name to Carolus Linnaeus when he published botanical papers in Latin. The name *graminifolia* refers to the grasslike leaves (from the outdated grass family name Graminae). This species is a near endemic and has only recently been reported from southern Georgia.

TRUMPET CREEPER
Campsis radicans (L.) Seem.
Trumpet Creeper family (Bignoniaceae)

Description: This vine uses adventitious roots produced along the stems to climb tree trunks and structures. The opposite, pinnately compound leaves are divided into 4–6 pairs of toothed, broadly or narrowly ovate leaflets. The flowers measure 3" long and 2" wide.

Bloom Season: April to October

Habitat/Range: Floodplain forests and disturbed sites south in Florida to Collier and Palm Beach Counties

Comments: *Campsis* refers to bent stamens. The name *radicans* alludes to the stems' rooting to trees and structures. It is widely cultivated for its showy flowers that attract ruby-throated hummingbirds and is a larval host for the plebeian sphinx moth. The sap may be irritating, giving rise to another common name, hellvine. Crossvine (*Bignonia capreolata*) has somewhat similar flowers, but it bears paired, lanceolate leaflets and climbs by tendrils with adhesive disks.

CARDINAL AIRPLANT
Tillandsia fasciculata Sw.
Pineapple family (Bromeliaceae)

Description: The leaves of this epiphyte range from 10"–20" long, forming a rosette. The inflorescence bears red, yellow, or green bracts, with tubular purple (rarely white) flowers emerging from behind the bracts. Each plant dies after flowering.

Bloom Season: All year

Habitat/Range: Upland forests, wooded swamps, and mangrove forests from Volusia, Orange, Polk, and Hillsborough Counties south into the Florida Keys (Monroe County)

Comments: *Tillandsia* honors Swedish botanist Elias Tillandz (1640–1693). The name *fasciculata* means "formed into a bundle" and alludes to the species' leaves. This is a state-listed endangered species due to the introduction of a Mexican bromeliad weevil (*Metamasius callizona*), first found in Florida in 1989. The weevil larvae destroy populations of this and other bromeliads by boring through the plants. Hummingbirds visit the flowers.

SEMAPHORE CACTUS
Consolea corallicola Small
(Also *Opuntia corallicola* [Small] Werderm.)
Cactus family (Cactaceae)

Description: This cactus may reach 6' tall, with flat, obovate pads (cladophylls) aligned on 1 plane. The pads and trunk are covered with wickedly sharp spines ranging from 1"–4" long. The red to red-orange flowers measure about ½" wide. Fruits are not produced.

Bloom Season: All year

Habitat/Range: Endemic to forests of the Florida Keys (Miami-Dade and Monroe Counties)

Comments: *Consolea* honors Italian botanist Michelangelo Console (1812–1897). The name *corallicola* means "growing on coral" and alludes to the coralline reef rock of the Florida Keys. This critically imperiled federal endangered cactus occurs naturally on only two islands in the Florida Keys, but efforts to establish it in other preserves in the Florida Keys are under way. It was first discovered in 1919 by botanist John Kunkel Small (1869–1938) on Big Pine Key.

CARDINAL FLOWER
Lobelia cardinalis L.
Bellflower family (Campanulaceae)

Description: Cardinal flower averages 2'–3' tall with hairy stems and toothed, lanceolate leaves averaging 1½"–2" long and ⅜"–¾" wide. The stems are topped with spikes of scarlet flowers, each with 3 spreading lower petals and 2 upper petals that unite into a tube at the base.

Bloom Season: July to November

Habitat/Range: Floodplain forests, spring runs, and riverbanks through the panhandle south to Hillsborough, Polk, and Indian River Counties

Comments: *Lobelia* honors Flemish herbalist Matthias de l'Obel (1538–1616). The name *cardinalis* refers to the cardinal-red flowers. Cardinal flower is dependent on hummingbirds to pollinate the flowers, and it is sometimes cultivated as a colorful addition to water gardens to attract them. Like other members of the genus, it is toxic if eaten in quantity and may cause vomiting, weakness, convulsions, and coma.

CORAL HONEYSUCKLE
Lonicera sempervirens L.
Honeysuckle family (Caprifoliaceae)

Description: This twining vine has opposite, mostly sessile leaves that are oblong to obovate on the newer stems. The clustered tubular, 1½"–2" flowers are typically red on the outside and yellow on the inside but may be all red, orange, or yellow.

Bloom Season: March to September

Habitat/Range: Floodplain forests through the panhandle south to Sarasota, Hardee, Highlands, and Orange Counties

Comments: *Lonicera* honors German herbalist Adam Lonitzer (1528–1586), who latinized his name to Adamus Lonicerus. The name *sempervirens* means "evergreen." This is a superb garden plant, with flowers that are highly attractive to hummingbirds and butterflies. The related and invasive Japanese honeysuckle (*Lonicera japonica*) is naturalized in Florida and has wider, fragrant blossoms with white, yellow, or pinkish lobes.

ROYAL CATCHFLY
Silene regia Sims
Pink family (Caryophyllaceae)

Description: The flowers of this 3'–4' perennial have a sticky calyx that traps flies and other small insects. Opposite sessile, lanceolate leaves measure 2"–4" long and 1"–1½" wide. Scarlet axillary flowers average 1" wide.

Bloom Season: June to August

Habitat/Range: Open woodlands of Jackson County

Comments: *Silene* is derived from Silenus, a folkloric man of the forest sometimes depicted as a drunk covered in foam, which relates to the many species in this group that are coated with a sticky secretion. When inebriated, Silenus was said to possess the wisdom of prophecy. The name *regia* means "royal." The flowers of this state-listed endangered species attract butterflies, sphinx moths, and hummingbirds. It was first described in 1815 by botanist John Sims (1749–1831) from plants collected in Missouri. The name catchfly relates to secretions on the plant that entrap flies.

MAN-IN-THE-GROUND
Ipomoea microdactyla Griseb.
Morning-Glory family (Convolvulaceae)

Description: The ovate or lanceolate leaves measure 2"–4" long and may be entire or palmately lobed. The trumpet-shaped flowers measure about 1½" long and 1"–1½" wide and range in color from rosy pink to carmine.

Bloom Season: April to December

Habitat/Range: Pine rocklands of southern Miami-Dade County

Comments: *Ipomoea* is Greek for "wormlike," alluding to the twining growth habit. The name *microdactyla* means "small fingers" and refers to the fingerlike projections on the tuberous root. The common name refers to the large root tuber that is similar to the related sweet potato (*Ipomoea batatas*). Native-plant enthusiasts in southern Florida sometimes cultivate this state-listed endangered species. Skipper butterflies crawl down the tube for nectar; the flowers are also visited by ruby-throated hummingbirds, bumblebees, and honeybees.

PAINTED LEAF

Euphorbia cyathophora Murray
(Also *Poinsettia cyathophora* [Murray] Bartling)
Spurge family (Euphorbiaceae)

Description: The leaves of this 10"–20" weedy, herbaceous species range from linear, lanceolate, ovate, to obovate, with larger leaf forms often fiddle-shaped, and measure 2"–4" long and ¼"–1¼" wide. The uppermost leaves are usually red at the base. Tiny male and female flower parts are in cup-shaped cyathia. The involucre has a solitary gland.

Bloom Season: All year

Habitat/Range: Dunes and disturbed sites throughout much of Florida but discontinuous in the northern counties

Comments: *Euphorbia* honors first-century Greek physician Euphorbus, who knew these plants were powerful laxatives. The name *cyathophora* means "cup bearing" and alludes to the cup-shaped cyathium, or "false flower." Another name is fire-on-the-mountain. The endemic *Euphorbia pinetorum* of Miami-Dade County and the Florida Keys has 3–4 glands on the involucre.

COASTAL INDIGO

Indigofera miniata Ortega
Pea family (Fabaceae)

Description: The hairy ¾"–1¼" leaves of this decumbent spreading species are compound with 5–9 leaflets. Red or salmon-pink flowers appear on axillary stems, and each flower measures about ⅜" long.

Bloom Season: April to September; all year in the southern counties

Habitat/Range: Pinelands and coastal habitats along Florida's east coast in St. Johns, Flagler, Volusia, Palm Beach, and Miami-Dade Counties into the Florida Keys (Monroe County); also Alachua, Levy, and Hernando Counties

Comments: *Indigofera* means "to bear indigo," referring to indigo dye. The name *miniata* alludes to the red flower color. Members of this genus were used to produce indigo dye, which is now made synthetically. Until recently, Florida plants had been referred to as an endemic variety (var. *florida*), but is now sunk under synonymy. Botanist Casimiro Gómez de Ortega (1740–1818) first described this species in 1798.

TRAILING RATANY

Krameria lanceolata Torr.
Ratany family (Krameriaceae)

Description: This odd species has hairy, spreading stems with sessile, lanceolate, hairy leaves. Each leaf averages ½"–1" long and ⅛"–¼" wide. The wine-red flowers are about ½" wide; spherical fruits are covered with sharp spines.

Bloom Season: May to July

Habitat/Range: Sandhills with scattered populations from Okaloosa, Walton, Liberty, and Suwannee Counties south to Hillsborough, Polk, and Highlands Counties

Comments: *Krameria* honors Austrian Army physician and botanist Johann Georg Heinrich Kramer (1684–1744). The name *lanceolata* refers to the lance-shaped leaves. The name ratany is derived from *ratânia* in the Andean Quechuan language, meaning "ground-creeping." The plants photosynthesize and also parasitize roots of nearby plants. The flowers produce oils collected by bees (*Centris* spp.) and then mixed with pollen as larval food. It is also called sandspur.

PINE LILY

Lilium catesbaei Walter
Lily family (Liliaceae)

Description: Pine lily reaches 20"–30" tall in flower, with lanceolate leaves 2"–3" long and ⅜"–½" wide, becoming smaller up the stem. A single flower (rarely 2) terminates the stem. The similar-looking sepals and petals range from 3"–4" long.

Bloom Season: August to January

Habitat/Range: Moist flatwoods and savannas from the panhandle south through the peninsula to Collier and Palm Beach Counties

Comments: *Lilium* is Latin for "lily." The name *catesbaei* honors English naturalist Mark Catesby (1682–1749), who collected plants in Virginia and the Carolinas. The lily family is well known in cultivation, and herbalists have used the blossoms and bulbs medicinally for centuries, especially for improving the memory and to soothe coughs and irritated eyes. Florida dusted skippers are fond of the nectar of this state-listed threatened species, which is also called Catesby's lily.

PANHANDLE LILY
Lilium iridollae M.K. Henry
Lily family (Liliaceae)

Description: The stems of this lily reach 4'–6' tall and have oblanceolate or obovate leaves measuring 2"–3½" long and ½"–1" wide, with small, rounded bumps on the veins and margins. The faintly fragrant, usually solitary flowers are nodding, with recurved, spotted sepals and petals to 4" long.

Bloom Season: July to September

Habitat/Range: Bogs, acidic swamps, and savannas of Escambia, Santa Rosa, Okaloosa, and Walton Counties in the western panhandle

Comments: In 1946 amateur botanist Mary K. Gibson Henry (1884–1967) gave this species the name *iridollae*, meaning "pot" and "rainbow" because she likened the flowers to "the pot of gold at the foot of my rainbow." She also penned, "I have long hoped that I might chance upon some attractive species which had remained unknown to science. This beautiful and delicately fragrant lily is all that I could have desired in my fondest anticipations."

TURKSCAP LILY
Lilium superbum L.
Lily family (Liliaceae)

Description: Stems of this lily can reach 9' tall and arise from subterranean bulbs. The leaves are elliptic or lanceolate, and the unscented flowers are nodding and range from yellowish orange to reddish purple, suffused with red distally and with magenta spots. The sepals and petals are sharply reflexed, with excerted stamens and magenta anthers.

Bloom Season: July to August

Habitat/Range: Pine barrens, openings in rich woods, swamp edges, streamsides, and moist meadows of Liberty, Leon, and Jefferson Counties

Comments: The name *superbum* means "superb." This is the largest native lily east of the Rocky Mountains and is a state-listed endangered species that was first described in 1762 by Carolus Linnaeus (1707–1778). The flowers are pollinated in Florida by several species of swallowtail butterflies. The common name relates to the similarity of the flowers to a type of Turkish headdress.

SCARLET ROSEMALLOW
Hibiscus coccineus Walter
Mallow family (Malvaceae)

Description: The smooth stems of this mallow die back in winter and then resprout from the base in springtime, reaching up to 10' tall. The palmate leaves are 4"–8" long and deeply cut into 5 lobes. The bright red (rarely white) flowers are axillary and measure about 6" wide.

Bloom Season: May to August

Habitat/Range: Freshwater swamps discontinuously from the panhandle south to Collier and Broward Counties

Comments: *Hibiscus* is said to come from the Greek *ibiscos,* for living in marshes with ibis. The name *coccineus* means "red," referring to the flowers. Although this species can be successfully cultivated in pots submerged in water or grown in water gardens, explanations might be in order for inquisitive neighbors or even the local police, because the leaves very closely resemble those of marijuana (*Cannabis sativa*). Hummingbirds visit the flowers for nectar and pollen.

FAIRY HIBISCUS
Hibiscus poeppigii (Spreng.) Garcke
Mallow family (Malvaceae)

Description: This small, shrubby hibiscus averages 3'–4' tall, with coarsely toothed, ovate leaves 1"–2" long and half as wide. Coarse hairs cover the stems and leaves. The scarlet flowers are pendent and measure about ¾" long. Seeds are wind dispersed.

Bloom Season: All year

Habitat/Range: Rockland hammocks of Miami-Dade County and the Florida Keys (Monroe County)

Comments: The name *poeppigii* honors German botanist and zoologist Eduard Friedrich Poeppig (1798–1868). This state-listed endangered species was first described in 1826 as *Achania poeppigii* by German botanist and physician Curt Polycarp Joachim Sprengel (1766–1833) but moved to the genus *Hibiscus* in 1850 by German botanist Christian August Friedrich Garcke (1819–1904). Hummingbirds visit the flowers and are effective pollinators. It is also called Poeppig's rosemallow.

COWHORN ORCHID
Cyrtopodium punctatum (L.) Lindl.
Orchid family (Orchidaceae)

Description: This impressive epiphytic orchid has long, cigar-shaped pseudobulbs and linear, pleated leaves that spread in a single plane. The leaves wither away in winter, leaving sharp-tipped sheaths that peel away with age. Each flower spike bears 30–50 flowers to about 1⅛" wide.

Bloom Season: March to May

Habitat/Range: Wooded swamps and mangrove forests from Lee County south to Miami-Dade County and the upper Florida Keys (Monroe County)

Comments: *Cyrtopodium* means "curved foot" and alludes to the curved column foot. The name *punctatum* refers to the spotted flowers. Botanist Abram Paschal Garber (1838–1881) discovered this orchid near Miami in 1867. In 1923 botanist John Kunkel Small (1869–1938) wrote about collecting a specimen in the Everglades with 201 pseudobulbs that took six men to carry. Also called cigar orchid, it is a state-listed endangered species.

FLORIDA ADDERSMOUTH ORCHID
Malaxis spicata Sw.
Orchid family (Orchidaceae)

Description: This species averages 2½"–6" tall and often grows semi-epiphytically on mossy stumps, logs, and tree bases. There are 2 (rarely 3) succulent, ovate leaves from 1"–3½" long and ½"–2" wide. The flower spike stands well above the leaves and bears greenish-orange flowers, each measuring about ¼" wide. Plants may flower successively for several months.

Bloom Season: August to March

Habitat/Range: Swamps and mesic forests from Wakulla, Hamilton, Columbia, and St. Johns Counties discontinuously south to Collier and (historically) Miami-Dade Counties

Comments: *Malaxis* is Greek for "softening," alluding to the soft and tender texture of the leaves. The name *spicata* relates to the spike of flowers. This orchid is easily overlooked when growing on stumps and logs that are covered with mosses, ferns, and even other orchids. Also see *Malaxis unifolia* under Brown and Green Flowers.

CHAPMAN'S FRINGED ORCHID
Platanthera chapmanii (Small) Luer
Orchid family (Orchidaceae)

Description: The leaves of this terrestrial orchid are typically linear-lanceolate, measuring 6"–8" long and ⅜"–1¼" wide. Brilliant orange flowers are grouped at the top of stems that reach 12"–24" tall. Each flower is about ½" tall.

Bloom Season: July to August

Habitat/Range: Moist to dry flatwoods and savannas, with scattered populations from Liberty and Franklin Counties east to Duval County and south to Marion County

Comments: *Platanthera* means "broad anther." The name *chapmanii* honors botanist Alvan Wentworth Chapman (1809–1899). This orchid had been considered a natural hybrid (*Platanthera* x *chapmanii*) but was later determined to be a distinct species. Although it is not known to hybridize with other species, it often grows in association with other members of the genus. The photograph was taken in the Ocala National Forest in Marion County.

YELLOW FRINGED ORCHID
Platanthera ciliaris (L.) Lindl.
Orchid family (Orchidaceae)

Description: This terrestrial orchid may reach 3' tall when it shows off its 30 to 60 frilly-lipped flowers grouped atop erect stems. The keeled, glossy, lanceolate leaves range from 3"–10" long and up to 2" wide. The orange to orange-yellow flowers are about ¾" long and ½" wide.

Bloom Season: June to September

Habitat/Range: Moist meadows, marshes, pine savannas, and flatwoods discontinuously through the panhandle and across the northern peninsula south to Sarasota, DeSoto, Highlands, and Volusia Counties

Comments: The name *ciliaris* is Latin for "eyelashes" and alludes to the frilly lip. Palamedes swallowtail butterflies are regular visitors to the flowers, probing their tongue down the curved nectar spur. This state-listed threatened species is the best reason to go out in the woods of central and northern Florida with your camera in the muggy heat of August.

CRESTED FRINGED ORCHID
Platanthera cristata (Michx.) Lindl.
Orchid family (Orchidaceae)

Description: Flowering plants can reach 8"–28" tall, with linear-lanceolate to linear-oblong leaves measuring 2"–8" long and ⅜"–1⅛" wide. The flowers are about ⅜" tall and as wide. The round lateral sepals stick out like ears.

Bloom Season: June to September

Habitat/Range: Prairies, pine savannas, marshes, and seepage slopes from the panhandle, with discontinuous populations scattered around the peninsula from Madison and Nassau Counties south to Orange and Manatee Counties

Comments: The name *cristata* relates to having tassel-like tips, or "crested," referring to the fringed lip. The best season to look for it is mid-July through August. The plant pictured was growing in a longleaf pine savanna in the Florida panhandle (Jefferson County). There are 2 natural hybrids involving this species: *Platanthera* x *canbyi* and *Platanthera* x *channellii*.

YELLOW FRINGELESS ORCHID
Platanthera integra (Nutt.) A. Gray ex L.C. Beck
Orchid family (Orchidaceae)

Description: The linear-lanceolate leaves clasp the stem. Flowering plants reach 10"–20" tall, with a 2"–3" tight cluster of saffron-yellow flowers. The flowers are about ⅜", with a nearly entire, finely serrated lip.

Bloom Season: June to September

Habitat/Range: Wet woods and pine savannas across the panhandle from Escambia County to Jackson, Liberty, and Wakulla Counties; also Nassau, Duval, Orange, Osceola, and Highlands Counties

Comments: The name *integra* means "whole" and relates to the fringeless lip. This species is also called frog-arrow, perhaps alluding to the somewhat arrow-shaped lip. The plant photographed was growing in a pitcherplant bog in the Apalachicola National Forest among flowering plants of sandbog deathcamas (*Zigadenus glaberrimus*). Hybrids involving this state-listed endangered species are unknown.

LEAFLESS BEAKED ORCHID
Sacoila lanceolata (Aubl.) Garay
Orchid family (Orchidaceae)

Description: The fleshy, lanceolate leaves average 4"–8" long and ¾"–3" wide, forming a basal rosette (absent when flowering). A stout, erect spike, to 12" tall or more, is topped with an arrangement of coral red (rarely green or yellow), ¾"–1" pubescent flowers.

Bloom Season: April to July

Habitat/Range: Meadows, pastures, and road-sides of Walton County and from Levy, Baker, and Flagler Counties south through mainland Florida

Comments: *Sacoila* alludes to the sac-shaped projection formed by the sepals and base of the column. The name *lanceolata* refers to the lanceolate leaves. This state-listed threatened species colonizes roadsides that have been spared from mowing. It was first collected in Florida in Lake County in 1894, and the long list of botanical synonyms attests to the many attempts to name the various flower color forms. The green-flowered form is also in this guide.

SCARLET LADIES'-TRESSES
Sacoila lanceolata (Aubl.) Garay var. *paludicola*
(Luer) Sauleda, et al.
Orchid family (Orchidaceae)

Description: The fleshy, lanceolate leaves average 4"–8" long and ¾"–3" wide, forming a basal rosette (present when flowering). An erect spike, to about 12" tall, is topped with ¾" scarlet pubescent flowers. The sepals are smaller than the typical variety.

Bloom Season: January to April

Habitat/Range: Hardwood forests and swamps in Sarasota, Collier, Broward, and Miami-Dade Counties

Comments: The name *paludicola* relates to the species' growing in swamps. Populations outside Collier County are suspect and were likely purposely introduced. In the 1960s, attempts were made to introduce it into Everglades National Park, without success. Natural populations are centered in and around the Fakahatchee and Corkscrew Swamps in Collier County. It is a state-listed threatened species, with a range that extends into the West Indies.

MULE-EAR ORCHID

Trichocentrum undulatum (Sw.) Ackerman
& M.W. Chase
Orchid family (Orchidaceae)

Description: The stiff, keeled leaves of this epiphytic orchid reach 3' long and 6" wide and are shaped like a mule's ear. The flower spike is 2'–4' long, bearing an open spray of very ornamental 1¼" flowers.

Bloom Season: March to May

Habitat/Range: Mangrove and buttonwood forests of mainland Monroe County

Comments: *Trichocentrum* relates to the nectarless spur of the flowers. The name *undulatum* refers to the undulating sepals and petals. This state-listed endangered orchid was first discovered in Florida in 1903 by botanists Alvah Augustus Eaton (1865–1908) and John J. Soar (1869–1951) in Miami-Dade County. It is extirpated in Miami-Dade County and is now restricted to remote areas of mainland Monroe County in Everglades National Park. It is being threatened by the larvae of an orchid fly (*Melanagromyza miamiensis*), which cause the flowering stems to abort.

HUMMINGBIRD-FLOWER

Macranthera flammea (W. Bartram) Pennell
Broomrape family (Orobanchaceae)

Description: This biennial hemiparasite reaches 5'–10' tall, with 4-angled stems and opposite, toothed and deeply lobed leaves that average 3"–5" long. Tubular flowers are 1"–1½" long, with 4 large, hairy stamens that extend well beyond the floral tube.

Bloom Season: July to September

Habitat/Range: Open woodlands and seepage bogs from Escambia County east to Leon, Liberty, and Franklin Counties in the Florida panhandle

Comments: *Macranthera* alludes to the species' large anthers. The name *flammea* means "flamered" and relates to the bright orange flowers. This state-listed endangered species produces haustoria on the roots to parasitize nearby trees. Like its name implies, the flowers are visited by hummingbirds but also by large butterflies, especially swallowtails. Other names are flameflower and Spanish princess.

STANDING-CYPRESS
Ipomopsis rubra (L.) Wherry
Phlox family (Polemoniaceae)

Description: This biennial has unbranched, leafy stems to 6' tall. The ¾"–1½", finely divided pinnate leaves are divided into feathery, threadlike divisions. The tubular flowers are about 1"–1½" long.

Bloom Season: June to August

Habitat/Range: Sandhills of Escambia, Jackson, and Leon Counties; also from Suwannee, Alachua, and Nassau Counties south to Sumter, Lake, and Brevard Counties

Comments: *Ipomopsis* alludes to the resemblance of the flowers to an *Ipomoea* (morning-glory). The name *rubra* means "red," for the flowers. Ruby-throated hummingbirds favor the flowers, and this species is often cultivated as a colorful addition to gardens well beyond its native range. It was placed in the genus *Ipomopsis* in 1936 by botanist Edgar Theodore Wherry (1885–1982). Another common name is Spanish larkspur. It ranges from Texas to Kentucky and North Carolina, and is naturalized northward into Canada.

ORANGE MILKWORT
Polygala lutea L.
Milkwort family (Polygalaceae)

Description: Orange milkwort is a biennial that averages 4"–8" tall, with thick ovate leaves ranging from ¾"–1½" long and half as wide. The somewhat cylindrical, ¾"–1" flower heads are in compact arrangements of orange to yellow flowers subtended by bracts of the same color.

Bloom Season: February to November

Habitat/Range: Flatwoods, bogs, and cypress pond margins throughout mainland Florida except Monroe and Miami-Dade Counties

Comments: *Polygala* means "much milk," in the fanciful belief that milkworts could increase lactation. The name *lutea* means "yellow," alluding to the yellow flower heads produced in parts of its range, where it is called yellow milkwort or yellow bachelor's button. In Florida the flower heads are typically orange and the plant is often found in open habitats with moist soils, where it may be hidden among grasses. An interesting common name is "swamp Cheetos."

143

WILD COLUMBINE
Aquilegia canadensis L.
Buttercup family (Ranunculaceae)

Description: The stems of wild columbine reach 12"–30" tall, with compound leaves divided into 3 lobed, obovate leaflets. The pendent, 1½"–2" flowers have red, petal-like sepals and yellow petals that fade into red.

Bloom Season: February to July

Habitat/Range: Mesic forests and riverbanks of Jackson, Liberty, and Washington Counties in the Florida panhandle

Comments: *Aquilegia* is from *aquila* ("eagle") for the shape of the spurs that resemble an eagle's talons. The name *canadensis* refers to Canada. Columbine relates to doves in the genus *Columbina* for the fanciful resemblance of the flowers to doves drinking. Other names for this state-listed endangered species include cluckies, meetinghouses, and jack-in-trousers. Native American men rubbed crushed seeds on their hands as a love charm. Damaged plants release toxic hydrogen cyanide. Hummingbirds visit the flowers.

INDIAN PINK
Spigelia marilandica (L.) L.
Strychnos family (Strychnaceae)

Description: The opposite, sessile, ovate to lanceolate leaves of this clump-forming 12"–18" species average 2½"–3" long and 1"–1½" wide and are conspicuously veined. The 1-sided inflorescence bears brilliant red, tubular flowers that constrict at the top and then flare open starlike, with a yellow interior.

Bloom Season: April to June

Habitat/Range: Moist woodlands and along wooded streambanks across the Florida panhandle (eight counties)

Comments: *Spigelia* honors Flemish anatomist and botanist Adrián van den Spiegel (1578–1625), who latinized his name to Adrianus Spigelius. The name *marilandica* refers to Maryland. Carolus Linnaeus (1707–1778) first described this species as *Lonicera marilandica* in 1753 but then moved it to the genus *Spigelia* in 1767. Look for it in spring at Florida Caverns State Park (Jackson County) along the walkway leading to the caverns. It is also called woodland pinkroot.

YELLOW FLOWERS

Canna flaccida

This section includes flowers ranging from pale cream to bright yellow. Some species have two-colored flowers, such as yellow and pink or yellow and white. If the predominant color is yellow, they are included here.

MANASOTA PAWPAW
Asimina manasota DeLaney
Custard-Apple family (Annonaceae)

Description: This elegant shrub reaches 3' tall, with curved (falcate) linear to linear-spatulate leaves measuring 5"–9" long and ⅜"–1" wide, with margins usually uprolled. Flowers are in axillary whorls, with pale yellow or maroon outer petals measuring ¾"–1" long. The sepals are creamy yellow when young and suffused with purple with age.

Bloom Season: April to May

Habitat/Range: Endemic to longleaf pine and turkey oak sandhills of Hardee, Manatee, and Sarasota Counties

Comments: *Asimina* is taken from *assimin*, a Native American word for pawpaw. The name *manasota* refers to Manatee and Sarasota Counties, where this species was first discovered by botanist Kris DeLaney (1951–) and named before he found a specimen in Hardee County. The name also promotes Manasota 88, an environmental organization dedicated to public land acquisitions in the area. See also *Asimina* x *bethanyensis*.

RUGEL'S FALSE PAWPAW
Deeringothamnus rugelii (B.L. Rob.) Small
Custard-Apple family (Annonaceae)

Description: Upright, seldom-branching stems reach about 8"–10" tall, with alternate, 1½"–3" oblong leaves. Solitary, pale yellow (rarely red) flowers appear in the leaf axils and are about ⅜" long.

Bloom Season: April to June

Habitat/Range: Endemic to sandy pine flatwoods in Volusia County

Comments: *Deeringothamnus* translates to "Deering's little shrub" and was named in 1924 by botanist John Kunkel Small (1869–1938) to honor his philanthropist friend, Charles Deering (1852–1927), whose father founded International Harvester. The name *rugelii* honors German-born botanist Ferdinand Ignatius Xavier Rugel (1806–1879). This federal endangered species grows solely in Immokalee sand within and around a Volusia County state forest. Fire is crucial to the species' long-term survival. It was first collected near New Smyrna (Volusia County) in May 1848.

PINELAND GOLDEN TRUMPET
Angadenia berteroi (A. DC.) Miers
Dogbane family (Apocynaceae)

Description: Pineland golden trumpet averages 6"–12" tall, often branching near the top. The opposite leaves are linear-oblong with curled margins, measuring 1"–2" long and ⅜"–½" wide. Trumpet-shaped ¾"–1½" blossoms are produced singly or several at a time at the branch tips.

Bloom Season: All year

Habitat/Range: Pine rocklands of Miami-Dade County and the Florida Keys (Monroe County)

Comments: *Angadenia* translates to "gland" and "vessel," alluding to the enclosed stigma. The name *berteroi* honors Italian botanist Carlo Luigi Guiseppe Bertero (1789–1831), who explored the neotropics. The sap of this state-listed threatened species can cause severe eye irritation as well as a blistering skin rash. In the Bahamas it has been used to ward off "intercourse taboo." Skippers are effective pollinators, but polkadot wasp moth larvae will strip the plant bare of leaves and flowers.

SAVANNAH MILKWEED
Asclepias pedicellata Walter
Dogbane family (Apocynaceae)

Description: This milkweed often gets overlooked due to its small stature, reaching only about 12" tall. The leaves are opposite, narrowly linear, and average ¾"–1½" long and about ⅛" wide. The yellowish flowers measure about ¼" long or slightly longer and are held on long pedicels in open, few-flowered clusters.

Bloom Season: March to September

Habitat/Range: Moist savannas from Walton County east and south through peninsular Florida

Comments: *Asclepias* was named for Aesculapius, Greek god of medicine. The name *pedicellata* refers to the long stalks (pedicels) of the flowers. British-American botanist Thomas Walter (1740–1789) described this species in 1788 from plants collected in South Carolina. It can easily go unnoticed when growing among competing vegetation, so check areas that have burned in the springtime, where it will be much more conspicuous.

WILD ALLAMANDA
Pentalinon luteum (L.) B.F. Hansen & Wunderlin
Dogbane family (Apocynaceae)

Description: The stems of this attractive, twining vine can climb high into trees. The glossy, opposite leaves are 2"–4" long and up to 2" wide, with trumpet-shaped 2" flowers clustered at the branch tips.

Bloom Season: April to November

Habitat/Range: Coastal and inland forest margins from St. Lucie and Lee Counties south through the Florida Keys

Comments: *Pentalinon* alludes to the 5 anther appendages, and *luteum* relates to the yellow flowers. Consuming the latex will cause burning of the mouth and throat, diarrhea, and convulsions, and may lead to heart failure. The sap burns sensitive skin and has been used as an arrow poison. This species is also called hammock viperstail. Despite its poisonous properties, it is cultivated for its showy display of flowers. The larvae of the polkadot wasp moth (oleander moth) may defoliate the entire plant.

GOLDEN-CLUB
Orontium aquaticum L.
Arum family (Araceae)

Description: The oval leaves average 6"–8" long and 3"–6" wide and have water-repelling qualities. The spatheless inflorescence is composed of a reddish stipe that terminates in a broad white stem below the yellow spadix. Minuscule, bisexual flowers are arranged along the tip of the spadix.

Bloom Season: December to June

Habitat/Range: Forested freshwater habitats through most of Florida south to Martin and Collier Counties

Comments: *Orontium* is said to be a name for a plant growing in Syria's Orontes River and used for this genus of plants by Carolus Linnaeus (1707–1778). The name *aquaticum* refers to the species' aquatic habitat. Native Americans dried and ground the seeds and rootstock of this species as a source of carbohydrates. Seeds microwaved in water for 5 minutes are said to have a "firm texture and pleasant nutty flavor," with no irritation from toxins usually associated with aroids.

WOOLLY DUTCHMAN'S-PIPE

Aristolochia tomentosa Sims
Pipevine family (Aristolochiaceae)

Description: This twining vine has ovate to reniform leaves reaching 8" long and 6" wide. The odd-looking, hairy axillary flowers are about ¾" long.

Bloom Season: February to May

Habitat/Range: Bottomland forests of Escambia and Santa Rosa Counties and from Holmes, Washington, and Bay Counties east to Gadsden and Liberty Counties in the Florida panhandle

Comments: *Aristolochia* means "best delivery," for the ancient use to aid childbirth. The name *tomentosa* refers to the dense, matted, soft hairs on the stems and leaves. This state-listed endangered species was named in 1811 by British physician and botanist John Sims (1749–1831). Hairs inside the floral tube point downward to keep insects from escaping until the flower is pollinated. They can then escape—if they survive long enough. It is a larval host plant of the pipevine and polydamas swallowtail butterflies.

CREEPING SPOTFLOWER

Acmella repens (Walter) Richard
(Also *Acmella oppositifolia* [Lam.] R.K. Jansen
var. *repens* [Walter] R.K. Jansen)
Aster family (Asteraceae)

Description: This species is usually prostrate, with opposite toothed, ovate leaves measuring ½"–1" long and ⅜" wide. The flower heads are ⅜"–½" wide.

Bloom Season: All year

Habitat/Range: Marshes and floodplains throughout most of mainland Florida

Comments: *Acmella* was taken from a Singhalese name for a plant now known as *Blainvillea acmella*. The name *repens* relates to the stems, which typically creep along the ground. Chewing the flower heads creates a tingling sensation of the mouth and tongue that lasts about 10 minutes. A related species in Brazil is called *abecadária* (alphabet plant) because it is thought to make babies speak more easily. It is eaten in the tropics as a mouth-tingling salad herb and chewed to relieve toothache.

149

COMMON LEOPARDBANE

Arnica acaulis (Walter) Britton, et al.
Aster family (Asteraceae)

Description: Common leopardbane can be recognized by its stemless, 2"–5" broadly elliptic or ovate leaves that form a basal rosette, its stems that are covered with glandular hairs, and the clasping stem leaves. The flower heads reach 2"–2½" across.

Bloom Season: March to June

Habitat/Range: Flatwoods of Jackson and Liberty Counties in the Florida panhandle

Comments: *Arnica* may have derived from the Greek *ptarmiké*, for a plant that invokes sneezing. The name *acaulis* means "stemless" or "with very short stems," referring either to the leaves or to non-flowering plants. This state-listed endangered species was first described in 1788 as *Doronicum acaule* by botanist Thomas Walter (1740–1789) but moved to the genus *Arnica* in 1888 by Nathaniel Lord Britton (1859–1934) and other collaborators. The name leopardbane is used for a variety of plants thought to ward off wild beasts.

COASTAL PLAIN HONEYCOMBHEAD

Balduina angustifolia (Pursh) B.L. Rob.
Aster family (Asteraceae)

Description: This biennial reaches 2'–5' tall when flowering in its second year. Basal leaves are linear and eventually disappear with age. The stem leaves are very narrow and range from ½"–2" long. The plant is branched at the top, with flower heads measuring 1½"–2" wide.

Bloom Season: All year

Habitat/Range: Scrub, dunes, and sandhills throughout most of mainland Florida

Comments: *Balduina* honors American botanist William Baldwin (1779–1819). The genus is spelled differently because there was no "w" in the Greek alphabet. The name *angustifolia* refers to the narrow leaves. The species was first described in 1814 as *Buphthalmum angustifolium* by botanist Frederick Traugott Pursh (1774–1820) but was moved to the genus *Balduina* in 1911 by botanist Benjamin Lincoln Robinson (1864–1935). Butterflies frequent the flowers.

ONEFLOWER HONEYCOMBHEAD
Balduina uniflora Nutt.
Aster family (Asteraceae)

Description: Unlike the previous species, there are few to no branches at the top of the main stem, typically with a single flower head topping each plant. Flower heads reach 2" across, with a yellow disk. When present, ray florets number 8–22.

Bloom Season: August to October

Habitat/Range: Flatwoods, bogs, and savannas throughout the Florida panhandle and from Hamilton, Columbia, and Alachua Counties east to Flagler, Duval, and Nassau Counties

Comments: The name *uniflora* means "one flower" but is a bit of a misnomer because it refers to the frequent absence of ray florets on the heads of flowers. Botanist Thomas Nuttall (1786–1859) first described this species in 1818. It is less common than the previous species and has a much more restricted range in the state. A third native species (*Balduina atropurpurea*) has purple disks and occurs in four northeastern Florida counties.

SOFT GREENEYES
Berlandiera pumila (Michx.) Nutt.
Aster family (Asteraceae)

Description: The hairy leaves of this 12"–30" perennial have crenate margins and are mostly oblong to ovate, reaching ¾"–1⅜" long and about ½" wide. The flower heads are 1¼"–2" wide, with deep yellow to orange-yellow ray corollas and reddish or maroon disk florets. The disk is soft to the touch.

Bloom Season: March to October

Habitat/Range: Sandhills across the Florida panhandle and northern peninsula south to Marion and Volusia Counties

Comments: Jean-Louis Berlandier (1805–1851) was a Belgian botanist and anthropologist who had a badger, frog, tortoise, 26 plant species, and the genus *Berlandiera* named in his honor. The name *pumila* means "dwarf." The most striking feature of this species is the strong chocolate perfume emitted from the flowers. Gardeners in northern Florida sometimes grow this species to attract a variety of butterflies.

FLORIDA GREENEYES
Berlandiera subacaulis (Nutt.) Nutt.
Aster family (Asteraceae)

Description: Florida greeneyes has alternate, deeply lobed or scalloped leaves that form a basal rosette. The leaves are mostly 1"–4½" long and downy beneath. The flower heads are held singly on a hairy stem that's 6"–20" tall. The disk is green with yellow disk florets arranged in a circle. The short ray flowers have a notched tip.

Bloom Season: All year

Habitat/Range: Endemic to sandy habitats nearly throughout Florida

Comments: The name *subacaulis* relates to the short stem of this species. It was first described in 1821 as *Silphium subacaule* by botanist Thomas Nuttall (1786–1859) but moved to the genus *Berlandiera* by Nuttall in 1841. It sometimes hybridizes with the previous species to form an endemic hybrid (*Berlandiera* x *humilis*), which has only been vouchered from St. Johns County. The genus comprises 4 species indigenous to the southern United States and Mexico.

BURMARIGOLD
Bidens laevis (L.) Britton, et al.
Aster family (Asteraceae)

Description: This perennial has entire, elliptic, sessile leaves ranging from 2"–4" long and ⅜"–1" wide. Flower heads average 1"–2" wide, with yellow ray and disk flowers.

Bloom Season: October to March

Habitat/Range: Wet meadows, marshes, and lake margins discontinuously scattered across much of mainland Florida

Comments: *Bidens* is Latin for "two-toothed," referring to the 2 teeth on the dry, 1-seeded achene. The name *laevis* means "smooth" and refers to the texture of the leaves. Seminoles used an infusion of the leaves to treat "sun sickness" and "fire sickness," both of which had to do with the eyes, headache, and body aches. Marsh beggarticks (*Bidens mitis*) has very similar flowers but differs by its serrate, pinnately divided leaves. Both species can form fields of yellow when in flower and are sometimes cultivated by water garden enthusiasts.

PINELAND RAYLESS GOLDENROD
Bigelowia nudata (Michx.) DC. ssp. *australis*
L.C. Anderson
Aster family (Asteraceae)

Description: The very narrow, alternate, 3-nerved basal leaves are linear-oblanceolate to narrowly spatulate, with relatively few small stem leaves. Discoid heads with vertical ranks of phyllaries are in flat-topped arrays with tiny yellow disk florets.

Bloom Season: Mostly October to May

Habitat/Range: Endemic to moist flatwoods in Bradford, Alachua, and Levy Counties and from Pasco, Sumter, Lake, and Flagler Counties south to Broward and Collier Counties

Comments: *Bigelowia* honors Massachusetts medical and botanical scholar Jacob Bigelow (1787–1879), who taught at Harvard University. The name *nudata* means "naked," alluding to the rayless flowers; *australis* refers to the subspecies' southern range. It may be easily mistaken for Coastal Plain yellowtops (*Flaveria linearis*) but it has opposite leaves, usually with serrate margins.

NUTTALL'S RAYLESS GOLDENROD
Bigelowia nuttallii L.C. Anderson
Aster family (Asteraceae)

Description: Plants have basal rosettes of narrowly linear, alternate 2"–5" leaves and form compact colonies by rhizome-like caudex branches. The rayless flowers are in terminal, flat-topped clusters with many small stem leaves.

Bloom Season: September to October

Habitat/Range: Thin soils on acidic sandstone outcrops in Washington County and sand pine scrub in Pinellas County

Comments: The name *nuttallii* honors English botanist Thomas Nuttall (1786–1859), who traveled in Florida in 1830. This state-listed endangered species was described in 1970 from plants collected in 1969 by Florida botanist Loran Crittendon Anderson (1936–) along the bank of the Ohoopee River in Tatnall County, Georgia. It is common in Texas and Louisiana, where it is sometimes cultivated in rock gardens, but in Florida it occurs in only two widely separated counties.

SEA OXEYE

Borrichia frutescens (L.) DC.
Aster family (Asteraceae)

Description: This species forms large rhizomatous colonies with 2'–4' stems lined with gray-green lanceolate, pubescent leaves measuring 1"–2" long and ½"–¾" wide. Flower heads measure ⅝"–1" across. The disk is stiff to the touch due to sharp involucral bracts.

Bloom Season: All year

Habitat/Range: Coastal strand and salt marshes through nearly all of Florida's coastal counties into the Florida Keys

Comments: *Borrichia* honors Danish botanist Ole Borch (1628–1690), who latinized his name to Olaus Borrichius. The name *frutescens* means "shrubby." Another common name is beach carnation. This species is used in coastal landscaping for its tolerance of dry, saline soils and its cheery, butterfly-attracting, daisy-like flowers, produced throughout the year. *Borrichia arborescens* has similar flowers but is not rhizomatous, the disk is soft to the touch, and it has dark green shiny leaves.

MOSIER'S FALSE BONESET

Brickellia mosieri (Small) Shinners
Aster family (Asteraceae)

Description: The 12"–36" stems are finely pubescent, with widely spaced alternate leaves to 1" long. The leaves are very narrowly linear, typically drooping or twisted, with revolute (curled under) margins. The flower heads are in open, branched clusters.

Bloom Season: April to September

Habitat/Range: Endemic to pine rocklands of Miami-Dade County

Comments: *Brickellia* honors Irish-born physician and naturalist John Brickell (1748–1809), who lived in Georgia. The name *mosieri* commemorates South Florida naturalist Charles A. Mosier (1871–1936). The name boneset relates to plants used to heal broken bones or to treat dengue (breakbone) fever. It is also called brickellbush. This species is quite similar to *Brickellia eupatorioides* of northern and central Florida, which has much wider, coarsely toothed leaves. The flower heads are practically identical.

GREEN-AND-GOLD
Chrysogonum virginianum L. var. *australe*
(Alexander ex Small) H.E. Ahles
Aster family (Asteraceae)

Description: This is a low, mat-forming species with colonies connected by underground rhizomes. The coarsely hairy leaves are elliptic-ovate and average about 2" long and 1" wide. The flower heads measure about 1½" across.

Bloom Season: February to May

Habitat/Range: Deciduous woodlands and floodplains of Walton, Jackson, Gadsden, and Leon Counties

Comments: *Chrysogonum* translates to "gold" and "knee" (or "joint"), referring to where the flower stems attach at the leaf axils (stem joints). The name *virginianum* relates to Virginia, where this species was first collected, and the varietal name *australe* means "southern." It is also called goldenstar and golden knee within its range across the eastern United States. The bright yellow flowers stand out like gold gems on the forest floor.

BUSH GOLDENROD
Chrysoma pauciflosculosa (Michx.) Greene
Aster family (Asteraceae)

Description: Diagnostic features of this 2'–3' bushy species are its fleshy alternate, narrowly elliptic leaves and young stems that are sticky. The leaves are grayish green and measure up to 2" long and ⅜" wide. Numerous small heads of flowers form a canopy over the tops of the leafy branches.

Bloom Season: October to December

Habitat/Range: Coastal dunes and sandhills from Escambia County east to Jackson, Liberty, and Wakulla Counties in the Florida panhandle

Comments: *Chrysoma* alludes to the yellow-gold heads of flowers. The name *pauciflosculosa* relates to the few woolly hairs on the fruits (cypselae). It was first described as *Solidago pauciflosculosa* by French botanist André Michaux (1746–1802), but the name wasn't published until 1803, a year after his death. American botanist Edward Lee Greene (1843–1915) moved it to the genus *Chrysoma* in 1895. It is the only member of the genus in the United States.

DELANEY'S GOLDENASTER

Chrysopsis delaneyi Wunderlin & Semple
Aster family (Asteraceae)

Description: The stems average 2'–3' tall and are lined with hairy, linear- or elliptic-oblong, clasping leaves. First-season rosettes have broadly spatulate leaves averaging 3"–5" long and about 1" wide near the tip, narrowing toward the base. Flower heads are 1"–1½" wide.

Bloom Season: November to January

Habitat/Range: Endemic to longleaf pine and turkey oak sandhills from Lake, Orange, and Brevard Counties to Highlands and Broward Counties

Comments: *Chrysopsis* means "gold appearance" and relates to the golden corollas. The name *delaneyi* honors botanist Kris DeLaney (1951–), who first collected the species in Highlands County in November 1987. It was described in 2003. This species is of conservation concern due to loss of habitat caused by agribusiness and urban sprawl. *Chrysopsis highlandsensis* has similar flowers, but the leaves are covered with white, woolly hairs.

SCRUBLAND GOLDENASTER

Chrysopsis subulata Small
Aster family (Asteraceae)

Description: The densely woolly, first-season basal leaves of this biennial are linear-oblanceolate. The numerous stem leaves during anthesis are mostly linear, covered with shaggy hairs, and average ½"–1¼" long and ⅛"–¼" wide. The flower heads are 1"–1¼" wide, with numerous curled green phyllaries.

Bloom Season: May to September

Habitat/Range: Endemic to sandy habitats on the Florida peninsula, mostly north of Lake Okeechobee

Comments: The name *subulata* means "awl-shaped" and relates to the leaves. There are eleven species in this genus in the United States, and all of them occur in Florida. This is the earliest species to flower and is 1 of 6 endemic species in Florida. Botanist John Kunkel Small (1869–1938) first collected this species in 1924 between Avon Park and Sebring (Highlands County). The plant photographed was in a vacant field next to the Avon Park Airport.

BULL THISTLE (YELLOW FORM)
Cirsium horridulum Michx.
Aster family (Asteraceae)

Description: The wickedly spiny, lobed or deeply incised leaves of this biennial reach 12" long and 2" wide, forming a basal rosette. The leaves on flowering stems are clasping, smaller, and not as deeply cut. The flower heads range from 2"–3" in diameter and vary from rosy purple, lavender, yellow, to white.

Bloom Season: All year

Habitat/Range: Pinelands and roadsides mostly in the northern Florida counties (yellow form)

Comments: *Cirsium* means "swollen vein," alluding to members of the genus used medicinally to treat varicose veins. The name *horridulum* means "prickly." The pink-flowered form is found statewide. In Greek mythology thistles appeared on Earth to grieve the loss of Daphnis, a shepherd said to be the creator of pastoral poetry. Other common names are purple thistle, yellow thistle, and bristle thistle. This species is also in the Pink Flowers section of this guide.

BAKER'S TICKSEED
Coreopsis bakeri E.E. Schill.
Aster family (Asteraceae)

Description: The narrowly linear to linear-oblanceolate leaves are infolded, unlobed, and glabrous on the upper surface. Those characteristics, plus molecular DNA and habitat, separate it from *Coreopsis lanceolata*. The flower heads average 1½" wide.

Bloom Season: March to April

Habitat/Range: Endemic to upland glade habitat with thin soils over limestone in Jackson County

Comments: *Coreopsis* means "tick-like," alluding to the seeds, which resemble ticks. The name *bakeri* honors Florida naturalist Wilson Baker (1940–) and was described by botanist Edward E. Schilling (1953–) in October 2015. The photograph was taken in a remnant glade at Florida Caverns State Park. Surveys were conducted in similar habitat in adjacent Gadsden County, but so far the species is known only as a narrow endemic in Jackson County. This is the newest addition to Florida's official state wildflower list.

FLORIDA TICKSEED
Coreopsis floridana E.B. Smith
Aster family (Asteraceae)

Description: The stems reach 36" tall, with narrowly elliptical, alternate leaves averaging 1½"–6" long and ⅛"–⅜" wide. The ray florets are typically twice notched at the tip, and the flower heads average 2" wide.

Bloom Season: Late September to February

Habitat/Range: Endemic to wet flatwoods from Walton County down Florida's west coast to Collier County and through the peninsula from Volusia County to Miami-Dade County

Comments: The name *floridana* relates to Florida. This species resembles a narrow-leaved form of *Coreopsis gladiata*, found from northern Florida to North Carolina and Mississippi, but differs by its short, deltoid outer phyllaries and its shorter and broader achenes. It is Florida's only endemic member of the genus, although some botanists still maintain it as a synonym of *Coreopsis gladiata*.

LANCELEAF TICKSEED
Coreopsis lanceolata L.
Aster family (Asteraceae)

Description: The lanceolate leaves may have 1 or 2 lateral lobes and range from 1¾"–5" long and ⅜"–¾" wide. The ray and disk flowers of this species are yellow.

Bloom Season: Mostly April to August

Habitat/Range: Sandy habitats and disturbed sites throughout the Florida panhandle; also Suwannee, Alachua, St. Johns, Lake, and Volusia Counties

Comments: The name *lanceolata* refers to the lance-shaped leaves. This species was introduced as a landscape plant in Japan and became so invasive that it is currently on the Ecological Society of Japan's 100 Worst Invasive Species list. *Coreopsis bakeri* in Jackson County is very similar, and some botanists still relegate it as a synonym of *Coreopsis lanceolata*. Bees and butterflies visit the small disk flowers and serve as pollinators. Buntings, sparrows, and goldfinches eat the seeds.

LEAVENWORTH'S TICKSEED
Coreopsis leavenworthii Torr. & A. Gray
Aster family (Asteraceae)

Description: Leavenworth's tickseed averages 10"–24" tall, with narrow, opposite leaves that average ½"–4" long and ⅟₁₆"–¼" wide, the lower leaves usually divided into 2 or more narrow segments. The flower heads average about 1" wide.

Bloom Season: All year

Habitat/Range: Flatwoods and savannas throughout Florida

Comments: The name *leavenworthii* honors Civil War Army surgeon and botanist Melines Conklin Leavenworth (1796–1862), who became one of the more important plant collectors in the southern United States. Seminoles used this species in an infusion to treat heat exhaustion. This is one of the most common native wildflowers used in roadside beautification projects in much of Florida. A shorter plant of peninsular Florida with linear, entire lower leaves has been referred to as *Coreopsis lewtonii* and may be resurrected as a valid species.

GREATER TICKSEED
Coreopsis major Walter
Aster family (Asteraceae)

Description: The opposite, 1"–4" leaves of this species are often divided into 3 narrowly lanceolate segments, giving the appearance of being in whorls along the stem. The flower heads are about 1¾" across. Flowering plants average 12"–30" tall.

Bloom Season: May to September

Habitat/Range: Sandhills of the western Florida panhandle from Jackson, Washington, and Walton Counties west to Escambia County

Comments: The name *major* means "greater" and relates to this species' wide range across the eastern United States. The leaf segments, which resemble 6 whorled leaves, are a diagnostic feature of this species. Members of this genus add splashes of color as carefree annuals or perennials in wildflower gardens for home landscapes, and some have been hybridized into double forms and garish colors for the nursery trade. They are very closely allied to the genus *Bidens*.

SLENDER SCRATCHDAISY

Croptilon divaricatum (Nutt.) Raf.
Aster family (Asteraceae)

Description: Stems of this annual may be sprawling or upright to 2' tall and are covered with stiff hairs. The narrowly lanceolate, serrate stem leaves are alternate, sessile, and 3-nerved, becoming bract-like near the heads. The flower heads average ⅜" wide.

Bloom Season: July to November

Habitat/Range: Openings of sandy woods, roadsides, and fencerows from Escambia County east to Duval and St. Johns Counties and south to Lake, Hillsborough, and Pinellas Counties

Comments: *Croptilon* means "scythe" and "feather," alluding to the featherlike appearance of the curved, pinnately toothed leaves of the type species. The name *divaricatum* relates to the species' spreading or straggling growth habit. The common name is for the stiff, scratchy hairs that cover the stems. Look for this annual along roadsides and other disturbed sites, where it often grows intermixed with weedy grasses.

SLENDER FLATTOP GOLDENROD

Euthamia caroliniana (L.) Greene ex Porter & Britton
Aster family (Asteraceae)

Description: The intricately branched, glabrous stems of this species are typically 24"–36" tall but may be much taller. The very narrowly linear leaves are 1"–2½" long, abundantly gland-dotted, and bent downward. The small flower heads are usually in flat-topped arrays and are often multilayered.

Bloom Season: August to December

Habitat/Range: Open, moist sandy soils, trailsides, and dunes throughout mainland Florida

Comments: *Euthamia* comes from Greek words meaning "well" and "crowded" and probably alludes to the crowded branching habit. The name *caroliniana* in this case refers to South Carolina, where this species was first collected. Small butterflies often visit the flowers, but it is practically unknown in cultivation. It was once placed in the genus *Solidago,* the true goldenrods, but was relegated to the genus *Euthamia* in 1894.

COASTAL PLAIN YELLOWTOPS

Flaveria linearis Lag.
Aster family (Asteraceae)

Description: This profusely branching, herbaceous perennial has narrowly linear, sessile, sometimes serrated leaves to about 4" long and ⅛"–¼" wide. The stems are often reddish purple with a flat-topped, spreading cluster of small disk flowers (5–10 per head; sometimes with a single ray flower).

Bloom Season: All year

Habitat/Range: Coastal and inland habitats from Jackson and St. Johns Counties discontinuously south to the Florida Keys (Monroe County)

Comments: *Flaveria* means "yellow" and refers to the yellow dye extracted from some species. The name *linearis* alludes to the narrow leaves. Florida gardeners cultivate this species because butterflies and bees are common sights around flowering plants. Four members of the genus are native to Florida, but this is by far the most abundant species, especially in recently burned prairies and along roadways that border its habitat.

LANCELEAF BLANKETFLOWER

Gaillardia aestivalis (Walter) H. Rock
Aster family (Asteraceae)

Description: The leaves of this perennial species have narrowly elliptic, obovate, or spatulate (usually toothed) blades that measure ¾"–2¼" long and ⅛"–⅝" wide. The heads have 6–12 deeply 3-lobed ray flowers that may be yellow, purple, pinkish, or white. Disk flowers may be yellow, purplish brown, or bicolored.

Bloom Season: June to October

Habitat/Range: Dry pinelands and prairies across the Florida panhandle south to Hardee and Highlands Counties

Comments: *Gaillardia* honors eighteenth-century French magistrate Gaillard de Merentonneau (apparently in error as Charentonneau). This species was first collected in South Carolina and described by British-American botanist Thomas Walter (1740–1789) and published in his *Flora Caroliniana* in 1788. Lanceleaf blanketflower is not as popular in cultivation as the following species.

BLANKETFLOWER

Gaillardia pulchella Foug.
Aster family (Asteraceae)

Description: Blanketflower is an annual, although it sometimes persists from seed in cultivation. It typically reaches 8"–14" tall, with oblong or spatula-shaped leaves that are usually entire but may be toothed, measuring about 2"–4" long and ⅜"–½" wide. The ray flowers are most often yellow to orange at the tips and reddish or purplish at the base.

Bloom Season: All year

Habitat/Range: Dunes, sandhills, and roadsides discontinuously scattered throughout Florida, including the Florida Keys

Comments: The name *pulchella* means "beautiful" and aptly describes the blossoms. This species is also called Indian blanket, and both common names allude to the colorful blankets woven by Native Americans. Another name is firewheel. This species is commonly seeded along Florida roadways for beautification projects, often escaping into adjacent habitats where it never naturally occurred.

SPANISH DAISY

Helenium amarum (Raf.) H. Rock
Aster family (Asteraceae)

Description: The narrowly linear leaves of Spanish daisy are smooth or sparsely hairy and sometimes deeply dissected. The flower heads are held above the leaves, and each head measures about ⅝"–1¼" wide, with toothed ray flowers that angle slightly downward.

Bloom Season: May to November

Habitat/Range: Sandy pinelands and open disturbed sites throughout mainland Florida

Comments: *Helenium* honors Helen of Troy, queen of Sparta, whose abduction by Prince Paris of Troy brought about the Trojan War. The name *amarum* refers to the bitter leaves, giving rise to the name bitterweed in parts of its native range. The botanical name was revised from *Gaillardia amara* in 1957 by botanist Howard Francis Leonard Rock (1925–1964). It is mostly associated with disturbed sandy soils, so look for it in abandoned fields or along trails that bisect its habitat.

PURPLEHEAD SNEEZEWEED
Helenium flexuosum Raf.
Aster family (Asteraceae)

Description: The sparsely hairy stems are strongly winged, with grooved flower stems. Oblong to lanceolate sessile leaves are 1"–5" long and average ¼"–½" wide. The plant reaches about 36" tall and is often branched in the upper half. The flower heads measure about ⅝" wide. Ray flowers may be present or absent.

Bloom Season: February to October

Habitat/Range: Wet flatwoods and floodplains discontinuously across the Florida panhandle and south to Hillsborough and Polk Counties, with a disjunct population in Everglades National Park (Miami-Dade County)

Comments: The name *flexuosum* refers to the flexible stems. It has been suggested that this species may be of hybrid origin. As is true of other members of the genus, the leaves taste bitter; neither deer nor rabbits will eat the plant. Small bees and butterflies visit the disk flowers. Other common names are bitterweed and Hélénie Nudiflore.

SOUTHEASTERN SNEEZEWEED
Helenium pinnatifidum (Nutt.) Rydb.
Aster family (Asteraceae)

Description: The basal leaves are pinnately divided partway to the midrib and are 2"–6" long. The flower heads are solitary on tall stems that rise from the center of the leafy rosette and stand 1'–2' tall or more. The flower heads average 1"–1½" wide, with notched ray flowers.

Bloom Season: All year

Habitat/Range: Freshwater wetlands and flatwoods through most of mainland Florida

Comments: The name *pinnatifidum* means "pinnately cut," referring to the leaves. Botanist Thomas Nuttall (1786–1859) described it as *Leptopoda pinnatifida* in 1841, but it was moved to the genus *Helenium* in 1915 by Swedish-born American botanist Per Axel Rydberg (1860–1931). The plant is toxic to livestock and is a principal cause of "spewing sickness" in cattle. The name sneezeweed is derived from Native Americans, who dried and powdered certain species to use as snuff.

SWAMP SUNFLOWER
Helianthus angustifolius L.
Aster family (Asteraceae)

Description: Swamp sunflower has very narrow leaves that curl under along the margins (revolute), measuring 2"–6" long and about ¼" wide. The showy flower heads measure 2" or more across.

Bloom Season: April to December, but mostly October to November

Habitat/Range: Marshes, wet flatwoods, and roadside ditches of Florida south to Lee, Glades, and Martin Counties

Comments: *Helianthus* means "sun flower." The name *angustifolius* alludes to the narrow leaves. Look for this species adorning roadsides and adjacent habitats in the fall months. It reaches 5' tall or more, so it is difficult to miss when in flower. Southeastern sunflower (*Helianthus agrestis*) is similar but with lanceolate to narrowly ovate leaves that are not strongly revolute. The naturalized muck sunflower (*Helianthus simulans*) also has similar flowers but with leaves that reach 6" long and 1" wide.

LAKESIDE SUNFLOWER
Helianthus carnosus Small
Aster family (Asteraceae)

Description: The unbranched, leafless stems of this sunflower may reach 24" tall when flowering. Lanceolate to linear leaves are mostly basal, opposite or alternate, and measure 4"–10" long and ½"–1" wide, with a white midvein. The flower heads average 2½"–3" across, with yellow disk flowers.

Bloom Season: July to October

Habitat/Range: Endemic to wet prairies and flatwoods of Duval, Flagler, Putnam, St. Johns, and Volusia Counties (historically in Clay County)

Comments: The name *carnosus* means "fleshy" and relates to the leaves. This state-listed endangered species was first collected in Duval County in July 1897 and is only known from northeastern Florida, where most of the existing populations are on unprotected private land. The common name alludes to the species' habit of growing along lake margins, but it will tolerate drier soils. Bees and butterflies frequent the disk flowers for nectar.

WEST COAST DUNE SUNFLOWER

Helianthus debilis (Nutt.) ssp. *vestitus*
(E. Watson) Heiser
Aster family (Asteraceae)

Description: The hairy stems of this subspecies are decumbent and form low mounds along coastal dunes. The leaves are coarsely and irregularly toothed, averaging 2"–4" long and half as wide. The flower heads are 2" wide.

Bloom Season: All year

Habitat/Range: Endemic to coastal and inland dunes from Pinellas and Hillsborough Counties south along Florida's west coast to Lee County

Comments: The name *debilis* means "weak" and alludes to the species' decumbent stems. The name *vestitus* means "covered" and relates to the soft hairs covering the stems. Another endemic subspecies (ssp. *cucumerifolius*) is scattered around Florida from Escambia County in the western panhandle to Sarasota County. East coast dune sunflower (*Helianthus debilis* ssp. *debilis*) ranges from southeastern Georgia south along the east coast to the Florida Keys. Flowers are identical.

CAMPHORWEED

Heterotheca subaxillaris (Lam.) Britton & Rusby
Aster family (Asteraceae)

Description: Camphorweed typically reaches about 2'–4' tall, with ovate to elliptic leaves ranging from ½"–2¾" long and ⅜"–2" wide. The larger basal leaves wither away before flowering. The leaf blades are entire or coarsely toothed and often undulating. The flower heads average 1" wide.

Bloom Season: All year

Habitat/Range: Sandhills, dunes, and pinelands throughout mainland Florida

Comments: *Heterotheca* means "different container," alluding to the dissimilar achene-like fruits called cypselae. The name *subaxillaris* refers to the floral heads produced near the leaf axils. A key to identifying this species is the strong odor of camphor from crushed leaves. Another member of the same family with a similar appearance and odor is camphor daisy (*Rayjacksonia phyllocephala*) of Florida's central west coast and the Florida Keys. Butterflies visit the flowers.

COASTAL PLAIN HAWKWEED
Hieracium megacephalon Nash
Aster family (Asteraceae)

Description: The leaves are elliptic to inversely egg shaped (obovate) and range from 1⅜"–3" long and about half as wide. The leaves and flowering stems are covered with coarse hairs, and the involucral bracts are ½" or longer. The ¾"–1" heads of flowers close by mid-afternoon and are produced in corymbs on stems to 18" tall.

Bloom Season: All year

Habitat/Range: Sandhills, flatwoods, and pinelands from Liberty and Franklin Counties south through the peninsula

Comments: *Hieracium* comes from *heirakos,* an ancient Greek word for "hawk," and relates to the fanciful belief by Pliny (AD 23–79) that hawks ate the plants to improve their vision. The name *megacephalon* means "large head" and refers to the heads of flowers, which are larger than those of related species. Queen-devil (*Hieracium gronovii*) produces flowers in panicles with shorter involucral bracts.

VIRGINIA DWARF DANDELION
Krigia virginica (L.) Willd.
Aster family (Asteraceae)

Description: The basal rosette of leaves of this annual may reach 6" across, but plants may flower when the rosette has only reached 1" wide, especially in dry sand. Oblanceolate leaves average 2"–2½" long and ½"–¾" wide, often pinnately cut, with shallow lobes. The flower heads are about ⅜"–½" wide.

Bloom Season: February to May

Habitat/Range: Pine flatwoods and disturbed sites across all northern Florida south to Pinellas, Hillsborough, Polk, Osceola, and Sarasota Counties

Comments: *Krigia* honors German physician and botanist David Krieg (1667–1713), who collected plants in the United States before moving to Riga in present-day Latvia to practice medicine but fell victim to the plague, or starvation, during the Russian invasion. The name *virginica* relates to Virginia, where this species was first collected. Two other native members of this genus occur in Florida.

BUTTERWEED

Packera glabella (Poir.) C. Jeffrey
(Also *Senecio glabellus* Poir.)
Aster family (Asteraceae)

Description: The toothed 2"–4" leaves of this suc-culent, weedy species are deeply and irregularly cut, reducing in size up the hollow, striated stems. The fragrant flower heads are produced in showy clusters, and each head is about ⅜"–½" wide.

Bloom Season: March to July

Habitat/Range: Marshes and other wet areas throughout the mainland except the northeastern counties

Comments: *Packera* honors Canadian botanist John G. Packer (1929–), professor emeritus, University of Alberta. The name *glabella* relates to the species' smooth (glabrous) leaves. Herbalists have used members of this genus medicinally for vari-ous gynecological ailments, but the leaves of this species contain high levels of alkaloids that can cause severe liver damage in humans if eaten and are also toxic to grazing livestock. It is frequent along roadsides that bisect wetlands.

SANDDUNE CINCHWEED

Pectis glaucescens (Cass.) D.J. Keil
Aster family (Asteraceae)

Description: This low-growing species has leaves that emit an intense aroma when crushed. The narrowly linear leaves are opposite, sessile, and typically about ¼"–½" long, with 2 rows of oil glands on the lower surface. The flower heads are ⅜" wide and distinctly stalked.

Bloom Season: All year

Habitat/Range: Dry disturbed sites of Hillsbor-ough, Polk, and Brevard Counties south through the Florida Keys

Comments: *Pectis* is Latin for "comb" and alludes to the comblike bristles along the leaf margins of the type species. The name *glaucescens* refers to the fine waxy coating on the stems (glaucous). It is also called tea blinkum in Florida and has been used in Jamaica to treat colds and tuberculosis. It is called *chinche hierba* (bedbug herb) in Puerto Rico for its use to repel bedbugs. Spreading cinchweed (*Pectis prostrata*) has wider leaves and sessile flower heads.

FLORIDA FALSE SUNFLOWER
Phoebanthus grandiflorus (Torr. & A. Gray)
S.F. Blake
Aster family (Asteraceae)

Description: The 30"–40" stems of this species bear linear or linear-lanceolate, alternate leaves that measure ¾"–1¾" long and ⅛"–⅜" wide. The flower heads may reach 3½" across. The phyllaries are appressed.

Bloom Season: March to November

Habitat/Range: Endemic to sandhills and pine flat-woods from Clay to Levy Counties south to Martin and Sarasota Counties; also Jackson County

Comments: *Phoebanthus* is from the Greek *phoebus* ("the sun") and *anthos* ("flower"). The name *grandiflorus* relates to the large heads of flowers. It was first described in 1842 as *Helianthella grandiflora*, but American botanist Sidney Fay Blake (1892–1959) moved it to the genus *Phoebanthus* in 1916. When in flower, this species is easy to see while you're driving down forest roads that bisect preserves within its range. The disk flowers attract a variety of nectar-seeking butterflies.

PINELAND FALSE SUNFLOWER
Phoebanthus tenuifolius (Torr. & A. Gray) S.F. Blake
Aster family (Asteraceae)

Description: Very narrow threadlike leaves appear up the entire length of the 20"–40" stems that usually branch near the top, with the branches terminating in showy flower heads that reach 3" across.

Bloom Season: April to September

Habitat/Range: Endemic to sandhills and flatwoods of Liberty, Franklin, Calhoun, and Gulf Counties in the Florida panhandle

Comments: The name *tenuifolius* means "slender leaves." This is a state-listed threatened species due to its limited range. A discovery made by Troy University biology professor Alvin R. Diamond (1962–) in 1985 in Escambia County, Alabama, was determined to be this species, but this station was later cleared and herbicided. The natural range of this and the previous species do not overlap. Pollinator-predator spiders are frequently seen waiting for prey on the flower heads.

ZIGZAG SILKGRASS

Pityopsis flexuosa (Nash) Small
Aster family (Asteraceae)

Description: Zigzagging stems average 12"–20" tall, with alternate, narrowly linear leaves from 1½"–2" long and ⅛"–¼" wide, becoming shorter and narrower up the stem. The flower heads are 1" across.

Bloom Season: September to October

Habitat/Range: Endemic to sandhills of Franklin, Liberty, Gadsden, Wakulla, Leon, and Jefferson Counties in the Florida panhandle

Comments: *Pityopsis* means "resembling a pine," alluding to the narrow leaves of the type species, which resemble a seedling pine (*Pinus*). The name *flexuosa* relates to the zigzagging stems. This state-listed endangered species has suffered mostly from fire suppression and development encroaching on its habitat. It was first described in 1896 as *Chrysopsis flexuosa* by botanist George Valentine Nash (1864–1921) but moved to the genus *Pityopsis* in 1933 by renowned botanist John Kunkel Small (1869–1938).

NARROWLEAF SILKGRASS

Pityopsis graminifolia (Michx.) Nutt.
(Also *Heterotheca graminifolia* [Michx.] Shinners)
Aster family (Asteraceae)

Description: The lower leaves of silkgrass are 4"–8" long and ¼"–½" wide, with smaller leaves up the stem. The flower heads are usually numerous, with bright yellow ray and disk flowers. The flower heads are ⅝"–¾" in diameter.

Bloom Season: All year

Habitat/Range: Pinelands and dry prairies throughout Florida

Comments: The name *graminifolia* refers to the grasslike leaves of this species. The plant is used medicinally to reduce fever and to treat boils, colds, and rheumatism. The leaves of plants in parts of central Florida are considerably wider than what is typical in other regions of Florida and may warrant further taxonomic scrutiny. It is sometimes cultivated by gardeners for its cheery flowers and butterfly-attracting attributes. Five members of the genus are native to Florida.

CAROLINA DESERTCHICORY
Pyrrhopappus carolinianus (Walter) DC.
Aster family (Asteraceae)

Description: This somewhat weedy annual is commonly seen in overgrown lots and along roadsides. The leaves are mostly lanceolate with entire margins or with 1 or 2 lobes near the base. The flower heads measure about 1"–1½" across.

Bloom Season: April to September

Habitat/Range: Sandy habitats and disturbed sites south in Florida to Sarasota, DeSoto, Highlands, and Indian River Counties

Comments: *Pyrrhopappus* is a combination of words meaning "yellowish red" and "pappus," referring to the color of the pappi (the modified calyx crowning the dry achene in the aster family). The name *carolinianus* refers to South Carolina, where the type specimen was collected near Williamsburg in 1927. The Cherokee used the plant medicinally to cleanse the blood; other Native American tribes ate the roots. The flowers are often visited by small diurnal moths.

PRAIRIE CONEFLOWER
Ratibida pinnata (Vent.) Barnhart
Aster family (Asteraceae)

Description: Stems of this species can reach 48" tall, with leaves divided into 3–9 toothed lobes. Each leaf measures up to 14" long and 6" wide. The showy heads of flowers are held well above the leaves at the apex of tall stems, each with 6–15 ray florets circling a purplish oblong disk. The tiny disk florets are yellow but may be purple toward the tips.

Bloom Season: May to October

Habitat/Range: Prairies and limestone outcrops in woodland openings of Gadsden and Jackson Counties in the Florida panhandle

Comments: *Ratibida* is believed to be a name used by Greek physician Pedanius Dioscorides (AD 40–90) as *rathibida*, for an aster found in Roman Dacia, an ancient province once located in present-day Romania. The name *pinnata* refers to the pinnate leaves. This species ranges across much of the eastern half of the United States into Ontario and is cultivated by gardeners.

BLACKEYED SUSAN
Rudbeckia hirta L.
Aster family (Asteraceae)

Description: This well-known species produces a rosette of coarse-haired, toothed 2"–4" leaves with smaller, clasping stem leaves. The ray florets may radiate outward from the cone-like central disk or arch downward.

Bloom Season: February to November

Habitat/Range: Sandhills and flatwoods throughout mainland Florida

Comments: *Rudbeckia* honors botany professor Olaus Rudbeck (1660–1740), whose most famous student was Carl Linneaus (1707–1778), who latinized his name to Carolus Linnaeus when he published botanical papers in Latin. The name *hirta* is for the coarsely hairy (hirsute) stems and leaves. The common name is believed to come from British colonists and is taken from the poem "Black-Eyed Susan" by John Gay (1685–1732). There are 9 members of this genus in Florida, but this is the most common and widespread species in the state and one of the most well-known wildflowers in America.

CUTLEAF CONEFLOWER
Rudbeckia laciniata L.
Aster family (Asteraceae)

Description: The lower leaves of this species reach 8" long or more and are on narrowly winged petioles (often drooping). The lower to middle leaves have 3–7 large, coarsely toothed lobes and are sometimes formed into 2 smaller divisions. The upper leaves are much smaller, lack lobes, and are either entire or toothed. The flower heads are 2"–3" across, with a green disk that turns yellowish and then brown as seeds ripen.

Bloom Season: June to September

Habitat/Range: Moist, open woodlands and floodplains of Walton, Liberty, Gadsden, Leon, and Levy Counties

Comments: The name *laciniata* relates to the leaves being divided into segments (laciniate). There are named cultivars of this species in the nursery trade, and some spread vigorously from rhizomes. The disk flowers attract nectar-seeking butterflies and bumblebees. This species ranges across the eastern United States into Canada.

BROWNEYED SUSAN

Rudbeckia triloba L.
Aster family (Asteraceae)

Description: The hairy stems are spreading, with ovate to elliptic leaves averaging 4"–8" long and ¾"–2" wide. The lower stem leaves may have 3–5 lobes. The flower heads measure about ¾"–⅞" across and are produced in panicles of 10–30 heads.

Bloom Season: April to October

Habitat/Range: Open fields and roadsides in Jackson, Calhoun, Wakulla, Citrus, and Levy Counties

Comments: The name *triloba* refers to the 3-lobed cauline (stem) leaves. The flowers of this species are smaller than other members of the genus in Florida. The flowers of this short-lived perennial attract a host of insects, including butterflies, moths, bees, beetles, and bee flies. The leaves provide forage for deer, rabbits, and other herbivores. It is a state-listed endangered species due to its limited range in Florida but is common in other parts of its range across the eastern United States. It prefers disturbed soils.

STARRY ROSINWEED

Silphium asteriscus L.
Aster family (Asteraceae)

Description: Stems may reach 36" tall, with hairy lanceolate basal leaves that average 2"–10" long and ¼"–2" wide. Flower heads average 2"–2½" across. The flower heads have 12–20 ray florets. Only the ray florets in *Silphium* produce seeds.

Bloom Season: April to October

Habitat/Range: Prairies, open forests, and roadsides from Escambia County to Lee County along the Gulf Coast

Comments: *Silphium* was the name of a plant depicted on coins in the ancient Greek city of Cyrene in present-day Libya. The name *asteriscus* relates to its resemblance to the genus *Asteriscus* of Europe, Africa, and the Middle East. The type specimen for Florida was collected in 1884 from Gadsden County by botanist Allan Hiram Curtiss (1845–1907). The name rosinweed relates to the plant resin, which smells of turpentine and is used for medicinal purposes as well as a breath freshener in chewing gum.

KIDNEYLEAF ROSINWEED
Silphium compositum Michx.
Aster family (Asteraceae)

Description: The alternate, roughly hairy (hispid) leaves are typically toothed, pinnately or palmately lobed, and range up to 14" long and 20" wide, with long petioles. The flower heads have 6–12 ray florets, and each head measures about 2" across.

Bloom Season: May to November

Habitat/Range: Open pine and oak forests, meadows, and roadsides across the Florida panhandle and discontinuously south in the peninsula to Pasco, Marion, and Flagler Counties

Comments: The name *compositum* means "compound" and relates to the species' deeply dissected leaves. This is a bold plant that cannot be missed, especially when in flower, but the plant looks somewhat similar to *Smallanthus uvedalia* (described next), which typically has winged petioles. French botanist André Michaux (1746–1802) first described this species, but the name wasn't published until the year following his untimely death.

HAIRY LEAFCUP
Smallanthus uvedalia (L.) Mack. ex Small
Aster family (Asteraceae)

Description: The 3- to 5-lobed opposite leaves of this species range to 12" or more in length and up to 10" wide, with petioles (usually winged) that reach 6" long. The stems may reach 6'–10' tall, with flower heads borne singly on long stems or in corymbs of 2–5 heads, each measuring about 1½"–2" across.

Bloom Season: All year

Habitat/Range: Moist woodlands across the Florida panhandle and south in the peninsula to Pinellas, Polk, Osceola, and Brevard Counties

Comments: *Smallanthus* commemorates American botanist John Kunkel Small (1869–1938). The name *uvedalia* was given to this plant by botanist Kenneth Kent Mackenzie (1877–1934) to honor English clergyman the Reverend Robert Uvedale (1642–1722), who tended a garden of exotic plants in the London Borough of Enfield. It is also called bear's paw due to the outline of the leaves.

BLUESTEM GOLDENROD
Solidago caesia L.
Aster family (Asteraceae)

Description: This goldenrod is usually unbranched, 1½'–3' tall; the central stem typically cants to one side. The elliptic to elliptic-oblong leaves are alternate and reach up to 5" long and ¾" wide. The flowers are in axillary clusters along the stems.

Bloom Season: May to November

Habitat/Range: Bluff forests across most of the Florida panhandle; also Suwannee County

Comments: *Solidago* refers to "becoming whole" or "strengthen" and likely relates to the species' healing properties in treating wounds, infections, kidney stones, and arthritis. The name *caesia* alludes to the light blue stems of some plants, especially as they age. According to folklore, goldenrods are believed to be able to point the way toward buried gold and can show where water is located underground. In northern climes it is believed that when the first goldenrod blooms, there will be frost in 6 weeks.

LEAVENWORTH'S GOLDENROD
Solidago leavenworthii Torr. & A. Gray
Aster family (Asteraceae)

Description: Good characteristics of this species are its lack of basal leaves and its pointed, non-twisted, serrate stem leaves. The stem leaves average 2"–3" long and ⅜"–½" wide and are bundled near the stem tips on young plants but line the stem on flowering specimens. Flowering plants average 3'–4' tall, with flowers in a some-what pyramidal array.

Bloom Season: May to December

Habitat/Range: Flatwoods, dunes, and disturbed sites from Jackson, Calhoun, and Liberty Counties in the Florida panhandle east and south through most of the peninsula

Comments: The name *leavenworthii* honors botanist Melines Conklin Leavenworth (1796–1862), who served as an army surgeon during the Civil War and became an important plant collector in the southern United States. Chapman's goldenrod (*Solidago chapmanii*) is similar but the stem leaves are twisted and not serrated.

SEASIDE GOLDENROD
Solidago sempervirens L.
Aster family (Asteraceae)

Description: The best field characteristic of this species is the basal rosette of large ovate to oblanceolate leaves that reach up to 16" long and 2½" wide (and are present when flowering). The tall inflorescence can reach 6' in height, with numerous side branches covered with ¼" flowers.

Bloom Season: All year

Habitat/Range: Coastal dunes and brackish and freshwater marshes through much of the Florida panhandle and from Nassau, Putnam, Marion, and Levy Counties south through the peninsula

Comments: The name *sempervirens* means "evergreen." The medicinal virtues of goldenrods have been known since the civilizations of ancient Rome and Greece and are one of the most effective treatments of urinary tract infections. Goldenrod species are the state flowers of Alabama, Kentucky, and Nebraska, and they are among the most well-known wildflowers across the United States.

WAND GOLDENROD
Solidago stricta Aiton
Aster family (Asteraceae)

Description: Wand goldenrod has a simple, straight, grooved stem, with the main leaves forming a basal rosette. The leaf blades are spatulate, to 6" long and 1" wide, tapering toward the base to a long petiole. The sessile, scalelike stem leaves are appressed to the stem. The flower spike is usually unbranched.

Bloom Season: All year

Habitat/Range: Pinelands, wet prairies, and margins of salt marshes throughout Florida

Comments: The name *stricta* means "erect" or "upright," referring to the flowering stem. One common misconception involving goldenrods is that they are the cause of allergies. Common ragweed (*Ambrosia artemisiifolia*) is the real culprit because it has airborne pollen, unlike goldenrods, and blooms in the same season. Among Florida's native goldenrods, this is the easiest species to identify due to its narrow, typically unbranched inflorescence.

SQUAREHEAD
Tetragonotheca helianthoides L.
Aster family (Asteraceae)

Description: The stems of this species average 12"–36" tall and are covered with long, soft, unmatted hairs (villous). The opposite leaves are lanceolate, ovate, or rhombic, coarsely toothed, and measure 3"–7" long and 1"–5" wide. The involucre is quadrangular, and the flower heads reach about 2" across.

Bloom Season: May to July

Habitat/Range: Sandhills and open woods across much of the Florida panhandle and discontinuously south in the peninsula to Citrus, Lake, and Highlands Counties

Comments: *Tetragonatheca* refers to the diagnostic, 4-angled involucre (the bracts surrounding a flower or flower cluster). The name *helianthoides* alludes to its close resemblance to a *Helianthus* (Asteraceae). Butterflies are fond of the nectar provided by the rather long disk flowers, which are also visited by bumblebees. This is the only member of the genus in Florida.

CHAPMAN'S CROWNBEARD
Verbesina chapmanii J.R. Coleman
Aster family (Asteraceae)

Description: The wingless stems reach 24"–32" tall, with mostly opposite, roughly hairy, toothed elliptic leaves to ⅜"–¾" long. Heads of deep yellow flowers terminate the stems.

Bloom Season: May to August

Habitat/Range: Endemic to pine flatwoods and bogs in Walton, Washington, Bay, Gulf, Liberty, and Franklin Counties in the Florida panhandle

Comments: *Verbesina* is a modification of the genus *Verbena*. The name *chapmanii* honors American botanist and physician Alvan Wentworth Chapman (1809–1899), who authored his *Flora of the Southern States* in 1860. Botanist James Robert Coleman (1934–) described this state-listed threatened species in 1972. The clusters of flowers look very much like some members of the genus *Palafoxia* (Asteraceae). Most populations are protected within the Apalachicola National Forest. Butterflies are attracted to the flowers.

PINELAND HELIOTROPE

Euploca polyphylla (Lehm.) J.I.M. Melo & Semir
(Also *Heliotropium polyphyllum* Lehm.)
Borage family (Boraginaceae)

Description: This species has erect or spreading stems with narrow, alternate elliptic leaves from ⅜"–¾" long to ⅛" wide. The flower spikes curl under at the tip with 5-lobed, yellow or white flowers, each about ¼" wide.

Bloom Season: All year

Habitat/Range: Pinelands and prairies of Escambia County and from Taylor and Flagler Counties south into the Florida Keys (Monroe County)

Comments: *Euploca* is Greek for "true" and "to plait" (braid), referring to the corolla. The name *polyphylla* means "many leaves." This species was moved to the genus *Euploca* from *Heliotropium* in 2009 by botanists José Iranildo Miranda de Melo and João Semir. The genus was established by botanist Thomas Nuttall (1786–1859) in 1837, included in *Heliotropium* by botanist Asa Gray (1810–1888), and reestablished in 2003 on the basis of molecular data.

FLORIDA PRICKLY-PEAR

Opuntia austrina Small
Cactus family (Cactaceae)

Description: This cactus has elliptic or obovate pads (stems) that reach 2"–8" long and 1"–3" wide, with sharp spines to 1¼". The flowers range from 2"–2½" wide and produce cone-shaped, reddish-purple 1"–2" fruits.

Bloom Season: March to July

Habitat/Range: Endemic to sandy habitats of peninsular Florida

Comments: Greek philosopher Theophrastus (372–287 BC) used the name *Opuntia* for a plant found near the ancient city of Opus in Greece, and it was later applied to this group of cacti in 1754 by botanist Philip Miller (1671–1771). The name *austrina* means "southern." This cactus has long been synonymized under *Opuntia humifusa*, but a 2012 University of Florida doctorate dissertation by botanist Lucas C. Majure (1981–) separates it as a distinct species. Cockspur (*Opuntia drummondii*) occurs in northeastern Florida; Keys jumping cactus (*Opuntia abjecta*) is found in the lower Florida Keys.

ERECT PRICKLY-PEAR
Opuntia stricta (Haw.) Haw.
Cactus family (Cactaceae)

Description: This cactus typically grows upright and may reach about 60" tall, or it may be spreading. It is much-branched, with succulent pads that may have no spines or have long, sharp, paired spines to 1½" long. The flowers average 2"–2½" wide. The obovoid fruits (berries) ripen reddish purple.

Bloom Season: February to August

Habitat/Range: Coastal habitats and relict shell mounds along both coastlines of Florida, including the Florida Keys

Comments: The name *stricta* means "erect" or "upright" and alludes to this species' growth habit. This state-listed threatened species was first described in 1803 by botanist Adrian Hardy Haworth (1768–1833) as *Cactus strictus* and moved to *Opuntia* by Haworth in 1812. Botanist John Kunkel Small (1869–1938) listed twenty-six native *Opuntia* species for Florida, while more reserved taxonomists recognize only three or six species in the state.

GOLDEN CANNA
Canna flaccida Salisb.
Canna family (Cannaceae)

Description: The broadly lanceolate leaves of this succulent herbaceous species range from 8"–24" long and 3"–6" wide, alternating along a fleshy 2'–4' stem. The showy, symmetric flowers are short-lived.

Bloom Season: March to November

Habitat/Range: Freshwater wetlands in Santa Rosa, Franklin, and Wakulla Counties and from Dixie, Alachua, and Nassau Counties south through mainland Florida

Comments: *Canna* is Greek for "reed." The name *flaccida* refers to the species' flaccid flowers. Larvae of the Brazilian skipper often defoliate native and cultivated canna species. The larvae cut two slits on the leaf blade and fold the flap over as a shelter to hide from predators in daytime and then feed at night, but orioles and other birds have figured out this ploy and pull the slits open to reveal the tasty morsel hiding inside. Seminoles placed the hard seeds in turtle shells to make ceremonial rattles.

PINEBARREN FROSTWEED

Crocanthemum corymbosum (Michx.) Britton
(Also *Helianthemum corymbosum* Michx.)
Rockrose family (Cistaceae)

Description: This species forms mounds, rarely more than about 10" tall. The leaves are linear-lanceolate and range from 1"–1¾" long and ¼"–⅜" wide. The flowers are in dense cymes, each about ⅝" wide, with petals that are squared off at the tip.

Bloom Season: March to August

Habitat/Range: Sandhills and dunes through most of mainland Florida

Comments: *Crocanthemum* means "saffron yellow flower." The name *corymbosum* refers to the arrangement of the flowers in a corymb, a flat-topped inflorescence with flowers that open from the outside inward. The genus *Crocanthemum* was split from the old-world genus *Helianthemum*. Some species produce flowers that open in the morning and then shed their petals in the after-noon (chasmogamous) but also produce self-fertile (cleistogamous) flowers along the branches.

FLORIDA SCRUB FROSTWEED

Crocanthemum nashii (Britton) Barnhart
(Also *Helianthemum nashii* Britton)
Rockrose family (Cistaceae)

Description: The narrow alternate leaves average 1"–1⅜" long and ¼"–⅜" wide and are covered with star-shaped hairs that create the appearance of being covered with hoarfrost, giving rise to the name frostweed. The elongated, branched, leafy inflorescence bears ⅝" flowers with somewhat more rounded petals than the previous species.

Bloom Season: February to August

Habitat/Range: Scrub habitat scattered throughout most of peninsular Florida

Comments: The name *nashii* honors New York Botanical Garden botanist and horticulturist George Valentine Nash (1864–1921). The name frostweed relates to species growing in cold temperate regions that form intricate patterns of ice crystals (called "frost flowers") on their stems near ground level after nighttime freezes. This species was first collected in 1894 near Eustis (Lake County).

COASTAL PLAIN ST. JOHN'S-WORT
Hypericum brachyphyllum (Spach) Steud.
Mangosteen family (Clusiaceae)

Description: The short, needlelike leaves of this erect 2'–4' shrubby species are strongly revolute (rolled toward the underside) and average ¼"–⅜" long. The attractive 5-petaled flowers are about ¾" wide and can completely cover the plant. Capsules are about ³⁄₁₆" long.

Bloom Season: April to September

Habitat/Range: Depressions in scrub, wet flatwoods, and savannas throughout most of mainland Florida

Comments: *Hypericum* means "above image" and relates to the custom of placing the flowers above images to ward off evil spirits in households and places of worship. The name *brachyphyllum* is descriptive of the very short leaves. Botanist Edouard Spach (1801–1879) described it as *Myriandra brachyphylla* in 1836. It resembles *Hypericum tenuifolium*, a smaller species with mostly decumbent, matted stems that are 6-angled in cross section.

ROUNDPOD ST. JOHN'S-WORT
Hypericum cistifolium Lam.
Mangosteen family (Clusiaceae)

Description: This shrubby species reaches 14"–36" tall, with 4-angled stems that bear linear-oblong, sessile leaves with underturned edges. The leaves measure 1"–3" long and about ⅓" wide. The stalked, 5-petaled ½" flowers are in loose corymbs.

Bloom Season: June to September

Habitat/Range: Wet flatwoods and freshwater marshes throughout mainland Florida

Comments: The name *cistifolium* refers to the resemblance of the leaves to those of a *Cistus* (Cistaceae). The species was first described by Jean-Baptiste Antoine Pierre de Monnet, Chevalier de Lamarck (1744–1829), in 1797. Several species of St. John's-wort are used as herbal treatments for various forms of depression and were once used as a charm against witchcraft and demons. Herbal tea made from St. John's-wort leaves is thought to help ease tensions by settling mild emotional imbalances and promoting a sense of calm.

ST. PETER'S-WORT

Hypericum crux-andreae (L.) Crantz
Mangosteen family (Clusiaceae)

Description: This is an erect shrub to 36" tall, with 4-petaled flowers at the branch tips. The oval or wedge-shaped, clasping leaves measure ½"–¾" wide and line the stems. The bark on older stems sheds off in strips.

Bloom Season: June to November

Habitat/Range: Flatwoods and seepage bogs of the Florida panhandle discontinuously south in the peninsula to Orange, Highlands, and Collier Counties

Comments: The specific epithet *crux-andreae* translates to "St. Andrew's cross," a common name now used for *Hypericum hypericoides*. The name St. Peter's-wort relates to Saint Peter, one of the twelve Apostles, who founded the early Christian Church of Antioch and whom Roman Emperor Nero Augustus Caesar (AD 37–68) crucified in AD 64. Saint Peter chose to be crucified upside down because he didn't feel worthy enough to be crucified in the same manner as Jesus. The devastating Great Fire of Rome occurred the same year.

HIGHLANDS SCRUB ST. JOHN'S-WORT

Hypericum cumulicola (Small) W.P. Adams
Mangosteen family (Clusiaceae)

Description: This species reaches 12"–28" tall and is branched at the base, with 3 or more erect stems lined with opposite, needlelike ¼" leaves. The flowers are in the upper forks of the stems.

Bloom Season: All year

Habitat/Range: Endemic to white sand scrub and rosemary balds of Polk and Highlands Counties

Comments: The name *cumulicola* means "dweller on a heap or mound," in this case, sand. This central Florida endemic was given federal endangered status in 1987, mostly due to habitat loss. Although recruitment increases after fire, the species prefers rosemary balds—a unique, open-scrub microhabitat with a relatively low frequency of fire. Botanist John Kunkel Small (1869–1938) named this species *Sanidophyllum cumulicola* in 1924, but it was moved to *Hypericum* in 1962 by botanist William Preston Adams (1930–). Bees are a principal pollinator.

181

EDISON'S ST. JOHN'S-WORT
Hypericum edisonianum (Small)
W.P. Adams & N. Robson
Mangosteen family (Clusiaceae)

Description: This species may reach 5' tall, with opposite gray-green leaves that measure ½"–⅝" long and ¼"–⅜" wide with conspicuous red glands at the base. The flowers average ⅞" wide.

Bloom Season: April to September

Habitat/Range: Endemic to wet depressions in scrub, cutthroat seeps, and seasonally wet prairies of Collier, DeSoto, Glades, Highlands, and Polk Counties

Comments: The name *edisonianum* commemorates famed inventor Thomas Alva Edison (1847–1931), who bought a winter home in Fort Myers, Florida, in 1885 as a gift to his second wife, Mina. This state-listed endangered species has suffered tremendous habitat loss from wetland drainage, agribusiness, and urban sprawl. Protection of its habitat, coupled with proper management through prescribed fire, is crucial to the long-term survival of this Florida endemic.

MARSH ST. JOHN'S-WORT
Hypericum fasciculatum Lam.
Mangosteen family (Clusiaceae)

Description: This shrubby species reaches 4' tall and has peeling, reddish or gray bark. The needle-like leaves are ⅜"–⅞" long and formed in bundles. The flowers average ⅝" wide, with 5 pinwheel-like petals.

Bloom Season: All year

Habitat/Range: Flatwoods and freshwater wetlands throughout mainland Florida

Comments: The name *fasciculatum* means "bundled," referring to the leaves. Members of this genus contain a chemical that reacts with light, so exposure to sun after drinking tea brewed from the flowers can result in severe sunburn. A long-held tradition is that picking St. John's-wort flowers on St. John's Day (June 24) foretells marriage for maidens. In Christian tradition, Saint John baptized Jesus along the bank of the Jordan River and was a major religious figure mentioned in the Christian Bible and the central religious text of Islam, the Koran.

ST. ANDREW'S-CROSS

Hypericum hypericoides (L.) Crantz
Mangosteen family (Clusiaceae)

Description: This species is diffusely branched, with reddish brown stems that are erect or decumbent. Leaves are linear to somewhat egg shaped, opposite, and measure about ⅜"–1" long and up to half as wide. The flowers measure about ¾"–1" long, with petals arranged in an X.

Bloom Season: May to December

Habitat/Range: Wet flatwoods and floodplains throughout mainland Florida

Comments: When botanist Carolus Linnaeus (1707–1778) first described this plant, he placed it in the genus *Ascyrum* and gave it the specific epithet *hypericoides* because he thought it resembled a *Hypericum*. The common name refers to the resemblance of the flowers to the diagonal cross (saltire) on which Saint Andrew was crucified in the first century. Saint Andrew became the patron saint of Scotland, and a saltire is proudly represented on the national flag.

SMOOTHBARK ST. JOHN'S-WORT

Hypericum lissophloeus W.P. Adams
Mangosteen family (Clusiaceae)

Description: This evergreen species may reach 12' tall, with drooping branches and narrowly linear, needlelike leaves averaging ½"–1" long. The bark on the upper stems is smooth and metallic gray or coppery, exfoliating on the lower stems like birch bark. The flowers are usually solitary in the leaf axils and measure about ⅝" wide.

Bloom Season: May to October

Habitat/Range: Endemic to pond margins and sinks of Bay and Washington Counties

Comments: The name *lissophloeus* means "smooth barked." The global range of this state-listed endangered species encompasses only two counties in the Florida panhandle. One of the prettiest species in the genus, its smooth, peeling bark and growth habit helps distinguish it from all other Florida species. Mature specimens often produce prop roots at the base, much like a red mangrove, to help stabilize the plant in mucky soils.

MYRTLELEAF ST. JOHN'S-WORT
Hypericum myrtifolium Lam.
Mangosteen family (Clusiaceae)

Description: This bushy species reaches 36" tall, with ovate to elliptic-ovate leaves ⅜"–1" long or more. The ovate sepals are leaflike, with obovate petals; the flowers average about ⅝" wide.

Bloom Season: April to December

Habitat/Range: Flatwoods and pond margins throughout much of mainland Florida

Comments: The name *myrtifolium* refers to the resemblance of the leaves to a myrtle (Myrtaceae). When taking St. John's-wort as a treatment for mild depression or simply as a mood elevator, avoid prolonged sun exposure—St. John's-wort may increase your risk of sunburn. It has also been reported that other prescription and over-the-counter medicines (such as birth control pills) become less effective when taking St. John's-wort. This is a large genus, with some Florida species preferring wet habitats and others thriving in desertlike scrub.

HAIRY ST. JOHN'S-WORT
Hypericum setosum L.
Mangosteen family (Clusiaceae)

Description: This hairy-stemmed species reaches about 26" tall, unbranched below, with narrowly ovate to narrowly oblong-elliptic ⅜"–⅝" bristly leaves lining the stems (sometimes appressed to the stems). The ½" flowers have 5 curved petals and are produced on short, terminal branches.

Bloom Season: May to September

Habitat/Range: Moist flatwoods and bogs from Escambia County discontinuously west to Nassau, Duval, and St. Johns Counties; also Pasco and Hillsborough Counties

Comments: The name *setosum* means "bristly" and alludes to the hairs on the plant's stems and leaves. The curved petals give the appearance of a twirling motion, a characteristic that makes it stand out among other members of the genus. St. John's-worts have been used medicinally for more than 2,000 years, mostly to treat depression and other mood disorders. Carolus Linnaeus (1707–1778) named this species in 1753.

ATLANTIC ST. JOHN'S-WORT
Hypericum tenuifolium Pursh
Mangosteen family (Clusiaceae)

Description: Compact mounds of stems reach 20" tall, often decumbent and forming mats, with needlelike, linear, clustered leaves to ⅜" long, but with smaller leaves produced in the axils of the longer leaves. Flowers are in terminal clusters and are about ⅜" wide.

Bloom Season: April to November

Habitat/Range: Low pinelands and prairies from Escambia County to Washington, Bay, and Franklin Counties in the Florida panhandle and from Duval, Alachua, and Hernando Counties south through the peninsula to Palm Beach and Collier Counties

Comments: The name *tenuifolium* relates to the species' slender leaves. Botanist John Kunkel Small (1879–1938) once wrote that the flowers of this species are so bright yellow that they irritate the eyes when growing in full sun. A poem dating to 1400 claimed "St. John's wort doth charm all witches away, if gathered at midnight on the saint's holy day."

FOURPETAL ST. JOHN'S-WORT
Hypericum tetrapetalum Lam.
Mangosteen family (Clusiaceae)

Description: The dull green clasping leaves are broadly ovate and paired in 2 sizes. The X-shaped flowers have 4 petals, with 2 outer sepals that resemble leaves and 2 narrower inner sepals. The flowers are about 1" wide and appear at the branch tips and in the leaf axils.

Bloom Season: All year

Habitat/Range: Wet flatwoods throughout much of mainland Florida but absent in some of the northernmost counties

Comments: The name *tetrapetalum* means "four petals." Early Christians made St. John's-worts a symbol of Saint John the Baptist because they flowered around June 24, St. John's Day. Members of the genus have long been used medicinally to promote healing of wounds because of their antibiotic properties. Flower extracts are antiviral, so medical researchers are testing their effectiveness against the deadly virus (HIV) that causes acquired immunodeficiency syndrome (AIDS).

FLORIDA BELLWORT
Uvularia floridana Chapm.
Autumn Crocus family (Colchicaceae)

Description: The plants reach 18" tall, with angled stems that branch once when flowering. Smooth, alternate, narrowly oval leaves have a waxy appearance and average 1½"–2¾" long and 1"–1½" wide. Nodding, pale yellow flowers are 1 per stem and about 1" long, subtended by a large, leafy bract.

Bloom Season: February to May

Habitat/Range: Deciduous forests of Jackson, Gadsden, Leon, and Nassau Counties

Comments: *Uvularia* is taken from *uvula*, the lobe hanging from the back of the soft palate of humans, and is a fanciful allusion to the pendent blossoms of the type species, *Uvularia perfoliata*. The name *floridana* relates to Florida, where plants were collected by botanist Alvan Wentworth Chapman (1809–1899) and described in 1860. It is a state-listed endangered species that ranges across the southeastern United States.

MERRYBELLS
Uvularia sessilifolia L.
Autumn Crocus family (Colchicaceae)

Description: Perennial stems of this species are typically 2-branched and reach 8"–14" tall with oval, sessile, lily-like leaves. The pendent, cream, bell-like flowers are single or in pairs. Unlike the previous species, there is no leafy bract subtending the flower, which is a key identifying feature.

Bloom Season: April to May

Habitat/Range: Deciduous floodplain forests and streambanks of Walton, Washington, Bay, Jackson, Gadsden, Calhoun, and Liberty Counties in the Florida panhandle

Comments: The name *sessilifolia* alludes to the sessile (stalkless) leaves. Other common names are spreading bellwort, sessileleaf bellwort, wild oats, and straw lily. The genus is sometimes included in the closely related Lily family (Liliaceae). A third species (*Uvularia perfoliata*), with stems that look like they perforate the leaves, occurs in Jackson, Gadsden, and Leon Counties.

OKEECHOBEE GOURD

Cucurbita okeechobeensis (Small) L.H. Bailey
Gourd family (Cucurbitaceae)

Description: This spreading or climbing, dioecious annual vine has coarsely hairy, alternate, heart-shaped toothed or lobed leaves that measure 4"–8" wide. Round, green, hard-shelled gourds measure 3"–3½", with irregular, light green and yellowish stripes. Flowers are 2"–2½" wide.

Bloom Season: January to September

Habitat/Range: Bottomland forests and wooded swamps of Volusia, Lake, Seminole, Glades, and Palm Beach Counties

Comments: *Cucurbita* is the Latin name for a gourd. The name *okeechobeensis* relates to Lake Okeechobee, where botanist John Kunkel Small (1869–1938) collected it on Torry Island (Palm Beach County) in November 1913. William Bartram (1739–1823) first reported it in 1774 along the St. Johns River in present-day Lake County. It is a state- and federal-listed endangered species. The gourds are edible but bitter tasting.

FLORIDA YAM

Dioscorea floridana Bartlett
Yam family (Dioscoreaceae)

Description: Heart-shaped leaves of this counter-clockwise-twining, tuberous vine reach 4½" long and 3½" wide, with axillary inflorescences bearing yellowish male and female flowers on separate plants. Rhizomes are yellow.

Bloom Season: April to August

Habitat/Range: Mesic forests from Gulf, Liberty, and Gadsden Counties discontinuously east and south to Hillsborough and Brevard Counties

Comments: *Dioscorea* is for Greek physician Pedanius Dioscorides (AD 40–90). The name *floridana* means "of Florida." It was described in 1910 by botanist Harley Harris Bartlett (1886–1960). The native *Dioscorea villosa* is similar but has brown rhizomes and white flowers. *Dioscorea bulbifera* and *D. alata* are invasive in Florida and have aerial bulbils. The yam of commerce is the African *Dioscorea rotundata*, but the word "yam" also refers to the sweet potato (*Ipomoea batatas*), a morning-glory.

TINTED WOODLAND SPURGE
Euphorbia commutata Engelm. ex A. Gray
Spurge family (Euphorbiaceae)

Description: The stems of this species may reach 16" tall, with obovate or spatulate leaves measuring up to 1¼" long and ¾" wide. Minuscule "false flowers" are subtended by opposite or whorled, kidney-shaped floral bracts that may be fused at the base. Subglobose fruits are 3-lobed to about ³⁄₁₆" wide.

Bloom Season: All year

Habitat/Range: Moist woodlands in Walton, Jackson, Gadsden, Levy, and Marion Counties

Comments: *Euphorbia* honors first-century Greek physician Euphorbus, who knew these plants were powerful laxatives. The name *commutata* means "altered" or "changed" and refers to its separation from another species. This state-listed endangered species is easily overlooked, even when in flower. It ranges across eastern North America into Ontario. As with related species, the inflorescence looks like a single flower.

WATER TOOTHLEAF
Stillingia aquatica Chapm.
Spurge family (Euphorbiaceae)

Description: This species has toothed, narrowly lanceolate leaves from 1"–3" long and up to ¾" wide but usually narrower. Flower stalks reach 4" tall and produce male flowers above and female flowers below. All parts exude milky sap when broken that can irritate the mouth and eyes.

Bloom Season: February to June

Habitat/Range: Floodplain swamps, mesic flatwoods, and pond margins from Santa Rosa County along the Gulf Coast to Dixie County and from Hernando, Lake, and Brevard Counties south through the peninsula

Comments: *Stillingia* honors English naturalist Benjamin Stillingfleet (1702–1771). When Stillingfleet died, his will stated that all his research papers were to be burned. The name *aquatica* means "of wetlands." This species is also called corkwood, because the stems float and were used as fishing corks. It was described in 1860 by botanist Alvan Wentworth Chapman (1809–1899).

QUEEN'S DELIGHT

Stillingia sylvatica L.
Spurge family (Euphorbiaceae)

Description: Queen's delight reaches 2' tall or more, with finely toothed, shiny, broadly lanceolate leaves that bleed white sap when broken. The leaves average 2"–3" long and up to 1¼" wide. Male and female flowers are on the same spike.

Bloom Season: All year

Habitat/Range: Sandhills and flatwoods throughout mainland Florida

Comments: The name *sylvatica* relates to the species' growing in wild places. Despite safety warnings and serious medical concerns, people take queen's delight in tablet form to treat liver disease, gallbladder disorders, constipation, and laryngitis and to induce vomiting. It was historically used medicinally to treat patients in terminal stages of syphilis. If eaten, it will cause violent vomiting and purging. The common name is said to relate to the imagined similarity of the erect inflorescence to male genitalia, with the word "queen" simply relating to a woman.

STICKY JOINTVETCH

Aeschynomene viscidula Michx.
Pea family (Fabaceae)

Description: The leaves of this low-growing species are divided into 3–7 small, hairy, ovate leaflets that close at night. The flowers are solitary, about ⁵⁄₁₆" wide, and are typically widely spaced along the stems. The jointed, hairy fruits are flattened on 1 side.

Bloom Season: May to December

Habitat/Range: Sandhills, scrub, and pinelands through most of mainland Florida north of Lake Okeechobee; disjunct in Miami-Dade County

Comments: *Aeschynomene* is Greek for "ashamed" and relates to the sensitive leaflets of some species that fold when touched. The name *viscidula* refers to the viscid, or sticky, hairs on the stems and leaves. The young leaves are used as larval food for the barred yellow, a common butterfly of pinelands. *Aeschynomene americana* has feathery leaflets and is common throughout Florida. *Aeschynomene pratensis* is endemic to the southern peninsula.

189

GOPHERWEED
Baptisia lanceolata (Walter) Elliott
Pea family (Fabaceae)

Description: The compound leaves of this long-lived perennial are divided into 3 lanceolate leaflets from 2"–4" long and ¾"–1¼" wide. Typical yellow pea flowers are either axillary or in terminal clusters of several flowers.

Bloom Season: March to May

Habitat/Range: Sandhills and flatwoods throughout the panhandle and in northeast Florida south to Volusia County; also Hernando, Hillsborough, Sarasota, and Polk Counties

Comments: *Baptisia* is taken from *bapto,* "to dip in dye," and the species was named by French botanist Étienne Pierre Ventenat (1757–1808) for the use of some members of this genus to make a blue dye. It was first described as *Sophora lanceolata* in 1788 by British-American botanist Thomas Walter (1740–1789). It is a larval host plant of the orange sulphur, clouded sulphur, frosted elfin, eastern tailed blue, hoary edge, and wild indigo duskywing butterflies in Florida.

PARTRIDGE PEA
Chamaecrista fasciculata (Michx.) Greene
Pea family (Fabaceae)

Description: This annual has stems and petioles with incurved hairs and reaches 12"–36" tall. The leaves are divided into numerous narrow, linear-oblong ½"–¾" leaflets; there are nectar glands at the base of the petioles. Flaccid, solitary flowers appear from the leaf axils with 5 unequal ½" petals, sometimes pale red at the base. The anthers are yellow.

Bloom Season: May to November

Habitat/Range: Sandhills, flatwoods, and dunes throughout mainland Florida

Comments: *Chamaecrista* means "on the ground" and "a crest." The name *fasciculata* means "clustered" or "bundled together." It is a larval host plant of the ceraunus blue, little sulphur, sleepy orange, and cloudless sulphur butterflies. The perennial Deering's partridge pea (*Chamaecrista deeringiana*) is typically less than 12" tall and has red anthers. Some botanists regard it as a synonym of *Chamaecrista fasciculata*.

BIG PINE PARTRIDGE PEA

Chamaecrista lineata (Sw.) Greene var. *keyensis*
(Pennell) H.S. Irwin & Barnaby
(Also *Chamaecrista keyensis* Pennell)
Pea family (Fabaceae)

Description: This perennial species reaches 30"
tall but is often low and sprawling, with compound
leaves covered in short hairs and with small petiole glands. The leaves measure 1"–1½" long, with
4–9 pairs of leaflets. The axillary flowers reach
about 1" wide and have reddish-purple anthers.

Bloom Season: All year

Habitat/Range: Endemic to pine rocklands of the
lower Florida Keys (Monroe County)

Comments: The name *lineata* alludes to the linear
striations on the leaflets; *keyensis* relates to the
Florida Keys. There was a collection in 1969 at
Black Point in Miami-Dade County by botanist
Robert. W. Long (1927–1976), but this species no
longer exists on the Florida mainland. It received
federal endangered status in October 2016. The
largest populations are on Big Pine Key in the
National Key Deer Refuge.

SENSITIVE PEA

Chamaecrista nictitans (L.) Moench var. *aspera*
(Muhl. ex Elliott) H.S. Irwin & Barnaby
Pea family (Fabaceae)

Description: This annual is covered in soft, shaggy
hairs, with stems that average 18"–30" tall. The
compound leaves are 1¼"–2¾" long and ⅜"–¾"
wide, with 7–32 small, hairy leaflets. The flowers
are less than ⅜" wide.

Bloom Season: Mostly July to September

Habitat/Range: Pine rocklands and flatwoods
throughout peninsular Florida into the Florida Keys
and sporadic in the panhandle, where it is replaced
by the nearly glabrous var. *nictitans*

Comments: The name *nictitans* means "blink-
ing" or "moving," relating to the leaves, which
fold against the rachis at night. The name *aspera*
means "rough," referring to the coarse hairs on the
stems and pods. The leaves serve as larval food for
the cloudless sulphur, little yellow, gray hairstreak,
and ceraunus blue butterflies. The Cherokee used
this species to treat spasms in infants.

FLORIDA ALICIA

Chapmannia floridana Torr. & A. Gray
Pea family (Fabaceae)

Description: The leaves of this perennial are divided into 3–9 leaflets, each 1"–2¼" long and mostly restricted to the lower half of the stems. Orangish-yellow ephemeral flowers average about ¾" wide. Sticky hairs cover the stems.

Bloom Season: April to October

Habitat/Range: Endemic to sandhills, scrub, and sandy roadsides from Clay County south to Collier County

Comments: *Chapmannia* was named in 1838 by two botanical titans of the time, John Torrey (1796–1873) and Asa Gray (1810–1888), to commemorate noted botanist Alvan Wentworth Chapman (1809–1899). The genus is represented by 4 species, but this is the only one in the United States. The name *floridana* means "of Florida." The common name alicia relates to nobility, or "noble kind." The stems die back in winter and resprout from the rootstock in springtime. The flowers open before sunrise and wilt by midday.

AVON PARK HAREBELLS

Crotalaria avonensis DeLaney & Wunderlin
Pea family (Fabaceae)

Description: The oval leaves of this perennial are covered with hairs and measure up to ¾" long; there are no stipules present at the base of the petioles. Plants have hairy stems that reach 1"–4" tall and typical yellow pea flowers, but with a short keel beak that curves back toward the standard.

Bloom Season: March to June

Habitat/Range: Endemic to scrub habitat of Polk and Highlands Counties

Comments: *Crotalaria* means "a rattle" and alludes to the seeds, which rattle inside the mature pods. The name *avonensis* refers to Avon Park (Highlands County) on the Lake Wales Ridge, where this species maintains a precarious existence and faces extinction without habitat preservation and proper management. It was described in 1989 by botanists Kris DeLaney (1951–) and Richard P. Wunderlin (1939–) and added to the federal endangered species list in 1996. It is critically imperiled.

LOW RATTLEBOX
Crotalaria pumila Ortega
Pea family (Fabaceae)

Description: Low mounds of stems may reach 12" tall, with compound leaves divided into 3 inversely egg-shaped leaflets that measure ¼"–⅜" long. The flower standard is oval, with thin red lines at the base. The keel is bent at a sharp right angle.

Bloom Season: All year

Habitat/Range: Pinelands and grassy areas in Alachua and Sarasota Counties and from Volusia and Collier Counties south through the coastal counties into the Florida Keys

Comments: The name *pumila* means "little," referring to the small stature of this species. This is a larval host plant of the day-flying bella moth, which has orangish-pink forewings marked with white bands and black spots. The bright pink hind wings create a flash of color when the moth takes flight. Adult bella moths exude a toxic, frothy spit to defend against predators. Spanish botanist Casimiro Gómez de Ortega first described this species in 1797.

RABBITBELLS
Crotalaria rotundifolia J.F. Gmel.
Pea family (Fabaceae)

Description: Rabbitbells has prostrate or slightly ascending hairy stems with oval or oblong leaves (hairy above) that measure ½"–1¼" long and ¼–½" wide. Stipules are present at the base of the petioles. The ⅜" flowers are often solitary on long stems; the keel beak projects upward and outward. The pods measure ¾"–1" long.

Bloom Season: All year

Habitat/Range: Flatwoods and sandhills throughout Florida

Comments: The name *rotundifolia* refers to the species' oval leaves. Rabbitbells closely resembles the endangered endemic Avon Park harebells (*Crotalaria avonensis*) described previously, but a key to separating it from this species is the absence of stipules at the base of the petiole. Both may be found growing together in Polk and Highlands Counties. *Crotalaria spectabilis* and *Crotalaria pallida* are tall, naturalized exotics found in disturbed sites throughout much of Florida.

TROPICAL PUFF
Neptunia pubescens Benth.
Pea family (Fabaceae)

Description: This spreading species has compound leaves divided into 3–4 pairs of segments that divide again into many tiny leaflets. The ½" clusters of flowers are on terminal stalks that reach 3½" long. The hairy pods are about 1" long and ⅜" wide.

Bloom Season: April to November

Habitat/Range: Flatwoods, margins of salt marshes, and disturbed sites discontinuously from the central coastal panhandle south through the peninsula into the Florida Keys

Comments: *Neptunia* honors Neptune, Roman god of the sea, and relates to members of this genus that grow in coastal habitats. The name *pubescens* alludes to the soft hairs (pubescence) covering the stems and leaves. The sensitive leaflets fold together at night and also close quickly when touched. Small bees visit the flowers and are effective pollinators. Some species are eaten as potherbs in tropical Asia.

BROWNHAIR SNOUTBEAN
Rhynchosia cinerea Nash
Pea family (Fabaceae)

Description: Brownhair snoutbean has 3-angled, trailing or prostrate stems that may reach 3' long and are covered with ash-colored hairs. Leaves are divided into 3 rounded, hairy leaflets. The terminal leaflet is largest and measures ⅝"–1" long and ½"–1⅛" wide. From 3–5 yellow, pealike ⅜" flowers are in clusters.

Bloom Season: March to November

Habitat/Range: Endemic to sandhills and scrub of peninsular Florida and the Florida Keys

Comments: *Rhynchosia* is Greek for "beak" and alludes to the beak-like keel petals. The name *cinerea* means "ash-colored" and refers to the hairs on the leaves. Of the 9 *Rhynchosia* species native to Florida, this is the only endemic. It is one of the first wildflowers to bloom after fire, so wildflower enthusiasts should check recently burned areas. Seven other members of this genus in Florida produce 3 leaflets; 2 species have a single leaflet.

ROYAL SNOUTBEAN
Rhynchosia cytisoides (Bertol.) Wilbur
Pea family (Fabaceae)

Description: This erect, open-branched, somewhat bushy species has scabrous compound leaves divided into 3 obovate leaflets that average about ¼"–½" long and ⅛"–¼" wide but may be larger. Flowers are typically solitary in the leaf axils and measure ½"–⅝" long.

Bloom Season: April to October

Habitat/Range: Sandhills, scrub, and dry, open forests from Escambia County east across the Florida panhandle to Gadsden, Wakulla, Liberty, and Taylor Counties

Comments: The name *cytisoides* alludes to this species' resemblance to a *Cytisus* (Fabaceae). Italian botanist Antonio Bertoloni (1775–1869) first described this species in 1850 as *Lespedeza cytisoides*. The easiest place to find this species within its Florida range is to look along the sides of dirt roads that bisect its habitat. The plant photographed was along a clay road in Blackwater River State Forest in Okaloosa County.

DOUBLEFORM SNOUTBEAN
Rhynchosia difformis (Elliott) DC.
Pea family (Fabaceae)

Description: The stems of this species are trailing or prostrate to about 40" in length. The leaves have 1 leaflet at the lower nodes, becoming 3-foliolate up the stems. The petioles are covered with coarse hairs; the elliptic leaflet blades are smooth above, hairy below. Flowers are in axillary clusters and measure about ⅜" wide and long.

Bloom Season: May to September

Habitat/Range: Sandhills of Walton County in the Florida panhandle discontinuously east and south in the peninsula to Hillsborough and Polk Counties

Comments: The name *difformis* relates to an unusual form compared to other members of the genus—in this case alluding to the species' dimorphic compound leaves that are 1-foliolate and 3-foliolate on the same plant. Members of this genus are sometimes utilized as larval host plants for the long-tailed skipper, a common wildland and urban butterfly in Florida.

MICHAUX'S SNOUTBEAN
Rhynchosia michauxii Vail
Pea family (Fabaceae)

Description: Diagnostic features of this species are its trailing habit, with only a single rounded leaflet (1-foliolate). All other trailing species of this genus in Florida are 3-foliolate. Flowers are in axillary clusters, each measuring about ⅜" long.

Bloom Season: All year

Habitat/Range: Sandhills and dry woodlands from Taylor, Alachua, and Clay Counties south through most of central Florida; disjunct in Okaloosa and Miami-Dade Counties

Comments: The name *michauxii* commemorates French botanist and explorer André Michaux (1746–1802), who succumbed to a tropical fever in Madagascar. It was described in 1895 by botanist Anna Murray Vail (1863–1955), who was a Columbia University student of botany professor Nathaniel Lord Britton (1859–1934) and would later become the first librarian of the New York Botanical Garden. This species also occurs in Georgia and North Carolina.

SIDEBEAK PENCILFLOWER
Stylosanthes biflora (L.) Britton, et al.
Pea family (Fabaceae)

Description: The stems of this erect or spreading perennial can reach nearly 24" long, with compound leaves divided into 3 ovate, elliptic, or lanceolate leaflets, each about ¾"–1½" long and ¼"–⅜" wide. The margins may be entire or with small spines (spinulose). The flowers are about ⅜" wide. The narrow seedpods have a hooked beak.

Bloom Season: May to November

Habitat/Range: Sandhills and flatwoods across the Florida panhandle south in the peninsula to Hillsborough, Polk, and Lee Counties

Comments: *Stylosanthes* translates to "pillar" and "flower," for the column-like style. The name *biflora* relates to the flowers, which often appear in pairs. The type specimen for Florida was collected in 1891 at DeFuniak Springs (Walton County). This and other species in this genus serve as larval food for the barred yellow, a common butterfly that occurs throughout Florida.

EVERGLADES KEY PENCILFLOWER

Stylosanthes calcicola Small
Pea family (Fabaceae)

Description: Slender, spreading stems bear compound leaves divided into 3 linear-elliptic, toothed leaflets measuring ⅜"–⅝" long and ⅛"–¼" wide. The flowers are about ³⁄₁₆" wide. Jointed pods produce 1 fertile seed; the terminal joint has a straight or moderately curved beak.

Bloom Season: All year

Habitat/Range: Pine rocklands of Miami-Dade County and the Florida Keys (Monroe County)

Comments: The name *calcicola* refers to the species' growing in limestone soils. This state-listed endangered species was first recorded in Florida in 1915 from the pinelands between Castellow Hammock and Ross Hammock in Miami-Dade County by botanist John Kunkel Small (1869–1938). Small described it in 1933 for his monumental work, *Manual of the Southeastern Flora*. The similar cheesytoes (*Stylosanthes hamata*) is naturalized in southern Florida and has larger flowers and pods with an incurved beak.

COWPEA

Vigna luteola (Jacq.) Benth.
Pea family (Fabaceae)

Description: Cowpea is a weedy vine with alternate compound leaves on long petioles. There are 3 lanceolate leaflets, each about 1½" long and ½"–¾" wide. The ¾" flowers are in few-flowered clusters at the top of angled stems that stand well above the foliage.

Bloom Season: All year

Habitat/Range: Mostly disturbed sites through peninsular Florida into the Florida Keys, and sporadic in the panhandle

Comments: *Vigna* honors Italian professor Dominicus Vigna (1581–1647), who wrote a commentary on Theophrastus in 1625. The name *luteola* means "yellow," referring to the flower color. Although cowpea is a larval host plant of the gray hairstreak, cassius blue, ceraunus blue, and long-tailed skipper butterflies, it is not purposely cultivated by gardeners because of its weedy tendencies. The plant is used in Polynesia to cure "ghost sickness," a perceived ailment caused by supernatural powers.

CAROLINA JESSAMINE
Gelsemium sempervirens (L.) W.T. Aiton
Gelsemium family (Gelsemiaceae)

Description: This twining, evergreen vine has stems to 20' long, with light green lanceolate leaves 1"–3" long and ½"–¾" wide. The fragrant, funnel-shaped flowers are about 1½" long.

Bloom Season: January to April

Habitat/Range: Deciduous forests south through Florida to Charlotte, Highlands, and Palm Beach Counties

Comments: *Gelsemium* is a latinized version of *gelsomino,* the Italian name for jasmine. The name *sempervirens* means "evergreen." There are only 3 species in this genus, and 2 occur in Florida (the third species is native to Asia). *Gelsemium rankinii* flowers are similar but are not aromatic, and it occurs mostly in the panhandle. Both species in Florida are highly toxic and may be fatal if ingested. Gelsemiaceae was separated from Bignoniaceae in 1994 and is distinguished principally by the lack of latex and stipules.

CAROLINA REDROOT
Lachnanthes caroliana (Lam.) Dandy
Bloodwort family (Haemodoraceae)

Description: The leaves of redroot are mostly basal, spreading in a fan like an iris. A flowering plant is typically 12"–24" tall, with an inflorescence covered in soft hairs. The flowers measure ⅜" wide.

Bloom Season: May to September

Habitat/Range: Wet, sunny habitats throughout mainland Florida

Comments: *Lachnanthes* means "wool flower" and alludes to the woolly inflorescence. The name *caroliana* refers to the Carolinas. Native Americans used redroot to achieve mental stimulation and to develop "a heroic attitude." A tonic made from the roots was said to cause "brilliancy and fearless expression of the eye." The common name relates to a red dye extracted from the roots and used by Native Americans to color hair and clothing, as noted in 1789 by naturalist William Bartram (1739–1823) during his travels.

FRINGED YELLOW STARGRASS

Hypoxis juncea Sm.
Yellow Stargrass family (Hypoxidaceae)

Description: The rushlike leaves of this species are rolled inward (involute). The leaves rarely exceed 8" long and ⅛" wide and have long hairs on the undersurface. The erect flower stalk is finely pubescent and topped by a single (rarely 2) star-like, ½" flower.

Bloom Season: All year

Habitat/Range: Flatwoods and low depressions through mainland Florida south to Palm Beach and Collier Counties

Comments: *Hypoxis* is a Greek name originally used for a plant with sour leaves. The name *juncea* refers to the resemblance of the leaves to a species of *Juncus* (rush). This species was first described in 1792 by English botanist James Edward Smith (1759–1828), who founded the Linnean Society of London in 1788 and became its first president. There are 4 other species of *Hypoxis* scattered about Florida, but stiff yellow stargrass (*Hypoxis rigida*) is found only in the central panhandle.

RICHWEED

Collinsonia canadensis L.
Mint family (Lamiaceae)

Description: The stems reach 3'–4' tall, with coarsely serrate, ovate leaves 3"–4" long and 2"–3" wide. Lemon-scented flowers are in a terminal raceme, each measuring about ⅝" long, with 2 exserted stamens.

Bloom Season: July to November

Habitat/Range: Calcareous ravine forests in Jackson, Calhoun, Leon, Jefferson, and Hamilton Counties

Comments: *Collinsonia* honors Peter Collinson (1693–1768), an avid gardener, a cloth merchant, and a Fellow of the Royal Society in London, England. The name *canadensis* relates to Canada, where Collinson discovered this species. The name richweed is for the rich soils it prefers. The black, fibrous roots have strong antioxidant properties and are still used medicinally to improve circulation and relieve throat congestion, including "preacher's throat," from talking long and loud. *Collinsonia serotina* has 4 stamens and occurs in northern Florida.

SPOTTED BEEBALM
Monarda punctata L.
Mint family (Lamiaceae)

Description: Spotted beebalm typically reaches 12"–30" tall, with toothed, aromatic 2"–3" leaves. Hairy, purple-dotted yellow (or white) flowers are in whorls subtended by pale to showy, pinkish-violet bracts.

Bloom Season: May to October

Habitat/Range: Dry habitats through much of Florida south to Collier and Palm Beach Counties

Comments: *Monarda* honors Spanish physician and botanist Nicolás Bautista Monardes (1493–1588), who wrote books on roses, citrus, and Greek medicine. He believed tobacco smoke was a cure for many diseases. The name *punctata* refers to the dots on the flowers. English naturalist John Banister (1654–1692) first collected this species in Virginia in 1680. It was used by the Seminole tribe in Florida as "death medicine," to be taken as a psychological remedy for grieving after a funeral. Bees and butterflies are attracted to the flowers.

YELLOW BUTTERWORT
Pinguicula lutea Walter
Bladderwort family (Lentibulariaceae)

Description: The viscid leaves measure ⅝"–2¼" long and overlap alternately to form a dense rosette. An erect flowering stem from 4"–12" tall is topped by 1–2 flowers that measure ¾"–1⅜" wide.

Bloom Season: March to June

Habitat/Range: Low pinelands and savannas throughout much of mainland Florida

Comments: *Pinguicula* alludes to the greasy texture of the leaf surface. The name *lutea* relates to the species' yellow flowers. This is a state-listed threatened species in Florida but may be locally abundant in the proper habitat, often growing in the company of other carnivorous plants. When small insects become stuck to the mucilage that coats the leaf surface, the leaf margins slowly curl over but never completely close. After the unfortunate bug is dissolved, the leaf margins unfurl. The plants were once used to curdle milk, giving rise to the common name butterwort.

HORNED BLADDERWORT
Utricularia cornuta Michx.
Bladderwort family (Lentibulariaceae)

Description: Horned bladderwort is a delicately branched aquatic species with creeping stems and thin, filamentous leaves. Tiny bladder-like traps are produced on the leaf margins. The erect, wiry, 4"–16" raceme bears 1–8 yellow flowers. Each flower measures about ⅝" and bears a prominent spur.

Bloom Season: All year

Habitat/Range: Freshwater wetlands and ponds throughout mainland Florida except in the northern peninsula

Comments: *Utricularia* is Latin for "little bag," alluding to the small, baglike traps on the leaves of all species in this genus. When a tiny aquatic organism triggers a trap, it is sucked inside, where digestive enzymes absorb nutrients from the prey. The name *cornuta* means "horned," referring to the curved spur of the flower. Although aquatic, it frequently flowers while stranded in mud. This and other species can form spreading colonies in shallow water.

ZIGZAG BLADDERWORT
Utricularia subulata L.
Bladderwort family (Lentibulariaceae)

Description: The delicate, threadlike stems of this minuscule carnivorous species creep along the bottom in shallow water or may be terrestrial in moist sand. Leaflike segments are either absent or narrowly linear to blossoms ⅜" long. The thin, erect raceme averages 1"–3" tall and is most often topped by a single blossom (or 2–8) that measures about ⅛"–³⁄₁₆" wide.

Bloom Season: April to December

Habitat/Range: Shallow water or moist soils throughout most of mainland Florida

Comments: The name *subulata* means "awl-shaped," referring to the spur. Although small in stature, flowering colonies of this species are quite attractive. When a plant produces numerous flowers, the stem zigzags to help support the weight. The highly specialized, diminutive traps capture nematodes and other tiny organisms that live in the soil. Some species have traps large enough to feed on mosquito larvae.

DIMPLED TROUTLILY

Erythronium umbilicatum C. Parks & Hardin
Lily family (Liliaceae)

Description: The paired, elliptic to ovate-lanceolate, irregularly mottled leaves of this species arise from an underground bulb and measure 2"–7" long and ¾"–1½" wide. The yellow petals and sepals may be tinged or splotched with reddish brown.

Bloom Season: February to April

Habitat/Range: Moist bottomland and slope forests of Liberty, Gadsden, and Leon Counties

Comments: *Erythronium* means "red" and refers to the flower color of the type species, *Erythronium dens-canis,* of central and southern Europe. The name *umbilicatum* alludes to having a navel and refers to the indented (umbilicate) apex of the capsules. The flowers are difficult to photograph because they face downward close to the ground. The flower photographed was growing on a steep slope near a stream in Gadsden County. The flowers do not open on overcast days, so choose a sunny day in February or March.

SMALL'S FLAX

Linum carteri Small var. *smallii* C.M. Rogers
Flax family (Linaceae)

Description: The narrow, glabrous, alternate leaves range from ½"–¾" long, with paired red glands at the base. The 6"–12" stems are sparingly branched, with forked flower spikes. The ¾" flowers have a diagnostic, mostly undivided style.

Bloom Season: Mostly February to April

Habitat/Range: Endemic to pinelands and prairies from Charlotte and Glades Counties south to mainland Monroe and Miami-Dade Counties

Comments: *Linum* is an ancient Latin name for flax and linen. The name *carteri* honors Pennsylvania botanist Joel Jackson Carter (1843–1912), who explored southern Florida with his botanist friend John Kunkel Small (1869–1938), whom the variety name *smallii* honors. This state-listed endangered species can be confused with pitted stripeseed (*Piriqueta caroliniana*) but it has wider leaves, hairy flower stalks, and lacks the pair of red glands at the leaf base.

FLORIDA YELLOW FLAX
Linum floridanum (Planch.) Trel.
Flax family (Linaceae)

Description: This glabrous species ranges from 8"–24" tall, with narrow, alternate, overlapping leaves facing upward on the stems. The leaves measure ½"–⅝" long and ⅛" wide. The ⅜" flowers are produced at or near the tips of the stems, with a distinctly 5-parted style.

Bloom Season: All year

Habitat/Range: Sandhills and flatwoods throughout most of mainland Florida

Comments: The name *floridanum* refers to Florida. Of the 9 native members of the genus in Florida, this is the most widespread species in the state. Botanist William Trelease (1857–1945) published the name *Linum floridanum* in 1887. Stiff yellow flax (*Linum medium* var. *texanum*) is similar but has glands on the margins of the inner sepals. Flax seed, linen, and linseed oil are derived from European and Mediterranean species. Larvae of the variegated fritillary butterfly feed on this and other members of the genus.

POOR MAN'S PATCH
Mentzelia floridana Nutt.
Stick Leaf family (Loasaceae)

Description: This ruderal species has ascending branches with hairy, ovate, alternate leaves that measure ¾"–2" long and half as wide. The 5-petaled flowers are solitary in the upper leaf axils and measure 1" wide.

Bloom Season: All year

Habitat/Range: Sandy coastal and inland dunes from Duval and Levy Counties south along both coasts and all counties below Lake Okeechobee, including the Florida Keys

Comments: *Mentzelia* honors German botanist Christian Mentzel (1622–1701). The name *floridana* means "of Florida." The leaves cling tightly to clothing and are difficult to remove. The barbed hairs can cut off the feet and legs of insects that alight on the leaves, which may be a ploy by the plant to utilize dead insects as fertilizer. The common name refers to downtrodden people who walk through fields of this plant, resulting in their clothes being covered with leaves, like patches.

COASTAL INDIAN MALLOW
Abutilon permolle (Willd.) Sweet
Mallow family (Malvaceae)

Description: This shrubby perennial has hairy stems and heart-shaped, velvety pubescent leaves that average 2"–4" long with a nearly equal width. The flowers are mostly solitary and measure about 1" wide. The ribbed fruits are cup shaped, flat on top, with seeds in tight chambers.

Bloom Season: All year

Habitat/Range: Coastal and inland disturbed sites from Broward and Collier Counties south through the Florida Keys; also Manatee County

Comments: *Abutilon* is taken from *aubutilun,* a name used by Arab philosopher and physician Avicenna (980–1037) for a mallow-like plant. The name *permolle* means "very softly pubescent" and is descriptive of the species' leaves. It was first described as *Sida permollis* in 1809 by German botanist Carl Ludwig von Willdenow (1765–1812). This genus comprises more than 100 species; some are important fiber plants in Asia.

COMMON FANPETALS
Sida ulmifolia Mill.
Mallow family (Malvaceae)

Description: The stems reach 12"–36" tall, with alternate, coarsely toothed leaves that average ¾"–1" long and ½"–¾" wide. The yellow to yellowish-orange, ½" flowers are on axillary stalks, with long hairs on the calyx.

Bloom Season: All year

Habitat/Range: Pinelands, salt marshes, and disturbed sites in the western and eastern panhandle south throughout the peninsula to the Florida Keys

Comments: *Sida* is a name used by Greek philosopher Theophrastus (372–287 BC) for a water lily but later used for this group of mallows. The name *ulmifolia* relates to the elm-like leaves. Gardeners should try to tolerate this weedy species, because it is a larval host for the common checkered-skipper and the tropical checkered-skipper butterflies. The stems of some species are used to make brooms; the leaves are high in protein but may cause elevated heart rate and blood pressure if eaten. It is also called wireweed.

YELLOW MEADOWBEAUTY
Rhexia lutea Walter
Melastome family (Melastomataceae)

Description: This species reaches 8"–14" tall, with bristly stems and narrow, linear, hairy leaves from ½"–¾" long and ⅛" wide. Flowers are ¾"–⅞" wide and produced at the branch tips.

Bloom Season: May to August

Habitat/Range: Savannas, flatwoods, and wet roadsides from Escambia County east to Leon and Wakulla Counties and from Baker and Nassau Counties south to Alachua, Putnam, and Volusia Counties

Comments: *Rhexia* is a name used by Roman scholar Pliny (AD 23—79) for a plant useful in treating ruptures. The name *lutea* means "yellow" and relates to the flowers. Yellow meadow-beauty often grows in association with species of *Ludwigia* (Onagraceae), which also have 4-petaled yellow flowers, so look for the telltale anthers, hairy leaves, and urn-shaped fruits of this species. It was described in 1788 by British-American botanist Thomas Walter (1740–1789).

GOLDEN COLICROOT
Aletris aurea Walter
Bog Asphodel family (Nartheciaceae)

Description: The elliptic to lanceolate basal leaves measure ¾"–3" long and ⅜"–¾" wide. The erect scape averages 10"–20" tall, with the upper half lined with rounded, mealy, golden-yellow flowers that measure about ¼" long.

Bloom Season: April to August

Habitat/Range: Savannas, flatwoods, and bogs from Escambia County west to Gadsden, Liberty, and Franklin Counties; also Columbia and Nassau Counties

Comments: Aletris was a legendary Greek slave woman who ground grain, so the genus *Aletris* relates to the mealy texture of the flowers. The name *aurea* means "golden-yellow" and alludes to the flower color. The Florida range of this and the following species overlap in northern peninsular Florida and the panhandle, but this species differs mainly by its smaller, rounded flowers. The roots of this group of plants were used as herbal remedies for various stomach ailments.

YELLOW COLICROOT
Aletris lutea Small
Bog Asphodel family (Nartheciaceae)

Description: The rosette of basal leaves is broadly linear, ranging from 1½"–6" long and ⅜"–⅞" wide. The scape stands 12" tall or more, with yellow flowers spaced along the top half. The flowers measure about ⅜" long and ⅛" wide and are covered with mealy bumps.

Bloom Season: February to September

Habitat/Range: Flatwoods, prairies, and open depressions throughout most of mainland Florida

Comments: The name *lutea* refers to the species' yellow flowers. The common name relates to its use as a bitter root-tea to treat colic, dysentery, rheumatism, and other ailments. An enterprising woman named Lydia Pinkham (1819–1883) created and marketed a popular alcoholic "women's tonic" made from the roots of white colicroot (*Aletris farinosa*) and other herbs to alleviate menstrual pain. This species ranges south into the Big Cypress National Preserve but is absent from Everglades National Park.

GOLDEN CREST
Lophiola aurea Ker Gawl.
Bog Asphodel family (Nartheciaceae)

Description: The flowering stems of this perennial species reach about 36" tall, with white, woolly hairs covering the inflorescence. The basal leaves are linear, 3"–16" long and up to ½" wide. The yellow flowers measure about ⅜" wide, with triangular, reflexed sepals and petals (tepals).

Bloom Season: April to July

Habitat/Range: Wet flatwoods, savannas, marshes, and roadside ditches from Escambia County east to Holmes, Jackson, Washington, Calhoun, Liberty, and Wakulla Counties in the Florida panhandle

Comments: *Lophiola* is from the Greek *lophia* ("a crest") and alludes to the pubescence on the upper surface of the sepals and petals. The name *aurea* refers to the golden yellow flowers. English botanist John Bellenden Ker Gawler (1764–1842) described this species in 1813. This genus has also been included in the Lily family (Liliaceae) and the Bloodroot family (Haemodoraceae).

AMERICAN LOTUS
Nelumbo lutea Willd.
Lotus family (Nelumbonaceae)

Description: The orbicular leaf blades are 8"–12" across and held above the water on stout petioles that connect in the center of the leaf blade. The showy, fragrant, 6" flowers are clear yellow and are held well above the leaves. The flat-topped seed heads are cone shaped and contain hard, spherical, ½" seeds.

Bloom Season: May to August

Habitat/Range: Lakes and canals of eastern North America south in Florida from Jackson and Gulf Counties to Glades and Broward Counties

Comments: *Nelumbo* is the Sinhalese name for the sacred lotus (*Nelumbo nucifera*) and translates to "holy lotus." The name *lutea* means "yellow" and relates to the flowers. The pink-flowered sacred lotus is naturalized in Florida and is one of Buddhism's most significant symbols of enlightenment and sexual purity, often depicted with godly deities sitting on the blossoms. It is considered a gentlemanly flower in Vietnam.

SPATTERDOCK
Nuphar advena (Aiton) Aiton f.
(Also *Nuphar lutea* [L.] Small)
Waterlily family (Nymphaeaceae)

Description: Spatterdock leaf blades typically stand above the water and measure 8"–12" long and 6"–8" wide, with a deep notch at the base. The flowers have 6–9 yellow sepals that form a cup. The true petals are small and scalelike, crowded among the stamens.

Bloom Season: All year

Habitat/Range: Freshwater habitats throughout most of mainland Florida

Comments: *Nuphar* comes from a name used by Pedanius Dioscorides (AD 40–90) for a medicinal plant. The name *advena* means "adventive" and relates to spreading from one place to another by any means (an immigrant). Spatterdock is an aggressive colonizer, often covering the entire water surface of ponds and canals. It is usually found in much deeper water than water lilies (*Nymphaea* ssp.). The seeds are an important food for waterfowl, and the leaves provide cover for fish and other aquatic life.

YELLOW WATERLILY
Nymphaea mexicana Zucc.
Waterlily family (Nymphaeaceae)

Description: The leaf blades of this species are deeply notched, green above, red below, and may reach up to 10" wide. The showy, 3"–4" flowers may be floating or held above the water surface and are open from midmorning to late afternoon.

Bloom Season: May to October

Habitat/Range: Ponds and streams in Wakulla, Alachua, and Duval Counties discontinuously south to Collier and Miami-Dade Counties

Comments: *Nymphaea* is Greek for "water nymph." The name *mexicana* refers to Mexico, where this species was first collected and named in 1832 by Joseph Gerhard Zuccarini (1797–1848), a German professor of botany at the University of Munich. The banana-like root tubers are an important food for canvasback ducks in their winter range. It hybridizes with the scented water lily (*Nymphaea odorata*) and forms a vigorous, sterile plant named *Nymphaea* x *thiona,* known from Brevard, Orange, and Wakulla Counties.

PONDSHORE PRIMROSEWILLOW
Ludwigia arcuata Walter
Evening Primrose family (Onagraceae)

Description: The prostrate, creeping stems root at the nodes and have short, hooked hairs. The opposite, sessile, oblanceolate leaves measure ⅜"–¾" long and ¼"–⅜" wide. Flowers are axillary on long, thin stalks and measure about ⅝" wide.

Bloom Season: April to November

Habitat/Range: Marshes and edges of lakes, rivers, and spring runs from Franklin, Wakulla, and Gadsden Counties south throughout much of the Florida peninsula to Collier County; also Walton and Duval Counties

Comments: *Ludwigia* honors German botanist and professor of medicine Christian Gottlieb Ludwig (1709–1773). The name *arcuata* means "arched" and alludes to the hooked stem hairs. British-American botanist Thomas Walter (1740–1789) first described this species in 1788 from plants collected in South Carolina. The mat-forming *Ludwigia repens* has wider leaves and tiny flowers.

SEASIDE PRIMROSEWILLOW

Ludwigia maritima R.M. Harper
Evening Primrose family (Onagraceae)

Description: Stems of this species are simple or with a few branches near the top. Stems range from 2'–3' tall and are usually reddish to golden with coarse hairs. Leaves are alternate, linear to lanceolate, and average 1"–3" long and ⅛" wide (sometimes red). The 1" flowers are axillary.

Bloom Season: May to November

Habitat/Range: Moist coastal and inland habitats throughout mainland Florida

Comments: The name *maritima* means "by the sea" and relates to this species' maritime habitat. Botanist Roland McMillan Harper (1878–1966) named this species in 1904 from plants collected in Georgia in August 1902. The similar southeastern primrosewillow (*Ludwigia linifolia*) has narrow leaves with 1" flowers. Mexican primrosewillow (*Ludwigia octovalvis*) is a common shrub seen along canal banks and roadside ditches with bright yellow, typically 4-petaled flowers to about 1½" wide.

HAIRY PRIMROSEWILLOW

Ludwigia pilosa Walter
Evening Primrose family (Onagraceae)

Description: This bushy species is copiously hairy throughout, with alternate, elliptic-lanceolate leaves to 3" long and ½" wide. The ½" flowers lack petals and are congested in the upper leaf axils. The nectary disk is bright yellow.

Bloom Season: June to November

Habitat/Range: Swamps and wet roadside ditches throughout the Florida panhandle and discontinuously south in the peninsula to Sarasota, Hardee, and Palm Beach Counties

Comments: The name *pilosa* refers to the long, soft, shaggy (pilose) hairs covering all parts of the plant. It ranges from North Carolina to Virginia south to Louisiana and Florida. Another species, *Ludwigia repens,* is a very common plant of wet areas, including damp roadside ditches, and can form dense mats, sometimes growing underwater. It has reddish stems and tiny, greenish-yellow flowers. There are 26 native members of the genus in Florida.

SUNDROPS

Oenothera fruticosa L.
Evening Primrose family (Onagraceae)

Description: This somewhat bushy herbaceous perennial may reach 30" tall, with narrowly lanceolate, entire or slightly toothed leaves. The 1¼"–1⅜" flowers may be cup shaped, with 4 or 5 petals that are notched at the tips. The club-shaped fruits are 4-angled.

Bloom Season: March to June

Habitat/Range: Flatwoods and hillsides from Nassau, Flagler, and Clay Counties disjunctly west across the panhandle to Escambia County

Comments: One translation of *Oenothera* is that it was taken from *oinos* (wine) and *thera* (imbibing), relating to its use in making wine "to make the heart merry." Other translations also involve wine. The name *fruticosa* describes this species' shrubby growth habit. It is widespread across eastern North America. The common name relates to the buds, which open as soon as the sun shines on them. It has been used medicinally to treat hemorrhoids and boils.

BARTRAM'S EVENING PRIMROSE

Oenothera grandiflora L'Hér. ex Aiton
Evening Primrose family (Onagraceae)

Description: Plants average 4'–6' tall with elliptic to lanceolate leaves from 1"–6" long and ¾"–1" wide. The highly perfumed flowers measure 2"–2¼" wide, opening at night and closing by midmorning

Bloom Season: June to November

Habitat/Range: Mesic woodlands, riverbanks, and roadsides from Escambia County to Walton County and in Leon, Wakulla, and Franklin Counties (escaped from cultivation in Alachua, Putnam, Lake, and Polk Counties)

Comments: The name *grandiflora* alludes to the species' large flowers. Although it was described in 1789 by French botanist and magistrate Charles Louis L'Héritier de Brutelle (1746–1800), American naturalist William Bartram (1739–1823) first collected it in Alabama in 1775 and planted it in his father's Pennsylvanian garden. There are 8 native species in Florida along with 3 naturalized exotics.

CUTLEAF EVENING PRIMROSE
Oenothera laciniata Hill
Evening Primrose family (Onagraceae)

Description: This trailing species has lobed leaves to 2" long and ⅜"–¾" wide. The flowers are ¾"–1" wide, with 4 petals and 4 petal-like sepals. The seed capsule is narrowly cylindrical, measuring ¾"–1½" long.

Bloom Season: All year

Habitat/Range: Sandy woods, fields, and roadsides throughout most of Florida

Comments: The name *laciniata* means "formed into narrow divisions," alluding to the leaf shape on some plants. The flowers open at dusk and close by late morning. Evening primroses are a natural source of gamma-lineolic acid, which promotes women's health, especially for premenstrual syndrome. The leaves are larval food of the gallium sphinx. The plant is especially noticeable along roadsides early in the morning, before the flowers close and wilt away by midmorning.

FLORIDA DANCING LADY ORCHID
Oncidium ensatum Lindl.
Orchid family (Orchidaceae)

Description: This orchid is usually terrestrial, with long, strap-shaped leaves from ½"–1" wide and up to 4' long, often spreading fanlike. The branched flower spike may exceed 7' tall, with many ¾"–1" flowers spaced up to 6" apart.

Bloom Season: April to August

Habitat/Range: Hardwood forests of Collier, Miami-Dade, and Monroe (mainland) Counties

Comments: *Oncidium* is Greek for "little swelling" and alludes to the warty calluses on the surface of the lip. The name *ensatum* means "swordlike," referring to the leaves. This state-listed endangered species was first discovered in Florida in 1903 and is now mostly restricted to Everglades National Park. Members of the genus offer no pollinator reward but mimic nectar-producing flowers in the Malpighia family (Malpighiaceae) to deceive potential insect pollinators. Its threats are illegal collecting and dry-season fires.

GYPSY-SPIKES

Platanthera flava (L.) Lindl.
Orchid family (Orchidaceae)

Description: This terrestrial orchid has 2–3 spreading or ascending, lanceolate or elliptic-oblong leaves that average 3"–8" long and ½"–1½" wide. Pale yellow to greenish-yellow flowers are about ¼" wide and subtended by a leafy bract.

Bloom Season: April to November

Habitat/Range: Mesic hardwood forests, wet meadows, and wooded swamps, with isolated populations in the central and eastern panhandle south in the peninsula from Dixie and Nassau Counties to Hillsborough and Polk Counties

Comments: *Platanthera* means "broad anther." The name *flava* means "pure yellow" and alludes to the flower color. This state-listed threatened species was first described in 1813 as *Habenaria herbiola*. It is quite unlike other members of the genus in Florida and is exceptionally difficult to find in dappled light because of its small stature and pale flowers. Another name is southern tubercled orchid.

DOLLAR ORCHID

Prosthechea boothiana (Lindl.) W.E. Higgins var. *erythronioides* (Small) W.E. Higgins
(Also *Encyclia boothiana* [Lindl.] Dressler)
Orchid family (Orchidaceae)

Description: From 1–3 linear-lanceolate leaves arise from flattened pseudobulbs and measure 2"–4" long and ½"–1" wide. The flowers are about ¾" across.

Bloom Season: August to October

Habitat/Range: Coastal hammocks and mangrove forests of Martin, Collier, Monroe (mainland and Keys), and Miami-Dade Counties

Comments: *Prosthechea* means "appendix" and refers to the appendage on the back of the column. The name *boothiana* honors English botanist William Beattie Booth (1804–1874) and *erythronioides* alludes to the resemblance of the flowers to a species of *Erythronium* (Liliaceae). The common name of this state-listed endangered species refers to the pseudobulbs being the size of a silver dollar. It was once abundant in coastal forests of the southern mainland and the Florida Keys.

DOWNY YELLOW FALSE FOXGLOVE
Aureolaria virginica (L.) Pennell
Broomrape family (Orobanchaceae)

Description: The downy, or pubescent, leaves are ovate to lanceolate and measure 2"–5" long and ¾"–1¼" wide. The 5-lobed flowers range from 1¼"–2" wide.

Bloom Season: April to August

Habitat/Range: Mesic woodlands of the central panhandle; also Clay County

Comments: *Aureolaria* is taken from Greek words meaning "golden" and "oak" and is believed to refer to the species' yellow flowers and because it can be hemiparasitic on the roots of oaks. A hemi-parasite parasitizes a host as well as photosynthe-sizes. Another common name is downy oak leach. The name *virginica* relates to Virginia, where it was first collected in 1919. Two other species in Florida (*Aureolaria flava* and *A. pectinata*) have overlapping ranges. The leaves produce a gummy liquid sticky enough to sometimes entrap insects. It has been used medicinally to treat dysentery and venomous snakebites and as a sedative.

CANADIAN LOUSEWORT
Pedicularis canadensis L.
Broomrape family (Orobanchaceae)

Description: A basal rosette is formed by lanceo-late, fernlike leaves with pinnate lobes and wavy margins, measuring up to 6" long and 1"–2" wide. A green to reddish-brown, leafy stalk reaches about 12" tall and is topped by a congested cluster of 2-lipped, yellow, ¾"–1" flowers, sometimes with a reddish upper lip.

Bloom Season: February to May

Habitat/Range: Calcareous woodlands in Walton, Washington, Jackson, Gadsden, Leon, and Clay Counties

Comments: *Pedicularis* is taken from *pediculus*, Latin for "louse." It was believed that the presence of this plant in pastures would produce lice on sheep. The name *canadensis* refers to Canada, where the species was first collected and later described in 1767 by Carolus Linnaeus (1707–1778). It is also called wood betony. Grasses growing near this plant are often stunted because of its parasitic habit.

PIEDMONT BLACKSENNA
Seymeria pectinata Pursh
Broomrape family (Orobanchaceae)

Description: Piedmont blacksenna reaches 8"–24" tall, with hairy stems, leaves, and flowers. The leaves are deeply divided and average ¾"–1¼" long. The flowers reach about ½" wide, and there are a series of red dots on the upper lobes.

Bloom Season: March to October

Habitat/Range: Scrub and sandhills throughout most of mainland Florida

Comments: *Seymeria* honors English naturalist Henry Seymer (1745–1800). The name *pectinata* is Latin for "comb," referring to the shape of the leaves. The species was described in 1814 by botanist Frederick Traugott Pursh (1774–1820). One other member of the genus in Florida is yaupon blacksenna (*Seymeria cassioides*), a species recently discovered to be a devastating root parasite on pines (*Pinus* spp.) of the southeastern United States that weakens or kills the trees. This genus was formerly in the Figwort family (Scrophulariaceae).

CREEPING WOODSORREL
Oxalis corniculata L.
Woodsorrel family (Oxalidaceae)

Description: Creeping woodsorrel has leaves that are divided into 3 rounded leaflets that somewhat resemble a shamrock. The creeping stems root at the nodes, forming extensive colonies. Flowers are about ½" wide and produce cylindrical capsules that forcefully discharge seeds long distances.

Bloom Season: All year

Habitat/Range: Disturbed sites and riverbanks throughout Florida.

Comments: *Oxalis* refers to the sour-tasting leaves that contain calcium oxalate. The name *corniculata* means "with small horns" and alludes to the projections on the seeds. This is a common weed of lawns and gardens but can be abundant along riverbanks and other moist habitats in Florida. The leaves are edible but can inhibit calcium intake if eaten in quantity. It has a cosmopolitan distribution and is considered an invasive weed in some regions. As a weed, it is very difficult to control.

MEXICAN PRICKLY POPPY
Argemone mexicana L.
Poppy family (Papaveraceae)

Description: Prickly poppy is a wickedly spiny biennial that averages 1'–3' tall. The deeply lobed, alternate leaves range from 3"–8" long, with sharp tips terminating each lobe and with sharp spines along the bottom of the midvein. The flowers have 6 bright yellow petals that form a tulip-like cup and average 1¼"–1½" wide. The sap is yellow.

Bloom Season: January to June

Habitat/Range: Disturbed soils of Escambia, Jackson, Franklin, and Leon Counties and throughout most of peninsular Florida into the Florida Keys

Comments: *Argemone* comes from a Greek name originally used for a poppy-like plant used to treat cataract of the eye. The name *mexicana* means "of Mexico." The latex is poisonous to grazing animals but is used to treat warts, malaria, and migraine headaches. Poisoning from consuming the latex causes extreme swelling of the legs. This species is related to the opium poppy (*Papaver somniferum*).

YELLOW PASSIONFLOWER
Passiflora lutea L.
Passionflower family (Passifloraceae)

Description: The light green leaves of this rhizomatous vine have 3 rounded lobes and measure 1"–2" long and 2"–3" wide. Axillary flowers measure about ¾" wide, with green sepals and greenish-yellow petals. The round fruits are purplish black.

Bloom Season: March to October

Habitat/Range: Mesic hammocks across the Florida panhandle discontinuously east to Duval and Clay Counties and south to Hernando and Lake Counties

Comments: *Passiflora* is Latin for "passion flower" and relates to the floral parts believed to symbolize the crucifixion of Christ. The name *lutea* means "yellow" and relates to the greenish-yellow petals. It is widespread across the eastern and midwestern United States and is the only native species with non-photosynthetic cotyledons that form underground (hypogeal). It is a larval host of the zebra longwing and gulf fritillary butterflies.

PITTED STRIPESEED

Piriqueta caroliniana (Walter) Urb.
(Also *Piriqueta cistoides* [L.] Griseb. ssp.
caroliniana [Walter] Arbo.)
Passionflower family (Passifloraceae)

Description: Stems from 4"–8" tall bear toothed, linear to elliptic-ovate leaves that may be smooth or pubescent and range from ¾"–2" long and ¼"–⅝" wide. Flowers average ¾" wide, with 5 stamens and 3 bushy-tipped stigmas.

Bloom Season: All year

Habitat/Range: Prairies and pinelands throughout Florida

Comments: *Piriqueta* is from a French Guiana name for a member of the genus. The name *caroliniana* means "of Carolina." Gulf fritillary butterflies sometimes use this species as a larval host plant. It can be confused with members of the genus *Linum*, which do not have bushy-tipped stigmas. A recent revision places the Turneraceae in the Passifloraceae, and current studies may separate this species into several other species, with 2 possibly being endemic to Florida.

BABY JUMP-UP

Mecardonia procumbens (Mill.) Small
Plantain family (Plantaginaceae)

Description: This prostrate species has opposite, toothed, ovate leaves averaging ½"–1" long and ⅜"–½" wide. Paired flowers are on long, axillary pedicels and nearly hidden by bracts. The flowers are ¼" wide.

Bloom Season: All year

Habitat/Range: Wet depressions and moist disturbed sites from Escambia, Jackson, and Leon Counties in the Florida panhandle and sporadic from Putnam and St. Johns Counties south into the Florida Keys

Comments: *Mecardonia* honors Antonio de Meca y Cardona, an eighteenth-century Spanish patron of the Barcelona Botanical Garden and marquis of Ciutadilla, a village in Spain. The name *procumbens* is for the species' procumbent, or reclining, growth habit. It was first described in 1768 as *Erinus procumbens* by botanist Philip Miller (1691–1771). Baby jump-up is a shortening of "baby jump up and kiss me." It is found on all continents except Antarctica.

TALL PINEBARREN MILKWORT
Polygala cymosa Walter
Milkwort family (Polygalaceae)

Description: The basal leaves are linear to linear-lanceolate and are present when flowering. Very few short, widely spaced, narrowly linear leaves appear on a flowering stem that reaches 24"–46" tall. Flowers are in terminal cymes, with each flower measuring about ³⁄₁₆" long.

Bloom Season: March to December

Habitat/Range: Wet pinelands, savannas, and cypress swamps throughout mainland Florida south to Charlotte, Highlands, Okeechobee, and Palm Beach Counties

Comments: *Polygala* means "much milk," in the fanciful belief that milkworts could increase lactation. The name *cymosa* relates to the flowers being produced in cymes (a broad, flat inflorescence with flowers that open from the center outward). Except for its height and different leaf shapes, this species is nearly identical to the shorter low pinebarren milkwort (*Polygala ramosa*).

CANDYROOT
Polygala nana (Michx.) DC.
Milkwort family (Polygalaceae)

Description: This biennial is only ¾"–2" tall, with spatulate, ¾"–2⅜" leaves that form a small rosette. The compact raceme measures about ³⁄₈"–¾" long and ³⁄₈"–½" wide. The tiny flowers are lemon yellow, with elliptic wings that are rolled inward (involute) at the tip.

Bloom Season: All year

Habitat/Range: Flatwoods, seepage bogs, and coastal swales throughout mainland Florida south to Broward and Collier Counties

Comments: The name *nana* alludes to the species' small stature. The name candyroot refers to the licorice-like flavor of the roots. Candyroot is very similar to the imperiled, endemic Small's milkwort (*Polygala smallii*) of southeastern Florida, which has oblong-lanceolate wings that are not rolled inward at the tip. In the counties where these 2 species both occur (Palm Beach, Martin, St. Lucie), Small's milkwort is mostly east of US 1, in sandy coastal habitats.

YELLOW MILKWORT

Polygala rugelii Shuttlew. ex Chapm.
Milkwort family (Polygalaceae)

Description: The basal leaves of this annual or biennial (sometimes perennial) species are in an irregular rosette but often not present when flowering. The leaves are spatulate (spatula-shaped), narrow at the base, and range from 1¼"–2¼" long and ¼"–½" wide. The rounded flower clusters are ⅜"–1¼" long and 1" wide, held on stems that may exceed 24" in height.

Bloom Season: March to November

Habitat/Range: Endemic to wet flatwoods of peninsular Florida

Comments: The name *rugelii* honors German-born botanist Ferdinand Ignatius Xavier Rugel (1806–1879), who collected in Florida, Cuba, and southern Appalachia. Yellow milkwort often grows in the company of other members of the genus and can be exceptionally abundant in the proper habitat, especially after fire. when it can turn flatwoods into fields of yellow.

REDSTEM PURSLANE

Portulaca rubricaulis Kunth
Purslane family (Portulacaceae)

Description: The fleshy red stems are ascending to erect and are lined with linear, hemispheric leaves that average ⅜"–½" long and no more than ⅛" wide. The flowers measure about ½"–⅝" wide.

Bloom Season: All year

Habitat/Range: Coastal berms, dunes, salt marshes, and shell mounds of Pinellas County and from Charlotte County south along the Gulf Coast into Miami-Dade County and the Florida Keys (Monroe County)

Comments: *Portulaca* means "little door" and refers to the lid of the capsule. The name *rubri-caulis* translates to "red stem." The species was first described in 1823 by botanist Karl Sigismund Kunth (1788–1850) from plants collected in Venezuela, the type locality. Populations in the West Indies may have flowers in tones of orange, salmon, or red. Some botanists have treated these as *Portulaca phaeosperma*; others say they are simply color forms of this species.

MARSH BUTTERCUP
Ranunculus hispidus Michx. var. *nitidus*
(Chapm.) T. Duncan
Buttercup family (Ranunculaceae)

Description: Decumbent stems bear basal, ovate to rhombic leaves with either 3 leaflets or merely 3-parted, each with 2–3 lobes. The blades average 1½"–2" long and 1"– 1½"wide, with smaller stem leaves. The flowers are ¾"–1" wide, with 5 petals.

Bloom Season: February to May

Habitat/Range: Wet woodlands from Jackson and Calhoun Counties east in the Florida panhandle to Leon and Wakulla Counties; also Nassau, Duval, Levy, Citrus, and Lake Counties in the peninsula

Comments: *Ranunculus* relates to the frog genus *Rana*, for the numerous frogs that reside in wetlands where buttercups often grow. The name *hispidus* refers to the bristly (hispid) stems, leaves, and sepals. The name *nitidus* means "shining," alluding to the lustrous flower petals. This is a genus of about 600 species; some are popular garden subjects, with numerous cultivars.

HARVEST-LICE
Agrimonia incisa Torr. & A. Gray
Rose family (Rosaceae)

Description: The hairy stems reach 36" tall, with pubescent, elliptic or oblanceolate compound leaves. The leaflets are deeply incised and measure ½"–1" long and ⅜"–½" wide, with glands on the lower surface. The flowers are ½" wide.

Bloom Season: August to October

Habitat/Range: Sandhills from Escambia County discontinuously east to Duval County and south to Hillsborough and Polk Counties

Comments: *Agrimonia* was taken from *argemonia*, a name used by Pliny (AD 23–79) for "cataract," and relates to the medicinal use of members of this genus to treat cataracts. The name *incisa* is descriptive of the incised leaflets of this state-listed threatened species. It was first described in 1840 by botanists John Torrey (1796–1873) and Asa Gray (1810–1888) from plants collected in Alabama. The common name relates to the hooked fruits that cling to clothing.

HOODED PITCHERPLANT
Sarracenia minor Walter
Pitcherplant family (Sarraceniaceae)

Description: The pitchers (traps) of this species have translucent spots that allow light to enter. The hooded pitchers are light green, often tinged with red at the top, and average 6"–10" tall. The flowers reach 2"–3" across.

Bloom Season: March to June

Habitat/Range: Bogs and wet flatwoods from Gadsden, Liberty, and Gulf Counties continuously east and south in the peninsula to Lake Okeechobee

Comments: *Sarracenia* honors French surgeon and botanist Michel Sarrazin (1659–1734), who immigrated to Canada in 1684 and was the first to state that this group of plants caught insects, an idea that was ridiculed until naturalist Charles Darwin (1809–1882) wrote about it in 1875. The name *minor* relates to the small stature of this species. Ants and other insects are attracted into the trap by light entering through translucent spots on the sides of the tube and then meet their demise.

GROUNDCHERRY
Physalis walteri Nutt.
Nightshade family (Solanaceae)

Description: Gray hairs cover the stems and leaves of this 6"–20" tall species. The ovate to lanceolate leaves are 1½"–4" long, with entire margins. The pendent, trumpet-shaped flowers range from ½"–¾" long and wide. The round, yellow fruits are encased in a lantern-like, papery calyx.

Bloom Season: All year

Habitat/Range: Coastal strand and pinelands through most of Florida but absent from some northern counties

Comments: *Physalis* is Greek for "bladder," alluding to the species' inflated calyx. The name *walteri* honors British-American botanist Thomas Walter (1740–1789). Some species are cultivated for their fruits and sold in markets under the name "husk tomato"; they were an important food long before the debut of the related tomato. Another species (*Physalis philadelphica*) is the tomatillo, popular in Mexican cuisine. This and other species in this genus are larval hosts of the Carolina sphinx moth.

HARPER'S BEAUTY

Harperocallis flava McDaniel
False Asphodel family (Tofieldiaceae)

Description: The narrowly linear, ribbed leaves are basal and reach up to 8½" long. Flower stems reach 24" tall, with terminal, solitary flowers bearing 3 petals and 3 sepals (tepals) measuring about 1½" across.

Bloom Season: April to May

Habitat/Range: Endemic to wet prairies, bogs, and moist roadsides of Bay, Franklin, and Liberty Counties

Comments: *Harperocallis* combines "Harper" and "beautiful" to honor botanist Roland MacMillan Harper (1878–1966) and to recognize this species' floral beauty. The name *flava* alludes to the yellow flowers. This federal endangered species is of critical conservation concern because of its small populations and very restricted range. It was first discovered near the town of Sumatra within Apalachicola National Forest in 1965 and described in 1968 by Mississippi State University botany professor Sidney T. McDaniel (1940–).

ROCKLAND LANTANA

Lantana depressa Small
Verbena family (Verbenaceae)

Description: This is a low-spreading shrub to 12" tall, with elliptic, glossy, roughly hairy, toothed leaves from ⅜"–1" long and ¼"–⅜" wide. The stems lack prickles. The tubular flowers open yellow and become tawny orange.

Bloom Season: All year

Habitat/Range: Endemic to pine rocklands of southern Miami-Dade County

Comments: Roman poet Publius Vergillius Maro, or Virgil (70–19 BC), called a plant with flexible stems *lenta viburna,* now known as *Viburnum lantana.* Linnaeus reapplied the species name to this group of plants. The name *depressa* refers to the prostrate growth habit. Various yellow-flowered low-growing hybrids and cultivars of exotic *lantanas* are erroneously sold in the Florida nursery trade as this endangered endemic species. It is threatened by gene pool contamination through hybridization with the invasive *Lantana strigocamara.*

ELLIOTT'S YELLOWEYED GRASS

Xyris elliottii Chapm.

Yelloweyed Grass family (Xyridaceae)

Description: This species grows in dense, low tufts and has narrow, flattened, fanlike leaves that resemble a miniature iris. The leaves range from 4"–10" tall and about ¼" wide. The scape is 1–2 ribbed and is topped by an ovoid to elliptic cone-like spike that bears 1–3 flowers, each with 3 petals that unfold in the morning.

Bloom Season: All year

Habitat/Range: Wet flatwoods, savannas, and bogs throughout mainland Florida

Comments: *Xyris* is taken from a Greek word meaning "razor" and refers to a species with leaves that resemble swords. The name *elliottii* honors American legislator, banker, and botanist Stephen Elliott (1771–1830) of South Carolina. There are 24 *Xyris* species native to Florida (4 are endemic); most of them have yellow flowers, making identifying them a challenge. Use a botanical key to compare leaf variation and flower size.

GREATER CALTROP

Kallstroemia maxima (L.) Hook. & Arn.

Caltrop family (Zygophyllaceae)

Description: The hairy stems are mostly prostrate with evenly pinnate, compound leaves bearing oblong-elliptic, hairy leaflets averaging ½"–¾" long. The flowers are about ½" wide. The fruits are covered with long hairs.

Bloom Season: All year

Habitat/Range: Coastal habitats and disturbed sites in Escambia County and scattered through much of peninsular Florida into the Florida Keys

Comments: *Kallstroemia* honors Anders Kallstroem (1733–1812), a contemporary of Tyrolean naturalist and physician Giovanni Antonio Scopoli (1723–1788). The name *maxima* means "largest" and alludes to this species' wide geographical range. The common name relates to the resemblance of the fruits of members of this family to a caltrop—an antipersonnel weapon with sharp metal spikes used as early as 331 BC to slow the advance of horses, war elephants, and foot soldiers.

BROWN AND GREEN FLOWERS

Epidendrum anceps

This section includes flowers that range from pale green to purplish brown. You may need to check the White or Yellow sections for very pale green or pale yellowish flowers if you cannot find what you are looking for here.

EASTERN POISON IVY
Toxicodendron radicans (L.) Kuntze
Cashew family (Anacardiaceae)

Description: This vine bears compound leaves with 3 entire or variously lobed leaflets reaching 1"–4" long and ½"–3" wide. Flowers are in axillary clusters and measure ¼" wide. Round ⅛" fruits ripen white.

Bloom Season: January to July

Habitat/Range: Hardwood forests, swamps, and pinelands throughout Florida

Comments: *Toxicodendron* means "poison tree." The name *radicans* refers to the roots, which attach to trees and buildings along the stem. The sap causes a blistering rash on sensitive people 24 hours or more after contact that may require hospitalization. Smoke from burning poison ivy can cause severe and even fatal respiratory difficulty. This species is related to mango, cashew, and pistachio. Eastern poison oak (*Toxicodendron pubescens*) occurs in northern Florida; poison sumac (*Toxicodendron vernix*) occurs in northern and central Florida. Birds eat the fruits without harm.

BALDWIN'S MILKWEED
Asclepias connivens Baldwin
Dogbane family (Apocynaceae)

Description: This unusual milkweed reaches 12"–24" tall, with linear-lanceolate, opposite, sessile leaves produced along arching stems. The leaves average 1"–3" long and ⅜"–½" wide. The green to greenish-yellow flowers are about 1" wide and clustered at the tips of the stems. The incurved hoods converge over the stigma.

Bloom Season: June to August

Habitat/Range: Wet flatwoods and bogs through most of the Florida panhandle and discontinuously south in the peninsula to Charlotte, Highlands, and Okeechobee Counties (historically in Miami-Dade County)

Comments: *Asclepias* was named for Aesculapius, Greek god of medicine. The name *connivens* refers to the conniving (converging) hoods over the stigma. The species was named in 1817 by American botanist William Baldwin (1779–1819). The flower size and shape make it easily distinguishable.

CURTISS' MILKWEED
Asclepias curtissii A. Gray
Dogbane family (Apocynaceae)

Description: The leaves of this milkweed are obovate or oblong and average 1"–2" long and ⅜"–½" wide. Flowers are in umbels at the upper nodes and are typical of the genus in shape, with the corona extending upward into hoods with small, incurved horns. The reflexed petals are green.

Bloom Season: May to October but peaking June to August

Habitat/Range: Endemic to white sand scrub and sandhills from Clay and Marion Counties south to Highlands and Broward Counties

Comments: The name *curtissii* commemorates noted Florida botanist Allan Hiram Curtiss (1845–1907). There are 5 Florida native plants named in honor of Curtiss. Skippers, duskywings, hairstreaks, and blues frequently visit the flowers and are likely pollinators. Ants and bee flies rob nectar. This state-listed endangered species is threatened by fire suppression and habitat loss from development and agribusiness.

PINELAND MILKWEED
Asclepias obovata Elliott
Dogbane family (Apocynaceae)

Description: The softly pubescent stems average 16"–30" tall, with opposite, hairy, obovate to elliptic leaves that measure 2"–4" long and ¾"–1¼" wide. The leaves are often wavy and have conspicuously netted veins. Flowers are in terminal umbels with green corolla lobes and yellowish-brown hoods.

Bloom Season: May to August

Habitat/Range: Sandhills and pinelands of the Florida panhandle from Escambia County east to Gadsden, Liberty, Gulf, Leon, and Taylor Counties

Comments: The name *obovata* alludes to the obovate (inversely egg-shaped) leaves. American legislator, banker, and botanist Stephen Elliott (1771–1830) first described this species in 1817. The feet or mouthparts of visiting insects, such as bees, ants, wasps, and butterflies, slip into the slits formed by adjacent anthers, pulling the pollen sacs free. Pollination takes place when this is repeated with another flower.

VELVETLEAF MILKWEED
Asclepias tomentosa Elliott
Dogbane family (Apocynaceae)

Description: This robust, 2'–3' species has softly pubescent, opposite, elliptic to oval leaves that average 2"–4" long and ¾"–1" wide, often with pinkish midveins. Greenish-white flowers are in large terminal or axillary clusters, each flower measuring about ⅜" long.

Bloom Season: April to August

Habitat/Range: Sandhills and dunes from Liberty and Franklin Counties east and south through the peninsula to Brevard, Highlands, and Collier Counties

Comments: The name *tomentosa* refers to the dense, matted (tomentose) hairs on the leaves. American legislator, banker, and botanist Stephen Elliott (1771–1830) first described this species in 1817 from plants collected in South Carolina. It is also called tuba milkweed for the tuba-like hoods on the flowers. After releasing its seeds to the wind in the fall, the plant dies back in winter then resprouts in early spring.

WHORLED MILKWEED
Asclepias verticillata L.
Dogbane family (Apocynaceae)

Description: The threadlike, whorled leaves of this rhizomatous species are a helpful key to identification. It reaches 2' tall, with leaves that are 2"–3" long and about ⅛" wide. Flowers may be white or tinged greenish white to pinkish brown, with sickle-shaped, white to pinkish horns that are curved inward. Seedpods measure 3"–4" long and ½" wide, splitting open along 1 side to release seeds to the wind.

Bloom Season: March to September

Habitat/Range: Sandhills and flatwoods through-out most of mainland Florida

Comments: The name *verticillata* relates to the whorled leaves. Nectar from the flowers attracts many kinds of bees, wasps, flies, beetles, moths, and small butterflies. The sap from milkweeds has been used in home remedies to treat snakebite and remove warts and also taken as a contraceptive. Butterfly larvae that feed on milkweeds become toxic to would-be predators.

GREEN COMET MILKWEED

Asclepias viridiflora Raf.
Dogbane family (Apocynaceae)

Description: The stems reach 8"–24" tall, with opposite, lanceolate to ovate, elliptic or oval leaves that measure 1½"–4½" long and 1"–3" wide. The corolla is circular in outline (rotate) with green, reflexed lobes.

Bloom Season: June to August

Habitat/Range: Open, calcareous woodlands of Gadsden and Jackson Counties

Comments: The name *viridiflora* means "green flowers," and the species was named in 1808 by self-educated polymath Constantine Samuel Rafinesque (1783–1840), who was born near Constantinople and later settled in Ohio. Although its native range encompasses nearly all the United States and Canada, it is a state-listed endangered species in Florida. Mammal herbivores such as deer, rabbits, cows, and horses avoid this and other milkweeds due to the bitter-tasting latex that contains toxic cardiac glycosides, but these glycosides are valuable in the treatment of heart disease.

GREEN ANTELOPEHORN

Asclepias viridis Walter
Dogbane family (Apocynaceae)

Description: This species is usually sprawling but may reach up to 24" tall. The leaves are narrowly oblong from 2½"–5" long and ½"–⅝" wide. The showy flowers are about ½" wide, with green petals and purplish stamens.

Bloom Season: February to September

Habitat/Range: Sandy pinelands of Gadsden and Liberty Counties through north-central Florida; also sandy pockets in pine rocklands of southern Miami-Dade County into the Florida Keys (Monroe County)

Comments: The name *viridis* refers to the green flowers. The common name is a fanciful allusion to the resemblance of the pods to the horns of some type of antelope. Despite its butterfly-attracting attributes as a larval host plant for monarch, queen, and soldier butterflies, and this species' clusters of very ornamental flowers, it is seldom cultivated. In the wild it is highly dependent on fire to maintain its existence.

SOUTHERN MILKWEED

Asclepias viridula Chapm.
Dogbane family (Apocynaceae)

Description: The erect stems are lined with hairs between the leaf nodes and have widely spaced, opposite, very narrowly linear 2"–4" leaves that often arch upward. The flowers are in terminal and axillary umbels, with 6–10 flowers per umbel, typically greenish white and sometimes blushed with purple.

Bloom Season: April to July

Habitat/Range: Flatwoods of the central panhandle and northeastern Florida counties

Comments: The name *viridula* means "somewhat green," relating to the greenish-white flower color. This is a state-listed threatened species due to its limited range in Florida and was first described in 1860 by American botanist and physician Alvan Wentworth Chapman (1809–1899), who authored his *Flora of the Southern States* in 1860. This milkweed is easiest to find in the months after fire has burned through its habitat, which reduces competition.

SANDHILL SPINY POD

Chthamalia pubiflora Decne.
(Also *Matelea pubiflora* [Decne.] Woodson)
Dogbane family (Apocynaceae)

Description: Vining stems average 20"–28" long, with hairy, heart-shaped, opposite leaves from 1"–2" long and ¾"–1¾" wide. The ⅜" flowers are densely hirsute internally. Cucumber-like pods bear short, soft spines.

Bloom Season: April to June

Habitat/Range: Sandhills from Madison, Suwannee, Columbia, and Clay Counties south to Hillsborough, Polk, and Highlands Counties

Comments: *Chthamalia* means "spreading on the ground." The name *pubiflora* means "hairy flowers." This state-listed endangered species was described in 1844 by botanist Joseph Decaisne (1807–1882) and moved to the genus *Matelea* in 1941 by botanist Robert Everard Woodson (1904–1963). Through a study of the evolution and systematics of American milkweed vines, Oklahoma State University botanist Angela McDonnell (1984–) moved it back to the genus *Chthamalia* in 2017.

ANGLE POD MILKVINE
Gonolobus suberosus (L.) R. Br.
Dogbane family (Apocynaceae)

Description: The opposite leaves of this vining species are somewhat heart shaped and measure 4"–6" wide. Axillary, star-shaped, ½"–⅝" flowers are usually multicolored, from maroon to brownish at the base and green or yellowish toward the tips.

Bloom Season: April to October

Habitat/Range: Woodlands across the Florida panhandle south through the peninsula to Charlotte, Lee, Glades, and Brevard Counties

Comments: *Gonolobus* refers to the angled pods. The name *suberosus* alludes to the corky bark. Botanist Robert Brown (1773–1858) relegated this species to the genus *Gonolobus* from *Cynanchum* in 1810. The flowers are self-incompatible and require cross-pollination by insects carrying pollinia from the flowers of one plant to another, so there is generally low fruit-set. There is much nomenclatural confusion regarding this state-listed threatened species.

ALABAMA MILKVINE
Matelea alabamensis (Vail) Woodson
Dogbane family (Apocynaceae)

Description: This perennial vine reaches 6' long, with cordate leaves to 6" long and 4½" wide. The green, 1" flowers have intricate venation and a yellow disk, and there is a star formed at the top of the column. The elongated, yellowish-green, 4" fruits are covered with soft spines.

Bloom Season: April to June

Habitat/Range: Deciduous woods and ravine slopes of Walton, Liberty, and Gadsden Counties

Comments: *Matelea* was named by French botanist Jean Baptiste Christophore Fusée Aublet (1720–1778) and is believed to be a French Guiana aboriginal name for the species Aublet described. The name *alabamensis* relates to Alabama, where this species was first collected and described in 1903 by botanist Anna Murray Vail (1863–1955) as *Vincetoxicum alabamense*. This state-listed endangered species ranges into Georgia and Alabama. The flowers are cross-pollinated by flies.

YELLOW CAROLINA MILKVINE
Matelea flavidula (Chapm.) Woodson
Dogbane family (Apocynaceae)

Description: Heart-shaped, opposite leaves on this vining species are about ¾"–1" long and ⅜"–½" wide. Yellowish-green, ¾" flowers are clustered in the leaf axils and followed by spiny pods.

Bloom Season: April to June

Habitat/Range: Deciduous bluff forests of Washington, Liberty, Gadsden, and Duval Counties

Comments: The name *flavidula* refers to the yellowish-green flowers. This state-listed endangered species was first described in 1878 as *Gonolobus flavidulus* by botanist Alvan Wentworth Chapman (1809–1899) but moved to the genus *Matelea* in 1941 by botanist Robert Everard Woodson (1904–1963). The name milkvine comes from the milky sap exuded from broken stems. Members of this genus need to have flowers present for positive identification. The flowers of this species closely resemble *Matelea alabamensis* but lack the star on the top of the column.

GULF COAST SWALLOWWORT
Pattalias palustre (Pursh) Fishbein
(Also *Cynanchum angustifolium* Persoon; *Seutera angustifolia* [Persoon] Fishbein & W.D. Stevens)
Dogbane family (Apocynaceae)

Description: The thin stems twine around low vegetation, with opposite, narrowly linear leaves averaging ½"–1" long. Broken stems exude white sap. The axillary clusters of ³⁄₁₆" flowers have creamy brown corolla lobes and pinkish coronas.

Bloom Season: April to October

Habitat/Range: Coastal strand and salt marshes along Florida's Gulf Coast and from St. Johns County south along the Atlantic coast into the Florida Keys

Comments: *Pattalias* is a Greek word referring to the unbranched horn of a 2-year-old stag and alludes to the columnar beak at the top of the style. The name *palustre* relates to growing in swampy ground. Oklahoma State University botanist Mark Fishbein (1962–) made the revision to *Pattalias palustre* in May 2017. The species is a larval host for queen butterflies.

GREENDRAGON
Arisaema dracontium (L.) Schott
Arum family (Araceae)

Description: Greendragon reaches about 12"–24" tall, with a single, dissected leaf blade to 30" long and 24" wide; each leaflet measures 5"–8" long and 1½"–2½" wide. The spadix reaches 6"–12" long and is nearly surrounded by the green spathe. Red-orange berries appear in late summer.

Bloom Season: March to July

Habitat/Range: Floodplain forests through much of the Florida panhandle south in the peninsula to Pasco, Sumter, Lake, Orange, and Brevard Counties (absent in the northeastern counties)

Comments: *Arisaema* refers to the red-spotted leaves on the type species. The name *dracontium* is Latin for "dragon-wort." The juice from the stems of *Arisaema* species will instantly stop the pain from small cuts. It was placed in the genus *Arisaema* in 1832 by Austrian botanist Heinrich Wilhelm Schott (1794–1865), regarded at the time as the foremost authority on the Araceae.

JACK-IN-THE-PULPIT
Arisaema triphyllum (L.) Schott
Arum family (Araceae)

Description: This aroid reaches up to 24" tall, with 1–2 long-petioled, compound leaves divided into 3 lanceolate leaflets, each measuring 6"–10" long and half as wide. The spadix is covered with minuscule flowers and arises from a sheath-like spathe that forms a hood. The spathe is green with white or brownish-purple stripes.

Bloom Season: February to July

Habitat/Range: Wet hammocks of Florida south to Collier and Palm Beach Counties

Comments: The name *triphyllum* relates to the 3 divisions of the leaves. The common name dates back to the 1300s, when the name Jack was used in the same manner as John is today—a man who has hired a prostitute. Apparently Jack (the spadix) is in the pulpit (the spathe) confessing his sins. Eating the plant will cause painful burning of the mouth. *Arisaema* species are often male when young and become female as they mature, or they can change sex in response to nutrients.

SEACOAST MARSH ELDER

Iva imbricata Walter
Aster family (Asteraceae)

Description: This species can form mounds of stems that are wider than tall. The ascending stems average 10"–20" tall and are lined with smooth, succulent leaves from 1"–1½" long and ⅜"–½" wide, becoming smaller up the stems. Male (staminate) and female (pistillate) flowers are together in the same head and encased by overlapping involucral bracts (phyllaries).

Bloom Season: June to October

Habitat/Range: Beach dunes, usually near the tideline, from Escambia County east to Franklin County and from Hillsborough and Duval Counties south along both coasts into the Florida Keys (Monroe County)

Comments: *Iva* is thought to allude to *Ajuga iva*, a mint with a similar leaf odor. The name *imbricata* refers to the overlapping (imbricate) floral bracts. The flowers are wind-pollinated, and the airborne pollen can cause allergic rhinitis (hay fever), like the related ragweeds (*Ambrosia* spp.).

WILD JOB'S TEARS

Onosmodium virginianum (L.) A. DC.
(Also *Lithospermum virginianum* L.)
Borage family (Boraginaceae)

Description: The 12"–24" stems of this perennial bear alternate, hairy, oblong to elliptic leaves that average 1"–5" long and ½"–1" wide. Flowers are in leafy, helicoid cymes and measure about ½" long.

Bloom Season: May to August

Habitat/Range: Sandhills, shell middens, and open woodlands south in Florida to Hillsborough, Polk, Highlands, Orange, and Volusia Counties

Comments: *Onosmodium* refers to resembling the related genus *Onosma*. The name *virginianum* relates to Virginia. The name Job's tears is also the name of a grass (*Coix lacryma-jobi*) with hard seeds that are kept in one's pocket to bring good fortune. This tradition dates to the central character in the biblical book of Job, rewarded by God for Job's patience after losing all that he held dear but never losing his faith. It is also called Virginia marbleseed and false gromwell.

SPANISH MOSS
Tillandsia usneoides (L.) L.
Pineapple family (Bromeliaceae)

Description: This rootless epiphyte produces slender, elongated stems and leaves clothed with silvery gray hairs. The threadlike strands hang in long clumps from trees, especially oaks and cypress. Inconspicuous, fragrant flowers appear in the leaf axils.

Bloom Season: April to August

Habitat/Range: A variety of wooded habitats, including residential trees, throughout Florida

Comments: *Tillandsia* honors Swedish botanist Elias Tillandz (1640–1693), who traveled by boat from Finland to Sweden but got so seasick he walked the 622 miles back. The name *usneoides* refers to the resemblance of the leaves to the lichen genus *Usnea*. Spanish moss has the widest natural range of any bromeliad and is a symbol of the southeastern United States. It is the larval host plant of the black-winged dahana moth and provides habitat for a species of jumping spider (*Pelegrina tillandsiae*).

PAPERY WHITLOW-WORT
Paronychia chartacea Fernald
Pink family (Caryophyllaceae)

Description: The wiry stems of this annual or short-lived perennial radiate horizontally from a taproot with tiny, revolute, triangular-ovate leaves. Numerous green to cream, minute flowers cover the plant.

Bloom Season: July to November

Habitat/Range: Endemic to rosemary and sand pine scrub of Bay and Washington Counties in the Florida panhandle and on the Lake Wales Ridge from Lake and Orange Counties south to Highlands County

Comments: *Paronychia* means "beside fingernail" and is also the medical term for a painful bacterial infection of the soft tissue surrounding a fingernail. Members of this genus were once used to treat this disease as well as a similar viral disease called whitlow, or felon. The name *chartacea* refers to the papery leaves. It is a federal endangered species and often occurs in fire lanes and trails that bisect its habitat.

BEACH TEA

Croton punctatus Jacq.
Spurge family (Euphorbiaceae)

Description: This small, bushy species averages 10"–24" tall, with ovate to elliptic, gray-green leaves measuring 1"–2" long and ½"–¾" wide and densely covered with star-shaped hairs. The inconspicuous flowers measure ³⁄₁₆" wide.

Bloom Season: All year

Habitat/Range: Beach dunes from Escambia County to Franklin County in the Florida panhandle and from Pinellas and Nassau Counties south along both coasts to Collier and Miami-Dade Counties

Comments: *Croton* refers to the resemblance of the seeds to a tick. The name *punctatus* refers to the dots covering the stems and leaves. This species occurs along coastal dunes from North Carolina to Texas and through the neotropics. A tea brewed from the leaves has been used in home remedies, hence the common name. It is also called gulf croton. Members of this genus have been used as a powerful purgative, but that use was discontinued when too many overdoses ended in coma and death.

DELTOID SPURGE

Euphorbia deltoidea Engelm. ex Chapm.
(Also *Chamaesyce deltoidea* [Engelm. ex Chapm.] Small)
Spurge family (Euphorbiaceae)

Description: This fire-dependent species forms small, dense mats across sandy pockets in pine rocklands. The leaves reach ⅛" wide, with incon-spicuous, yellowish-green "false flowers."

Bloom Season: All year

Habitat/Range: Endemic to pine rocklands of southern Miami-Dade County

Comments: *Euphorbia* honors first-century Greek physician Euphorbus, who knew these plants were powerful laxatives. The name *deltoidea* alludes to the deltoid leaves. This federal endangered spe-cies occurs solely in remnant pine rockland parcels east of Everglades National Park. *Euphorbia deltoi-dea* ssp. *pinetorum*, with ascending, hairy stems and leaves, occurs south and west of the range of the deltoid spurge, into Everglades National Park. *Euphorbia deltoidea* ssp. *serpyllum*, with grayish-green leaves, is endemic to Big Pine Key.

INDIAN CUCUMBERROOT

Medeola virginiana L.
Lily family (Liliaceae)

Description: Rhizomatous stems reach 10"–30" tall, woolly white when young, and topped by a whorl of 5–9 sessile leaf blades measuring 3"–6" long and 1"–2" wide. The small flowers have curled, yellowish-green sepals and petals.

Bloom Season: April to June

Habitat/Range: Rich, mesic, deciduous forests of Santa Rosa, Okaloosa, Liberty, Gadsden, and Leon Counties

Comments: *Medeola* was named for Medea, a mythical Greek sorceress and granddaughter of the sun god Helios, who later married Jason, as told in the play by Euripides (480–406 BC). The name *virginiana* is for Virginia, where this species was first collected and later described in 1753. This state-listed endangered species has long been aligned with *Trillium* but was moved to the Liliaceae in 1987 by Soviet-Armenian botanist Armen Leonovich Takhtajan (1910–2009). The fresh rhizomes are edible and taste like cucumbers.

FLORIDA FEATHERSHANK

Schoenocaulon dubium (Michx.) Small
Melanthium family (Melanthiaceae)

Description: The basal leaves are channeled, elongated, and very narrowly linear to about 8"–12" long and ⅛" wide. The bluish-green scape reaches 12"–30" tall, the upper portion lined with small flowers bearing extended stamens.

Bloom Season: April to August

Habitat/Range: Endemic to sandhill and scrub habitat from Gilchrist, Alachua, and Putnam Counties south into Highlands, Martin, Palm Beach, and Broward Counties

Comments: *Schoenocaulon* refers to the stems that resemble those of a *Schoenus* (Cyperaceae). The name *dubium* means "dubious" (doubtful) and relates to this species not conforming to the characteristics of other members of the family. Botanist André Michaux (1746–1802) first described it as *Helonias dubia,* published the year following his untimely death in Madagascar. The genus ranges from the United States south to Peru.

BUTTERFLY ORCHID
Encyclia tampensis (Lindl.) Small
Orchid family (Orchidaceae)

Description: The hard, round or egg-shaped pseudobulbs are topped by 1–3 linear-lanceolate leaves from 3"–12" long and ⅜"–¾" wide. Fragrant, ¾" flowers typically have greenish-brown sepals and petals with a white lip marked with a purple blotch or streaks, but there is much variation.

Bloom Season: Mostly May to July

Habitat/Range: Hardwood forests and wooded swamps from Levy, Putnam, and Flagler Counties south through the Florida Keys

Comments: *Encyclia* means "to encircle," alluding to the lateral lobes of the lip that encircle the column. The name *tampensis* refers to the Tampa Bay area, where it was first discovered in 1846. This is Florida's most common epiphytic orchid and can be found growing on a variety of trees, including mangroves. This species also occurs in the Bahamas. The common name relates to the flowers' resembling small butterflies hovering above the plant.

DINGY STAR ORCHID
Epidendrum anceps Jacq.
(Also *Epidendrum amphistomum* A. Rich.)
Orchid family (Orchidaceae)

Description: The leafy stems of this epiphytic orchid average 12"–24" long, with alternate, elliptic leaves measuring 2"–6" long and ½"–1½" wide. The leaves are usually green but may be burgundy. The brown to greenish-brown, ⅜" flowers form a ball at the tip of the branches.

Bloom Season: November to July

Habitat/Range: Hardwood swamps from Lee and Broward Counties south through the Florida mainland

Comments: *Epidendrum* means "on tree" and alludes to the epiphytic habit of many orchids in this genus. The name *anceps* means "two-edged," alluding to the flattened peduncle. This orchid was first discovered in Florida at Gobbler's Head (Collier County) in 1904. The flowers smell like overripe vegetables at night and are pollinated by male nocturnal moths. It is a state-listed endangered species principally due to habitat loss and illegal collecting.

FLORIDA JADE ORCHID
Epidendrum floridense Hágsater
(Also *Epidendrum difforme* Jacq., misapplied)
Orchid family (Orchidaceae)

Description: This epiphyte has pendent stems with thick, glossy, elliptic leaves that average ¾"–1¼" long and ⅜"–½" wide. Flowers are in terminal umbels and measure about ⅝" wide.

Bloom Season: August to November

Habitat/Range: Hardwood forests and wooded swamps from Lee and Palm Beach Counties south through the Florida mainland (disjunct in Polk County)

Comments: The name *floridense* refers to Florida, the geographical location of the type specimen collected in July 1992 in the Fakahatchee Swamp (Collier County) by botanist Eric Hágsater (1945–). This state-listed endangered species was first discovered in Florida by Abram Paschal Garber (1838–1881) in 1877 near Miami (Miami-Dade County), when it was thought to be *Epidendrum difforme*, a similar species native to the neotropics. It is also called Florida star orchid.

GREEN-FLY ORCHID
Epidendrum magnoliae Muhl.
(Also *Epidendrum conopseum* R. Br.)
Orchid family (Orchidaceae)

Description: The stems of this epiphyte bear narrowly elliptic leaves ranging from 2"–3½" long and ⅜"–½" wide. The small greenish flowers measure ½"–⅝" wide.

Bloom Season: August to February

Habitat/Range: Hardwood forests and wooded swamps throughout much of the Florida panhandle and south in the peninsula to Manatee, Hardee, Highlands, Osceola, and Brevard Counties

Comments: The name *magnoliae* relates to this species' preference for growing on southern magnolia (*Magnolia grandiflora*) in the northern parts of its range. When growing on live oak (*Quercus virginiana*), it is often hidden by ferns. It occurs farther north than any other epiphytic orchid in the Western Hemisphere and has been used in hybridizing to breed cold tolerance into tropical orchids, without much success. The flowers emit a sweet fragrance at night and are visited by moths.

STIFF STAR ORCHID
Epidendrum rigidum Jacq.
Orchid family (Orchidaceae)

Description: The creeping stems of this epiphyte form large colonies on tree branches. The elliptic, leathery leaves measure 1"–3¼" long and ¼"–⅜" wide. The flowers reach about ¼" wide and alternate along zigzagging, sheathed terminal spikes.

Bloom Season: October to May

Habitat/Range: Hardwood forests and wooded swamps of Lee, Collier, Hendry, Palm Beach, Broward, and Miami-Dade Counties

Comments: The name *rigidum* refers to the somewhat stiff flowers. This orchid is locally common but is often hidden on the host tree by resurrection fern (*Pleopeltis polypodioides*). Botanist Allan Hiram Curtiss (1845–1907) first discovered this species in Florida near Miami in 1877. It grows on a variety of trees, sometimes high up on the trunks and branches of cypress (*Taxodium*). It was first collected and described from Martinique in 1760 by botanist Nikolaus Joseph von Jacquin (1727–1817).

WILD COCO
Eulophia alta (L.) Fawc. & Rendle
Orchid family (Orchidaceae)

Description: Wild coco has erect, pleated, lanceolate leaves that arise from a corm. The leaves are typically 1'–2' long and 1"–2" wide. The tall flower spike is lined with 20–50 flowers with green to purple sepals and petals. The crested, 3-lobed lip is maroon.

Bloom Season: September to November

Habitat/Range: Forest edges, prairie margins, and along roadsides from Flagler, Orange, and Pasco Counties south through the peninsula

Comments: *Eulophia* refers to the crest on the lip of the flower. The name *alta* means "tall." Wild coco was first discovered in Florida by botanist Alvan Wentworth Chapman (1809–1899) in 1875. The related, invasive Chinese crown orchid (*Eulophia graminea*) has smaller flowers, a pink-centered white lip, and a large corm with grasslike leaves. It occurs through the southern half of Florida and is spreading rapidly in mulched areas.

TOOTHPETAL ORCHID
Habenaria floribunda Lindl.
(Also *Habenaria odontopetala* Rchb. f.)
Orchid family (Orchidaceae)

Description: This species produces a rosette of fleshy, elliptic leaves from 3"–6" long and ¾"–1¼" wide. Green, ⅜" flowers are on a 10"–24" erect stem. There is a toothlike projection at the base of each petal.

Bloom Season: September to February

Habitat/Range: Hardwood forests and swamps in northeastern Florida and from Levy, Marion, and Volusia Counties south through the peninsula

Comments: *Habenaria* means "rein," for the rein-like spur. The name floribunda refers to the abundance of flowers. This is Florida's most common terrestrial orchid, forming large colonies in the humus of forests or growing on rotting stumps and floating logs in swamps. The blossoms fill the night air in forests with sweet perfume. Seminoles used the plant in funeral processions to help ward off evil spirits and "to strengthen medicine men."

WATER SPIDER ORCHID
Habenaria repens Nutt.
Orchid family (Orchidaceae)

Description: The fleshy, lanceolate leaves of this terrestrial or semiaquatic orchid are 3"–6" long and ½"–1" wide. Spindly, ⅜" green flowers are crowded on an erect, terminal spike. The dorsal sepal is shallowly concave, with thin, spreading, lateral sepals; the lip is greenish, with a descending central lobe.

Bloom Season: Sporadically all year

Habitat/Range: Freshwater wetlands, pond margins, and wet roadside ditches throughout most of mainland Florida

Comments: The name *repens* means "creeping," in reference to the species' growth habit. This orchid often grows among floating vegetation, especially in rafts of invasive water-hyacinth (*Eichhornia crassipes*), or it may form floating mats on its own. It requires permanently wet soil in terrestrial environments and can form spreading populations. Botanist Thomas Nuttall (1786–1859) first described it in 1818.

CRESTED CORALROOT
Hexalectris spicata (Walter) Barnhart
Orchid family (Orchidaceae)

Description: This saprophytic orchid consists entirely of a spike of flowers that emerges from an underground coralloid (brittle and branching) root that lives in symbiosis with fungus in the humus. The flowering spike may reach 18" tall, with ½" flowers.

Bloom Season: April to August

Habitat/Range: Dry, open forests, with populations scattered around the Florida panhandle and peninsula south to Pasco, Lake, and Indian River Counties; also Sarasota and Lee Counties

Comments: *Hexalectris* means "six" and "cock," alluding to the number of projections on the lip that resemble a cock's comb. The name *spicata* refers to the spike of flowers. This attractive, state-listed endangered species grows in the sandy humus of forests in association with oaks, pines, and junipers. Squirrels and armadillos dig up and eat the roots, alerted to their presence by the flowering stems.

GREEN ADDERSMOUTH
Malaxis unifolia Michx.
Orchid family (Orchidaceae)

Description: Plants are typically 3"–6" tall, with a single, ovate leaf measuring 2½"–3½" long and 1½"–2¼" wide. The raceme of green, ⅛" blossoms elongates as anthesis progresses.

Bloom Season: March to May in Florida

Habitat/Range: Hardwood forests and wetland margins through much of the Florida panhandle east to Leon and Wakulla Counties and also Alachua, Marion, and Hernando Counties

Comments: *Malaxis* is Greek for "softening," alluding to the soft and tender texture of the leaves. The name *unifolia* relates to the single leaf produced by this species. This is a state-listed endangered species due to its scarcity and limited range in Florida and is listed as endangered throughout much of its North American range. See the Red and Orange Flowers section for *Malaxis spicata*. They are the only 2 members of this genus in Florida.

COPPER LADIES'-TRESSES

Mesadenus lucayanus (Britton) Schltr.
Orchid family (Orchidaceae)

Description: The pale green to grayish-green, elliptic to oblanceolate leaves form a small rosette and measure ½"–4" long and ⅜"–1⅛" wide. Flower stalks average 8"–10" tall, the upper half lined with coppery, ⅛" flowers.

Bloom Season: December to March

Habitat/Range: Hardwood forests of Citrus, Duval, Manatee, Martin, and Volusia Counties (historically Miami-Dade County)

Comments: *Mesadenus* means "middle gland." The name *lucayanus* refers to the Lucayans, the original inhabitants of the Bahamas before the arrival of Europeans. Charles Mosier (1871–1936) and John Kunkel Small (1869–1938) first discovered this orchid in Florida in 1915 on Elliott Key (Miami-Dade County). It ranks as one of the most difficult orchids to find because the flowering stems blend in perfectly with the leaf litter on the forest floor. This species has also been placed in the genus *Spiranthes*.

CRESTLESS PLUME ORCHID

Orthochilus ecristatus (Fernald) Bytebier
(Also *Pteroglossaspis ecristata* [Fernald] Rolfe)
Orchid family (Orchidaceae)

Description: Flowering stems of this species can reach 5' tall, with erect, linear-lanceolate leaves measuring 6"–30" long and ½"–1¼" wide. The flowers measure about ⅝" across, and the sepals and petals form a hood over the lip.

Bloom Season: August to October

Habitat/Range: Pinelands, oak barrens, and scrub in Santa Rosa, Wakulla, and Leon Counties south through most of the peninsula

Comments: *Orthochilus* is from the Greek *orthos*, meaning "straight" or "upright," and *cheilos*, "a lip." The name *ecristatus* means "without a crest," for the crestless lip of the flowers. Phylogenetic studies in 2014 and 2015 moved this species into the genus *Orthochilus*. Plants in Florida with purplish flowers and described as var. *pottsii* have no taxonomic validity. It is a state-listed endangered species due to habitat loss.

GREEN WOOD ORCHID
Platanthera clavellata (Michx.) Luer
Orchid family (Orchidaceae)

Description: The fleshy, linear-oblong to elliptic leaf measures 3"–7" long and ½"–1" wide. Pale green to dull yellowish-green flowers appear on the upper half of a stem that averages 5"–10" tall. Each flower is about ⅜" long.

Bloom Season: June to August

Habitat/Range: Bogs and low woods of Santa Rosa, Calhoun, Liberty, Gadsden, and Wakulla Counties

Comments: *Platanthera* means "broad anther." The name *clavellata* refers to the club-shaped (clavate) spur. This orchid is decidedly cold tolerant and ranges across the eastern half of the United States and Canada. The presence of a series of forward-pointing lateral projections on the column has led some taxonomists to suggest it should be placed in the genus *Habenaria* along with *Platanthera integra* and *P. nivea*, which share the same characteristic, but this is not widely accepted. It is also called green reinorchid.

YELLOWSPIKE ORCHID
Polystachya concreta (Jacq.) Garay & H.R. Sweet
Orchid family (Orchidaceae)

Description: The thin, narrowly oblong to elliptic leaves of this epiphytic orchid average 4"–8" long and ⅜"–1¼" wide. The hooded green to yellowish ¼" flowers are on terminal spikes, often with numerous branchlets.

Bloom Season: July to December

Habitat/Range: Wooded swamps, hammocks, and mangrove forests in Hardee, DeSoto, Highlands, and Martin Counties and from Lee, Collier, and Broward Counties south into the Florida Keys (Monroe County)

Comments: *Polystachya* means "many spikes" and refers to the branchlets on the inflorescence. The name *concreta* is Latin for "grown together" and alludes to the flower parts. This state-listed endangered species may be locally common and is inadvertently pollinated by small, iridescent-green halictid bees as they harvest the starchy lip hairs. It ranges from Africa into Florida and the neotropics.

MRS. BRITTON'S SHADOW WITCH
Ponthieva brittoniae Ames
Orchid family (Orchidaceae)

Description: Flowering plants average 4"–8" tall, with elliptic to ovate leaves that average 2" long and ½" wide but may be leafless when flowering. The flowers reach about ⅜" wide.

Bloom Season: January to March

Habitat/Range: In and around limestone sinks in pine rocklands of Miami-Dade County

Comments: *Ponthieva* honors Henri de Ponthieu, an eighteenth-century West Indian Huguenot who sent plant specimens to British botanist Sir Joseph Banks (1743–1820). The name *brittoniae* honors Elizabeth Britton (1858–1934), wife of Nathaniel Lord Britton (1859–1934) and leading founder of the New York Botanical Garden. First found in Florida in 1909 near Perrine, today this critically imperiled endangered species is found only on Long Pine Key in Everglades National Park, where it is extraordinarily rare and exceptionally difficult to find. It is also found in Cuba and the Bahamas.

HAIRY SHADOW WITCH
Ponthieva racemosa (Walter) C. Mohr
Orchid family (Orchidaceae)

Description: The rosette of elliptic to oblanceolate leaves of this terrestrial orchid measure 2"–4" long and ½"–1" wide, and are present at flowering. From 20–35 green and white hairy flowers are arranged on a hairy spike, each measuring about ¼" wide and held nearly horizontal. The sepals and petals are conspicuously green striped.

Bloom Season: October to January

Habitat/Range: Shady forests and swamps from Bay and Jackson Counties east and south through most of the Florida peninsula

Comments: The name *racemosa* refers to the raceme of flowers. This orchid can form large rhizomatous colonies under proper conditions. Small, iridescent halictid bees have been observed visiting the flowers and are likely pollinators. The species ranges across the southeastern United States from Virginia and Tennessee to Texas. The flowers resemble Halloween ghouls when viewed up close.

LEAFLESS BEAKED ORCHID (GREEN FORM)
Sacoila lanceolata (Aubl.) Garay forma *albidaviridis* Catling & Sheviak
Orchid family (Orchidaceae)

Description: The fleshy, lanceolate leaves average 4"–8" long and ¾"–3" wide, forming a basal rosette (absent when flowering). A stout, erect spike, to 12" tall or more, is topped with an arrangement of pubescent, green, white-lipped, ¾"–1" flowers.

Bloom Season: April to July

Habitat/Range: Meadows, pastures, and road-sides of Walton County and from Levy, Baker, and Flagler Counties south through mainland Florida

Comments: *Sacoila* alludes to the sac-shaped projection formed by the sepals and base of the column. The name *lanceolata* refers to the lanceo-late leaves, and the form *albidaviridis* translates to "white-green." The species is commonly seen along roadsides and was first collected in Florida in Lake County in 1894, but this green form appears to be more common in the southernmost counties within its Florida range.

CRANEFLY ORCHID
Tipularia discolor (Pursh) Nutt.
Orchid family (Orchidaceae)

Description: A single, velvety, ovate leaf arises from the ground in winter from underground tubers. The leaves are green to greenish purple above, often purple on the underside, and measure 3"–4" long and 2"–2½" wide. The flowering stem is 9"–12" tall, typically with 2 dozen or more lopsided, green or purplish-green, ⅜" flowers.

Bloom Season: August to September

Habitat/Range: Deciduous woods across the Florida panhandle and in Suwannee, Columbia, Alachua, and Marion Counties

Comments: *Tipularia* was taken from the crane fly genus *Tipula* because the flowers appear to resemble crippled crane flies. The name *discolor* means "of two colors" and relates to the 2-toned leaves. This state-listed threatened species is difficult to find in the dappled light of forests. The photograph was taken on a rainy day in August in the Ocala National Forest in Marion County.

WORMVINE ORCHID
Vanilla barbellata Richb. f.
Orchid family (Orchidaceae)

Description: The green or orange stems of this leafless, vining orchid are smooth, ⅜"–½" thick, and root to trees at the nodes. The fragrant flowers measure 2"–2½" wide.

Bloom Season: April to July

Habitat/Range: Coastal hammocks and mangrove forests of Biscayne National Park (Miami-Dade County); also Monroe County on the mainland and the Florida Keys

Comments: *Vanilla* is from the Spanish *vainilla*, or "small pod," in reference to the bean-like seed capsules. The name *barbellata* means "somewhat bearded" and alludes to the small bristles on the lip of this state-listed endangered species. Despite periodic hurricanes that ravage southern Florida's coastlines, this orchid still survives in mangrove-buttonwood associations around the Flamingo area of Everglades National Park and in protected areas of the Florida Keys. The similar *Vanilla dilloniana* has deciduous lanceolate leaves on the fresh growth and flowers that are lined with red around the entire lip. Presumed extirpated in Florida, *Vanilla dilloniana* was documented in the early 1900s in the hammocks around Coconut Grove (Miami-Dade County) and at "Cape Sable" (Monroe County), which is presumed to be around the Flamingo area in present-day Everglades National Park.

DUSKY VANILLA
Vanilla phaeantha Rchb. f.
Orchid family (Orchidaceae)

Description: The ½" wide, zigzagging stems of this vining orchid may exceed 20' in length. The oblong leaves reach 5" long and 1½" wide, with clusters of 3"–4" flowers emerging from the leaf axils. Only 1 or 2 flowers open at a time.

Bloom Season: April to July

Habitat/Range: Forested swamps of Collier and Miami-Dade Counties

Comments: The name *phaeantha* means "dusky flower," alluding to its shadowy cast. The species' population is centered in Collier County, but there is a small population in Everglades National Park. This state-listed endangered species closely resembles *Vanilla planifolia,* the source of vanilla flavoring used in baking and puddings. *Vanilla planifolia* is naturalized in forests of southern Florida, where it climbs high into trees, but the stems do not zigzag like this species. *Vanilla mexicana* of Martin and Miami-Dade Counties has green sepals and petals and a pure white lip.

CORKYSTEM PASSIONFLOWER
Passiflora suberosa L.
Passionflower family (Passifloraceae)

Description: This small vine has corky outgrowths on mature stems and climbs by tendrils. The alternate leaves vary in size and shape, ranging from 1"–4" long, and may be linear, lanceolate, and sometimes lobed. The flowers are ½" wide.

Bloom Season: All year

Habitat/Range: Hammocks, pinelands, and coastal strand from Dixie and Duval Counties south into the Florida Keys

Comments: *Passiflora* is Latin for "passion flower" and relates to the crucifixion of Jesus. The name *suberosa* means "corky-barked." This is a preferred larval host plant of the zebra longwing, Julia, and gulf fritillary butterflies. A recent treatment for the *Flora of North America* concludes that the correct name for Florida plants is *Passiflora pallida*, but University of South Florida taxonomists disagree, citing intergrades of flower size and other inconsistencies used to separate the 2 species.

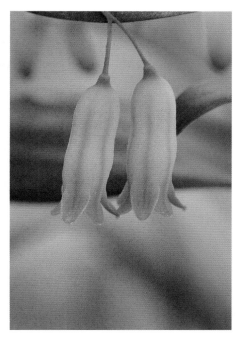

SCRUB BUCKWHEAT

Eriogonum floridanum Small
(Also *Eriogonum longifolium* Nutt. var.
gnaphalifolium Gand.)
Buckwheat family (Polygonaceae)

Description: The basal leaves range from 6"–10" long and ½"–¾" wide (green above, white below). Flowering plants reach 2'–3' tall, with alternate leaves and terminal clusters of wooly, starlike, ½" flowers.

Bloom Season: April to November

Habitat/Range: Endemic to sandhills and scrub in Putnam, Marion, Sumter, Lake, Seminole, Orange, Osceola, Polk, and Highlands Counties

Comments: *Eriogonum* means "wool-knee" and alludes to the woolly stems and swollen joints of *Eriogonum tomentosum*. The name *floridanum* refers to Florida, where this species was first collected in 1903 by botanist John Kunkel Small (1869–1938). Bees and wasps are the principal pollinators of this state endangered and federal threatened species. Prospectors in the Great Plains believed silver deposits occurred wherever *Eriogonum longifolium* grew.

SMOOTH SOLOMON'S SEAL

Polygonatum biflorum (Walter) Elliott
Butcher's Broom family (Ruscaceae)

Description: Smooth, alternate, lanceolate leaf blades measure 2"–10" long. Paired, axillary, tubular flowers reach ½"–¾" long and have 6 lobes. Blue berries measure ⅜" wide.

Bloom Season: March to May

Habitat/Range: Mixed deciduous woods scattered across the Florida panhandle to the north-central peninsula from Escambia County to Hernando and Lake Counties

Comments: *Polygonatum* alludes to the many joints of the rhizomes. The name *biflorum* is descriptive of the paired flowers. The species was first collected in South Carolina in 1788. The common name is said to have come from the scars on the rhizomes, which resemble the ancient Hebrew seal of King Solomon of Israel, or from the hexagram engraved on the bottom of cups (called Solomon's seal) in ancient Arab tradition, and depicted by the 6 lobes of the flowers. The hexagram later became a symbol of Judaism (Star of David).

YELLOW PITCHERPLANT
Sarracenia flava L.
Pitcherplant family (Sarraceniaceae)

Description: The yellowish-green (rarely red) leaves are modified into tall, 2'–3' traps, with a hood extending over the opening. The green to yellow flowers are nodding and average 2½" wide.

Bloom Season: April to July

Habitat/Range: Wet pine savannas, cypress swamps, bogs, and seepage slopes from Escambia County east to Leon and Wakulla Counties in the Florida panhandle; also Hamilton, Columbia, and Alachua Counties

Comments: *Sarracenia* honors French surgeon and botanist Michel Sarrazin (1659–1734), who was among the first to suggest that this group of plants caught insects. The name *flava* means "yellow," for the mature flowers. Insects are lured to the traps with scent from extrafloral nectaries. The inside wall of the trap is slippery, causing the insects to fall into the enzyme-rich liquid, where they are dissolved. This species forms extensive colonies.

WHITETOP PITCHERPLANT
Sarracenia leucophylla Raf.
Pitcherplant family (Sarraceniaceae)

Description: The leaves are modified into tall, 2'–3' traps that are white above, green below, with netlike venation and a hood (operculum) extending over the opening. The red to maroon flowers are 2½"–3" wide.

Bloom Season: May to July

Habitat/Range: Bogs and wet pine savannas of the Florida panhandle from Escambia County east to Leon, Liberty, and Franklin Counties

Comments: The name *leucophylla* means "white-leaved" and alludes to the white upper portion of the leaves (pitcher-like traps). It is a state-listed endangered species. Extrafloral nectaries on the lip of the traps lure insects, but the nectar of at least 1 species is narcotic and causes the stupefied insect to fall into the pitcher. The hood over the entrance helps keep rain out and also deters flying insects from escaping. Look inside the traps for pitcherplant moths hanging onto the sides.

PARROT PITCHERPLANT

Sarracenia psittacina Michx.
Pitcherplant family (Sarraceniaceae)

Description: The decumbent, 5"–8" pitchers of this species are variously pigmented with green, red, or yellow. Flowers are yellowish green or red.

Bloom Season: April to August

Habitat/Range: Bogs, seeps, and wet roadsides from Escambia County west to Leon and Wakulla Counties; also Baker and Nassau Counties

Comments: The name *psittacina* alludes to the resemblance of the traps to the head of a parrot (psittacine). The pitchers of this state-listed threatened species have white "windows" on the walls to allow light to enter so that insects think they are exits. The hood conceals an opening that is lined with nectar and designed to lure insects into a rounded chamber leading into a narrowing tunnel with crisscrossed hairs that prevent escape. The hapless bug eventually slips into liquid that contains digestive enzymes. This species also ranges from Georgia to Louisiana.

EARLEAF GREENBRIER

Smilax auriculata Walter
Smilax family (Smilacaceae)

Description: This wickedly thorny vine uses its long stems to scramble across other vegetation. The leaves typically have ear-like basal lobes, often with pale white mottling. The fragrant flowers are in clusters and measure ¼"–⅜" wide.

Bloom Season: All year

Habitat/Range: Pinelands, sandhills, hardwood forests, and thickets throughout mainland Florida

Comments: *Smilax* comes from *smilakos,* a name used by Pliny (AD 23–79) for an evergreen oak. Smilax is also a mythological Greek nymph who fell hopelessly in love with a mortal, so the gods changed her into a brambly vine. The name *auriculata* refers to the ear-like lobes on the leaves. This species makes travel through its habitat painful, especially if you are foolish enough to wear shorts. The young, tender stems can be eaten raw or cooked; the rhizomes of *Smilax ornata* are the source of sarsaparilla and root beer.

BLUERIDGE CARRIONFLOWER

Smilax lasioneura Hook.
Smilax family (Smilacaceae)

Description: This thornless annual bears many tendrils and may climb to 6' high. Dull, ovate leaf blades measure 1½"–3" long and 1¼"–2" wide, pale green and pubescent below, and with petioles shorter than the blade. Tiny green, unisexual flowers are in globose umbels.

Bloom Season: April to August

Habitat/Range: Deciduous woods of Jackson, Calhoun, Liberty, Gadsden, Leon, Jefferson, and Alachua Counties

Comments: The name *lasioneura* means "woolly veins," for the hairs on the veins on the underside of the leaves. It was named in 1840 by William Jackson Hooker (1785–1865) from plants collected in Saskatchewan (Canada). It has also been placed in the genera *Coprosmanthus* and *Nemexia*. This species resembles *Smilax ecirrhata*, which is typically erect and with rudimentary tendrils. The common name relates to the odor of rotten meat produced by the flowers of some species.

CROOMIA

Croomia pauciflora (Nutt.) Torr.
Stemona family (Stemonaceae)

Description: This rhizomatous species reaches about 12" tall, with 2"–3" heart-shaped (cordate) leaves arranged at the top of succulent stems. Tiny 4-petaled green flowers are axillary on threadlike stems hidden by the leaves.

Bloom Season: March to June

Habitat/Range: Moist bluff forests and wooded slopes of Gadsden and Liberty Counties in the Florida panhandle

Comments: *Croomia* commemorates Hardy Bryan Croom (1797–1837), a wealthy plantation owner who bought 640 acres of land east of Tallahassee in March 1836 but died at sea near Cape Hatteras, North Carolina, in 1837 after the wreck of the steamship *Home*. Croom was interested in Florida botany and is credited with the discovery of this species. The name *pauciflora* means "few flowers." This genus of 3 species is represented in China, Japan, and the southeastern United States. It has been included in the Yam family (Dioscoreaceae).

WHITE FLOWERS

Argemone albiflora

This section is for either pure white flowers or flowers with white as the dominant color. Some flowers produce albino morphs, so you may need to check other color sections if you do not find what you are looking for here.

CAROLINA SCALYSTEM
Elytraria caroliniensis (J.F. Gmel.) Pers.
Acanthus family (Acanthaceae)

Description: A basal rosette comprises spatulate leaves that measure 4"–6" long and up to ½" wide with a white or pinkish midvein. The 6"–8" scape is covered with small scales, becoming cone-like at the apex, with a single, 5-lobed, ⅜" flower.

Bloom Season: February to November

Habitat/Range: Flatwoods, wet pinelands, and floodplains through much of peninsular Florida west in the panhandle to Holmes, Washington, and Calhoun Counties

Comments: *Elytraria* is Greek for "sheath" or "vagina," referring to the flowers and fruits enclosed by bracts. The name *caroliniensis* relates to South Carolina, where this species was first collected in 1791. Some botanists separate this species into 2 varieties, with var. *angustifolia* being endemic to southern Florida, but the current consensus is that there is just a single variable species in the state.

NIGHTFLOWERING WILD PETUNIA
Ruellia noctiflora (Nees) A. Gray
Acanthus family (Acanthaceae)

Description: The 10"–16" hairy stems are purplish with oval, bluntly pointed, opposite, 1½"–2¾" leaves covered with coarse hairs. The flowers reach 3"–4" wide, with a floral tube to 3½" long, and may be flecked with pink.

Bloom Season: May to August

Habitat/Range: Wet flatwoods and bogs of the central panhandle and the northeastern Florida counties

Comments: *Ruellia* honors French herbalist Jean de la Ruelle (1474–1537), who also went by Jean Ruel and later latinized his name to Joannes Ruellius. The name *noctiflora* relates to the species' nocturnal flowers. Hybridizing experiments indicate this state-listed endangered species is closely allied to *Ruellia caroliniensis*. It was first described in 1824 by American naturalist John LeConte (1784–1860) as *Ruellia tubiflora*. Sphinx moths pollinate the flowers at night; and the flowers fall off shortly after sunrise.

YELLOW BRACTSPIKE

Yeatesia viridiflora (Nees) Small
Acanthus family (Acanthaceae)

Description: This species may reach 24" tall but is usually shorter. The leaves are elliptic to elliptic-lanceolate, 2"–6" long, with white, pale purple, or pink, somewhat 2-lipped flowers that measure about ½" across.

Bloom Season: May to August

Habitat/Range: Shaded streambanks and deciduous forests of Jackson, Gadsden, Liberty, and Jefferson Counties in the Florida panhandle

Comments: *Yeatesia* honors Georgia state geologist William Smith Yeates (1856–1908), who authored an 1896 report on gold deposits in Georgia. The puzzling name *viridiflora* means "green flowers," so perhaps the original specimen had green-tinted flowers or the name was meant to be *viridifolia* (green leaves). The widely used common name is also puzzling, because the bracts are not yellow. German botanist Christian Gottfried Daniel Nees von Esenbeck (1776–1858) described it in 1847.

ADAM'S NEEDLE

Yucca filamentosa L.
Agave family (Agavaceae)

Description: This unmistakable species produces a 2'–3' rosette of stiff, swordlike, sharp-tipped leaves to 30" long and 4" wide, with many curled filaments along the margins. Flowering spikes reaching 6'–8' tall have showy, creamy white, nodding flowers, each about 2" long.

Bloom Season: April to July

Habitat/Range: Sandhills and dry forests south in Florida to Lee, Glades, and Broward Counties

Comments: *Yucca* is taken from the Taino word *yuca* (cassava), for the root of *Manihot esculenta* (Euphorbiaceae) and mistakenly applied to this group of plants. The name *filamentosa* relates to the leaf filaments. Biblical stories have it that Adam and Eve used the sharp leaf tips of a yucca to sew fig leaves together to cover their nakedness after committing the first sin. *Yucca gloriosa* is larger, with no leaf filaments. *Yucca aloifolia* has dark green, sharp-tipped leaves and reaches 10' tall.

LANCELEAF ARROWHEAD
Sagittaria lancifolia L.
Water Plantain family (Alismataceae)

Description: The lanceolate leaves spread fanlike, with a leaf blade to 16" long and 4" wide, or leaf blades may be entirely absent. The flowers are in whorls of 3, each with 3 petals. The female flowers are uppermost on the spike.

Bloom Season: All year

Habitat/Range: Freshwater wetlands across most of Florida, with scattered populations in the panhandle

Comments: *Sagittaria* is Latin for "an arrow," relating to the leaf shape of some species. The name *lancifolia* is for the lance-shaped leaf blades of this common species. There are 9 native species in this genus in Florida, along with 1 subspecies and 2 varieties. The flowers are similar, but location, leaf shape, and flower size help narrow the choices. Duck potato is another common name and refers to the tubers being eaten by ducks after breaking away from the roots and floating to the surface. Another species in this genus with large flowers, *Sagittaria latifolia*, has wide, arrowhead-shaped leaves.

CROWPOISON
Nothoscordum bivalve (L.) Britton
Garlic family (Alliaceae)

Description: From 1–4 narrow, linear, grass-like leaves reach about 12" long and arise from rounded bulbs. The odorless flowers have 6 white tepals with a red or purplish midvein and measure ⅝"–⅞" across.

Bloom Season: March to December

Habitat/Range: Moist woods and disturbed sites across most of the panhandle south to Hernando, Marion, Orange, and Brevard Counties; also Lee County

Comments: *Nothoscordum* is Greek for "false garlic," referring to its resemblance to the culinary herb. The name *bivalve* relates to the 2 valves in the seedpods. The Cherokee extracted a poison from this plant to kill crows eating their crops. This genus was previously placed in the Lily family (Liliaceae) and also the Amaryllis family (Amaryllidaceae). Flower buds may not open on overcast days, and more plants bloom in spring than at any other time of year. False garlic is another common name.

COTTONWEED

Froelichia floridana (Nutt.) Moq.
Amaranth family (Amaranthaceae)

Description: Sparingly branched, pubescent stems of this species reach 4' tall, with opposite, narrowly elliptic to oblanceolate leaves along the lower stem reaching up to 4" long and ¾" wide. Terminal spikes of white, woolly flowers are 1½"–3" long.

Bloom Season: May to October

Habitat/Range: Sandhills, scrub, and disturbed sites across nearly all mainland Florida

Comments: *Froelichia* honors German botanist Joseph Aloys von Frölich (1766–1841). The name *floridana* refers to Florida, but the type specimen collected in 1818 by botanist Thomas Nuttall (1786–1859) was from Georgia. Nuttall named it *Oplotheca floridana*, but it was later moved to the genus *Froelichia* by French naturalist Christian Horace Bénédict Alfred Moquin-Tandon (1804–1863). This species is often seen in open sandy areas, including citrus groves and roadsides. Another common name is plains snakecotton.

JUBA BUSH

Iresine diffusa Humb. & Bonpl. ex Willd.
Amaranth family (Amaranthaceae)

Description: The smooth stems are much-branched, with opposite, ovate to lanceolate leaves measuring ⅝"–4½" long and ⅜"–2" wide. The stems and leaves are sometimes red. Tiny flowers are in an airy, diffusely branched panicle.

Bloom Season: All year

Habitat/Range: Dry disturbed sites and coastal strand in Jackson, Liberty, and Leon Counties south through most of the peninsula into the Florida Keys

Comments: *Iresine* relates to the long, cottony hairs encircling the calyx. The name *diffusa* alludes to the diffuse branching habit. Juba is a mesmerizing step dance performed by Afro-Caribbean slaves and a name given to this plant in the West Indies because the inflorescence dances in the wind. Another name is bloodleaf. It is sold in tropical American markets for medicinal use in treating coughs, colds, and colic. The species is a larval host plant for the Hayhurst's scallopwing butterfly.

STRING-LILY
Crinum americanum L.
Amaryllis family (Amaryllidaceae)

Description: The succulent strap-like leaves of this amaryllis emerge from a deep-rooted bulb and average 1'–2' long and 1"–2" wide, becoming flat near the tip. The showy, fragrant flowers have radially symmetrical sepals and petals that measure 2½"–5½" long and ½"–⅝" wide.

Bloom Season: All year

Habitat/Range: Freshwater wetlands through much of mainland Florida, but mostly in the central and southern peninsula

Comments: *Crinum* is a Greek name for "lily." The name *americanum* means "of America." This species is called seven sisters in parts of its range because it was believed that the flower clusters resemble the Pleiades, a star cluster said to represent the 7 daughters of Atlas and Pleione. Sphinx moths dust their wings with pollen while sipping nectar and are effective pollinators. The entire plant may be eaten to the ground by the voracious feeding of the flightless lubber grasshopper.

FLORIDA PANHANDLE SPIDERLILY
Hymenocallis choctawensis Traub
Amaryllis family (Amaryllidaceae)

Description: The dark green, deciduous, strap-shaped leaves measure 14"–24" long and 1"–2" wide, arising from a rhizomatous underground bulb. From 1–8 highly fragrant flowers, with a yellowish central eye and 4"–5" tepals, open sequentially over a period of weeks.

Bloom Season: May to August

Habitat/Range: Floodplain forests, swamps, and riverbanks from Escambia County east through Franklin, Liberty, and Gadsden Counties

Comments: *Hymenocallis* means "beautiful membrane" and relates to the hymen-like membrane between the stamens. The name *choctawensis* relates to the Choctaw tribe of Native Americans originally from the southeastern United States (Louisiana, Mississippi, Alabama, and Florida). The range of this spiderlily encompasses southwest Georgia, the Florida panhandle, and across southern Alabama, Mississippi, and Louisiana.

BEACH SPIDERLILY

Hymenocallis latifolia (Mill.) M. Roem.
Amaryllis family (Amaryllidaceae)

Description: The long strap-shaped leaves reach 30"–36" long and 2½"–4" wide, arising from a fleshy underground bulb. The flowers are in terminal clusters atop a fleshy stalk to 48" tall or more. The sepals and petals (tepals) are lax, with the petals slightly wider than the sepals. The anthers are red-orange.

Bloom Season: June to October

Habitat/Range: Beach dunes and mangrove forests from Pinellas, Hillsborough, and Volusia Counties discontinuously south along both coasts into the Florida Keys; also on dunes of Franklin County in the Florida panhandle

Comments: The name *latifolia* means "wide leaves." This species is conspicuous among the vegetation that shares its habitat along beach dunes. Swarms of lubber grasshoppers can eat the leaves down to the ground. This is the largest member of the genus in Florida and is sometimes planted in urban landscapes.

ALLIGATORLILY

Hymenocallis palmeri S. Watson
Amaryllis family (Amaryllidaceae)

Description: This species has deciduous, strap-shaped leaves 6"–16" long and up to ½" wide. The fragrant, solitary flowers have 3 widely spreading, linear petals and 3 petal-like sepals measuring 2"–3" long that spread beneath a thin, cuplike membrane connecting the stamen filaments.

Bloom Season: May to October

Habitat/Range: Endemic to freshwater marshes and wet prairies of Bradford and Duval Counties and from Brevard County across to Pinellas County south throughout the peninsula

Comments: The name *palmeri* honors botanist Edward Palmer (1829–1911). Sphinx moths are effective pollinators and receive pollen on their wings as they probe their proboscis down the nectar tube. The pollen is then transferred to the next flower the moth visits. This species is easiest seen flowering in the months following spring fires, when there is little competing vegetation.

PUNTA GORDA SPIDERLILY

Hymenocallis puntagordensis Traub
Amaryllis family (Amaryllidaceae)

Description: The leathery leaves measure 10"–27" long and ¾"–1¼" wide. A fleshy 10"–14" scape bears 3–5 fragrant flowers that open sequentially (up to 3 at a time), with narrow sepals and petals and a small, membranous central cup.

Bloom Season: August to September

Habitat/Range: Endemic to margins of roadside ditches and disturbed pine flatwoods of Charlotte County

Comments: The name *puntagordensis* relates to the city of Punta Gorda in Charlotte County, where it was first collected and later described in 1962 by botanist Hamilton Paul Traub (1890–1983). In 2012 University of Florida botanist Daniel B. Ward (1933–2016) attempted to rename it *Hymenocallis latifolia* var. *puntagordensis*, but that opinion was not widely accepted. This species is on the brink of extinction and deserves further taxonomic review for state and federal protection.

TREAT'S ZEPHYRLILY

Zephyranthes atamasca (L.) Herb. var. *treatiae* (S. Watson) Meerow
Amaryllis family (Amaryllidaceae)

Description: The glossy leaves reach ³⁄₁₆" wide with erect, white or pinkish flowers that measure 1½"–2½" tall. The stigma exceeds the anthers.

Bloom Season: January to May

Habitat/Range: Wet flatwoods and meadows from Jefferson, Taylor, and Dixie Counties over to Nassau County discontinuously south to Manatee, Hardee, Highlands, Osceola, and Volusia Counties

Comments: Zephyrus is the Greek god of the west wind, so *Zephyranthes* translates to "west wind flower," alluding to the winds that bring spring rains and flowers. The name *atamasca* is thought to be derived from the Virginia Algonquian word *ätamäsku*, or "under grass," relating to the underground bulbs. The name *treatiae* honors Mary Lua Adella Davis Treat (1830–1923), who corresponded with Charles Darwin. It is a state-listed threatened species.

SIMPSON'S ZEPHYRLILY

Zephyranthes simpsonii Chapm.
Amaryllis family (Amaryllidaceae)

Description: The leaves of this species average 12"–20" long and ⅟₁₆"–⅛" wide. The funnel-shaped flowers are white or pink-tinged with pink stripes on the back of the sepals. The stigma is shorter than or equal to the anthers.

Bloom Season: Mostly April to May

Habitat/Range: Wet flatwoods from Levy, Marion, and Volusia Counties south to Collier and Palm Beach Counties

Comments: The name *simpsonii* honors Illinois botanist Joseph Herman Simpson (1841–1918), who collected plants in Florida. Its range overlaps in Central Florida with the previous species, but the very narrow leaves and a stigma that is shorter than or equal to the anthers are diagnostic. It is a state-listed threatened species principally due to habitat loss and fire suppression. There is hardly a prettier sight than a field of native zephyrlilies blooming after a fire.

BETHANY PAWPAW

Asimina x *bethanyensis* DeLaney
Custard-Apple family (Annonaceae)

Description: This shrubby hybrid is intermediate in appearance between its parents, *Asimina manasota* and *A. reticulata*, but it more closely resembles *A. manasota*. Leaves are slightly curved and average 3"–5" long and ½"–⅝" wide. Showy flowers with a somewhat fetid odor appear on the growth of the current season and measure 2"–2½" wide.

Bloom Season: March to April

Habitat/Range: Endemic to longleaf pine and turkey oak sandhills of Manatee County, including pasturelands on former sandhills wherever both parents occur

Comments: *Asimina* is taken from *assimin,* a Native American word for pawpaw. The name *bethanyensis* refers to the Bethany Church region near Myakka City (Manatee County), where this endemic hybrid was first discovered by botanist Kris DeLaney (1951–). *Asimina manasota* is critically imperiled; if it becomes extinct, so will this endemic hybrid.

259

FLAG PAWPAW
Asimina obovata (Willd.) Nash
Custard-Apple family (Annonaceae)

Description: This shrubby species reaches 6' tall or more and has an open branching habit. It has conspicuous red hairs on new shoots, petioles, and the veins on the undersides of the leaves. Leaves are obovate to oblanceolate and measure 1½"–5" long and 1"–2" wide. The flowers, with obovate petals that measure 2"–3" long and 1¼"–1¾" wide, have a lemon fragrance.

Bloom Season: March to May

Habitat/Range: Endemic to sand ridges and scrub from Levy, Alachua, Clay, and Flagler Counties south to Hillsborough, Polk, Glades, and St. Lucie Counties

Comments: The name *obovata* describes the obovate (inversely egg-shaped) leaves and petals of the flowers. This is a frequent and conspicuous resident of sandhills and scrub, and the snow-white flowers can easily be seen from roadways that bisect its habitat. The sweet, banana-like fruits reach 3" long and are a favorite of Florida black bears.

PYGMY PAWPAW
Asimina pygmea (W. Bartram) Dunal
Custard-Apple family (Annonaceae)

Description: This sparingly branched shrub has reddish brown stems with red, appressed hairs and reaches about 12" tall. Leaves are obovate to lanceolate, often ascending, and average 2"–4" long. The fetid flowers are about ½" long, with white to maroon outer petals and deep maroon inner petals.

Bloom Season: March to November

Habitat/Range: Sandhills and pinelands from Madison and Taylor Counties east to Nassau County and south through Manatee, Polk, Osceola, and Brevard Counties

Comments: The name *pygmea* relates to the plant and flowers being dwarf in size. Another name is dwarf pawpaw. The species was first collected and named *Annona pygmea* in 1791 by famed American naturalist William Bartram (1739–1823), who was called *puc puggee* ("flower hunter") by Ahaya the Cowkeeper, chief of the Alachua tribe of the Seminole. Botanist Michel Felix Dunal (1789–1856) moved it to *Asimina* in 1817.

NETTED PAWPAW

Asimina reticulata Shuttlew. ex Chapm.
Custard-Apple family (Annonaceae)

Description: This 1'–4' shrubby species has oblong, fleshy leaves that average 1½"–4" long and 1" wide, with netted venation and orange hairs. The outer petals are creamy white, sometimes with pale brown lines, and measure about 1½" long and 1" wide. The 1½"–1¾" cylindrical fruits are yellowish green.

Bloom Season: January to May

Habitat/Range: Flatwoods from Levy, Bradford, and Flagler Counties south to Collier and Miami-Dade Counties; also Hamilton County

Comments: The name *reticulata* means "netted" and alludes to the leaf veins. The local name dog-banana relates to the resemblance of the fruits to a dog's scrotum, and the species was once placed in the genus *Orchidocarpum,* or "testicle fruit." The larvae of the pawpaw sphinx moth and the zebra swallowtail butterfly feed on the leaves, and the plant is sometimes cultivated to attract the swallowtails to urban gardens.

LAKE JACKSON PAWPAW

Asimina spatulata (Kral) D.B. Ward
Custard-Apple family (Annonaceae)

Description: The stems may reach 4' tall, with narrow, leathery leaves up to 8" long and ¼"–½" wide, or spatulate leaves to 2" long and ¾" wide. The axillary flowers are solitary on the current new growth. The edible, oblong fruits ripen yellowish green.

Bloom Season: April to November

Habitat/Range: Sandhills, flatwoods, and scrub in the Florida panhandle from Okaloosa County east to Hamilton, Suwannee, Lafayette, and Dixie Counties

Comments: The name *spatulata* refers to the spatulate leaves. Some people develop a rash from contact with pawpaw fruits, so handle them with care. This species is similar to *Asimina angustifolia*, which occurs east of the Suwannee River. The common name relates to Lake Jackson (Leon County), where the type specimen was collected in 1957 by Alabama botanist Robert Kral (1926–). A hybrid called *Asimina* x *kralii* honors Kral.

ROYAL FALSE PAWPAW
Deeringothamnus pulchellus Small
Custard-Apple family (Annonaceae)

Description: This unusual plant reaches 8"–12" tall, with arching stems emerging from a very large taproot. The leathery, oblong leaves are 1"–2½" long and ½"–¾" wide. Fragrant, creamy white to pinkish axillary flowers are solitary, with 6–10 petals measuring ½"–1" long.

Bloom Season: March to May

Habitat/Range: Endemic to flatwoods with moist sandy soils in Charlotte, Lee, and Orange Counties

Comments: *Deeringothamnus* translates to "Deering's little shrub" and was named in 1924 by botanist John Kunkel Small (1869–1938) to honor his philanthropist friend, Charles Deering (1852–1927), whose father founded International Harvester. Deering funded many of Small's botanical expeditions in Florida. In return, Small collected orchids, cactus, and other plants for Deering's 212-acre estate in Buena Vista, Florida, and later his 444-acre estate along Biscayne Bay south of Miami. The name *pulchellus* means "beautiful." The blossoms emit a sweet jasmine-like odor, and the plant is triggered into bloom by fire. It sometimes hybridizes with members of the genus *Asimina,* the pawpaws. Some botanists regard this species as a variety of *Asimina rugelii* (var. *pulchellus*). Another name is white squirrel-banana, for the fruits that are said to resemble the testicles of a squirrel.

COASTAL PLAIN ANGELICA

Angelica dentata (Chapm. ex Torr. & A. Gray)
J.M. Coult. & Rose
Carrot family (Apiaceae)

Description: Smooth, erect stems reach 24"–36"
tall, with leaves on long petioles. Each leaf is
divided into several lanceolate, coarsely-toothed
leaflets. Showy umbels are composed of up to a
dozen smaller clusters of tiny flowers.

Bloom Season: April to December

Habitat/Range: Sandhills and pine flatwoods
from Bay, Calhoun, and Jackson Counties east to
Franklin, Wakulla, and Leon Counties

Comments: *Angelica* is Latin for "angel" and
alludes to the healing properties of members
of the genus. The name *dentata* refers to the
outward-pointing (dentate) teeth on the leaflet
margins. This species is only known from Florida's
central panhandle and 4 small populations in Georgia. It is pollinated by bees and wasps and serves
as larval food for the black swallowtail butterfly.
One other species (*Angelica venenosa*) occurs in
four panhandle counties.

SPOTTED WATER HEMLOCK

Cicuta maculata L.
Carrot family (Apiaceae)

Description: This species reaches 6' tall, with hollow, herbaceous stems often mottled with purple.
The pinnately compound, alternate leaves measure
6"–10" long and 2"–6" wide, with opposite, lanceolate, toothed leaflets. Flowers are ⅛" wide in
umbels to 6" across.

Bloom Season: May to October

Habitat/Range: Freshwater habitats throughout
much of Florida but centered in the central and
north-central counties

Comments: *Cicuta* is Latin for poison hemlock
(*Conium maculatum*), which was used to execute
Greek philosopher Socrates (ca. 470–399 BC)
after he was charged by the government with
lack of religious respect and corruption of youth.
The name *maculata* means "spotted," referring to
the mottled stems. The plant contains powerful
neurotoxins and can be fatal even in small doses if
eaten. Despite its toxins, it is a favored larval host
plant of the black swallowtail butterfly.

SCRUB ERYNGO
Eryngium cuneifolium Small
Carrot family (Apiaceae)

Description: Flowering stems reach 12"–30" tall and branch near the top. The basal leaves have 3–5 coarse teeth at the tips of the wedge-shaped, reticulate-veined leaf blades. Small, cylindrical white flowers with powder blue anthers are in ⅜" heads subtended by bristly bracts.

Bloom Season: August to November

Habitat/Range: Endemic to white-sand scrub on the Lake Wales Ridge in Highlands County

Comments: *Eryngium* is from *eryngion,* the Greek name for *Eryngium campestre.* The name *cuneifolium* refers to the wedge-shaped leaves. This federal endangered species is restricted to a 24-mile strip of the Lake Wales Ridge between Sebring and the Archbold Biological Station in Lake Placid, where it can be locally abundant in fire lanes that bisect its habitat. Botanists John Kunkel Small (1869–1938) and Charles A. Mosier (1871–1936) first discovered it in 1927.

BUTTON ERYNGO
Eryngium yuccifolium Michx.
Carrot family (Apiaceae)

Description: This species has weak bristles on the margins of its narrowly linear leaves. The leaves are 6"–24" long and ½"–1" wide, becoming smaller up the flowering stem. Flower heads are on branched stalks that may reach 5' tall. The globose, ¾" heads of flowers have bracts that are bristly to the touch.

Bloom Season: May to September

Habitat/Range: Pinelands, prairies, and flatwoods throughout mainland Florida

Comments: The name *yuccifolium* relates to the leaves, which very much resemble those of a *Yucca* (Agavaceae). A concoction prepared from the roots of this species became the ceremonial "black drink" of the Seminole tribe in southern Florida, which replaced their emetic black drink made from *Ilex vomitoria* after they fled to the Everglades region in the 1800s during the Seminole Wars. This change was due to *Ilex vomitoria* not being indigenous to South Florida.

WATER DROPWORT

Tiedemannia filiformis (Walter) Feist &
S.R. Downie
(Also *Oxypolis filiformis* [Walter] Britton)
Carrot family (Apiaceae)

Description: This herbaceous species reaches
12"–36" tall, with succulent stems and alternate,
very narrowly linear leaves. The ³⁄₁₆" flowers are in
compound umbels, like an umbrella.

Bloom Season: All year

Habitat/Range: Freshwater wetlands and roadside
ditches throughout mainland Florida

Comments: *Tiedemannia* honors German professor
of anatomy and physiology Friedrich Tiedemann
(1781–1861). The name *filiformis* is for the
threadlike (filiform) leaves. Another name is water
cowbane, but there is no evidence the species
is toxic to cattle. It was moved from the genus
Oxypolis to *Tiedemannia* in 2012. A related species, *Ptilimnium capillaceum*, is much smaller, with
tiny flowers. Many members of this family serve
as larval host plants for the black swallowtail, a
butterfly that is common throughout Florida.

FLORIDA MILKWEED

Asclepias feayi Chapm. ex A. Gray
Dogbane family (Apocynaceae)

Description: This species dies back in winter,
resprouting in spring with stems 8"–20" tall and
narrowly linear, opposite leaves 2"–3" long. The
starlike flowers measure about ⁵⁄₈" wide.

Bloom Season: March to August

Habitat/Range: Endemic to sandhills and scrubby
flatwoods in Clay County and from Pasco, Lake,
Orange, and Brevard Counties south to Collier,
Glades, and Indian River Counties

Comments: *Asclepias* was named for Aesculapius,
Greek god of medicine, who was killed by Zeus
with a lightning bolt. The symbol for Aesculapius,
a snake twined around a shaft, is still used today
as a symbol of medicine. The name *feayi* honors
physician and botanist William T. Féay (1803–
1879). The species is also called Feay's milkweed
and can be found growing in open, sandy areas in
association with wiregrass (*Aristida stricta*). It was
first described in 1877.

SANDHILL MILKWEED
Asclepias humistrata Walter
Dogbane family (Apocynaceae)

Description: The stems of this milkweed may ascend to 18" tall, with pink-veined, opposite leaves that reach 5"–7" long and 3"–4" wide. Flowers are in umbels with white hoods and tan to pinkish, reflexed sepals. The 3"–5" pods are typically paired and stand erect.

Bloom Season: February to August

Habitat/Range: Pinelands, sandhills, scrub, and pasturelands south in Florida to Manatee, Highlands, Osceola, and Volusia Counties

Comments: The name *humistrata* relates to the sprawling growth habit. This colorful and attractive species is commonly seen in pastures because the plant is distasteful and toxic to livestock. White sap exudes from broken stems and leaves. It is sometimes cultivated within its native range as a larval host plant to attract monarch and queen butterflies but requires full sun and well-drained, sandy soil to succeed. Another common name is pinewoods milkweed.

LONGLEAF MILKWEED
Asclepias longifolia Michx.
Dogbane family (Apocynaceae)

Description: The long, narrow leaves of this species may reach 6" long and ⅛"–⅜" wide. The leaves have small hairs on the veins of the lower surface and scattered hairs on the upper surface. All parts exude milky sap if broken. The corolla lobes are pinkish purple with white bases and are strongly reflexed.

Bloom Season: February to September

Habitat/Range: Wet soils of pinelands and prairies scattered through the panhandle and peninsula

Comments: The name *longifolia* means "long leaved." Monarch and queen butterfly larvae are specialized to feed on milkweeds despite the plants' chemical defenses. Birds that attempt to eat their larvae find them distasteful and even toxic. There are 21 native milkweeds in Florida; 2 are endemic to the state. This species is found in Florida's wet prairies but is difficult to see even in bloom. Although attractive, it is seldom cultivated by gardeners.

WHITE SWAMP MILKWEED

Asclepias perennis Walter
Dogbane family (Apocynaceae)

Description: This milkweed reaches 12"–24" tall, with narrowly elliptic, opposite leaves that measure 3"–5" long and ½"–1½" wide. The stem is purplish with white (or blushed pink) ⅛" flowers in axillary clusters that average 1¼"–2" across. Unopened buds have a prominent pink spot on the top center.

Bloom Season: May to September

Habitat/Range: Floodplains, marshes, and roadside ditches south in Florida to Sarasota, DeSoto, Osceola, and Volusia Counties

Comments: The name *perennis* means "perennial." The species prefers shady, wet habitats and requires moist soil for successful cultivation. Stems root wherever they touch the ground, forming clonal colonies. Rose milkweed (*Asclepias incarnata*) is also called swamp milkweed and shares the same habitat, but it has larger, pink flowers. A milkweed flower essence is used in India to incarnate the soul and help strengthen self-esteem.

RED-RING MILKWEED

Asclepias variegata L.
Dogbane family (Apocynaceae)

Description: The broadly oblong to ovate leaves are opposite, measuring 3"–4" long and 1"–1½" wide, with undulating margins. Many-flowered umbels are crowded with waxy, white or pink-tinged, sweetly fragrant flowers that typically have a pink, purple, or red ring around the center of the corolla. Broken stems and leaves produce milky sap.

Bloom Season: March to June

Habitat/Range: Mesic hammocks from Santa Rosa County east to Walton County and from Jackson and Calhoun Counties east to Hamilton County

Comments: The name *variegata* means "variegated" and refers to the 2 colors on the flowers. The leaves are also 2-toned, being dark green above and pale below. This species is often found in more shaded situations than other members of the genus. Its range extends from Ontario and New England to Illinois, Oklahoma, and Texas south into the Florida panhandle, where it is local.

FRAGRANT SWALLOWWORT
Cynanchum northropiae (Schltr.) Alain
Dogbane family (Apocynaceae)

Description: The stems of fragrant swallow-wort twine around stems of shrubs in dry coastal habitats. The opposite, oblong-lanceolate leaves are ⅝"–1½" long and ⅜"–½" wide. All parts exude milky sap when broken. The fragrant ⅜" flowers are in axillary clusters.

Bloom Season: All year

Habitat/Range: Coastal strand of Brevard, Indian River, and Miami-Dade Counties through the Florida Keys (Monroe County)

Comments: *Cynanchum* translates to "dog strangler" and alludes to species that are poisonous to dogs. The name *northropiae* honors American botany professor Alice Rich Northrop (1864–1922). She is best known for advocating access to nature for school children in New York City. The flowers of this species fill the air surrounding the plants with perfume. Easy places to see this species are along the nature trails at Long Key and Bahia Honda State Parks in the Florida Keys.

DEVIL'S-POTATO
Echites umbellata Jacq.
Dogbane family (Apocynaceae)

Description: The paired, opposite leaves of this twining vine are oblong-elliptic, measuring 1½"–4" long and 1"–2" wide and spaced far apart along the stem. The trumpet-shaped flowers are creamy white with 5 curved lobes and measure 1½"–2" wide. The cylindrical, 6"–8" seedpods extend outward from each other, like horns.

Bloom Season: All year

Habitat/Range: Pinelands from Brevard County south through the coastal counties to Monroe County (mainland and Keys)

Comments: *Echites* is Greek for "viper," alluding to the snakelike, twining stems and the species' toxic nature. The name *umbellata* refers to the umbels of flowers. The common name is fair warning to not eat the poisonous, tuberous root. This is a larval host plant of the stunning, day-flying, red-white-and-blue, faithful beauty moth. The larvae are scarlet with iridescent blue spots designed to warn birds of their toxicity.

BALDWIN'S MILKVINE

Matelea baldwyniana (Sweet) Woodson
Dogbane family (Apocynaceae)

Description: The broadly ovate leaf blades of this vining species measure 2½"–5½" long and are deeply cordate (heart-shaped) at the base. The often branched, axillary flowering stems are topped with clusters of 5-lobed, ½" flowers. The corona lobes are cut ⅔ of their length into 2 linear teeth. Dry, dehiscent fruits are covered with soft spines.

Bloom Season: April to August

Habitat/Range: Bluff forests of Jackson and Gadsden Counties in the upper central panhandle

Comments: *Matelea* was named by French botanist Jean Baptiste Christophore Fusée Aublet (1720–1778) and is believed to be a French Guiana aboriginal name for the species Aublet described. Despite the spelling of the name, *baldwyniana* commemorates American physician and botanist William Baldwin (1779–1819). This is a state-listed endangered species due to its limited range in Florida.

BLODGETT'S SWALLOWWORT

Metastelma blodgettii A. Gray
(Also *Cynanchum blodgettii* [A. Gray] Shinners)
Dogbane family (Apocynaceae)

Description: This petite vine twines through low vegetation and bears opposite, lanceolate leaves that measure about ½" long and ¼" wide and exude white sap when broken. The small, 5-lobed flowers are in clusters along the stem and measure about ¼" long.

Bloom Season: March to October

Habitat/Range: Pinelands of Collier and Miami-Dade Counties south through the Florida Keys (Monroe County)

Comments: *Metastelma* is Greek and refers to the parted corona. The name *blodgettii* honors botanist John Loomis Blodgett (1809–1853), regarded as the most important figure in southern Florida's early botanical history. This is a state-listed threatened species due to its limited Florida range. Noted American botanist and Harvard University professor Asa Gray (1810–1888) first described this species in 1877.

MANGROVE RUBBERVINE

Rhabdadenia biflora (Jacq.) Müll. Arg.
Dogbane family (Apocynaceae)

Description: This is a high-climbing, twining vine with flexible stems and opposite, oblong leaves 2"–4" long and ⅝"–1" wide, often with pink veins. The 5-lobed, trumpet-shaped flowers are about 1½" wide, usually in pairs, and sometimes blushed with pink.

Bloom Season: Mostly May to August

Habitat/Range: Mangrove forests and cypress swamps from Brevard and Sarasota Counties south along both coasts into the Florida Keys

Comments: *Rhabdadenia* means "wand gland" and alludes to the slender pods. The name *biflora* relates to the often paired flowers. This species was named *Echites biflorus* in 1760 by botanist Nikolaus Joseph von Jacquin (1727–1817) but was moved to the genus *Rhabdadenia* in 1860 by Johannes Müller Argoviensis (1828–1896). Many members of the dogbane family are poisonous to eat; symptoms include dizziness, nausea, heart failure, and death.

WHITE TWINEVINE

Sarcostemma clausum (Jacq.) Roem. & Schult.
Dogbane family (Apocynaceae)

Description: White twinevine forms entanglements of twining stems that reach 10' long or more. All parts exude milky sap when broken. The oblong to linear leaves are opposite and measure 1"–3" long and ⅜"–¾" wide. Fragrant, hairy, 5-lobed flowers measure ⅜" wide.

Bloom Season: June to January

Habitat/Range: Coastal strand, cypress swamps, and mangrove swamps from Hillsborough, Polk, Orange, Seminole, and Brevard Counties south through the Florida Keys

Comments: *Sarcostemma* refers to the stems that twine around one another like a wreath or garland. The name *clausum* means "closed" or "shut" and is thought to allude to the flower buds or seedpods. This and other milkweeds are larval host plants of soldier, monarch, and queen butterflies. The species was first described as *Asclepias clausa* in 1760 by European botanist Nikolaus Joseph von Jacquin (1727–1817).

SPOONFLOWER
Peltandra sagittifolia (Michx.) Morong
Arum family (Araceae)

Description: The arrow-shaped leaf blades of this aroid average 5"–10" long and 2"–4" wide, with pinkish to green mottled petioles. The spathe measures 1½"–3" tall to 1¼"–2" wide. The mature fruits are red.

Bloom Season: April to July

Habitat/Range: Acidic freshwater wetlands and roadside ditches from Escambia County east to Holmes, Washington, Calhoun, and Bay Counties and from Taylor, Columbia, and Nassau Counties discontinuously south to Hillsborough, Hardee, and Highlands Counties

Comments: *Peltandra* refers to "a shield" and "stamens," alluding to the shield (spathe) surrounding the spadix that bears the flowers. The name *sagittifolia* relates to the sagittate (arrow-shaped) leaf blades. The species is sometimes cultivated by aroid enthusiasts but requires reliably moist soil or to be grown in a water garden. An extinct species (*Peltandra complicata*) is known from fossil records in Florida.

GREEN ARROW ARUM
Peltandra virginica (L.) Schott
Arum family (Araceae)

Description: This wetland species has arrow-shaped leaf blades on long, fleshy petioles. The inflorescence is typical of the arum family, with a long, cylindrical spadix enveloped by a leaflike bract called a spathe. The spathe is green with white margins; the spadix is covered with minuscule white to yellowish flowers. The fruits are green to purplish.

Bloom Season: All year

Habitat/Range: Swamps, marshes, and roadside ditches throughout most of mainland Florida

Comments: The name *virginica* relates to Virginia, where this species was first collected. The name *arrow arum* is for the arrow-shaped (sagittate) leaf blades. The species was moved from the Linnaean genus *Arum* to the genus *Peltandra* in 1832 by Austrian botanist Heinrich Wilhelm Schott (1794–1865), who is best known for his comprehensive work with aroids. This genus is restricted to eastern North America.

MARSH PENNYWORT
Hydrocotyle umbellata L.
Aralia family (Araliaceae)

Description: The leaf petiole averages 1½"–2" tall and is topped by a circular, 1"–1½" wide leaf blade with scalloped margins. Flowers are in umbels with individual flowers measuring about ⅛" wide.

Bloom Season: All year

Habitat/Range: Freshwater wetlands and other wet habitats, including roadsides and canal banks, throughout Florida

Comments: *Hydrocotyle* means "water" and "a small cup," alluding to the cup-shaped leaves of the type species (*Hydrocotyle vulgaris*), which hold water. The name *umbellata* relates to the umbels of flowers. It is sometimes placed in the Carrot family (Apiaceae). This common species can form extensive, stoloniferous colonies, especially along wet roadsides, where the low-growing plants escape mowing. Of the 6 species in Florida, 2 are naturalized exotics. The common name pennywort is also used for *Centella asiatica*, as is coinwort.

HAMMOCK SNAKEROOT
Ageratina jucunda (Greene) Clewell & Wooten
Aster family (Asteraceae)

Description: This branching perennial herb is 1½'– 3' tall, with coarsely serrate, narrowly rhombic leaves that measure ¾"–1¼" long and ⅝"–1" wide. Flowers are in small heads averaging ⅜" wide.

Bloom Season: September to January

Habitat/Range: Sand pine scrub, wooded sand ridges, dunes, hammocks, and roadsides from Gadsden, Leon, and Wakulla Counties east and south through mainland Florida

Comments: *Ageratina* is a diminutive of the genus *Ageratum*. The name *jucunda* means "agreeable" or "pleasing" and alludes to the attractiveness of a flowering plant. The name snakeroot relates to the root's use by Native Americans to treat venomous snakebite, with doubtful success. Small butterflies visit the flowers, especially crescents, blues, hairstreaks, and skippers. Two other species (*Ageratina altissima* and *A. aromatica*) occur mostly in the panhandle.

SOUTHERN INDIAN PLANTAIN

Arnoglossum diversifolium (Torr. & A. Gray) H. Rob.
Aster family (Asteraceae)

Description: The slightly grooved and angled stems of this species range from 3' to 6' tall and are branched near the top. The toothed lower leaf blades are cordate to ovate and measure 3"–4" long, with smaller and more deeply toothed upper stem leaves. The ½" flower heads are surrounded by white, winged bracts (phyllaries). The flowers range from white to lavender.

Bloom Season: May to September

Habitat/Range: Openings in floodplain forests of Walton, Holmes, Washington, Jackson, Calhoun, Leon, Levy, and Putnam Counties

Comments: *Arnoglossum* translates to "lamb tongue" and is an ancient Greek name for plantain (*Plantago major*). The name *diversifolium* alludes to the diversely shaped leaves of this species. It also ranges into Georgia and Alabama. A state-listed threatened species in Florida, it occurs mostly in the panhandle.

FLORIDA INDIAN PLANTAIN

Arnoglossum floridanum (A. Gray) H. Rob
Aster family (Asteraceae)

Description: The 5-ribbed stems of this species reach 3' tall and are much branched near the top. The ovate to elliptic basal leaves typically have 5 main veins radiating from the base and range from 3"–7" long. The smaller, ovate stem (cauline) leaves have scalloped (crenulate) margins. Flowers are white to pale green and are surrounded by green, winged bracts (phyllaries).

Bloom Season: May to September

Habitat/Range: Endemic to sandhills from Taylor, Madison, Hamilton, Columbia, and Duval Counties south through Sarasota, Manatee, Highlands, Hardee, and St. Lucie Counties

Comments: The name *floridanum* relates to Florida. Another common name is Florida cacalia. There are 6 native members of this genus in Florida; this is one of 2 endemic species. Bees and butterflies visit the flowers. This genus was once included in the Plantain family (Plantaginaceae).

OVATELEAF INDIAN PLANTAIN
Arnoglossum ovatum (Walter) H. Rob.
Aster family (Asteraceae)

Description: The basal leaves are variable and range from ovate to narrowly lanceolate, reaching up to 10" long, with entire margins. Stem (cauline) leaves are smaller. The flowers are white to greenish, with white or purple-tinged involucral bracts (phyllaries).

Bloom Season: August to October

Habitat/Range: Wet pine flatwoods, savannas, bogs, and roadside ditches discontinuously throughout mainland Florida

Comments: The name *ovatum* relates to the ovate (egg-shaped) leaves. This highly variable species ranges across the southeastern United States from North Carolina to Texas and has the widest range of any other species in Florida. Butterflies visit the flowers regularly. The name Indian plantain relates to the plantain-shaped leaves of *Arnoglossum plantagineum* and the medicinal and culinary uses by indigenous peoples of North America.

GEORGIA INDIAN PLANTAIN
Arnoglossum sulcatum (Fernald) H. Rob.
Aster family (Asteraceae)

Description: The stems of this 2'–4' species are strongly grooved, with broadly ovate or elliptic leaf blades to 6" long on petioles up to 16" in length. The flowers are white to greenish, sometimes suffused with purple.

Bloom Season: August to November

Habitat/Range: Wet clearings, roadside ditches, and seepage slopes from Escambia County east to Bay, Liberty, and Leon Counties in the Florida panhandle

Comments: The name *sulcatum* means "furrowed" or "grooved" (sulcate) and relates to the stems. This attractive species ranges from Georgia and Alabama into the adjacent Florida panhandle. There are 8 species native to the United States; 6 are in Florida. The Cherokee powdered the leaves of a related species (*Arnoglossum atriplicifolium*) and sprinkled it as a condiment on food. The leaves were also used as a poultice to remove toxins from cuts.

SPANISH NEEDLES

Bidens alba (L.) DC.
Aster family (Asteraceae)

Description: This weedy species has finely toothed leaves that are mostly opposite along angled stems. The simple or pinnately 3- to 7-lobed leaves average 1"–2" long; the flower heads are about 1" wide. The dry, needlelike seeds (achenes) cling to fur and clothing.

Bloom Season: All year

Habitat/Range: Disturbed sites throughout Florida

Comments: *Bidens* is Latin for "two toothed," alluding to the 2 teeth on the achene. The name *alba* means "white," referring to the ray flowers. Bahamians use the plant as a tea for "cooling the blood," to "cure a sick stomach," and to rid children of worms. If applied to a small cut, the clear sap will stop the bleeding. The edible leaves are high in iron but taste resiny. Soaking them in water overnight helps make them more palatable. This weedy species is worth tolerating because butterflies favor the flowers, plus it is a larval host plant of the dainty sulphur butterfly.

PINELAND DAISY

Chaptalia tomentosa Vent.
Aster family (Asteraceae)

Description: The elliptic leaves of this species are green above, densely white tomentose below, and form a basal rosette of leaves averaging 2"–4" long and ¾"–1¼" wide. The 1" flower heads top a 4"–12" leafless stem. The flower heads close and nod at night, becoming open and erect by midday.

Bloom Season: November to May

Habitat/Range: Wet flatwoods through most of Florida south to Collier and Broward Counties

Comments: *Chaptalia* honors French chemist and statesman Jean-Antoine-Claude Chaptal (1756–1831), who developed the process of adding sugar to pressed grape juice to raise the alcohol content of wine. The name *tomentosa* refers to the densely woolly (tomentose) hairs on the under-sides of the leaves. French botanist André Michaux (1746–1802) introduced this species to France as a garden wildflower, and it is cultivated in the West Indies for use as a tea to invoke the Devil during séances.

FALSE DAISY

Eclipta prostrata (L.) L.
Aster family (Asteraceae)

Description: This open-branched, weedy, herbaceous species is typically less than 24" tall, with opposite, sessile, lanceolate, sparsely toothed, hairy leaves from 1½"–4" long and ⅜"–1" wide. The flower heads are ⅜" across.

Bloom Season: All year

Habitat/Range: Ruderal wet places, marshes, floodplain forests, and roadside ditches throughout Florida

Comments: *Eclipta* means "a failing" and alludes to the near absence of pappus on the achenes. The name *prostrata* relates to its prostrate growth habit. This species is native to the New World but has been introduced throughout the Old World, perhaps from seeds contaminating livestock feed. It is used medicinally as a liver tonic, to treat athlete's foot, and to help rejuvenate scalps to counteract baldness. It is also used to treat scorpion stings and venomous snakebite. A decoction of the plant is used as a blue-black hair dye and for tattoos.

OAKLEAF FLEABANE

Erigeron quercifolius Lam.
Aster family (Asteraceae)

Description: The lobed, hairy leaves range from 2"–7" long and ⅝"–1½" wide, forming a rosette with smaller leaves up the flowering stem. The ⅜"–½" flower heads are in open clusters at the top of branching stems. The ray flowers are narrowly linear and number 100 or more per head.

Bloom Season: All year

Habitat/Range: Pinelands, prairies, and disturbed sites throughout Florida

Comments: *Erigeron* is Greek for "woolly" and "old man," alluding to the woolly heads of some species. The name *quercifolius* relates to the similarity of the leaves to oaks in the genus *Quercus*. The ray florets can vary among populations from white to blue to pink. The common name fleabane relates to several plants used as a flea repellent by placing their leaves in bedding. This is one of Florida's most frequently encountered wildflowers and is often found growing along trailsides and unmowed road swales.

PRAIRIE FLEABANE
Erigeron strigosus Muhl. ex Willd.
Aster family (Asteraceae)

Description: This annual reaches 10"–24" tall, with ascending hairs on the stems. The spatulate to linear basal leaves reach 1"–6" long and up to ½" wide. The flower heads measure about ½" wide.

Bloom Season: April to November

Habitat/Range: Flatwoods, bogs, and wet roadsides across the panhandle south to Hillsborough, DeSoto, Highlands, and Osceola Counties

Comments: The name *strigosus* refers to the sharp, straight, appressed (strigose) hairs on the stem. The stems of the previous species are covered with long, soft, unmatted (villous) hairs. This species also has fewer and wider ray florets than oakleaf fleabane. German-American botanist Gotthilf Heinrich Ernst Muhlenberg (1753–1815) first described this species, but his initial description did not satisfy the rules for valid publication; botanist Carl Ludwig Willdenow (1765–1812) corrected it in 1803.

EARLY WHITETOP FLEABANE
Erigeron vernus (L.) Torr. & A. Gray
Aster family (Asteraceae)

Description: The oblanceolate or spatulate leaves of this species form ground-hugging rosettes that spread by underground rhizomes. The flower heads measure about ⅝" wide, with many narrow ray flowers and yellow disk flowers. The flowering stems reach 10"–20" tall and are branched near the top.

Bloom Season: March to August

Habitat/Range: Pine flatwoods, bogs, and savannas throughout mainland Florida

Comments: The name *vernus* refers to the vernal equinox and relates to the species' springtime flowering; the common name also relates to its early appearance in spring. This species can be abundant in the proper habitat. A common usage to repel bugs involved burning the plants so that insects will "waste away in smoke." The leaves of some members of this genus were used in bedding as a flea deterrent; others were used to treat snakebite. Small bees and butterflies visit the flowers.

MOHR'S THOROUGHWORT

Eupatorium mohrii Greene
Aster family (Asteraceae)

Description: The stems of this species arise from tuberous rhizomes and are densely branched near the top. Oblanceolate, sessile, 3-nerved leaves measure ¾"–3" long and ¼"–⅝" wide. Flower heads cover the top of the plant in flat-topped arrays.

Bloom Season: May to November

Habitat/Range: Flatwoods throughout mainland Florida

Comments: *Eupatorium* honors Mithridates Eupator (132–63 BC), King of Pontus (now northeastern Iran), who married his sister, Laodice, and received notoriety for using a member of this genus as a poison antidote. The name *mohrii* honors German botanist Charles Theodore Mohr (1824–1901), who immigrated to the United States in 1848 and authored *Plant Life in Alabama*, published the year he died. This butterfly-attracting species was described in 1901 by American botanist Edward Lee Greene (1843–1915). There are 17 *Eupatorium* species in Florida.

SPOONLEAVED BARBARA'S BUTTONS

Marshallia obovata (Walter) Beadle & F.E. Boynton
Aster family (Asteraceae)

Description: The mostly basal, obovate leaves range from 1"–3½" long and ½"–1" wide (widest toward the apex), each with 3 conspicuous veins. Leafless flower stalks stand 10"–24" tall and are topped by a single head of disk flowers that reaches 1" wide.

Bloom Season: April to June

Habitat/Range: Pinelands and sandhills of Jackson County in the central panhandle

Comments: *Marshallia* honors American botanist Moses Marshall (1758–1813), cousin of famed naturalist John Bartram (1699–1777). The name *obovata* relates to the obovate (spoon-shaped) leaves. This species ranges across the southeastern states but occurs in only 2 state preserves within Jackson County. One other species that ranges into Jackson County is *Marshallia graminifolia* (see the Pink Flowers section in this guide). *Marshallia ramosa* is similar but occurs only in Clay and Washington Counties.

SNOW SQUARESTEM

Melanthera nivea (L.) Small
Aster family (Asteraceae)

Description: This is a trailing plant, or bushy to 3'
or more, with square stems. The coarsely toothed
to entire, ¾"–1¼" leaves are arrow shaped, with
the basal lobes held at right angles to the midrib.
Spherical ⅝" flower clusters are on long stems.
The anthers are black.

Bloom Season: All year

Habitat/Range: Flatwoods, prairies, and edges
of forests from Walton County east and south
through mainland Florida and into the Florida Keys

Comments: *Melanthera* translates to "black
anther." The name *nivea* means "snow white,"
referring to the flower heads. Venezuelan hunters
rub the leaves on their face in the belief that doing
so will make them better marksmen. Spanish
names include *cabeza negra* (black head) and
clavel blanco (white carnation). Florida gardeners
sometimes cultivate this species because of its
ease of care and because the flowers attract a
wide variety of butterflies.

CLIMBING HEMPVINE

Mikania scandens (L.) Willd.
Aster family (Asteraceae)

Description: This twining vine has angled stems
and somewhat triangular, opposite leaves that are
irregularly and sharply lobed. The leaves average
¾"–1¼" long and equally wide, but may be larger
in shade. Cylindrical flower heads are in flat-
topped clusters composed of small, fragrant disk
flowers that reach ½" long.

Bloom Season: All year

Habitat/Range: Forest margins, pinelands, prairies, and coastal strand throughout Florida

Comments: *Mikania* honors Austrian-Czech
botanist and professor Joseph Gottfried Mikan
(1743–1814), who taught botany at the University
of Prague. The name *scandens* means "climbing"
and relates to its growth habit. Gardeners should
take special note of this vine because flowering
plants attract a riot of nectar-seeking butterflies;
plus it is a larval host plant of the little metalmark
butterfly and the scarlet-bodied wasp moth.

PINEBARREN WHITETOP ASTER
Oclemena reticulata (Pursh) G.L. Nesom
Aster family (Asteraceae)

Description: Stems of this leafy species typically reach 12"–18" tall, with nearly sessile, toothed or entire, elliptic-oblong to ovate-elliptic leaves from 1"–4" long and ⅜"–1¼" wide. Flower heads are about 1" wide.

Bloom Season: April to June

Habitat/Range: Wet flatwoods from Walton County discontinuously east and south to Lee, Glades, and Martin Counties

Comments: Botanist Edward Lee Greene (1842–1915) created the genus *Oclemena* in 1903 with unknown derivation. A New York steamship named *Oclemena* sank in the St. Lawrence River in 1897, just 6 years before this genus was named, so perhaps Greene meant to commemorate that ship for some reason. The name *reticulata* refers to the netlike leaf venation. The first Florida collection of this species was in 1874 along the Indian River in Brevard County by botanist Ed Palmer (1831–1911).

FEAY'S PALAFOX
Palafoxia feayi A. Gray
Aster family (Asteraceae)

Description: The leaf blades of this somewhat lanky, 4'–8' species are narrowly elliptic to ovate, with heads of white to pinkish, dark-anthered, tubular flowers terminating the stems. Each flower averages ½" long and ⅛" wide.

Bloom Season: August to November but sporadically all year

Habitat/Range: Endemic to sandhills and scrub from Marion, Lake, and Volusia Counties south through the mainland

Comments: *Palafoxia* honors Spanish patriot José Rebolledo de Palafox y Melci (1776–1847), duke of Saragossa, who fought against Napoleon's armies. This species was described in 1877 by American botanist Asa Gray (1810–1888), who named it to honor physician and botanist William T. Féay (1803–1879). The flowers of this tall, attractive species are visited by an array of butterflies and other insects. It prefers dry, sunny situations. See the Pink Flowers section for *Palafoxia integrifolia*.

STINKING CAMPHORWEED

Pluchea foetida (L.) DC.
Aster family (Asteraceae)

Description: The typically unbranched stems reach 12"–18" tall, with toothed, elliptic to ovate leaves measuring 1½"–4" long and ½"–1½" wide, clasping at the base and often canted upward along the stem. The leaves have an objectionable odor when crushed. Flower heads are in terminal clusters, each head measuring ¼" wide.

Bloom Season: May to October

Habitat/Range: Freshwater wetlands and ditches throughout mainland Florida south to Palm Beach and Collier Counties

Comments: *Pluchea* honors French abbot and naturalist Noël-Antoine Pluche (1688–1761), who believed that nature was created solely to admire. The name *foetida* refers to the fetid odor of the leaves when crushed. Carolus Linnaeus (1707–1778) described this species as *Baccharis foetida* in 1753, but Swiss botanist Augustin Pyramus de Candolle (1778–1841) moved it to the genus *Pluchea* in 1836. Bees and butterflies visit the flowers.

TENNESSEE LEAFCUP

Polymnia laevigata Beadle
Aster family (Asteraceae)

Description: The lower leaves of this species reach 6"–12" long and 4"–6" wide and are deeply and raggedly cut with pointed lobes, reducing in size up the stem with few or no lobes. The 3'–6' stems are glabrous (smooth). The flower heads are about ½" wide, subtended by a whorl of leafy bracts, and with 3-toothed ray florets and male disk florets.

Bloom Season: June to July

Habitat/Range: Damp, shaded woodlands of Jackson County in the Florida panhandle

Comments: *Polymnia* relates to the mythological Greek muse Polymnia, daughter of Zeus and Mnemosyne and the inspirational goddess of sacred music and dance. The name *laevigata* means "smooth," for the glabrous stems. The common name relates to where the type specimen was collected in 1897 (Franklin County, Tennessee) by botanist Chauncery Delos Beadle (1866–1950). It is a state-listed endangered species in Florida due to its limited range.

SNAKEROOT

Prenanthes serpentaria Pursh
(Also *Nabalas serpentarius* [Pursh] Hook.)
Aster family (Asteraceae)

Description: The stems of this species are usually about 2' tall but have been recorded to 6' in height. The lower leaves often have paired side lobes and are typically 2"–4" long and half as wide. The nodding flower heads measure about ⅝"–1¼" long and range from white to yellow (green basally) with scandent hairs.

Bloom Season: October to December

Habitat/Range: Deciduous woods across the panhandle east to Jefferson, Hamilton, Nassau, and Duval Counties

Comments: *Prenanthes* means "drooping flower." The name *serpentaria* relates to the plant's use as a cure for snakebite and as a snake repellent. William Byrd II (1674–1744), founder of Richmond, Virginia, wrote in 1728: "If you smear your hands with the juice of it, you may handle the viper safely." Quite a few native plants were touted as cures or treatments for venomous snakebites, but none have proved effective. It is also called cankerweed and lionsfoot.

RABBIT TOBACCO

Pterocaulon pycnostachyum (Michx.) Elliott
Aster family (Asteraceae)

Description: This species has woolly, winged stems that reach 8"–24" tall with alternate, often shallowly toothed, lanceolate leaves from 1½"–4" long. The leaves are green above, woolly white below, with a white midvein. Flowers are creamy white and densely packed in cone-shaped clusters along an erect or arching spike.

Bloom Season: All year

Habitat/Range: Flatwoods, pinelands, and disturbed sites throughout Florida

Comments: *Pterocaulon* means "winged stem," and *pycnostachyum* refers to the densely packed flowers on the spike. The plant's black, tuberous roots yield black sap and are poisonous to eat. Another common name is blackroot. The name rabbit tobacco means "wild tobacco" and has nothing to do with a bunny. The leaves have been smoked in the absence of tobacco and contain coumarin, used medicinally as an anticoagulant and in rat poison. Butterflies visit the flowers.

DIXIE ASTER

Sericocarpus tortifolius (Michx.) Nees
Aster family (Asteraceae)

Description: Plants reach 12"–48" tall, with hairy stems and leaves that wither by flowering time. The leaves are obovate and measure ⅜"–1½" long and ⅛"–⅜" wide and have hairy upper surfaces, often with the margins curled and the blades twisted upward. The flower heads are about ½" wide.

Bloom Season: May to October

Habitat/Range: Sandhills, flatwoods, and forest margins throughout most of mainland Florida

Comments: *Sericocarpus* means "silky fruit" and relates to the silky pubescence on the achene (a dry, 1-seeded fruit of the Asteraceae). The name *tortifolius* refers to the twisted or contorted leaves. Small butterflies, especially crescents, hairstreaks, and skippers, visit the flowers. Another name is whitetop aster. It is the only member of the genus in peninsular Florida, but *Sericocarpus asteroides* occurs from Escambia County to Walton County in the Florida panhandle. It is also called cankerweed and lionsfoot.

RICE BUTTON ASTER

Symphyotrichum dumosum (L.) G.L. Nesom
Aster family (Asteraceae)

Description: The narrowly linear to linear-lanceolate leaves are entire or slightly toothed and are typically ½"–1½" long and ⅛"–¼" wide, with winged, clasping petioles (or sessile). The ½"–¾" flower heads have white to lavender rays and yellow disks.

Bloom Season: All year

Habitat/Range: Pinelands and prairies throughout most of mainland Florida into the Florida Keys

Comments: *Symphyotrichum* is Greek for "junction" and "hair," perhaps alluding to the bristles on the European cultivar used to describe the genus. The name *dumosum* means "bushy." The plant spreads by rhizomes and is extremely variable, Some botanists have attempted to separate it into more than one species or with many varieties. It is a good candidate for cultivation by gardeners. Butterflies visit the flowers for nectar, and this is a larval host plant of the pearl crescent butterfly.

SMOOTH WHITE OLDFIELD ASTER
Symphyotrichum racemosum (Elliott) G.L. Nesom
Aster family (Asteraceae)

Description: The spatulate or oblanceolate leaves of this rhizomatous species are thin, often with curled margins, and measure up to 1½" long and ½" wide, usually with smaller leaves in the axils. The flower heads measure about ¾" wide, with clear, cream disk florets, becoming pink to reddish.

Bloom Season: August to October

Habitat/Range: Moist to wet soils in Okaloosa, Holmes, Jackson, Calhoun, Liberty, Gadsden, Leon, Nassau, and Alachua Counties

Comments: The name *racemosum* relates to the raceme of flowers. The species was first described as *Aster racemosus* by American legislator, banker, and botanist Stephen Elliott (1771–1830) of South Carolina but was relegated to the genus *Symphyotrichum* by botanist Guy L. Nesom (1945–) in 1995. This species is infrequently encountered but may form colonies connected by long, underground rhizomes.

SIMMONDS' ASTER
Symphyotrichum simmondsii (Small) G.L. Nesom
Aster family (Asteraceae)

Description: This colonial species bears numerous entire, narrowly linear stem leaves from 1"–2" long and ⅛" or less wide. The oblanceolate basal leaves and lower stem leaves are coarsely toothed and measure 4"–6" long and ½"–¾" wide. The flowers average 1" wide, with ray florets that may be white, pale violet, or lavender.

Bloom Season: October to January

Habitat/Range: Wet flatwoods and lake margins throughout most of mainland Florida

Comments: The name *simmondsii* honors Edward Simmonds (1866–1931), director of the Plant Introduction Field Station in Miami in the early part of the twentieth-century. The species was first collected in Florida in 1909 by botanists John Kunkel Small (1869–1938) and Joel Jackson Carter (1843–1912) in what is now Everglades National Park. Small named it *Aster simmondsii* in 1913; botanist Guy L. Nesom (1945–) moved it to *Symphyotrichum* in 1995.

WHITE CROWNBEARD

Verbesina virginica L.
(Also *Verbesina laciniata* [Poir.] Nutt.)
Aster family (Asteraceae)

Description: The stems are prominently winged and may reach 6' in height, with 6"–8" alternate, irregularly lobed leaves that are rough to the touch. The upper leaves are smaller. The ⅝"–¾" flower heads are in terminal, branching clusters.

Bloom Season: May to November

Habitat/Range: Forest margins, pinelands, and coastal strand discontinuously across the panhandle and northern Florida south throughout the peninsula

Comments: *Verbesina* is a modification of the genus *Verbena*. The name *virginica* means "of Virginia." This plant dies back in winter and resprouts vigorously in springtime. Another common name is frostweed, relating to its sprouting shortly after the last frost of winter. It deserves horticultural attention because the flowers are a popular nectar source for butterflies, especially hairstreaks and skippers.

MAYAPPLE

Podophyllum peltatum L.
Barberry family (Berberidaceae)

Description: This rhizomatous species has deeply lobed, peltate leaves that average 8"–10" across and produces flowering and non-flowering stems within a colony. The flowers are pendent, hidden by the leaves, and measure about 1¾" wide. Yellow fruits average 2" long and 1¼" wide.

Bloom Season: February to May

Habitat/Range: Calcareous woodlands of Jackson County

Comments: *Podophyllum* means "foot" and "leaf," referring to the leaf shape. The name *peltatum* refers to the peltate (shield-shaped) leaves. This state-listed endangered species is known in Florida only from Florida Caverns State Park in Jackson County. The ripe fruits are reportedly edible but all other parts of the plant are toxic. Extracts from the plant are used medicinally to treat testicular cancer and a form of lung cancer. The species ranges north into Canada and west to Iowa, Kansas, and Nebraska.

WILD COMFREY

Andersonglossum virginianum (L.) J.I. Cohen
(Also *Cynoglossum virginianum* L.)
Borage family (Boraginaceae)

Description: The basal leaves have long petioles and form a rosette when young, with leaf blades averaging 4"–6" long and half as wide. Stem leaves are smaller. Flowers are in loose cymes and measure about ⅜" wide.

Bloom Season: February to July

Habitat/Range: Deciduous woodlands of Jackson, Liberty, and Gadsden Counties

Comments: *Andersonglossum* honors University of Michigan botanist William Russell Anderson (1942–2013), and *glossum* relates to the segregation from *Cynoglossum*. The name *virginianum* means "of Virginia." DNA sequencing revealed that North American species of *Cynoglossum* are distinct from old-world species, so a new genus was published for new-world species in 2015. It is related to the culinary herb comfrey, but alkaloids in wild comfrey have caused tumors in laboratory rats, so eating it is not advised.

SCORPIONTAIL

Heliotropium angiospermum Murray
Borage family (Boraginaceae)

Description: The lanceolate leaves of this shrubby, 3'–4' species measure 1"–6" long and ½"–2" wide. The ⅛" flowers are in 2 ranks on spikes that curl under at the tips.

Bloom Season: All year

Habitat/Range: Coastal strand and shell mounds from Volusia, Pinellas, and Hillsborough Counties south along the coast and throughout southern Florida below Lake Okeechobee, including the Florida Keys

Comments: *Heliotropium* means "turning toward the sun" and refers to the directional growth of a plant in response to sunlight (heliotropism). The name *angiospermum* means "with enclosed seeds." Adult male butterflies take alkaloids from the flower nectar and turn them into pheromones. Although butterfly gardeners in Florida often grow this species, it will spread beyond its bounds from seed. Some species are not safe to eat—alkaloids in the leaves have been linked to cancer.

SEASIDE HELIOTROPE

Heliotropium curassavicum L.
Borage family (Boraginaceae)

Description: Prostrate or ascending stems spread outward from the base and are lined with bluish to grayish-green fleshy leaves from ½"–1½" long and ¼"–⅜" wide. Inflorescences are coiled, double rows of yellow- or purple-centered white, ³⁄₁₆" flowers.

Bloom Season: All year

Habitat/Range: Beach strand, tidal marshes, mangrove forests, and moist disturbed sites of Franklin County and from Levy, Putnam, and Volusia Counties south along both coasts into the Florida Keys (Monroe County)

Comments: The name *curassavicum* means "of Curaçao," a Dutch island nation in the West Indies. In the neotropics the plant is eaten in salads and as a potherb, dried as a tea substitute, and the ashes are used as a salt substitute, but some members of this family contain alkaloids that have a negative cumulative effect on body organs. Monarch and queen butterflies are highly attracted to the flowers.

COASTAL SEA ROCKET

Cakile lanceolata (Willd.) O.E. Schulz
Mustard family (Brassicaceae)

Description: This bushy seashore plant reaches 2' tall with cylindrical, corky pods. The fleshy, lanceolate leaves are usually coarsely toothed and average 2"–4" long and ⅜" wide. The flowers are about ⅜" wide, with 4 petals.

Bloom Season: All year

Habitat/Range: Beach dunes along Florida's coastlines, including the Florida Keys

Comments: *Cakile* is from an Arabic name, *qaqulleh*. The name *lanceolata* is for the lance-shaped leaves. The raw or boiled leaves and green pods are edible and are high in vitamin C. The plant is called pork bush in the Bahamas and is served with pork dishes. The name sea rocket relates to *rochette*, an Italian word for arugula, or garden rocket, commonly eaten in salads. Seedpods break in half; the upper half is taken away by tides, while seeds in the lower half germinate near the parent plant. This species is a larval host of the great southern white butterfly.

CUTLEAF TOOTHCUP
Cardamine concatenata (Michx.) O. Schwarz
Mustard family (Brassicaceae)

Description: This species reaches 10" tall, with persistent basal leaves and seasonal leaves on the fertile stems. Stem leaves are in whorls, each measuring up to 3" long and wide and palmately divided into 3–5 toothed lobes. White to pinkish, 4-petaled flowers are ½" wide.

Bloom Season: January to March

Habitat/Range: Mesic hardwood forests and floodplains of Jackson, Gadsden, and Liberty Counties in the Florida panhandle

Comments: *Cardamine* comes from *kardamon,* the Greek name for a type of cress (Brassicaceae). The name *concatenata* means "linking together" and alludes to the palmately-divided leaves. The species was relegated to the genus *Cardamine* in 1939 by German botanist Otto Schwarz (1900–1983). Bees and butterflies visit the flowers, and cabbage white butterflies use it for larval food. Now-extinct passenger pigeons once used the tubers as a food source.

PINELAND CATCHFLY
Polanisia tenuifolia Torr. & A. Gray
Mustard family (Brassicaceae)

Description: The narrowly linear, revolute leaves measure ½"–2" long and are covered with glandular hairs. The flowers measure about ⅜" wide, with white oblong petals and pale yellow reflexed sepals.

Bloom Season: March to September

Habitat/Range: Scrub, dry pinelands, and sandhills in Jackson and Liberty Counties and from Levy, Clay, and Brevard Counties discontinuously south to Collier and Miami-Dade Counties

Comments: *Polanisia* refers to the flowers' many unequal stamens. The name *tenuifolia* describes the slender leaves. The name catchfly relates to small insects, such as flies, that get stuck to the viscid secretions of the stems and leaves. This species is not insectivorous, but the insects offer nutrients for the plant when the leaves fall off with their deceased cargo and decompose beneath the plant. Some botanists place it in the Cleome family (Cleomaceae).

CARTER'S PINELANDCRESS
Warea carteri Small
Mustard family (Brassicaceae)

Description: This annual herb may reach 5' tall but is usually half that height. Spatulate or obovate leaves measure ⅜"–1¼" long and ⅛"–⅜" wide. White, ⅜" flowers bearing 4 inward-curving petals are in rounded clusters.

Bloom Season: All year

Habitat/Range: Endemic to sandhills and scrub of Highlands, Lake, and Polk Counties (historically in Brevard, Glades, and Miami-Dade Counties but presumed extirpated)

Comments: *Warea* honors botanist Nathaniel A. Ware (1789–1854), who became a member of the American Philosophical Society in 1823. The name *carteri* honors botanist Joel Jackson Carter (1843–1912), who often tagged along with noted botanist John Kunkel Small (1869–1938) on trips to Florida. Together they collected the type specimen of this species in Miami-Dade County in 1903. This federal endangered species is locally common along portions of the Lake Wales Ridge.

SOUTHERN BLUETHREAD
Burmannia capitata (J.F. Gmel.) Mart.
Burmannia family (Burmanniaceae)

Description: A frail, mostly leafless stem stands 2"–4" tall and is topped by a tight cluster of 3-ribbed, tubular, ¼" flowers that barely open at the apex. Basal leaves are minuscule.

Bloom Season: May to December

Habitat/Range: Wet flatwoods, bogs, and pond margins nearly throughout mainland Florida

Comments: Dutch botanist Johannes Burman (1797–1779) worked on his *Flora of Ceylon* with Carolus Linnaeus (1707–1778), who later honored Burman with the naming of the genus *Burmannia*. The name *capitata* is taken from "captitate," either for the flowers aggregated in a dense cluster or for the globular swelling at the apex of the flowers. The species was moved to the genus *Burmannia* from *Vogelia* in 1824 by German botanist Carl Friedrich Philipp von Martius (1794–1868). Blue-thread (*Burmannia biflora*) has tiny flowers with blue wings and is found through most of Florida.

ALLEGHENY SPURGE

Pachysandra procumbens Michx.
Boxwood family (Buxaceae)

Description: The mottled, ovate leaves of this rhizomatous species are coarsely toothed at the apex and measure 1½"–3" long and 1"–1½" wide. Female flowers are at the bottom of the inflorescence, with male flowers congested above. The flowers are often hidden in the leaf litter of the forest floor.

Bloom Season: February to April

Habitat/Range: In leaf mold and humus of moist woods in Jackson County in the Florida panhandle

Comments: *Pachysandra* refers to the thick stamens (filaments). The name *procumbens* relates to the species' trailing growth habit. This state-listed endangered species forms a shrubby ground cover in the shade of forests, spreading by rhizomes to create a dense carpet. It is typically leafless when flowering. It is popular as a shade-tolerant ground cover in the nursery trade within its native range, from North Carolina and Virginia to Texas.

BARBWIRE CACTUS

Acanthocereus tetragonus (L.) Hummelinck
Cactus family (Cactaceae)

Description: This vine-like cactus has long, 3- or 4-angled stems armed with regularly spaced clusters of sharp spines. It may have stems that reach 12' or more and measure 2"–3" wide. The nocturnal flowers are 4" wide and sweetly fragrant. The red, ovoid fruits measure 2" wide.

Bloom Season: May to August

Habitat/Range: Dry coastal hammocks from Lee and St. Lucie Counties south through the Florida Keys

Comments: *Acanthocereus* is descriptive of the stems being thorny and waxy. The name *tetragonus* relates to the plant's 4-angled stems, but they may be 3-angled. This threatened species forms impenetrable thickets in coastal forests and is seldom seen in flower, even by the most dedicated wildflower enthusiast, because it blooms at night among intolerable swarms of salt marsh mosquitoes. Endangered Key Largo woodrats sometimes eat the stems down to the central core.

WEST COAST PRICKLY-APPLE

Harrisia aboriginum Small ex Britton & Rose
Cactus family (Cactaceae)

Description: The ribbed, cylindrical stems of this cactus average 6'–10' long and are lined with clusters of sharp ¼"–⅜" spines. The nocturnal flowers measure 4" wide, with toothed margins at the tip of the inner petals. The round, 2" fruits are yellow.

Bloom Season: May to October

Habitat/Range: Endemic to coastal berms and shell mounds of Manatee, Sarasota, and Lee Counties

Comments: *Harrisia* honors Irish botanist William H. Harris (1860–1920). The name *aboriginum* relates to the plant's habit of growing on aboriginal shell mounds. This critically imperiled federal endangered cactus is vulnerable to hurricanes and rising sea levels. The best keys to telling it apart from the following species is its range on the west coast of Florida and the fruit color. It tends to prefer the shelly soils of aboriginal shell mounds and middens created by the now-extinct Calusa Indians.

INDIAN RIVER PRICKLY-APPLE

Harrisia fragrans Small ex Britton & Rose
Cactus family (Cactaceae)

Description: The ribbed stems of this cactus average 6'–16' long and are lined with clusters of sharp ½"–¾" spines. The nocturnal flowers measure 4" wide, with entire margins at the tip of the inner petals. The 2" globose fruits are red.

Bloom Season: May to October

Habitat/Range: Endemic to coastal habitats from Volusia County south to the Florida Keys

Comments: The name *fragrans* refers to the floral scent. Like the previous species, this critically imperiled federal endangered cactus is vulnerable to hurricanes and sea level rise. It can be found in scrubby coastal hammocks bordering salt marsh habitat, tidal rock barrens, and coastal shell mounds. The flowers open several hours after sunset and close long before sunrise, so it takes true dedication, or total insanity, to be in its habitat at night with dense swarms of salt marsh mosquitoes.

KEYS TREE CACTUS

Pilosocereus robinii (Lem.) Byles & G.D. Rowley
Cactus family (Cactaceae)

Description: This columnar cactus can reach 20'
or more in height. Its stems are typically 10-ribbed,
3"–4" in diameter, and armed with clusters of
sharp spines. The 2" flowers open at dusk and
close after dawn. The red fruits are 1¼"–2" wide.

Bloom Season: April to October

Habitat/Range: Rocky tropical hammocks of the
Florida Keys (Monroe County)

Comments: *Pilosocereus* means "with soft straight
spreading hairs" and "waxy." The name *robinii*
honors French biologist Charles-Philippe Robin
(1821–1885), who studied plants in Cuba. The
flowers of this federal endangered cactus fill
the night air with a funky garlic odor meant to
attract nocturnal beetles. The similar *Pilosocereus
polygonus* occurs as a single clonal population on
Key Largo in John Pennekamp Coral Reef State
Park. It was first discovered in 1992 by botanist
Joe O'Brien (1964–).

WHITE LOBELIA

Lobelia paludosa Nutt.
Bellflower family (Campanulaceae)

Description: This water-loving species produces
nearly leafless flowering stems to about 24" tall,
with narrowly lanceolate leaves tufted at the base.
The basal leaves measure 2"–6" long and ⅜"–½"
wide, with a white midrib. Flowers are about
½" wide and slightly longer, sometimes lightly
blushed with pale violet.

Bloom Season: March to September

Habitat/Range: Wet flatwoods from Washington
and Bay Counties east and south throughout the
Florida mainland

Comments: *Lobelia* honors Flemish herbalist Matthias de l'Obel (1538–1616). The name *paludosa*
means "marsh loving." This species was first
described by English botanist Thomas Nuttall
(1786–1859) in 1818. Look for white lobelia in
open, wet habitats, sometimes emerging from
standing water. It somewhat resembles white-
flowered forms of *Lobelia brevifolia* but has
shorter leaves and does not occur in peninsular
Florida.

FLORIDA NAILWORT
Paronychia discoveryi DeLaney
Pink family (Caryophyllaceae)

Description: This perennial forms spreading mats with mostly sessile, linear-oblanceolate, ¼"–⅜" leaves. Tiny white, 5-lobed flowers open in succession.

Bloom Season: May to November

Habitat/Range: Endemic to oak scrub and inland dunes in Brevard, Hardee, Lake, Orange, St. Johns, and Volusia Counties

Comments: *Paronychia* means "beside fingernail" and is the medical term for a painful bacterial infection surrounding a fingernail. Nailworts were used to treat this disease as well as a viral infection called whitlow. The name *discoveryi* is for the *Discovery* space shuttle and crew, inspired by the species' discovery in 1988 near the Kennedy Space Center in Brevard County. Botanist Kris DeLaney (1951–) thought it ironic that missiles were being sent into outer space to search for life on other planets and here was a new plant species within sight of the launch pads.

SAND SQUARES
Paronychia patula Shinners
Pink family (Caryophyllaceae)

Description: The tiny flowers of this species are arranged in an interesting geometric pattern atop spreading, diffusely branched stems. The linear-oblong to oblanceolate leaf blades average ¼"–⅜" long and are less than ⅛" wide.

Bloom Season: June to November

Habitat/Range: Sandhills and open fields across the panhandle south through the central and western peninsula to Hillsborough, Polk, and Highlands Counties

Comments: The name *patula* relates to the species' spreading growth habit. Geometric flower patterns are unique to this genus in Florida. It was named *Siphonychia diffusa* in 1860 but was renamed *Paronychia patula* in 1962 by botanist Lloyd Herbert Shinners (1981–1971). There are 8 members of this genus in Florida, and 2 of them are endemic to the state. Rugel's nailwort (*Paronychia rugelii*) is similar but has slightly larger flowers and a single, branched, ascendant stem.

GOPHER APPLE
Geobalanus oblongifolius Michx.
(Also *Licania michauxii* Prance)
Coco Plum family (Chrysobalanaceae)

Description: This species is typically only about 6"–8" tall, forming extensive rhizomatous colonies. The oblong leaves average 2"–3" long and ½"–1" wide. Terminal clusters of white to yellowish, ⅜" flowers produce oval, off-white, 1" fruits.

Bloom Season: March to August

Habitat/Range: Sandhills, scrubby flatwoods, and pinelands throughout Florida

Comments: *Geobalanus* means "earth acorn" and relates to the fruits being developed near the ground. The name *oblongifolius* refers to the oblong leaves. The common name relates to the edible fruits being produced at eye level to a gopher tortoise. Florida Atlantic University botany professor Daniel F. Austin (1944–2015) wrote that the fruits taste "like a new plastic shower curtain smells." Recent taxonomic revisions have relegated this species back to the genus *Geobalanus* from *Licania*.

HEAVENLY TRUMPETS
Calystegia sepium (L.) R. Br. ssp. *limnophila* (Greene) Brummitt
Morning-Glory family (Convolvulaceae)

Description: This twining vine bears broad or narrow, arrow-shaped, pubescent leaves ranging from 2"–4" long and ¾"–2" wide. White (rarely pink) funnel-shaped flowers measure 2"–3" wide, typically with thin green nectar guides leading into the throat. Each flower lasts only a single day.

Bloom Season: March to September

Habitat/Range: Freshwater marshes and wet disturbed sites throughout mainland Florida

Comments: *Calystegia* means "calyx cover" and refers to the diagnostic bracts that conceal the calyx. The name *sepium* means "growing in hedges," and *limnophila* translates to "swamp loving." *Calystegia catesbeiana* of Jackson County in the Florida panhandle has velvety leaves with flowers in the lower leaf axils. Attempts have been made to include this genus within the closely related genus *Convolvulus*.

SCALDWEED
Cuscuta gronovii Willd. ex Schult.
Morning-Glory family (Convolvulaceae)

Description: Dodders are parasitic on a wide variety of plants, including grasses, by producing haustoria that tap into the vascular system of the host. The flowers reach about ¼" wide, with rounded corolla lobes and orange, threadlike stems.

Bloom Season: July to November

Habitat/Range: Wet hammocks and flatwoods south in Florida to Brevard and Collier Counties

Comments: *Cuscuta* translates to "tangled wisp of hair." The name *gronovii* honors Swedish botanist Jan Frederik Gronovius (1686–1762). Dodder seedlings die quickly if they cannot make contact with a host plant, which they locate by detecting pheromones, and are even capable of determining the most desirable host. They are basically freeloaders that take nutrients from their host while producing nothing themselves. The name scaldweed alludes to the plant's use to treat burns from hot liquid.

CAROLINA PONYSFOOT
Dichondra carolinensis Michx.
Morning-Glory family (Convolvulaceae)

Description: Ponysfoot has a creeping growth habit and can form an extensive 1"–2" tall ground cover. The reniform (kidney-shaped) leaves average about 1" long and wide, with ½"–⅝" white to greenish-white flowers.

Bloom Season: December to May

Habitat/Range: Mesic hammocks, floodplain forests, and disturbed sites throughout mainland Florida

Comments: *Dichondra* translates to "double" and "grain of corn," referring to the 2 capsules. The name *carolinensis* means "of Carolina." This is a common lawn weed in the southeastern United States. It was first collected in South Carolina and described by French botanist and explorer André Michaux (1746–1802), who succumbed to a tropical fever in Madagascar the year before the name was published. A similar species, *Dichondra micrantha*, with smaller flowers is sporadically naturalized in Florida.

GRISEBACH'S DWARF MORNING-GLORY

Evolvulus grisebachii Peter
Morning-Glory family (Convolvulaceae)

Description: The ¼"–⅜" elliptic leaves of this spreading species are covered with long, shaggy hairs. The axillary flowers are about ⅜" wide and appear on stems that lie flat on the ground.

Bloom Season: All year

Habitat/Range: Pine rocklands of Big Pine Key in the lower Florida Keys (Monroe County)

Comments: *Evolvulus* means "lacking" and "twining," referring to the non-twining stems. The name *grisebachii* honors German botanist and phytogeographer August Heinrich Rudolf Grisebach (1814–1879), who authored his *Flora of the British West Indian Islands* in 1864. This species was first described by botanist Albert Peter (1853–1937) in 1891. The best place to see this state-listed endangered species is along rocky road swales that bisect pine rockland habitat in the National Key Deer Refuge on Big Pine Key. The lilliputian Key deer are a bonus.

SILVER DWARF MORNING-GLORY

Evolvulus sericeus Sw.
Morning-Glory family (Convolvulaceae)

Description: The thin stems of this small species are ascending or decumbent, reaching up to 12" long. Leaf blades are linear to oblong, from ½"–1" long, and pointed at both ends. Flowers are white (rarely bluish) and measure ⅜" wide.

Bloom Season: April to October

Habitat/Range: Pinelands, wet flatwoods, and roadsides sporadically across the panhandle and northern Florida, then from Levy, Alachua, and Flagler Counties south through the peninsula

Comments: The name *sericeus* means "silky" and refers to the silky hairs that cover the stems and leaves. Botanist Olof Swartz (1760–1818) first described this species in 1788 from plants collected in Jamaica. This species is used in Mexico to treat burns and was called *havay ak* ("leprosy vine") by the Mayans. There are about 100 species of *Evolvulus*, mostly found in the Americas. Some are popular garden subjects.

MOONFLOWER

Ipomoea alba L.
Morning-Glory family (Convolvulaceae)

Description: This twining vine may reach 20' or more in length and can cover the canopy of trees. The alternate, heart-shaped leaves are entire or with 3–5 lobes. The flowers reach 3"–4" across, with cream or greenish nectar guides radiating into the throat.

Bloom Season: All year

Habitat/Range: Coastal and inland forests through much of peninsular Florida and the Florida Keys

Comments: *Ipomoea* means "wormlike" and alludes to the twining habit of some species. The name *alba* means "white." The flowers open at night and emit a heady scent to attract sphinx moths as pollinators and close shortly after sunrise. The seeds of some species were used in Mexico to cause hallucinations for divination and prophecy. In a curious mix of native beliefs and Christianity, the seeds are ground by a virgin in a ritual that is accompanied by prayer and then consumed at night after more prayer.

BEACH MORNING-GLORY

Ipomoea imperati (Vahl) Griseb.
(Also *Ipomoea stolonifera* J.F. Gmel.)
Morning-Glory family (Convolvulaceae)

Description: The rounded, alternate leaves of this trailing vine reach about 2" long and may be violin-shaped, with 3–7 rounded lobes. The trumpet-shaped flowers reach about 2" wide and close by midday.

Bloom Season: April to December

Habitat/Range: Sandy beaches along both coasts of Florida

Comments: The name *imperati* honors Italian apothecary and naturalist Ferrante Imperato (1550–1625) who was among the first to correctly describe how fossils were formed. This vine is important as a dune stabilizer by trapping drifting sand. It seems to sense the high-tide line and will change its direction of growth back toward the dunes. It is used medicinally in Asia to treat jellyfish stings. Beach moonflower (*Ipomoea violacea*) has white flowers and also grows on Florida beaches, but lacks the yellow center.

MAN-OF-THE-EARTH

Ipomoea pandurata (L.) G. Mey.
Morning-Glory family (Convolvulaceae)

Description: The stems of this vine may reach 30' long, with fiddle-shaped (pandurate) or heart-shaped leaves that measure 4"–6" long and 2½"–3½" wide. The flowers average 3"–3¼" wide. Reddish-brown seeds have hairy margins.

Bloom Season: May to October

Habitat/Range: Woodlands of Florida south to St. Lucie, Highlands, and Lee Counties

Comments: The name *pandurata* means "fiddle-shaped" and describes the leaf shape on some plants. The common name relates to the large underground, tuberous root (to 30 pounds.), which is edible when cooked but bitter compared to the related sweet potato (*Ipomoea batatas*). The species was named *Convolvulus panduratus* in 1753 by Carolus Linnaeus (1707–1778) but moved into the genus *Ipomoea* in 1818 by German botanist Georg Friedrich Wilhelm Meyer (1782–1856). The flowers open before dawn and close in the afternoon except on overcast days.

PINELAND CLUSTERVINE

Jacquemontia curtissii Peter ex Hallier f.
Morning-Glory family (Convolvulaceae)

Description: This vining species has alternate, elliptic leaves that measure ½"–⅞" long and ¼"–⅜" wide. The flowers measure ⅝"–¾" wide and are white, pink, or blushed with violet. The outer sepals are rounded.

Bloom Season: All year

Habitat/Range: Endemic to pinelands in Martin, Hendry, Collier, Monroe (mainland), and Miami-Dade Counties

Comments: *Jacquemontia* honors botanist Victor Vincelas Jacquemont (1801–1832), who traveled to India in 1828 to collect plant and animal specimens but died of cholera in Bombay at the age of 31. German botanist Gustav Albert Peter (1853–1937 named this species to commemorate botanist Allan Hiram Curtiss (1845–1907). An easy place to see this state-listed threatened species is along the Long Pine Key Nature Trail or the Pineland Trail in Everglades National Park, where it twines around low vegetation.

HAVANA CLUSTERVINE

Jacquemontia havanensis (Jacq.) Urb.
Morning-Glory family (Convolvulaceae)

Description: This semi-woody twining vine has alternate, linear to elliptic-ovate leaves to ½" long and ⅜" wide. The flowers measure ⅝"–¾" wide and may be slightly blushed with pink. The outer sepals are pointed.

Bloom Season: All year

Habitat/Range: Rockland hammock margins and coastal berms of the Florida Keys

Comments: The name *havanensis* is for Havana, Cuba, near where this species was first collected and described as *Convolvulus havanensis* in 1767 by Dutch botanist Nikolaus Joseph Freiherr von Jacquin (1727–1817). This critically imperiled, state-listed endangered species is present in Florida only in Dagny Johnson Key Largo Hammocks Botanical State Park in the upper Florida Keys and Bahia Honda State Park in the lower Florida Keys. It also occurs in the neotropics and is the only white-flowered member of the genus in the Florida Keys.

BEACH CLUSTERVINE

Jacquemontia reclinata House ex Small
Morning-Glory family (Convolvulaceae)

Description: The stems spread across open sand or creep through other dune vegetation. The oval, alternate leaves are rounded with notched tips and measure ½"–1" long and ⅜"–½" wide. The ⅝"–¾" flowers are often pinkish at the base and have hairy outer sepals.

Bloom Season: All year

Habitat/Range: Endemic to beach dunes along the Atlantic coastline of Martin, Palm Beach, Broward, and Miami-Dade Counties

Comments: The name *reclinata* refers to the species' reclining habit. Beach clustervine is a federal endangered species, and efforts to augment existing populations, or reintroduce plants into protected areas where it has been extirpated, have been made through the endangered species program at Fairchild Tropical Botanic Garden in Coral Gables, Florida. It is threatened by sea level rise, coastal development, and hurricanes. The photo is from Key Biscayne.

SHOWY DAWNFLOWER
Stylisma abdita Myint
Morning-Glory family (Convolvulaceae)

Description: The relatively short stems trail along the ground, with alternate, narrow, conspicuously hairy leaves measuring ½"–1" long and ¼"–⅜" wide. The ½" flowers open at dawn.

Bloom Season: April to December

Habitat/Range: Endemic to scrub habitat from Clay County to Collier County

Comments: *Stylisma* is Greek for "pillar" and refers to the style (a structure in female flower parts). The name *abdita* means "concealed" and relates to this plant often being hidden by others. Showy dawnflower is a state-listed endangered species first collected in 1961 at Gold Head Branch State Park in Clay County and described in 1966 by University of Florida botanist Tin Myint (1936–).

COASTAL PLAIN DAWNFLOWER
Stylisma patens (Desr.) Myint
Morning-Glory family (Convolvulaceae)

Description: The stems of this species spread close to the ground in all directions from the rootstock, bearing narrowly linear leaves measuring about 1"–2" long and ⅛"–¼" wide. The flowers are ¾"–1" wide, opening at dawn and closing by midafternoon.

Bloom Season: April to October

Habitat/Range: Sandhills and scrub across the Florida panhandle, continuously east and south in the peninsula to Volusia, Orange, Osceola, Polk, Highlands, and Manatee Counties

Comments: The name *patens* means "spreading" and relates to the species' growth habit. French botanist Louis Auguste Joseph Desrousseaux (1753–1838) described this species in 1792 as *Convolvulus patens*. The flowers last a part of a day but are replaced by new flowers at dawn the next morning. Small bees, wasps, and ants visit the flowers, but bees appear to be the pollinators. This is the most widespread species of this genus in Florida.

HAIRY DAWNFLOWER

Stylisma villosa (Nash) House
Morning-Glory family (Convolvulaceae)

Description: The leaves of this trailing species
are oblong to elliptic, averaging about 1"–1½"
long and ½" wide or more. The flowers are very
similar to the previous species, so check leaf
characteristics.

Bloom Season: May to November

Habitat/Range: Sandhills and scrub, with discontinuous populations through mainland Florida

Comments: The name *villosa* refers to the long,
soft hairs on the leaves (villous). Botanist George
Valentine Nash (1864–1921) first described this
species as *Breweria villosa* in 1895, but it was
moved to the genus *Stylisma* in 1907 by botanist
Homer Doliver House (1878–1949). There are 5
members of this genus in Florida, including the
previous endemic species. Wasps and ants visit
the flowers, but bees appear to be the principal
pollinators. The related *Evolvulus sericeus* has
similar-looking but slightly smaller flowers.

STARRUSH WHITETOP

Rhynchospora colorata (L.) H. Pfeiff.
Sedge family (Cyperaceae)

Description: This species forms rhizomatous colonies with spreading to erect, very narrowly linear
leaves. Inflorescences are solitary, with leafy
bracts that are white at the base, green apically,
and typically held horizontally.

Bloom Season: All year

Habitat/Range: Wet flatwoods, prairies, and moist
roadsides throughout peninsular Florida, with scattered populations across the panhandle

Comments: *Rhynchospora* is Greek for "snout
seed." The name *colorata* refers to the colored
floral bracts. Botanist Hans Heinrich Pfeiffer (b.
1890) moved this species to the genus *Rhynchospora* in 1935. It is very similar to Florida whitetop
(*Rhynchospora floridensis*) of Highlands, Collier,
Miami-Dade, and Monroe Counties, which differs
principally by forming non-rhizomatous tufts. There
are 53 other members of this genus in Florida
called beaksedges.

SANDSWAMP WHITETOP
Rhynchospora latifolia (Baldwin) W.W. Thomas
Sedge family (Cyperaceae)

Description: Flowering plants may reach about 30" tall, with linear leaves that measure about ¼" wide. The flowering stems overtop the leaves and are terminated by showy, green-tipped, white floral bracts surrounding clusters of inconspicuous flowers. The bracts are typically drooping.

Bloom Season: March to December

Habitat/Range: Wet flatwoods through the panhandle to Jefferson County and from Columbia, Baker, and Nassau Counties south through the peninsula

Comments: The name *latifolia* refers to the broad leaves of this species compared to others. This species was moved to the genus *Rhynchospora* from *Dichromena* in 1984 by botanist William Wayt Thomas (1951–). Most members of this family are pollinated by wind, but whitetops are insect pollinated and use their showy floral bracts to draw the attention of insects to the tiny flowers.

WATER SUNDEW
Drosera intermedia Hayne
Sundew family (Droseraceae)

Description: Typical of the genus, the spoon-shaped leaf blades of this carnivorous species are covered with gland-tipped hairs that entrap and digest small insects. The petioles are long, and the short-lived ¼" flowers are in a single rank up a naked stem to 4" tall. Plants may form floating rafts.

Bloom Season: April to September

Habitat/Range: Bogs, lakeshores, pond margins, and flooded roadside ditches across the panhandle south to Pasco, Polk, Osceola, and Highlands Counties

Comments: *Drosera* means "dewy" and relates to the dew-like leaf secretions. The name *intermedia* relates to characteristics that are intermediate among other species. This state-listed threatened species was first described in 1801 by German botanist Friedrich Gottlob Hayne (1763–1832) from plants collected near Hamburg, Germany. It ranges across Europe through the neotropics.

TARFLOWER
Bejaria racemosa Vent.
Heath family (Ericaceae)

Description: This shrubby species reaches 6'–8' tall, with obovate leaves from 1"–2" long and ½"–1" wide. It blooms at an early age, and the showy flowers have 7 narrow, spatula-shaped petals that are white or pinkish with pink bases.

Bloom Season: Mostly May to June

Habitat/Range: Flatwoods from Taylor, Lafayette, Baker, and Nassau Counties south through the peninsula

Comments: Carolus Linneaus (1707–1778) created the genus to honor eighteenth-century botanist José Béjar, but Linnaeus mistook the *j* in Béjar's name for an *f* and named the genus *Befaria*, which remained until it was corrected by Étienne Pierre Ventenat (1757–1808) when he described this species in 1800. The name *racemosa* refers to the raceme of flowers. The buds and backside of the flower petals are sticky and were once used as flypaper in homes because they entrap insects. This woody shrub is included in this guide because it is so conspicuous when in flower.

TRAILING ARBUTUS
Epigaea repens L.
Heath family (Ericaceae)

Description: The stems of this species trail close to the ground, with young branches covered with long, shaggy hairs. The hairy, alternate leaves are ovate-elliptic, from 1"–3" long and ⅝"–2" wide. The intensely fragrant flowers are about ⁵⁄₁₆" wide.

Bloom Season: February to July

Habitat/Range: Deciduous forests of Escambia, Santa Rosa, Okaloosa, and Liberty Counties in the Florida panhandle

Comments: *Epigaea* means "upon earth" and relates to the species' creeping growth habit. The name *repens* means "creeping" and also refers to the growth habit. It is called mayflower and ground laurel in parts of its native range across eastern North America and was named the state flower of Massachusetts in 1918. In Florida it is a state-listed endangered species because of its rarity and limited range within the state. It was photographed in the Apalachicola Bluffs and Ravines Preserve (Liberty County).

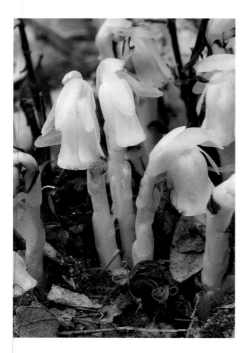

INDIANPIPES
Monotropa uniflora L.
Heath family (Ericaceae)

Description: This ephemeral species lacks chlorophyll and appears in tight clusters of white or pinkish succulent stems that stand 2"–8" tall. Flowers are white or pinkish and usually nodding. The plants turn black as they age.

Bloom Season: July to March

Habitat/Range: Scrub and mesic hammocks from Escambia County east to Leon and Wakulla Counties and from Suwannee, Columbia, and Duval Counties south to Palm Beach and Collier Counties

Comments: *Monotropa* means "one turn" and refers to the recurved top of the stem. The name *uniflora* relates to the single flower. Other names are convulsion-root, corpse-plant, and eyebright. The plant was used medicinally by indigenous people in the Americas to relieve sore eyes and to treat spasms and fainting spells. The roots contain fungi that form a web through decomposing leaf litter and parasitize the roots of trees, providing sugars for the plant.

SHINY BLUEBERRY
Vaccinium myrsinites Lam.
Heath family (Ericaceae)

Description: The glossy leaves of this low, bushy, rhizomatous species are obovate to elliptic and reach about ⅜" long and ⅛"–¼" wide. The globose, ¼" flowers are white or pink, with ⁵⁄₁₆" fruits that ripen blue.

Bloom Season: January to April

Habitat/Range: Scrubby flatwoods and pinelands throughout mainland Florida

Comments: *Vaccinium* is Latin for "blueberry." The name *myrsinites* relates to the myrtle-like leaves. The species was first described in 1783 by French naturalist Jean Baptiste Antoine Pierre de Monnet de Lamarck (1744–1829) from plants collected in 1799 near St. Augustine, Florida (St. Johns County). The fruits of this blueberry are very tasty and a source of food for a wide variety of birds and mammals, including wild turkeys, quail, and black bears. It is native throughout the southeastern United States and forms vast colonies.

FLATTENED PIPEWORT

Eriocaulon compressum Lam.
Pipewort family (Eriocaulaceae)

Description: The linear leaves taper gradually to a very slender apex (attenuate) and may reach 12" long. The flower heads are chalky white and flattened, measuring about ⅝" across, and are on top of stems that reach 12"–27" tall.

Bloom Season: November to June

Habitat/Range: Wet flatwoods and marshes throughout mainland Florida

Comments: *Eriocaulon* means "woolly stem," referring to the woolly hairs that line the flowering stems. The name *compressum* alludes to the compressed, or flattened, flower heads. The flower heads on this species are soft to the touch. This is the most aquatic member of this genus in Florida, often growing in standing water. Female flowers are often sterile. The species was described in 1789 by French naturalist Jean Baptiste Antoine Pierre de Monnet de Lamarck (1744–1829). Its range is mostly centered in the southeastern United States.

TENANGLE PIPEWORT

Eriocaulon decangulare L.
Pipewort family (Eriocaulaceae)

Description: The linear, basal leaves of this species are arranged in a spiral. The angled scape ranges from 12"–40" tall and is topped by a compact head of tiny flowers that form a rounded, or slightly compressed, white ball. The flower heads on this species are firm to the touch.

Bloom Season: May to October

Habitat/Range: Freshwater wetlands and flatwoods throughout mainland Florida

Comments: The name *decangulare* means "ten angled," referring to the typical number of angles on the flowering stem. It prefers strong sunlight, so it benefits from fire burning off competing vegetation. There are 6 members of this genus in Florida but there are more than 400 species worldwide, mostly distributed in tropical regions of southern Asia and the Americas. This species is native across the eastern United States south into Mexico and Nicaragua.

YELLOW HATPINS

Syngonanthus flavidulus (Michx.) Ruhland
Pipewort family (Eriocaulaceae)

Description: Narrowly linear, recurved, shiny leaves measure ¾"–1¼" long and form small tufts in moist, sandy soils. Minuscule flowers are borne in globose heads that appear as small, white buttons on slender stems held well above the leaves. The bracts below the heads are dull yellow, and each head bears both male and female flowers.

Bloom Season: February to July

Habitat/Range: Wet flatwoods, pond margins, and prairies throughout mainland Florida

Comments: *Syngonanthus* means "joined together" and "flower," alluding to the fused petals of the female flowers. The name *flavidulus* refers to the pale yellow floral bracts. German botanist and plant physiologist Eugen Otto Wilhelm Ruhland (1878–1960) moved this species from *Eriocaulon* to *Syngonanthus* in 1903. The fungus genus *Ruhlandiella* is named in honor of Ruhland, but his specialty was the Eriocaulaceae.

STINGING NETTLE

Cnidoscolus stimulosus (Michx.) Engelm. & A. Gray
Spurge family (Euphorbiaceae)

Description: Stinging hairs cover the stems and leaves of this species. It is usually less than 12" tall, with 3- or 5-lobed leaves, often irregularly dissected, and typically 3"–6" long and 2"–4" wide. The ½" flowers are fragrant.

Bloom Season: All year

Habitat/Range: Sandy habitats throughout Florida

Comments: *Cnidoscolus* is Greek for "nettle thorn." The name *stimulosus* means "tormenting" or "stinging," referring to the stinging hairs. Contact with the hairs will result in an intense stinging or burning sensation followed by a red rash that may leave the skin discolored for weeks. If left alone, the stinging will eventually dissipate, but scratching makes it worse. Placing tape over the affected area and pulling it off will remove the stinging hairs. The root is edible, and the leaves taste like spinach when cooked.

SILVER CROTON

Croton argyranthemus Michx.
Spurge family (Euphorbiaceae)

Description: This species reaches 12" tall and has rusty-brown, hairy stems and elliptic, gland-dotted leaves to 2" long and ½" wide, with pale to silvery undersides. Male and female flowers are together on the same plant and measure up to ¼" wide. The plant may emit a faint skunk-like odor.

Bloom Season: March to September

Habitat/Range: Sandhills and scrub from Escambia County east across the panhandle and northern peninsula south to Pinellas, Hillsborough, Polk, and Osceola Counties

Comments: *Croton* refers to the resemblance of the seeds to a tick. The name *argyranthemus* alludes to the silvery flowers. A tea was prepared from the leaves to cure colic, diarrhea, sore throat, and ulcers. The species is a larval host plant of the goatweed leafwing butterfly. *Croton glandulosus* is an annual with similar flowers, but it has smooth or coarsely hairy leaves and occurs in pinelands and on beach dunes.

PINELAND CROTON

Croton linearis Jacq.
Spurge family (Euphorbiaceae)

Description: This species averages 2'–4' tall, with linear, alternate leaves that are green above and covered with silvery or golden hairs below. The leaves are ¾"–2" long to about ¼" wide. The ¼" male and female flowers are on separate plants.

Bloom Season: All year

Habitat/Range: Pinelands from St. Lucie County south through the Atlantic coastal counties to Big Pine Key in the lower Florida Keys

Comments: The name *linearis* refers to the linear leaves. This is the larval host plant of 2 endangered butterflies: the Florida leafwing and Bartram's scrub-hairstreak, both of which occur on Long Pine Key in Everglades National Park. Plants in this genus contain poisonous alkaloids but are sometimes used medicinally. The smaller rushfoil (*Croton michauxii*), with linear leaves that reach 1" long and ¼" wide, inhabits scrub and sandhills south to Charlotte, Glades, and Palm Beach Counties.

LESSER FLORIDA SPURGE
Euphorbia polyphylla Engelm. ex Chapm.
Spurge family (Euphorbiaceae)

Description: The glabrous stems of this perennial species reach 8"–12" tall, with wirelike stems and narrowly linear leaves ranging from ¼"–½" long and up to ⅛" wide. The ³⁄₁₆" "false flowers" are in loose panicles.

Bloom Season: All year

Habitat/Range: Endemic to sandhills and flat-woods from Hillsborough, Polk, Lake, Seminole, and Brevard Counties south to Collier and Miami-Dade Counties

Comments: *Euphorbia* honors first-century Greek physician Euphorbus, who knew these plants were powerful laxatives. The name *polyphylla* refers to the many leaves on the plant. Botanist Allan Hiram Curtiss (1845–1907) first discovered this species in Brevard County in 1892. This species is common but inconspicuous, so it is best to look for it in the first few months after fire has burned away competing vegetation. It has been erroneously reported from Louisiana.

WHITE WILD INDIGO
Baptisia alba (L.) Vent.
Pea family (Fabaceae)

Description: The compound leaves are divided into 3 elliptic to ovate leaflets that may reach about 2" long and ¾" wide. The scentless, white, ½" flowers in erect racemes are strikingly pretty.

Bloom Season: March to June

Habitat/Range: Flatwoods and riverbanks across much of the Florida panhandle east to Hamilton, Suwannee, Lafayette, and Dixie Counties and south in the peninsula to Citrus and Lake Counties

Comments: *Baptisia* means "to dip in dye," and was named by French botanist Étienne Pierre Ventenat (1757–1808) for the use of some members of this genus to make a blue dye. The name *alba* alludes to the white flowers. It is a larval host of the wild indigo duskywing butterfly. It has been used medicinally by Native Americans to treat rheumatism and swelling, as well as to counteract venomous snakebite. This species is easy to see from car windows on a drive through its habitat.

COINVINE
Dalbergia ecastaphyllum (L.) Taub.
Pea family (Fabaceae)

Description: This sprawling, somewhat vine-like species has branches that scramble over nearby vegetation or spread horizontally across the ground. Each leaflet is elliptic to ovate and measures 2"–3" long with a nearly equal width. The white (or blushed with pink), ⅜" flowers are in axillary clusters. The pods are circular and flat (like a coin).

Bloom Season: April to November

Habitat/Range: Coastal strand and shell middens in Seminole and Brevard Counties and in Pinellas and Hillsborough Counties, south along both coasts into the Florida Keys

Comments: *Dalbergia* honors Swedish brothers Carl Gustav Dahlberg (1721–1781), who sent plant specimens to Carolus Linnaeus from Surinam, and Nils Ericsson Dahlberg (1736–1820), a student of Linnaeus. The name *ecastaphyllum* refers to the single leaflet. The species is a larval host for the statira sulphur butterfly but is seldom cultivated by gardeners.

SUMMER FAREWELL
Dalea pinnata (J.F. Gmel.) Barneby
Pea family (Fabaceae)

Description: Plants average 2'–4' tall, with compound leaves divided into 5–9 threadlike leaflets. Flowers are in rounded heads and cover the tops of the plants.

Bloom Season: September to November

Habitat/Range: Sandhills and open, sandy woods from Okaloosa County east to Nassau County and south to Hillsborough, Hardee, Highlands, and Martin Counties

Comments: *Dalea* commemorates English physician and botanist Samuel Dale (1659–1739). The name *pinnata* alludes to the pinnately compound leaves. This species blooms in autumn as it bids farewell to summer. The endemic var. *adenopoda* has folded, elliptic-lanceolate leaves and occurs in the southern half of mainland Florida; var. *trifoliata* bears 3 threadlike leaflets and occurs in the Florida panhandle. Butterflies visit the flowers for nectar, and the species is a larval host of the southern dogface butterfly.

CREAM TICKTREFOIL
Desmodium ochroleucum M.A. Curtis ex Canby
Pea family (Fabaceae)

Description: This decumbent vine has leaves divided into 3 ovate leaflets that measure 1"–2⅛" long with a nearly equal width (the terminal leaflet is largest). The white to cream flowers are about ½" long. The fruit segments are flattened and cling to clothing.

Bloom Season: September to October

Habitat/Range: Open woodlands of Jackson County

Comments: *Desmodium* means "chain" and "to resemble," referring to the jointed pods. The name *ochroleucum* translates to "pale yellow" and "white," alluding to the creamy flower color. This species ranges from New Jersey to Missouri and Mississippi but is a state-listed endangered species in Florida due to its limited range in Jackson County. It is the rarest of the 19 native members of this genus in Florida. Like many legumes, it benefits from fire and soil disturbance. The flowers open in midmorning.

ELLIOTT'S MILKPEA
Galactia elliottii Nutt.
Pea family (Fabaceae)

Description: This twining species has leaves with up to 9 oblong leaflets and axillary flowers borne on long stems (peduncles). The pealike flowers are showy and measure ½"–⅝" wide. The narrow ½"–1" pods are densely covered with short appressed hairs.

Bloom Season: April to November

Habitat/Range: Pinelands and flatwoods in Bay and Taylor Counties and from Columbia, Alachua, and Nassau Counties south to Collier and Palm Beach Counties; also the Florida Keys

Comments: *Galactia* means "milky," a name first used in 1756 to describe a species with milky sap. The name *elliottii* honors American legislator, banker, and botanist Stephen Elliott (1771–1830) of South Carolina. The species is a larval host plant of the zarucco duskywing and northern cloudywing butterflies in Florida. Some species of *Tephrosia* have similar flowers. Native Americans used milkpeas medicinally.

SCURF HOARYPEA

Tephrosia chrysophylla Pursh
Pea family (Fabaceae)

Description: The branched stems are ground-hugging, with compound leaves typically bearing 5–7 widely obovate leaflets from ½"–1⅛" long and ⅜"–¾" wide. The leaflets are yellowish green above, with appressed silky hairs below. The red flower buds open white and measure about ½" wide, turning pale pink in the afternoon.

Bloom Season: May to October

Habitat/Range: Sandhills and clayhills throughout much of mainland Florida

Comments: *Tephrosia* means "hoary" or "ash-colored," relating to the grayish pubescence on the leaves of some species in this genus. The name *chrysophylla* means "with golden leaves" and refers to the yellow hairs on the leaves. The species was described in 1814 by German-American botanist Frederick Traugott Pursh (1774–1820) from plants collected in Georgia. Pursh died a destitute alcoholic in Montreal, Canada. Members of this genus were used by the Creeks to treat "loss of manhood."

SANDHILL TIPPITOES

Tephrosia mysteriosa DeLaney
Pea family (Fabaceae)

Description: The tawny hirsute stems are prostrate, with 7–11 mostly elliptic, olive green leaflets that measure about ½" long and ⅜" wide. There are strigose hairs covering the lower leaf surface, and the margins are hairy. Flat, red buds open white and measure about ½" wide, turning light pink in the afternoon.

Bloom Season: May to October

Habitat/Range: Endemic to sandhills (yellow sand) on the Lake Wales Ridge and Mount Dora Ridge in Marion, Lake, Polk, and Highlands Counties

Comments: The name *mysteriosa* relates to the species' discovery by Avon Park botanist Kris DeLaney (1951–), who thought it was mysterious that it could have existed for so long without being recognized as a distinct species by other botanists. It very much resembles *Tephrosia chrysophylla* but differs by its overall appearance, maximum leaflet count, leaflet shape, color, branching pattern, and geographic location.

SPIKED HOARYPEA
Tephrosia spicata (Walter) Torr. & A. Gray
Pea family (Fabaceae)

Description: The stems, leaves, and floral parts are copiously pubescent, with leaves that are divided into 5–15 oval or elliptic leaflets from ½"–1" long and ⅜"–½" wide. The flowers open white and turn reddish or purple by late afternoon. The closed buds are bright red.

Bloom Season: May to October

Habitat/Range: Pinelands and dry woods throughout most of mainland Florida

Comments: The name *spicata* relates to the long (spicate) flower stem. The name "hoarypea" comes from the pubescence on the leaves of some species that creates the appearance of being covered with hoarfrost, or frozen dew. The seeds of hoarypeas are high in protein and a favorite food of bobwhites, ground doves, mourning doves, and wild turkeys. The plant photographed was in the Julington-Durbin Creek Preserve in Duval County. Larvae of the northern cloudywing butterfly feed on the leaves.

FOURLEAF VETCH
Vicia acutifolia Elliott
Pea family (Fabaceae)

Description: The thin stems of this species often spread across other vegetation and have evenly pinnately compound leaves, typically with 4 very narrow leaflets that measure ½"–1" long. The white to lavender flowers are about ¼" wide. The pods are up to 1⅛" long.

Bloom Season: December to August

Habitat/Range: Pond and river margins, wet woods, and roadsides in Santa Rosa County and from Franklin to Union and Nassau Counties south throughout the peninsula

Comments: *Vicia* is said to be an ancient Latin name for "vetch," but it has also been translated as "to bind," in reference to its stems. The name *acutifolia* refers to the acute leaflets (tapering to a sharp point). The flower buds of this species open in the afternoon and are easily passed by because of their small size. It is most often found climbing over low vegetation, especially along trailsides that bisect its habitat.

OCALA VETCH

Vicia ocalensis R.K. Godfrey & Kral
Pea family (Fabaceae)

Description: This 3'–4' vine has compound leaves, typically with 6, narrowly oblong leaflets that range from 1⅛"–2" long. The white or very pale lavender flowers are ¼" wide. The pods reach 1½"–1¾" long.

Bloom Season: April to July

Habitat/Range: Endemic to streambanks and spring runs of Lake and Marion Counties

Comments: The name *ocalensis* refers to Ocala, Florida (Marion County), where this species was first collected along Juniper Springs Creek and described in 1958 by botanists Robert Kenneth Godfrey (1911–2000) and Robert Kral (1926–). It is a state-listed endangered species with a single population known outside of the Ocala National Forest in Marion County. Vetches are larval hosts of the clouded sulphur butterfly. A poultice from the leaves of vetches was used by Native Americans to treat spider bites, while the seeds were regarded as an aphrodisiac and good luck charms.

WHITE SCREWSTEM

Bartonia verna (Michx.) Raf. ex Barton
Gentian family (Gentianaceae)

Description: Frail, nearly leafless stems stand 2"–4" tall, topped by a 4-lobed (rarely 6), white, ⅛" flower. The stems are sometimes loosely branched near the top.

Bloom Season: November to May

Habitat/Range: Wet flatwoods and bogs throughout most of mainland Florida south to Collier and Broward Counties

Comments: *Bartonia* honors botanist Benjamin Smith Barton (1766–1815), a trained physician best known as a professional naturalist and author of the first book on botany written in the United States. The name *verna* means "of the spring," in reference to the species' springtime flowering, although in Florida it blooms from late fall into spring. It was first described as *Centaurella verna* by French botanist André Michaux (1746–1802) but not published until the year after his untimely death in Madagascar. This species is difficult to find due to its small stature, often hidden among grasses.

WIREGRASS GENTIAN
Gentiana pennelliana Fernald
Gentian family (Gentianaceae)

Description: Opposite, narrowly linear leaves measure ¾"–1¼" long on 4"–10" stems topped with a solitary, 5-lobed flower measuring 1¼"–2½" long and about 1" wide.

Bloom Season: November to February

Habitat/Range: Endemic to wet savannas and flatwoods from Walton County east to Leon and Wakulla Counties in the Florida panhandle

Comments: *Gentiana* is for King Gentius of Illyria, who ruled the Ardiaean State (present-day western Balkans) from 181–168 BC, and who promoted the medicinal virtues of Mediterranean gentians. The name *pennelliana* honors botanist Francis Whittier Pennell (1886–1952), who was the associate curator of the New York Botanical Garden from 1914 to 1921. This state-listed endangered species often grows in association with wiregrass (*Aristida stricta*), a common grass of Southern flatwoods and sandhills. The flowers will not open on overcast days.

STRIPED GENTIAN
Gentiana villosa L.
Gentian family (Gentianaceae)

Description: The stems reach 24" tall, with opposite, sessile, spatulate or obovate leaves from 2"–4" long and half as wide. The bell-shaped, 2" flowers are in terminal clusters and lined with green stripes, often blushed with purple.

Bloom Season: October to December

Habitat/Range: Sandhills and dry woods of Escambia, Santa Rosa, Jackson, Liberty, Leon, and Madison Counties

Comments: The name *villosa* relates to shaggy hairs, but nothing about this plant is hairy. Another name, Sampson's snakeroot, alludes to the plant's use to treat snakebite, but it was also used to make a bitter tonic. Elwyn Brooks White, author of *Charlotte's Web*, wrote about gentian root at the age of 84, saying it was "the path to the good life." The medicinal values of gentians were first found recorded on papyrus within an Egyptian tomb that dated to 1100 BC.

SHORTLEAF ROSEGENTIAN
Sabatia brevifolia Raf.
Gentian family (Gentianaceae)

Description: This annual typically reaches 4"–8" tall but may be much taller. The narrowly linear leaves are ascending and are sometimes appressed to the stem, reaching 1" long and barely ⅛" wide. The flowers are white (never pink) with a greenish-yellow center and average ⅞" wide. The upper branches are alternate.

Bloom Season: March to September

Habitat/Range: Flatwoods and brackish marshes throughout Florida south to Collier and Palm Beach Counties

Comments: *Sabatia* honors eighteenth-century Italian botanist Liberato Sabbati, who was the keeper of the botanical garden in Rome. The name *brevifolia* refers to the short leaves of this species. It is also called quinine herb and quinine flower, relating to its use to treat malaria. This species lacks the jagged red line at the base of the corolla lobes found on white forms of *Sabatia stellaris*, which very often shares its habitat.

LANCELEAF ROSEGENTIAN
Sabatia difformis (L.) Druce
Gentian family (Gentianaceae)

Description: This species may reach 30" tall, with an angular upper stem and opposite branching. The leaves are mostly lanceolate but may be ovate with prominent parallel veins. The flowers measure 1"–1¼" wide and are in branched, terminal clusters.

Bloom Season: May to August

Habitat/Range: Moist savannas and wet fields in the Florida panhandle and from Columbia to Nassau Counties south to Sarasota, DeSoto, and Highlands Counties

Comments: The name *difformis* means "two forms" and relates to the lateral flowers that typically have 5 corolla lobes, while the terminal flowers may be 6-lobed. Carolus Linnaeus (1707–1778) first described this species in 1753 as *Swertia difformis*, but it was moved to the genus *Sabatia* in 1914 by English botanist George Claridge Druce (1850–1932). Druce helped found the Ashmolean Natural History Society of Oxfordshire, England, in 1880.

LARGELEAF ROSEGENTIAN
Sabatia macrophylla Hook.
Gentian family (Gentianaceae)

Description: This species averages 20"–30" tall, with opposite, sessile, elliptic-lanceolate to ovate-lanceolate upper leaves. The leaf blades measure ¾"–2½" long and ½"–1" wide. Flowers can be numerous on branched inflorescences and measure ½"–¾" wide, with 5 (rarely 4) corolla lobes.

Bloom Season: May to September

Habitat/Range: Wet pinelands and bogs across the panhandle from Escambia County east to Gadsden and Wakulla Counties and also northeast Florida from Clay and Columbia Counties to Nassau County

Comments: The name *macrophylla* describes the large leaves of this species. British systematic botanist William Jackson Hooker (1785–1865) first described this species in 1836 from plants collected in St. Tammany Parish, Louisiana. Hooker's herbarium gained international acclaim, and in 1841 he was appointed director of the Royal Botanic Gardens, Kew.

PARASITIC GHOSTPLANT
Voyria parasitica (Schltdl. & Cham.)
Ruyters & Maas.
Gentian family (Gentianaceae)

Description: This species typically reaches 3"–6" tall, branching near the top of very frail stems that lack chlorophyll. The flowers range from beige to off-white and are about ⅜" long and 3⁄16" wide.

Bloom Season: March to October

Habitat/Range: Tropical hardwood hammocks of Miami-Dade County and the Florida Keys (Monroe County)

Comments: *Voyria* is a name from French Guiana. The name *parasitica* refers to the plant's deriving its nutrients from fungi that it parasitizes, a trait called myco-heterotrophy. This state-listed endangered species forms localized colonies but can easily be overlooked because it blends in perfectly with the leaf litter, where it is loosely rooted on the forest floor. It ranges into the Bahamas, Greater Antilles, Mexico, and Central America. Some members of this genus are used medicinally to treat chronic indigestion (dyspepsia).

INKBERRY

Scaevola plumieri (L.) Vahl
Goodenia family (Goodeniaceae)

Description: This mounding plant averages
24"–36" tall, with thick, dark green, glossy leaves
from 2"–4" long and 1"–1½" wide. The 5-lobed
flowers may be tinted with violet. The ½" fruits
are black.

Bloom Season: All year

Habitat/Range: Beach dunes from Pinellas and
Brevard Counties south along both coasts into the
Florida Keys

Comments: *Scaevola* means "left handed" and
is symbolic of the left hand of legendary sixth-
century Roman hero Gaius Mucius Scaevola, who
burned off his right hand in an altar fire to prove
his courage to Etruscan king Lars Porsena after
an assassination attempt, convincing Porsena to
make peace with Rome. The name *plumieri* honors
French botanist Charles Plumier (1646–1704). Gulls
and beach crabs eat the fruits of this state-listed
threatened species. The larger and invasive exotic
beach naupaka (*Scaevola taccada*) has light green
leaves and white fruits.

WHITE SUNNYBELL

Schoenolirion albiflorum (Raf.) R.R. Gates
Hyacinth family (Hyacinthaceae)

Description: White sunnybell does not have bulbs
like other species in this genus. The leaves are
coarsely fibrous, each measuring 10"–18" long and
¼" wide. A simple or branched inflorescence bears
white or greenish white flowers that measure
about ⅜" wide and are usually spaced 2" or more
apart.

Bloom Season: March to September

Habitat/Range: Marshy pinelands and wet prairies
in the central panhandle and from northeastern
Florida discontinuously south to Miami-Dade and
mainland Monroe Counties

Comments: *Schoenolirion* is taken from Greek
words meaning "rush," and "white lily." The
name *albiflorum* alludes to the white flowers of
this species. Another species with yellow flowers
(*Schoenolirion croceum*) occurs in freshwater
wetlands of northern Florida. This species is never
abundant, even in prime habitat. It is sometimes
included in the Lily family (Liliaceae).

AMERICAN FROG-BIT
Limnobium spongia (Bosc) Rich. ex Steud.
Frog-bit family (Hydrocharitaceae)

Description: The leaves of this species are floating or may be emersed when stranded or when growing in dense vegetation. The leaf blades are orbicular, cordate at the base, and measure up to 3" wide. Male flowers have 9–18 exserted stamens; female flowers bear 3–4 petals. Flowering usually occurs on plants with emersed leaves.

Bloom Season: March to November

Habitat/Range: Slow-moving water of streams, lakes, and roadside ditches from Gadsden, Liberty, and Franklin Counties south in the peninsula to Indian River, Glades, and Collier Counties

Comments: *Limnobium* means "living in pools." The name *spongia* relates to the spongy (aerenchymous) tissue on the bottom of the floating leaves that creates buoyancy. Emersed leaves lack this tissue. At first glance, the leaves of this species can be mistaken for the invasive water-hyacinth (*Eichhornia crassipes*).

BROWNE'S SAVORY
Clinopodium brownei (Sw.) Kuntze
Mint family (Lamiaceae)

Description: This mat-forming ground cover has opposite, ovate, toothed leaves that average ¾"–1¼" long and ½"–¾" wide. Stalked, axillary flowers are about ¼" wide, often with purple blushing.

Bloom Season: All year

Habitat/Range: Wet pine flatwoods, streambanks, and damp roadsides from Jackson and Bay Counties discontinuously east and south through the peninsula

Comments: *Clinopodium* means "bed" and "little foot," for the reclining habit of the type species. The name *brownei* honors Irish botanist and physician Patrick Browne (1720–1790), who moved to Jamaica in 1746. The plant is cultivated as a ground cover for damp soils and for the aquarium trade. The leaves produce a strong peppermint odor when crushed and can be used to brew a minty herbal tea. It very closely resembles the non-native, naturalized *Lindernia crustacea* (Linderniaceae), which has no minty odor.

SHORTLEAF FALSE ROSEMARY

Conradina brevifolia Shinners
Mint family (Lamiaceae)

Description: This subshrub reaches 2'–3' tall, with needlelike, highly aromatic leaves to about ⅜" long, formed in dense clusters along the branches. The ⅜" flowers range from white to pale lavender, with purple spots on the lip.

Bloom Season: All year, but mostly April to August

Habitat/Range: Endemic to white sand scrub on the Lake Wales Ridge in Highlands and Polk Counties

Comments: *Conradina* honors American botanist Solomon White Conrad (1779–1831). The name *brevifolia* relates to the species' short leaves. This rare, endemic, state and federal endangered species was described in 1962 by botanist Lloyd Herbert Shinners (1918–1971). Some botanists include it as a synonym of the comparatively widespread *Conradina canescens* of Georgia, Alabama, and the Florida panhandle, but it differs by its habitat, shorter leaves, and greater number of flowers per axil.

MUSKY BUSHMINT

Hyptis alata (Raf.) Shinners
Mint family (Lamiaceae)

Description: The square stems average 36"–48" tall with opposite, lanceolate, coarsely toothed leaves that measure 1½"–4" long and ½"–1½" wide. Axillary flower heads are ringed by small, white flowers with a 3-lobed lip dotted with pink or purple.

Bloom Season: All year

Habitat/Range: Low pinelands and marshes throughout mainland Florida

Comments: *Hyptis* means "turned back" and refers to the flower's resupinate lip. The name *alata* translates to "winged" and alludes to the leaf blades that narrow into petiole-like bases. The leaves have a musky odor when crushed, unlike the fresh minty scent typical of the family. It was first described as *Pycnanthemum alatum* in 1817 by Greek polymath Constantine Samuel Rafinesque (1783–1840) but was moved into the genus *Hyptis* in 1962 by American botanist Lloyd Herbert Shinners (1918–1971). The flowers attract butterflies.

WHITE BIRDS-IN-A-NEST
Macbridea alba Chapm.
Mint family (Lamiaceae)

Description: The hairy stems reach 24" tall and are terminated with a head-like inflorescence subtended by closely appressed bracts. Leaves are oblanceolate to spatulate, thick, hairy, and mostly in 6–8 pairs. The flowers measure 1"–1¼" long.

Bloom Season: June to September

Habitat/Range: Endemic to wet flatwoods and bogs of Liberty, Franklin, Gulf, and Bay Counties

Comments: American botanist Stephen Elliott (1771–1830) named the genus *Macbridea* in 1818 to honor botanist James Macbride (1784–1817), the year after his untimely death from yellow fever at the age of 33. The name *alba* refers to the white flowers, described as "bedsheet white." Protected populations of this state endangered and federal threatened species occur in the St. Joseph Buffer Preserve, Lathrop Bayou, Box-R Wildlife Management Area, Tate's Hell State Forest, and Apalachicola National Forest.

LOVE VINE
Cassytha filiformis L.
Laurel family (Lauraceae)

Description: The stems of this parasitic vine are yellowish green but become orange in full sun. Inconspicuous white flowers produce small, white, pearl-like fruits. The plant is found parasitizing woody shrubs and herbaceous species.

Bloom Season: All year

Habitat/Range: Coastal dunes, sandhills, pinelands, and forest margins from Pinellas, Hillsborough, Polk, Osceola, and Brevard Counties south through the Florida Keys (disjunct in Taylor County)

Comments: *Cassytha* is a Greek word for a parasitic plant. The name *filiformis* means "threadlike" and alludes to the stems. This plant somewhat resembles dodders (*Cuscuta* spp.) in the morning-glory family, but, besides the flower differences, the stems of love vine are fragrant when crushed, which typifies the laurel family. The name love vine relates to a tea brewed from the stems in the Bahamas that is believed to be an aphrodisiac.

CHAPMAN'S BUTTERWORT
Pinguicula planifolia Chapm.
Bladderwort family (Lentibulariaceae)

Description: The flat, oblong or elliptic leaves form a compact, ground-hugging rosette averaging 2"–3" across that is sometimes submerged. The scape stands 4"–5" tall, topped by a solitary blue or white flower to about 1" wide.

Bloom Season: January to April

Habitat/Range: Seepage bogs from Escambia County east to Jackson, Liberty, and Wakulla Counties

Comments: *Pinguicula* alludes to the greasy texture of the leaf surface. The name *planifolia* refers to the flat leaves. The greasy-feeling leaves of this insectivorous state-listed threatened species may be solid red or green; the flowers range from various shades of white to blue, with mixed flower colors in the same colony. It is also called swamp butterwort and was described in 1897 by botanist Alvan Wentworth Chapman (1809–1899). It ranges across southern Alabama to Mississippi.

PIEDMONT BLADDERWORT
Utricularia olivacea C. Wright ex Griseb.
Bladderwort family (Lentibulariaceae)

Description: The flowers of this carnivorous species are smaller than a pinhead and stand just above the water surface attached to olive green, algae-like floating mats.

Bloom Season: September to March

Habitat/Range: Ponds and ditches of Bay, Franklin, Wakulla, and Leon Counties in the panhandle and Putnam, Seminole, Brevard, Hillsborough, and Highlands Counties in the peninsula

Comments: *Utricularia* is Latin for "small bag," referring to the traps on the stems. The name *olivacea* refers to the olive green mats of stems. Due to its exceptionally small flowers, this plant is extremely difficult to find without close scrutiny of slimy-looking mats at the water surface. The minuscule traps target microscopic aquatic organisms. The species was first discovered in Cuba by botanist Charles Wright (1811–1885) and described in 1866.

SWAMP HORNPOD

Mitreola sessilifolia (J.F. Gmel.) G. Don
Logania family (Loganiaceae)

Description: Smooth, reddish stems of this annual stand 6"–18" tall and are lined with opposite, sessile, ovate leaves with toothed margins. Tiny flowers are in scorpioid arrangements at the tips of the stems.

Bloom Season: All year

Habitat/Range: Pine flatwoods, seepage slopes, wet prairies, depressions, and other wet habitats through most of Florida

Comments: *Mitreola* alludes to the miter-shaped capsule. The name *sessilifolia* is for the sessile (stemless) leaves. This is a common plant of wet areas, often growing in shallow water. The species was first described in 1791 as *Cynoctonum sessilifolium* by German naturalist Johann Friedrich Gmelin (1748–1804). He is noted for discovering the redfin pickerel in 1789. Members of this family contain strychnine and other harmful alkaloids, so eating them is not advised. There are 2 other similar species in Florida.

BLADDERMALLOW

Herissantia crispa (L.) Brizicky
Mallow family (Malvaceae)

Description: Bladdermallow reaches about 3' tall but often has a sprawling, almost vinelike habit. The heart-shaped, 1½"–2½" leaves are softly fuzzy with scalloped margins; the ½" flowers may be white or pale yellow with dark yellow at the base of the petals. The hairy, lantern-like capsules are ribbed and enclose hard, black, kidney-shaped seeds.

Bloom Season: All year

Habitat/Range: Coastal habitats of Brevard, Hillsborough, Lee, Collier, Miami-Dade, and Monroe Counties (including the Florida Keys)

Comments: *Herissantia* honors French physician, naturalist, and poet Louis Antoine Prospère Hérissant (1745–1769). The name *crispa* alludes to the irregularly waved capsule margins. This species is a larval host plant of the gray hairstreak and mallow scrub-hairstreak butterflies but it is seldom purposely cultivated by butterfly gardeners. The flowers open by midday.

COMFORTROOT

Hibiscus aculeatus Walter
Mallow family (Malvaceae)

Description: The stems may reach 6'–9' tall, with toothed, palmately divided leaves, sometimes resembling those of a maple (Acer). The overlapping petals are creamy white with a reddish-purple base, fading to pale yellow and then pink as the flower ages. The flowers measure 4"–5" wide.

Bloom Season: May to October

Habitat/Range: Upland bogs, pinelands, and ditches across the Florida panhandle west to Dixie, Alachua, Clay, Duval, and Nassau Counties, and also Lake County

Comments: *Hibiscus* is said to come from the Greek *ibiscos*, for living in marshes with ibis. The name *aculeatus* refers to the hooked prickles on the stems and leaves that will stick upon contact with skin, fur, and clothing. Hummingbirds visit the flowers for nectar and pollen. The common name is for the mucilaginous roots having comforting properties; they have been used as a soothing herbal tea to calm the mentally disturbed.

CRIMSONEYED ROSEMALLOW

Hibiscus moscheutos L.
Mallow family (Malvaceae)

Description: Stems of this mallow reach 5'–8' tall, dying back in winter and resprouting in spring. The 3"–8" leaves are ovate or lanceolate, shallowly toothed, and may have 2 or more lobes. The petals are typically white with a crimson base but are blushed with pink in parts of this species' range. The flowers average 7"–9" across.

Bloom Season: May to September

Habitat/Range: Inland wetlands, coastal tidal marshes, and wet roadsides across the Florida panhandle and south in the peninsula to Levy, Marion, and Lake Counties

Comments: The name *moscheutos* means "musky-scented" and alludes to the crushed leaves. The flowers are visited by hummingbirds, but bumblebees are the principal pollinators. A tea brewed from the leaves was used "to loosen coughs and relieve sore throats, especially if honey is added to each dose." It was also used to relieve irritation of the bowels and kidneys.

ALLIGATOR FLAG
Thalia geniculata L.
Arrowroot family (Marantaceae)

Description: This species reaches 6'–9' tall, with broad, lanceolate leaf blades from 12"–36" long and to 12" wide, attached to long petioles. The flowers are 1" long and ½" wide on pendent, zigzagging stems.

Bloom Season: May to November

Habitat/Range: Freshwater wetlands throughout most of the Florida peninsula and in Gulf, Franklin, and Wakulla Counties

Comments: *Thalia* honors German physician and botanist Johannes Thal (1542–1583), who wrote *A Flora of the Harz Mountains*, the highest mountain range in northern Germany. The name *geniculata* means "bent sharply like a knee" and refers to the angle of the leaf blade where it attaches to the petiole. The common name alludes to the leaves waving back and forth like flags as alligators push their way through the plants. It is a larval host plant of the Brazilian skipper and the saddleback and Io moths, both with stinging caterpillars.

FLY-POISON
Amianthium muscitoxicum (Walter) A. Gray
Melanthium family (Melanthiaceae)

Description: The leaves of this species are grasslike, measuring about ¼" wide and 12" long. Flowering stalks are erect, reaching 6"–10" tall, with ¼" flowers crowded at the top in a somewhat pyramidal arrangement. The flowers turn green after being pollinated.

Bloom Season: February to August

Habitat/Range: Flatwoods, pine savannas, and bogs from Escambia County east to Leon and Wakulla Counties in the Florida panhandle

Comments: *Amianthium* translates to "pure flower" and alludes to the absence of glands on the calyx and corolla. The name *muscitoxicum* means "fly poison." The leaves and bulbs are poisonous, especially to livestock, and the Cherokee used the plants to kill unwanted animals around their villages. The nectar kills flies but not butterflies. Another common name is stagger-grass, because cattle that eat the plant will stagger around before dying.

FAIRYWAND

Chamaelirium luteum (L.) A. Gray
Melanthium family (Melanthiaceae)

Description: Male (staminate) and female (pistillate) flowers are produced on separate plants (dioecious); female plants produce more leaves. The leaves are spatulate to oblanceolate and measure 2"–8" long and ½"–2" wide, with broad petioles. The flowers of both sexes are white.

Bloom Season: April to August

Habitat/Range: Rich deciduous woods discontinuously from Escambia County east to Leon and Wakulla Counties in the Florida panhandle and discontinuously from Duval County to Hillsborough County in the peninsula

Comments: *Chamaelirium* means "on the ground" and "lily" and relates to this species' original inclusion in the Lily family (Liliaceae). The name *luteum* means "yellow" and describes the color of the flowers as they age. It is also called devil's-bit and rattlesnake-root. The roots are used in folk medicine and are called starwort or unicorn root. The photo is of a male plant.

OSCEOLA'S PLUME

Stenanthium densum (Desr.) Zomlefer & Judd
Melanthium family (Melanthiaceae)

Description: This species may reach 30" tall at flowering. The flowers are congested in a terminal cluster, and each flower measures about ⅜" wide (white to pink). The leaves are grasslike, narrowly linear, and reach 10" long or more.

Bloom Season: March to June

Habitat/Range: Wet flatwoods across the panhandle and from Suwannee to Nassau Counties south to Sarasota, Manatee, Hardee, Glades, and St. Lucie Counties

Comments: *Stenanthium* means "narrow flower," alluding to the narrow sepals and petals. The name *densum* relates to the congested flowers. Native Americans used the plant to poison crows feeding on crops; it is also extremely toxic to people and grazing livestock. The common name relates to the resemblance of the inflorescence to the plume feathers worn by Osceola (1804–1838), war chief of the Seminole tribe during the Second Seminole War.

VIRGINIA BUNCHFLOWER
Veratrum virginicum (L.) W.T. Aiton
Melanthium family (Melanthiaceae)

Description: The basal leaves are linear-lanceolate and average 6"–10" long and ½"–¾" wide, with a hairy central stem to about 36" tall. The flowers are in terminal clusters and measure about ¾" across.

Bloom Season: May to September

Habitat/Range: Wet flatwoods in widely separated locations in the panhandle; isolated in Nassau and Putnam Counties; and in a band across Pasco, Hillsborough, Polk, and Osceola Counties

Comments: *Veratrum* translates to "true black" and alludes to the black rhizomes of some species. The name *virginicum* refers to Virginia, where this species was first collected. All parts of the plant, especially the black rhizomes, contain steroid alkaloids that cause severe vomiting, abdominal pain, hypotension, cardiac arrest, and even death if eaten. Another common name is false-hellebore.

SANDBOG DEATHCAMAS
Zigadenus glaberrimus Michx.
Melanthium family (Melanthiaceae)

Description: This rhizomatous species reaches 2'–4' tall, with mostly basal leaves that are linear in shape with parallel venation. Flowers are about 1" wide, white to cream, with paired greenish-yellow glands on each tepal, forming a ring.

Bloom Season: July to September

Habitat/Range: Wet flatwoods, bogs, and savannas in the Florida panhandle from Escambia County to Walton and Holmes Counties and from Calhoun and Gulf Counties to Leon and Wakulla Counties

Comments: *Zigadenus* refers to the paired floral glands on each sepal and petal (tepals). The name *glaberrimus* alludes to the glabrous inflorescence. The name deathcamas relates to the similar looking camas (*Camassia*), a species related to asparagus with edible bulbs, so the name deathcamas is intended to alert people of the plant's toxicity. All parts can cause convulsions and death if eaten.

APALACHICOLA MEADOWBEAUTY
Rhexia parviflora Chapm.
Melastome family (Melastomataceae)

Description: This species averages 8"–12" tall, with mostly smooth, square stems except for hairs at the leaf nodes. The opposite, hairy leaves are ½"–1" long, with small teeth along the margins. The flowers are about ¾" wide.

Bloom Season: April to October

Habitat/Range: Wooded swamps and bogs from Santa Rosa County to Wakulla County in the Florida panhandle

Comments: *Rhexia* is a name used by Roman scholar Pliny (AD 23–79) for a plant useful in treating ruptures. The name *parviflora* relates to the few flowers produced by this species. It is a state-listed endangered species due to its limited range and rarity in Florida. There are 10 *Rhexia* species in Florida; 8 of them have pink flowers and 1 species has yellow flowers. Although this is the only white-flowered species of the genus in Florida, some of the pink-flowered species commonly have white flowers.

FLOATING HEART
Nymphoides aquatica (J.F. Gmel.) Kuntze
Bogbean family (Menyanthaceae)

Description: The floating, ovate leaves of this aquatic species measure 4"–6" wide and are conspicuously roughened on the lower surface. Thickened roots are often at the base of the flowering stalks that appear from the node just below the leaf blade. The ⅜"–½" flowers are held just above the water surface.

Bloom Season: All year

Habitat/Range: Swamps, ponds, lakes, and canals throughout much of mainland Florida

Comments: *Nymphoides* refers to the similarity of this genus to *Nymphaea*, the waterlilies. The name *aquatica* relates to the species' aquatic habitat. This plant is sold in the aquarium trade as "banana lily" because of the banana-like clusters of swollen roots beneath the leaf blades. The similar crested floating heart (*Nymphoides cristata*) is naturalized from Asia and has a wavy crest on the corolla lobes and leaves typically mottled with purple.

BRACTED COLICROOT
Aletris bracteata Northr.
Bog Asphodel family (Nartheciaceae)

Description: The linear-lanceolate, grayish-green, leaves form a basal rosette and measure 2"–6" long to about ⅜" wide and resemble a miniature agave in appearance. Flowers reach ¼" long with spreading lobes and appear on the top third of an erect, 19"–23" scape.

Bloom Season: February to July

Habitat/Range: Pine rocklands of southern Miami-Dade County and Monroe County (mainland and Florida Keys)

Comments: Aletris was a legendary Greek slave woman who ground grain, so the genus *Aletris* relates to the mealy texture of the flowers. The name *bracteata* relates to the bracts that subtend the flowers. It is a state-listed endangered species first described in 1902 by American botany professor Alice Rich Northrop (1864–1922). She is best known for advocating access to nature for school children in New York City. This is the only member of the genus in Everglades National Park.

SOUTHERN COLICROOT
Aletris obovata Nash ex Small
Bog Asphodel family (Nartheciaceae)

Description: The bright green, elliptic to lanceolate basal leaves measure 1⅜"–4" long and ⅜"–1" wide. The obovoid (reverse egg-shaped) flowers are white to creamy white, sometimes tipped with orange, and reach ⅜" long. The flowers turn inward at the tip.

Bloom Season: March to July

Habitat/Range: Moist flatwoods and savannas from Leon, Liberty, and Franklin Counties across the northern peninsula and south to Citrus, Marion, Putnam, and Flagler Counties

Comments: The name *obovata* relates to the obovoid shape of the flowers. White colicroot (*Aletris farinosa*) has longer flowers that do not turn inward at the tip and is known only in Florida from Escambia and Jackson Counties. This genus is sometimes included in the Lily family (Liliaceae). Although *Aletris* species have been used to treat colic, they are now believed to have narcotic properties that can induce colic.

JAMESON'S WATERLILY
Nymphaea jamesoniana Planch.
Waterlily family (Nymphaeaceae)

Description: The elliptic leaves are green above and below, sometimes with darker green flecks, and measure up to 9" long and 7½" wide, with conspicuous weblike veins. The 3" flowers are usually floating, with uniformly green sepals and 12, 16, or 20 creamy white petals.

Bloom Season: August to November

Habitat/Range: Shallow water of marshes, canals, flooded ditches, and retention ponds in Levy, Citrus, Hillsborough, Sarasota, DeSoto, Charlotte, and Lee Counties

Comments: *Nymphaea* is Greek for "water nymph." According to Greek mythology, water nymphs, or naiads, are female spirits that inhabit and preside over lakes, streams, rivers, and springs. The name *jamesoniana* honors Scottish botanist William Jameson (1796–1873), who first collected this species in Guayaquil, Ecuador, in March 1846 and then described in 1852 by botanist Jules Émile Planchon (1823–1889). The flowers of this state-listed endangered species are seldom seen because they open late at night and close by dawn, beckoning nocturnal pollinators (probably beetles). It is well worth losing a little sleep to see this waterlily in flower.

WHITE WATERLILY
Nymphaea odorata Ait.
Waterlily family (Nymphaeaceae)

Description: The round, floating leaf blades reach 6"–10" wide, with a narrow basal cleft. The solitary, heavily perfumed, 3"–4" flowers open by midmorning and close by late afternoon. The white petals may be blushed with pink; the flowers typically float on the water surface.

Bloom Season: February to November

Habitat/Range: Freshwater ponds, lakes, swamps, and canals throughout mainland Florida

Comments: The name *odorata* refers to the fragrant blossoms, and this species is regarded as the most fragrant of all waterlilies. It is sometimes used to create fascinating hybrids for the water garden trade. Waterlily and lotus flowers held a prominent place in the art and mythology of Egyptian, Chinese, and Mayan cultures, and the rhizomes of some species contain psychotropic properties used as a hallucinogen to communicate with spirits of the dead. Beetles are pollinators.

JUG ORCHID
Aspidogyne querceticola (Lindl.) Meneguzzo
(Also *Erythrodes querceticola* [Lindl.] Ames;
Platythelys querceticola [Lindl.] Garay)
Orchid family (Orchidaceae)

Description: The frail, succulent stems of this diminutive, terrestrial species average 3"–6" tall and are lined with alternating lanceolate leaves averaging ⅜"–½" long and ¼"–⅜" wide. The flowers are barely ⅛" wide.

Bloom Season: June to February

Habitat/Range: Mesic forests and wooded swamps in Jackson, Liberty, and Wakulla Counties in the Florida panhandle and discontinuously south through the peninsula into the Florida Keys

Comments: *Aspidogyne* is from the Greek *aspidus*, "shield," and *gyne*, for the female reproductive parts. The name *querceticola* relates to the species most often being found growing among oaks in the genus *Quercus*. In 2012 Brazilian botanist Thiago E. C. Meneguzzo merged *Platythelys* with *Aspidogyne*, so this is a new name for this Florida orchid.

CARTER'S ORCHID
Basiphyllaea corallicola (Small) Ames
Orchid family (Orchidaceae)

Description: This terrestrial orchid bears a single, narrow leaf to about 1" long and ⅛" wide. The flower stem stands about 3"–6" tall and is topped by 1–3 flower buds that rarely open because they are pollinated in bud (cleistogamous).

Bloom Season: October to November

Habitat/Range: Pine rocklands and hammock margins of southern Miami-Dade County and Big Pine Key (Monroe County)

Comments: *Basiphyllaea* refers to the basal leaf. The name *corallicola* relates to growing on coral (oolitic limestone). Botanist Joel Jackson Carter (1843–1912) first discovered this endangered orchid in Florida in 1903 while bouncing along on a horse-drawn wagon across Longview Prairie south of Miami with botanists Alvah Augustus Eaton (1865–1908) and John Kunkel Small (1869–1938). Eaton was upset because he had switched seats with Carter that day. Even in flower it is difficult to find.

COSTA RICAN LADIES'-TRESSES
Beloglottis costaricensis (Rchb. f.) Schltr.
Orchid family (Orchidaceae)

Description: The ovate to elliptic leaves form a ground-hugging basal rosette that may not be present when flowering. The flowering stems are covered with glandular hairs and reach 4"–5" tall with small, ³⁄₁₆" flowers that have a green stripe on the sepals and petals.

Bloom Season: March to May

Habitat/Range: Tropical hardwood hammocks of southern Miami-Dade County

Comments: *Beloglottis* means "arrow" and "tongue" and presumably alludes to the shape of the lip. The name *costaricensis* relates to Costa Rica. This state-listed endangered species has disappeared from historical locations in Miami-Dade County, probably due to lowering of the water table. It is currently known from only a few locations within Everglades National Park. It also ranges through the West Indies, Mexico, and Central America. It was once included in the genus *Spiranthes.*

SPRING CORALROOT

Corallorhiza wisteriana Conrad
Orchid family (Orchidaceae)

Description: Leafless, frail, reddish or brown flowering stems emerge from an underground, branched rhizome, with flowers that are only about ¼" wide. The sepals are purplish-brown (sometimes greenish or pink) with a pure white, purple-dotted lip.

Bloom Season: December to April in Florida

Habitat/Range: In rich leaf litter of deciduous forests south in Florida to Lee, Highlands, and Indian River Counties

Comments: *Corallorhiza* means "coral root," alluding to the coral-like appearance of the rhizomes. The name *wisteriana* honors botanist Charles J. Wister (1782–1865), who first discovered this species in Pennsylvania. Botanist Solomon White Conrad (1770–1831) described it in 1829. It takes a trained eye, or sheer luck, to find it because it blends in with leaf litter so well. Armadillos are a threat to this orchid by rooting around in search of the underground rhizomes.

GHOST ORCHID

Dendrophylax lindenii (Lindl.) Benth. ex Rolfe
Orchid family (Orchidaceae)

Description: The photosynthetic roots of this leafless epiphyte are flecked with white and radiate outward like spokes on a wheel. The growing tips are green. The 3"–4" flowers are solitary or paired (rarely clustered).

Bloom Season: May to August

Habitat/Range: Forested swamps, strands, and sloughs of Collier, Hendry, and Lee Counties

Comments: *Dendrophylax* translates to "tree guardian," for the epiphytic habit. The name *lindenii* honors Belgian botanist Jean Jules Linden (1817–1898), who discovered this orchid in Cuba in 1844. Botanist Allan Hiram Curtiss (1845–1907) discovered it in Florida in 1880, and in 1885 naturalist Charles Torrey Simpson (1846–1932) found it growing on royal palms (*Roystonea regia*) along the Rodgers River in what is now Everglades National Park. This state-listed endangered species is pollinated by a sphinx moth (*Cocyctius antaeus*).

SPURRED NEOTTIA

Eltroplectris calcarata (Sw.) Garay & Sweet
Orchid family (Orchidaceae)

Description: The silky, elliptic leaf blades on long petioles range from 4"–6" long and 1½"–2½" wide. The 2" flowers are arranged on an erect spike. The sepals and petals are linear-lanceolate, with a recurved frilly lip.

Bloom Season: December to March

Habitat/Range: Hardwood forests of Broward, Miami-Dade, and Collier Counties (historically Highlands County)

Comments: *Eltroplectris* and *calcarata* both refer to the free-hanging nectar spur. This state-listed endangered species occurs in Everglades National Park (Miami-Dade County) and is known from the Fakahatchee Swamp and the Picayune Strand (Collier County), plus it was vouchered in Broward County in 2009. It has disappeared from Miami-Dade County east of Everglades National Park, and feral hogs have exterminated it from Highlands Hammock State Park (Highlands County). It is likely pollinated by moths.

NIGHT-SCENTED ORCHID

Epidendrum nocturnum Jacq.
Orchid family (Orchidaceae)

Description: The reedlike leafy stems of this epiphyte reach 3' long, with elliptic, leathery leaves that measure 3"–5" long and ½"–1" wide. The lip is 3-lobed, with 2 winglike lateral lobes and a narrow, pointed central lobe.

Bloom Season: July to December

Habitat/Range: Hardwood forests and swamps from Martin and Lee Counties south through the Florida mainland

Comments: *Epidendrum* means "on tree" and alludes to the epiphytic habit. The name *nocturnum* is for the captivating scent emitted by the flowers at night. The pungent, medicinal perfume attracts sphinx moths that hover hummingbird-like in front of the flowers at dusk and after dark. The pollinia stick to the head of the moth as it sips nectar and is then transferred to another flower. Botanist Abram Paschal Garber (1838–1881) first discovered this state-listed endangered species in Florida in 1877.

MICHAUX'S ORCHID
Habenaria quinqueseta (Michx.) Eaton
Orchid family (Orchidaceae)

Description: Flowering plants are 6"–14" tall, with 2"–6" long and ¾"–1" wide succulent, lanceolate leaves alternating up the stem. The ¾" flowers are spindly; the white lip is in 3 threadlike divisions, with a spur that measures 2"–4" long.

Bloom Season: August to January

Habitat/Range: Marshes and wet pinelands throughout most of mainland Florida

Comments: *Habenaria* means "rein," for the rein-like spur on the type species. The name *quinque-seta* means "five bristles," for the narrow portions of the calyx and corolla. The common name is for botanist André Michaux (1746–1802), who first described this species as *Orchis quinqueseta*. A similar long-spurred species (*Habenaria macro-ceratitis*) is sometimes treated as a variety of this species. It also closely resembles the rare, endangered *Habenaria distans* of southwest Florida, with leaves in a basal rosette.

HATCHET ORCHID
Pelexia adnata (Sw.) Poit ex Rich.
Orchid family (Orchidaceae)

Description: The elliptic leaves average 2½"–4½" long and 1¼"–2" wide, often with white spots. Flowers are ¼" wide on a hairy, erect spike rang-ing from 6"–10" tall.

Bloom Season: March to June

Habitat/Range: In humus or on mossy logs in hardwood swamps of Collier County (presumed extirpated in Miami-Dade County)

Comments: *Pelexia* means "helmet" and refers to the dorsal sepal, which is united with 2 petals to form a hood. The name *adnata* refers to the lateral sepals that clasp the column foot. This tropical species was first discovered in Florida by the author in 1978 in a Miami-Dade County hammock, but by 1985 the colony had died out. A new colony was found in 2004 in the Fakahatchee Swamp (Collier County) by Florida state park biologist Mike Owen (1960–) and AmeriCorps volunteer Karen Relish (1963–). More colonies have been found there recently. The Spanish name is *hachuela* ("hatchet").

WHITE FRINGED ORCHID

Platanthera blephariglottis (Willd.) Lindl. var. *conspicua* (Nash) Luer
Orchid family (Orchidaceae)

Description: When flowering, this orchid can reach 30" tall but is more typically 12"–16" in height. Lanceolate, keeled, glossy leaves average 3"–8" long and ¾"–1½" wide. Individual flowers are ½"–¾" long.

Bloom Season: August to October

Habitat/Range: Wet prairies, pine savannas, and marshes through much of northern and central Florida south to Manatee, Highlands, and Brevard Counties

Comments: *Platanthera* means "broad anther." The name *blephariglottis* translates to "tongue like an eyelid," in reference to the frilly lip, and the name *conspicua* alludes to the species' conspicuous flowers. It is a state-listed threatened species mostly due to habitat loss. It hybridizes in Florida with *Platanthera ciliaris* and also with *Platanthera cristata*. Some taxonomists give it species status as *Platanthera conspicua*.

SNOWY ORCHID

Platanthera nivea (Nutt.) Luer
Orchid family (Orchidaceae)

Description: This terrestrial orchid has keeled, lanceolate leaves that measure 2"–8" long and ¼"–⅜" wide. The erect stalk produces 20–50 glistening flowers arranged cylindrically, with individual flowers measuring about ¼" long and ⅛" wide. The narrow lip is bent backward at the center. The floral scent is reminiscent of grape jelly.

Bloom Season: May to June

Habitat/Range: Wet flatwoods and savannas scattered throughout much of mainland Florida

Comments: The name *nivea* means "snowy," alluding to the sparkling, snow-white flowers. Some botanists place this species in the genus *Habenaria*. It has a very short bloom period, and the key to finding it is to look in wet habitats that have recently burned. It often blooms in standing water and skips flowering in dry years. It is a state-listed threatened species principally due to habitat degradation from drainage.

LONG-LIPPED LADIES'-TRESSES
Spiranthes longilabris Lindl.
Orchid family (Orchidaceae)

Description: From 3–5 linear-lanceolate leaves measure 3"–6" long, but these may not be present when flowering. The pubescent flowers are ⁵⁄₁₆" wide, with a long lip diffused with yellow. The lateral sepals spread out horizontally.

Bloom Season: November to December

Habitat/Range: Flatwoods and prairies discontinuously through mainland Florida; most common in the southern half of the peninsula

Comments: *Spiranthes* translates to "coil flower," alluding to the spiraling flower arrangement of many species in this genus. The name *longilabris* refers to the long lip (labellum) of the flower. This state-listed threatened species reaches the Big Cypress National Preserve but is absent from Everglades National Park. It was first described in 1840 from plants collected in Louisiana. *Spiranthes igniorchis* has very similar flowers and is believed to be endemic to Polk and Okeechobee Counties.

FRAGRANT LADIES'-TRESSES
Spiranthes odorata (Nutt.) Lindl.
Orchid family (Orchidaceae)

Description: This aquatic or semiaquatic orchid is typically 10"–12" tall when in flower but can be much taller. The leaves are narrowly lanceolate and measure 3"–6" long and ½"–¾" wide. The flower spike is lined with very fragrant, ¼" flowers.

Bloom Season: Mostly October to December

Habitat/Range: Freshwater wetlands throughout much of mainland Florida

Comments: The name *odorata* means "with an odor," referring to the tantalizingly sweet perfume that emanates from the flowers. This species often blooms in standing water but may be found in wet soil of cypress domes and wooded swamps. When the plant is in standing water, it is well worth getting your feet wet to savor its fragrance. It was once regarded as a variety (var. *odorata*) of the similar *Spiranthes cernua*, known only from Liberty County in Florida. Also called marsh ladies'-tresses, it ranges from Delaware to Texas.

GREENVEIN LADIES'-TRESSES
Spiranthes praecox (Walter) S. Watson
Orchid family (Orchidaceae)

Description: The linear to linear-lanceolate leaves of this terrestrial orchid are spreading and average 4"–8" long and ¼"–½" wide. The flowers may be loosely or tightly spiraled, usually with a series of thin green lines on the lip.

Bloom Season: February to June

Habitat/Range: Flatwoods and pine savannas of mainland Florida south to Collier and Broward Counties

Comments: The name *praecox* means "untimely" and refers to the species' early bloom season. Plants with pure white lips are common in the southernmost counties within its Florida range, and a population in north-central Florida has pale green flowers. A plant of woodlands with green markings on the lip was named *Spiranthes sylvatica*, but recent molecular DNA research places it under synonymy with *Spiranthes praecox*. Two other species, *Spiranthes amesiana* and *S. eatonii*, also are no longer valid.

LITTLE PEARL-TWIST
Spiranthes tuberosa Raf.
Orchid family (Orchidaceae)

Description: The ovate leaves range from ¾"–2" long and ⅜"–¾" wide but are absent when flowering. The flowers spiral around the top portion of a thin, erect spike, with each flower measuring about 3⁄16" long.

Bloom Season: June to September

Habitat/Range: Dry, sandy pinelands, scrub, and savannas discontinuously across the Florida panhandle south in the peninsula to Lee, Highlands, and Indian River Counties

Comments: The name *tuberosa* alludes to the plant's underground tubers. This state-listed threatened species has tiny flowers, so close scrutiny of its habitat during anthesis is required to locate it. It has a propensity to grow in cemeteries with sandy soils, but also check natural habitats that have recently burned. The species ranges from New England to Texas and was first described in 1833 from plants collected in New Jersey. The common name relates to the spiraling pearl-white flowers.

SPRING LADIES'-TRESSES

Spiranthes vernalis Engelm. & A. Gray
Orchid family (Orchidaceae)

Description: The linear leaves average 4"–6" long and up to ⅜" wide. The erect flower spike is covered with pointed hairs and is lined with ¼" flowers, usually with some degree of spiraling, but some plants hold the flowers in a single rank. It averages 6"–10" tall when in flower.

Bloom Season: February to May

Habitat/Range: Flatwoods, prairies, and roadsides throughout mainland Florida

Comments: The name *vernalis* relates to the vernal equinox, or springtime, in reference to the species' flowering season. This is one of the most common terrestrial orchids in Florida. It is frequent along mowed road swales and in open prairies, and its early flowering season helps separate it from other white-flowered species, especially the very similar lacelip ladies'-tresses (*Spiranthes laciniata*), which typically blooms in summer, after this species has finished flowering.

DANCING LADY ORCHID

Tolumnia bahamensis (Nash ex Britton & Millsp.) Braem
(Also *Oncidium bahamense* Nash ex Britton & Millsp.)
Orchid family (Orchidaceae)

Description: This semi-epiphytic orchid bears 3–7 fan-shaped leaves from 6"–10" long and ¼"–⅜" wide. The inflorescence can reach 30" long, with flowers measuring ½"–¾" wide. The flowers are somewhat unpleasantly scented.

Bloom Season: April to June

Habitat/Range: Scrub and sandhill thickets of Martin and Palm Beach Counties

Comments: *Tolumnia* honors Lars Tolumnius (d. 428 BC), king of Veii in Etruria, northwest of present-day Rome. His name in Etruscan was Larth Tulumnes. The name *bahamensis* means "of the Bahamas," where this species was first collected at Eight Mile Rock on Grand Bahama in 1905. This state-listed endangered species is typically found at the bases of Florida rosemary (*Ceratiola ericoides*) or myrtle oak (*Quercus myrtifolia*) and is well concealed when not in flower.

WITHLACOOCHEE NODDINGCAPS
Triphora craigheadii Luer
Orchid family (Orchidaceae)

Description: A fragile, succulent stem averages 1"–2" tall, with 1–4 broadly ovate ⅜" leaves that are dark green above and purple below. Flowers are about ³⁄₁₆" wide and last only 2 hours in the morning. Plants often produce 2 buds that open a week apart.

Bloom Season: June to July

Habitat/Range: Endemic to mesic forests of Citrus, Sumter, Hernando, Highlands, and Collier Counties

Comments: *Triphora* means "threefold" and "bearing," alluding to the 3 flowers or the 3 crests on the lip of the type species. The name *craigheadii* honors Everglades National Park biologist Frank C. Craighead (1890–1982). This state-listed endangered species was described in 1966 by physician and botanist Carlyle A. Luer (1922–) from plants found in the Withlacoochee State Forest in 1965. It takes sheer luck to catch this orchid with an open flower, but the buds stand erect the day before they open.

GENTIAN NODDINGCAPS
Triphora gentianoides (Sw.) Ames & Schltr.
Orchid family (Orchidaceae)

Description: The succulent greenish-brown stems are usually found in small colonies, each stem standing about 3"–4" tall and topped by erect to arching, self-pollinating flowers that are slightly gaping. The stems arise from cylindric, subterranean tuberoids. Bract-like leaves partially sheath the stem.

Bloom Season: June to August

Habitat/Range: Shaded, sandy soils in landscapes and in leaf litter along wooded trails from Pinellas and St. Lucie Counties south along both coasts to Collier and Miami-Dade Counties

Comments: The name *gentianoides* relates to the species' resemblance to a member of the Gentian family (Gentianaceae). This somewhat weedy little orchid shows up in shaded mulch or in rich, sandy soil of garden landscapes. It often goes unrecognized and may likely occur in many more counties, where it has yet to be vouchered. It ranges into the neotropics.

THREE BIRDS ORCHID

Triphora trianthophoros (Sw.) Rydb.
Orchid family (Orchidaceae)

Description: The succulent stems of this orchid bear 2–6 ovate, ¼"–⅜" leaves. The ½"–⅝" flowers are nodding in bud but typically face upward when open and then nod again after closing.

Bloom Season: July to October

Habitat/Range: Hardwood forests of Leon County and then through the center of the state from Suwannee and Columbia Counties south to Hernando, Lake, and Orange Counties; also Highlands County

Comments: The name *trianthophoros* relates to the species' often having 3 flowers open at the same time, which is also reflected in the common name. Botanist Kanchi N. Gandhi (1948–), senior nomenclatural registrar of the Harvard University herbaria, noted in 2007 that the original spelling of the specific epithet was *trianthophoros*, not *trianthophora*, as it is usually spelled. Individual populations all bloom at the same time, offering the best chance for pollination.

BLUESTEM PRICKLY POPPY

Argemone albiflora Hornem.
Poppy family (Papaveraceae)

Description: The bluish-green, deeply to shallowly lobed leaves of this very prickly plant range from 2"–10" long and 1½"–3½" wide. The flowers are about 2" wide.

Bloom Season: April to June

Habitat/Range: Disturbed sites through much of the panhandle and peninsula south to Sarasota, DeSoto, and Brevard Counties; also vouchered from Broward County

Comments: *Argemone* is from a Greek name for a poppy-like plant used to treat cataract of the eye. The name *albiflora* relates to the white flowers. The latex has been used to treat warts and cold sores, and the seeds were used to induce vomiting, but misuse can be fatal. The species was named in 1815 by Danish botanist Jens Wilken Hornemann (1770–1841), whose views on flowers were inspirational to his friend Hans Christian Andersen (1805–1875) in the tale "Little Ida's Flowers." It is sometimes cultivated in Scandinavia.

BLOODROOT
Sanguinaria canadensis L.
Poppy family (Papaveraceae)

Description: The solitary leaf of this 3"–6" species is mostly palmately 5–7 lobed with scalloped margins, averaging 3"–4" wide (sometimes folded around the flower stem). The nectar-less flowers are 1"–2¼" wide, with alternating smaller petals. The sap is orange to red.

Bloom Season: January to May

Habitat/Range: Mesic forests and stream slopes of Walton, Washington, Jackson, Liberty, Gadsden, Leon, and Hamilton Counties

Comments: *Sanguinaria* is from the Latin *sanguis* ("blood"), in reference to the color of the sap. The name *canadensis* relates to Canada, where it was first collected and later described in 1753 by Carolus Linnaeus (1707–1778). The species is used medicinally to treat tapeworms, ulcers, fever, coughs, irregular menstrual periods, and cramps but is considered unsafe by the USDA. The sap is ill-advisedly used for face paint, and the seeds are used as love charms. Seeds are dispersed by ants.

CAROLINA GRASS-OF-PARNASSUS
Parnassia caroliniana Michx.
Grass-of-Parnassus family (Parnassiaceae)

Description: Basal leaves are oval with long petioles; the stem leaves are clasping, with cordate (heart-shaped) leaf blades. The flowers are on tall stalks, and each flower averages 1¼" across. The flowers have 3-parted, sterile stamens that are tipped with fake nectaries to attract pollinators through deceit.

Bloom Season: October to December

Habitat/Range: Mesic longleaf pine and wiregrass savannas of Liberty and Franklin Counties in the Florida panhandle

Comments: *Parnassia* was named for Mount Parnassus in Greece. It is said that cattle grazing on the mountain relished eating *Parnassia palustris*, so the ancient Greeks made it an "honorary grass." The name *caroliniana* relates to South Carolina, where the type specimen was collected and later described in 1803. It is regarded as an imperiled species in North Carolina.

GRASS-OF-PARNASSUS

Parnassia grandifolia DC.
Grass-of-Parnassus family (Parnassiaceae)

Description: The oval, slightly succulent, shiny leaf blades of this rhizomatous perennial are 1½"–4" long, with long petioles. Flowers measure 1½" wide, with intricate green, brown, or yellow venation on the petals.

Bloom Season: November to December

Habitat/Range: Shaded streambanks and cypress bogs in Liberty, Franklin, Putnam, and Marion Counties

Comments: The name *grandifolia* relates to the large leaves compared to other species in the genus. It is also called bog-stars. Some members of this genus live in arctic and alpine regions and are a symbol of the Highland Scottish Clan MacLea, formally recognized in 2003. There are 3 parnassia flowers on the British flag of Cumberland County, adopted in December 2012. This genus has previously been included in the Saxifrage family (Saxifragaceae) and the Stafftree family (Celastraceae).

KEYS PASSIONFLOWER

Passiflora multiflora L.
Passionflower family (Passifloraceae)

Description: This high-climbing, woody vine has softly pubescent, oblong leaves from 2"–2½" long and ¾"–1" wide. The ½" flowers are in axillary clusters and are followed by dark blue, globose, ⁵⁄₁₆" fruits.

Bloom Season: November to March

Habitat/Range: Tropical hardwood hammocks of the Florida Keys (Miami-Dade and Monroe Counties)

Comments: *Passiflora* is Latin for "passion flower" and relates to the crucifixion of Jesus. When Spanish physician Nicolás Monardes (1493–1588) published his herbal in 1574, he called these plants *Flos Passionis*, or "flower of passion." Ever since then the plants have become intertwined with mystical Christian beliefs that the flower parts depict the crucifixion of Christ. The name *multiflora* relates to the multiple flowers. This state-listed endangered species is most common in the upper Florida Keys. It also ranges into the West Indies.

PALE PASSIONFLOWER
Passiflora pallens Poepp. ex Mast.
Passionflower family (Passifloraceae)

Description: The evenly 3-lobed, light green leaves measure 1"–3" long and equally wide, with rounded lobes. The showy flowers are 2" wide and produce oval, yellow, 2" fruits. It climbs by tendrils.

Bloom Season: All year

Habitat/Range: Hardwood hammocks of Broward, Collier, Miami-Dade, and mainland Monroe Counties

Comments: The name *pallens* refers to the pale flower color of this state-listed endangered species. It is only sparingly cultivated by native-plant aficionados in the southernmost counties of Florida. It is not popular with butterfly gardeners because heliconian butterflies very rarely use it as larval food, and it tends to be rather short-lived. It is also called pineland passionflower, even though it is not fire tolerant and, therefore, is rarely found in pinelands. Its natural range extends into Cuba and Hispaniola.

GOATSFOOT
Passiflora sexflora Juss.
Passionflower family (Passifloraceae)

Description: The leaf blades of this vine are shaped somewhat like a goat's foot, densely pubescent, and range from 2½"–5" wide and about half as long. The leaves are opposite tendrils used for climbing; the clustered flowers measure ⅜"–½" wide, with greenish-white sepals and white petals. Fruits are subglobose, blue-black, and about ⅜" wide.

Bloom Season: October to March

Habitat/Range: Margins and canopy gaps of tropical hardwood hammocks in Miami-Dade County

Comments: The name *sexflora* refers to the clusters of 6 flowers that some plants produce. This species may disappear from areas but then reappear vigorously following soil disturbance, from either hurricanes or mechanical disturbance. Reintroduction efforts spearheaded by Fairchild Tropical Botanic Garden in Coral Gables have been successful at reestablishing it in areas where it historically occurred.

BRANCHED HEDGEHYSSOP

Gratiola ramosa Walter
Plantain family (Plantaginaceae)

Description: The branched, pubescent stems of this species reach 4"–12" tall, with opposite, oblong to ovate leaves that average ⅜"–⅞" long and about ¼" wide. The leaves are widely clasping, with coarse teeth along the margins. The tubular flowers are about ½"–⅝" long.

Bloom Season: All year

Habitat/Range: Flatwoods, pond margins, and open marshes throughout mainland Florida

Comments: *Gratiola* means "agreeableness" or "pleasantness" and is said to allude to the genus's medicinal qualities. The name *ramosa* means "branched." Some species have a long history of medicinal uses in Europe, and the related hyssop (*Hyssopus officinalis*) from Europe and the Middle East is mentioned numerous times in the Bible. It was named in 1788 by British-American botanist Thomas Walter (1740–1789). It is at its height of flowering during the summer rainy season.

PENINSULA AXILFLOWER

Mecardonia acuminata (Walter) Small ssp.
peninsularis (Pennell) Rossow
Plantain family (Plantaginaceae)

Description: This diffusely branched subspecies has angled stems with toothed leaves to about ¼" wide and between ½"–1" long. The 5-lobed, tubular flowers are on long, ascending stems, with the posterior lobes of the flowers united about ⅔ of the length.

Bloom Season: April to November

Habitat/Range: Endemic to marshes and moist pinelands in Lafayette County and from Levy, Marion, Lake, and Volusia Counties south to the Florida Keys

Comments: *Mecardonia* honors Antonio de Meca y Cardona, an eighteenth-century Spanish patron of the Barcelona Botanical Garden and marquis of Ciutadilla, a village in Spain. The name *acuminata* means "tapering to a long narrow point," referring to the leaf blades; *peninsularis* means "growing on a peninsula," in this case, Florida. Two other non-endemic subspecies occur in Florida.

WHITE BEARDTONGUE

Penstemon multiflorus (Benth.) Chapm. ex Small
Plantain family (Plantaginaceae)

Description: The opposite, elliptical stem leaves
of this 2'–3' species are gray-green, often with a
reddish midvein, and measure about 1"–2" long
and ⅜"–½" wide. The basal leaves are larger.
White (sometimes pinkish), tubular flowers average 1" long and ¾" wide and have a 3-lobed lip.

Bloom Season: April to September

Habitat/Range: Sandhills and flatwoods throughout much of Florida, including the Florida Keys

Comments: *Penstemon* means "five" and "stamen," alluding to the 4 fertile stamens and 1
sterile stamen on the type species of the genus.
The name *multiflorus* describes its many flowers.
This is the most frequent member of the genus
in Florida. The name beardtongue relates to the
hairs at the mouth of the corolla, which resemble
a bearded tongue. There are hundreds of species
and cultivars of *Penstemon* in the nursery trade.

ROUGH HEDGEHYSSOP

Sophronanthe hispida Benth. ex Lindl.
(Also *Gratiola hispida* [Benth. ex Lindl.] Pollard)
Plantain family (Plantaginaceae)

Description: The very narrow, needlelike leaves
are coarsely hairy (hispid) and measure ¼"–½"
long, crowded along the stems. The leaves are
often curled under at the margins (revolute). The
flowers measure about ½" wide and appear along
the stems.

Bloom Season: May to November

Habitat/Range: Dry flatwoods and scrub throughout much of mainland Florida

Comments: *Sophronanthe* means "modest flower."
The name *hispida* refers to the coarse hairs on
the leaves. The plant resembles wild pennyroyal
(*Piloblephis rigida*), but the leaves have no minty
odor. The Hebrew name *hyssop* refers to a plant
with purging qualities. The species was described
in 1836 by botanist George Bentham (1800–1884)
from plants collected near Apalachicola (Franklin
County). It was moved to *Gratiola* in 1897 and back
to *Sophronanthe* in 2008.

DOCTORBUSH

Plumbago zeylanica L.
(Also *Plumbago scandens* L.)
Leadwort family (Plumbaginaceae)

Description: Vinelike stems reach 3' long or more, with alternate, elliptic-lanceolate leaves ranging from 1¼"–4" long and up to 2⅜" wide. The white, tubular flowers are about ⅝" wide with blue anthers. The prism-shaped, linear fruits cling to hair and clothing.

Bloom Season: All year

Habitat/Range: Coastal strand and open disturbed sites from Levy and Volusia Counties south along both coasts through the Florida Keys

Comments: *Plumbago* was a name used by Dioscorides (ca. AD 40–90), for both a type of metal and a plant, hence the name leadwort. The name *zeylanica* means "of Ceylon," modern-day Sri Lanka. Leaves and roots cause reddening and blistering of the skin, giving rise to the Spanish name *malacara* (bad face). This is a larval host plant of the cassius blue butterfly. The nonnative blue plumbago (*Plumbago auriculata*) is naturalized in Florida.

BACHELOR'S BUTTON

Polygala balduinii Nutt.
Milkwort family (Polygalaceae)

Description: The stems reach 8"–24" tall and are often branched near the base, with lanceolate upper leaves. Small flowers are on erect stems in rounded, terminal clusters.

Bloom Season: All year

Habitat/Range: Wet pinelands, prairies, and coastal swales throughout much of mainland Florida but absent in most of the northern border counties

Comments: *Polygala* means "much milk," in the belief that milkworts could increase milk flow in cattle. Flemish physician Rembert Dodoens (1517–1585) wrote of milkworts in 1578 that they "engendreth plentie of milk; therefore it is good to be used of nurses that lack milk." The name *balduinii* honors American botanist William Baldwin (1779–1819). The name bachelor's button comes from Victorian times, when it was fashionable for single men to put flowers in buttonholes of their jacket to signify their availability.

BOYKIN'S MILKWORT
Polygala boykinii Nutt.
Milkwort family (Polygalaceae)

Description: The leaves vary greatly, from obovate to elliptic-obovate for the lower leaves and linear to linear-lanceolate for the upper leaves. Flowering plants average 6"–10" tall but may be twice that height. Tiny white or greenish-white flowers line the upper several inches of the erect, unbranched stems, held well above the foliage.

Bloom Season: All year

Habitat/Range: Prairies and flatwoods from Jackson, Calhoun, Gadsden, Leon, and Taylor Counties south along the coastal counties of the west coast to Miami-Dade County and into the Florida Keys

Comments: English botanist Thomas Nuttall (1786–1859), who traveled in Florida, named this species in 1834 to honor Georgia plantation owner and field botanist Samuel Boykin (1786–1846). The flowers of this species are conspicuously smaller in the southern portions of its Florida range than they are to the north.

COASTAL PLAIN MILKWORT
Polygala setacea Michx.
Milkwort family (Polygalaceae)

Description: Very slender, simple or sparsely branched stems typically stand 6"–8" tall and are topped by cylindric racemes of very small flowers that require magnification to appreciate. The flowers have 2 white wings with a mustard-yellow, bristly lip. The scalelike leaves are linear, tapering gradually from the base to the apex.

Bloom Season: All year

Habitat/Range: Flatwoods and bogs from Bay, Liberty, and Leon Counties east and south throughout mainland Florida

Comments: The name *setacea* means "bristled" and relates to the stems. Members of this genus have been used medicinally for depression, insomnia, coughs, and even venomous snakebite. French botanist André Michaux (1746–1802) collected and described this species from North Carolina in 1802, but the name wasn't published until 1803, a year after he died of a tropical fever during an expedition to Madagascar.

WATERPEPPER

Persicaria hydropiperoides (Michx.) Small
(Also *Polygonum hydropiperoides* Michx.)
Buckwheat family (Polygonaceae)

Description: Flowering plants reach 10"–36" tall
or more, with alternate, lanceolate leaves measuring 2½"–6" long and ½"–1½" wide. The petioles
form a sheath around the stem. The ⅛" flowers are
on axillary stalks.

Bloom Season: All year

Habitat/Range: Freshwater wetlands and roadside
ditches throughout mainland Florida

Comments: *Persicaria* relates to the similarity of
the leaves of the type species (*Persicaria hydropiper*) to the leaves of a peach (*Prunus persica*). The
name *hydropiperoides* alludes to the resemblance
of this species to *Persicaria hydropiper*. It is also
called swamp smartweed. The names waterpepper
and smartweed allude to the hot, peppery taste of
the leaves. It has been used to treat uterine and
intestinal bleeding and as a fish poison. There
are 11 native species in Florida and 5 naturalized
exotics.

TALL JOINTWEED

Polygonella gracilis Meisn.
Buckwheat family (Polygonaceae)

Description: The wispy stems of this species
reach 4'–6' tall, branched near the top, with
oblong, spatulate, or linear-spatulate leaves to 1"
long that are not present when flowering. Flowers
are about ⅛" wide.

Bloom Season: June to December

Habitat/Range: Sandhills, scrub, and dunes
throughout much of mainland Florida

Comments: *Polygonella* is a diminutive of
Polygonum and refers to the many swollen nodes
on the stem. The name *gracilis* means "grace-
ful" or "slender" and relates to the stems of
this species. English botanist Thomas Nuttall
(1786–1859) first described this species in 1818 as
Polygonum gracile, and Swiss botanist Carl Daniel
Friedrich Meisner (1800–1874) relegated it to the
genus *Polygonella* in 1856. This species closely
resembles the endemic *Polygonella basiramia* of
Polk and Highlands Counties, but it branches into
many stems near the ground.

LARGELEAF JOINTWEED
Polygonella macrophylla Small
Buckwheat family (Polygonaceae)

Description: The leathery, bluish-green, somewhat spoon-shaped leaves of this species reach 1½"–2" long and are widest near the tip. The white (pink or red) flowers are on erect spikes.

Bloom Season: Mostly October

Habitat/Range: Coastal dunes and scrub ridges from Escambia County east to Walton, Bay, and Franklin Counties in the Florida panhandle

Comments: The name *macrophylla* refers to the large leaves of this species. This state-listed threatened species was described in 1896 by American botanist John Kunkel Small (1869–1938) from plants collected in Franklin County. Small was an eminent botanist of the southeastern United States who spent a great deal of time in Florida. Populations of this species in the vicinity of Carabelle, Florida (Franklin County), have red or pinkish flowers. The plant photographed was in Henderson Beach State Park in Walton County.

SANDLACE
Polygonella myriophylla (Small) Horton
Buckwheat family (Polygonaceae)

Description: The zigzagging stems of this species form low mats, rooting at the nodes, with numerous needlelike, ¼" leaves that are pungently aromatic when crushed. The tiny flowers are in compact, rounded clusters, and each flower measures about ⅜" wide.

Bloom Season: All year

Habitat/Range: Endemic to sand pine scrub along the Lake Wales, Lake Henry, and Winter Haven sand ridges of central Florida

Comments: The name *myriophylla* alludes to the plant's many leaves. This state and federal endangered species was described by botanist John Kunkel Small in 1924 and has been vouchered in Highlands, Orange, Osceola, and Polk Counties. It requires fire to create or maintain openings in its sand pine scrub habitat, so one of its most serious threats is fire suppression. Other threats include habitat loss from development, agriculture, and destructives phosphate strip mines.

OCTOBER FLOWER

Polygonella polygama (Vent.) Engelm. & A. Gray
Buckwheat family (Polygonaceae)

Description: This perennial subshrub has narrowly to broadly spatulate leaves that average ½" long and ¼" wide. Flowers are about ³⁄₁₆" wide and are on short, diffusely-branched stems that cover the plant. Male and female flowers are on separate plants (dioecious).

Bloom Season: August to November

Habitat/Range: Sandhills, flatwoods, and scrub throughout much of mainland Florida

Comments: The name *polygama* refers to "many" and "marriage" (as in polygamy), relating to the many flowers of 2 different sexes. French botanist Étienne Pierre Ventenat (1757–1808) described this species in 1800 as *Polygonum polygamum*. The endemic var. *brachystachya* has leaves that are only about ¹⁄₁₆" wide and is restricted to about a dozen counties in southern and lower central Florida. The common name relates to the month it typically can be found flowering.

KIDNEYLEAF MUDPLANTAIN

Heteranthera reniformis Ruiz & Pav.
Pickerelweed family (Pontederiaceae)

Description: The procumbent, spreading stems of this species are often submerged, with a basal rosette of linear leaves and kidney-shaped, petiolate leaves that average 1" long and 1½" wide and have long, succulent petioles. The leaf blades are either emersed or floating. The inflorescences bear 1–8 short-lived flowers, with the terminal flower often reaching above the tip of the spathe.

Bloom Season: June to October

Habitat/Range: Streams, marshes, and wet roadside ditches in Escambia, Santa Rosa, Bay, Marion, and Highlands Counties

Comments: *Heteranthera* means "different" and "anther," alluding to the different size and shape of the anthers. The name *reniformis* means "kidney-shaped" and relates to the leaf blades. The plant photographed was in a roadside ditch near Archbold Biological Station (Highlands County), where it has yet to be vouchered.

GLADE WINDFLOWER

Anemone berlandieri Pritz.
Buttercup family (Ranunculaceae)

Description: Stems may reach 20" tall, with basal leaves divided into 3 toothed, deeply 3-lobed leaflets. Solitary flowers are at the top of the stem and measure about 1"–1¼" wide, subtended by long, narrow, leaflike bracts.

Bloom Season: February to May

Habitat/Range: Dry woodlands and roadsides in Jackson, Taylor, Dixie, Alachua, Levy, and Citrus Counties

Comments: *Anemone* is from the Greek *anemos* ("wind"). In Greek mythology, young and handsome Adonis, who was born from a myrrh tree, was gored by a wild boar sent by the jealous goddess Artemis. Adonis died in the arms of Aphrodite, who so loved him that she sprinkled nectar on his blood and out sprang the blood-red *Anemone coronaria*, with petals that blow off easily in the wind. The name *berlandieri* honors Belgian botanist and anthropologist Jean-Louis Berlandier (1805–1851). The species is also called tenpetal thimbleweed.

EASTERN FALSE RUE ANEMONE

Enemion biternatum Raf.
Buttercup family (Ranunculaceae)

Description: The sparingly-branched, reddish-green, smooth stems reach about 12" tall and have ternately-divided compound leaves and irregularly 2- to 3-lobed leaflets that are deeply notched at the tips. The leaflets reach 1" long and ¾" wide. Flowers have 5 sepals and are about ¾" across. Petals are absent.

Bloom Season: February to May

Habitat/Range: Rich, mesic, deciduous forests and streambanks in Jackson and Washington Counties in the Florida panhandle

Comments: *Enemion* is a name used by Greek physician Pedanius Dioscorides (AD 40–90) for an anemone. The name *biternatum* refers to the leaves being twice divided into 3s. It is a state-listed endangered species due to its limited range in Florida and is the only member of the genus in the state. Look for it along the trails in Florida Caverns State Park in Jackson County.

RUE ANEMONE

Thalictrum thalictroides (L.) A.J. Eames & B. Boivin
Buttercup family (Ranunculaceae)

Description: Erect stems arise from black, tuberous roots and reach 4"–12" tall, with leaves that are twice ternately compound. The 3-lobed leaflets are widely ovate to nearly round and measure ½"–1" wide. The 1"–1½" flowers have 5–10 petal-like sepals.

Bloom Season: January to June

Habitat/Range: Deciduous forests of Liberty, Gadsden, and Leon Counties

Comments: *Thalictrum* describes a plant with divided leaves and was used by Greek physician Pedanius Dioscorides (AD 40–90) for this genus. When Carolus Linnaeus (1707–1778) described this species as an *Anemone*, he chose the name *thalictroides*, or "resembling a *Thalictrum*." Botanists Arthur Johnson Eames (1881–1969) and Joseph Robert Bernard Boivin (1916–1985) moved it to the genus *Thalictrum* in 1957. A shrubby species, *Thalictrum revolutum*, is also found in the Florida panhandle.

VIRGINIA STRAWBERRY

Fragaria virginiana Mill.
Rose family (Rosaceae)

Description: This stoloniferous perennial bears trifoliate leaves on long petioles, with obovate to elliptic-obovate, coarsely toothed leaflets measuring ¾"–2" long and ½"–1¼" wide. The flowers are 1"–1¼" wide. The red fruits (strawberries) are about 1" long and ¾" wide.

Bloom Season: April to July

Habitat/Range: Open woodlands of Jackson and Leon Counties in the Florida panhandle

Comments: *Fragaria* is Latin for "possessing fragrance" and alludes to the sweet-smelling strawberry fruits. The name *virginiana* relates to Virginia, where the type specimen was collected and described by botanist Philip Miller (1691–1771). Some sources cite Antoine Nicolas Duchesne (1747–1827) as the author, but he referred to members of this genus as "constant races" and not species; therefore his names are invalid. It was hybridized with another species to produce the commercial strawberry.

SOUTHERN DEWBERRY

Rubus trivialis Michx.
Rose family (Rosaceae)

Description: The coarsely hairy stems of this trailing species are armed with stout thorns. The compound leaves have 3–5 serrated leaflets that are mostly elliptic to narrowly ovate. The solitary flowers range from white to pinkish and measure about 1" wide.

Bloom Season: January to May

Habitat/Range: Sandy flatwoods throughout most of mainland Florida

Comments: *Rubus* is an ancient name of the blackberry. The name *trivialis* means "ordinary" and relates to the species' being common throughout its range. There are 3 other blackberry species native to Florida, but this species and the sand blackberry (*Rubus cuneifolius*) are the most common and widespread. The fruits can be eaten raw and are a favorite of the Florida black bear, gray fox, and a variety of birds, including American robins and wild turkeys. Larvae of the blackberry looper and the stinging caterpillars of the lo moth feed on the leaves.

VIRGINIA BUTTONWEED

Diodia virginiana L.
Madder family (Rubiaceae)

Description: The stems are typically reddish green and reach 8"–24" long, with pubescent lanceolate, opposite leaves that range from ¾"–2½" long and ⅜" wide. Solitary, hairy, 4-lobed white flowers are produced in the leaf axils and average ⅜" wide. The red or green fruits are oblong.

Bloom Season: March to September

Habitat/Range: Freshwater wetlands throughout mainland Florida

Comments: *Diodia* is Greek for "thoroughfare" and was so named because some members of this genus often grow along waysides. The name *virginiana* means "of Virginia." This family includes some well-known cultivated plants, including gardenia, pentas, coffee, ixora, and jasmine. This species occurs in every county in Florida and is sometimes found colonizing overwatered lawns. It is often seen along flooded ditches, wet roadsides, pond margins, and riverbanks.

INNOCENCE OR FAIRY FOOTPRINTS

Houstonia procumbens (J.F. Gmel.) Standl.
Madder family (Rubiaceae)

Description: The elliptic to oval leaves of this creeping, ground-hugging perennial average ¼"–⅜" wide and perhaps slightly longer. The 4-lobed flowers measure about ½" across and sometimes have blue markings. The flowers can be terminal or axillary and barely extend above the leaves.

Bloom Season: All year but mostly fall

Habitat/Range: Sandhills, dunes, and moist flatwoods throughout mainland Florida

Comments: *Houstonia* honors Scottish botanist William Houstoun (1695–1733), who collected plants in the neotropics but died unexpectedly of heat stroke in Jamaica. His name is sometimes spelled Houston. The name *procumbens* refers to the species' procumbent growth habit. The name innocence relates to the pure white flowers, which represent purity. It also produces cleistogamous, or self-fertile, flowers underground, helping ensure the plant's survival.

PARTRIDGEBERRY

Mitchella repens L.
Madder family (Rubiaceae)

Description: This small, trailing plant roots along the stems and forms prostrate mats of dark green leaves in shady forests. The leaves are ½"–¾" long and about as wide. The fragrant, 4-lobed, hairy flowers are ½" across and produced in pairs. Rounded fruits are red, each with 2 bright red spots.

Bloom Season: March to November

Habitat/Range: Woodlands of Florida south to Charlotte, Glades, and Martin Counties

Comments: *Mitchella* was named to honor physician and botanist John Mitchell (1711–1768), who lived in Virginia and corresponded with Carolus Linnaeus (1707–1778). Mitchell thought a plant they were discussing was a species of *Chamaedaphe* (Ericaceae), so Linnaeus commemorated Mitchell's error by naming this genus for him. The name *repens* means "creeping." The leaves have been used to brew "a very good tea" that was believed to have medicinal values.

EVERGLADES KEY FALSE BUTTONWEED

Spermacoce neoterminalis Govaerts
(Also *Spermacoce terminalis* [Small]
Kartesz & Gandhi)
Madder family (Rubiaceae)

Description: Stems reach 12" tall, with linear, opposite leaves that average ½"–1" long and ⅛"–³⁄₁₆" wide. Flowers are in round, terminal clusters, or with a second, smaller cluster in the axil of the next pair of leaves down the stem.

Bloom Season: All year

Habitat/Range: Endemic to pinelands and coastal habitats south of Lake Okeechobee to the Florida Keys (Monroe County)

Comments: *Spermacoce* is Greek for "seed point," referring to the sharp calyx teeth. The name *neoterminalis* alludes to the species' range in the New World and the terminal clusters of flowers. Some taxonomists have attempted to relegate this species as a synonym of the naturalized exotic *Spermacoce verticillata*, which differs by its smaller flower clusters present in all the leaf axils and its preference for disturbed sites.

FLORIDA BEARGRASS

Nolina atopocarpa Bartlett
Butcher's Broom family (Ruscaceae)

Description: The narrowly linear leaves of Florida beargrass are wiry, arching or erect, and form a leafy rosette from a bulb-like base. The leaves reach 36" or more in length and have serrated margins. The tall scape (sometimes branched) is lined with ¼" flowers that are often spaced widely apart.

Bloom Season: June to August

Habitat/Range: Endemic to wet flatwoods from St. Johns County south along the coast to Brevard County and in Liberty, Franklin, Orange, Charlotte, and Lee Counties

Comments: *Nolina* honors French arboriculturist Abbé Charles-Pierre Nolin (1717–1796). The name *atopocarpa* relates to the asymmetrical fruit. Botanist Harley Harris Bartlett (1886–1960) first described this species in 1909 from plants collected in 1896 near Eau Gallie (Brevard County) by botanist Allan Hiram Curtiss (1845–1907). It is a state-listed threatened species.

BRITTON'S BEARGRASS
Nolina brittoniana Nash
Butcher's Broom family (Ruscaceae)

Description: The minutely toothed, narrow leaves vary from 28"–40" long and up to ⅜" wide, forming a basal rosette. A central spike rises up to 6' tall and is lined with ⅜" flowers. Male and female flowers are sometimes produced on separate plants.

Bloom Season: March to May

Habitat/Range: Endemic to sandhills and scrub from Marion and Lake Counties to Highlands and Hernando Counties

Comments: The name *brittoniana* honors American taxonomist Nathaniel Lord Britton (1859–1934), who helped found the New York Botanical Garden. It is a federal endangered species and is quite rare even in prime habitat. Threats to its existence include habitat degradation and fire suppression. The genus *Nolina* is a taxonomic quagmire, having been placed in the Agavaceae, Asparagaceae, Convallariaceae, Dracaenaceae, Hyacinthaceae, and Nolinaceae families and now the Ruscaceae.

WATER PIMPERNEL
Samolus ebracteatus Kunth
Brookweed family (Samolaceae)

Description: The rosette of spoon-shaped, grayish-green, 1"–3" leaves with red veins makes this plant easy to identify when not in flower. The ⅜" flowers line the top portion of the erect spike.

Bloom Season: All year

Habitat/Range: Freshwater and brackish marshes, flatwoods, and marshes, from Gulf County and Volusia County south along both coasts into the Florida Keys

Comments: *Samolus* is of Celtic origin and is the name of a plant that grows in wet places and was used by Druids to treat diseases of cows and pigs. According to legend, to be effective the plants must be gathered with the left hand while fasting. The name *ebracteatus* means "without bracts." This species was described in 1818 from plants collected by botanist Karl Sigismund Kunth (1788–1850) in Cuba, where it is sometimes eaten as famine food. Seaside brookweed (*Samolus valerandi* ssp. *parviflorus*) has tiny flowers on nearly naked stems.

LIZARD'S TAIL
Saururus cernuus L.
Lizardstail family (Saururaceae)

Description: The stems are often bronze, and average 12"–18" tall with heart-shaped leaves that measure 4"–6" long and 1½"–2½" wide. The leaves are aromatic when crushed. The spikes of small, fragrant flowers arch to some degree.

Bloom Season: October to July

Habitat/Range: Freshwater wetlands throughout mainland Florida

Comments: *Saururus* is Greek for "lizard tail" and alludes to the shape of the inflorescence. The name *cernuus* means "drooping" or "nodding," in reference to the lax tip of the inflorescence. This species makes a wonderful addition to water gardens or if you have a propensity to overwater container plants. It spreads by rhizomes, and the flowers are attractive to butterflies and small bees. A cultivar in the nursery trade called Hertford Streaker has yellowish-white leaves and 2-toned green mottling in the center of each leaf blade.

GOATWEED
Capraria biflora L.
Figwort family (Scrophulariaceae)

Description: This somewhat shrubby herbaceous species averages 12"–36" tall, with alternate, narrowly lanceolate, coarsely-toothed leaves averaging ½"–2" long and ¼"–½" wide. Paired flowers emerge from the leaf axils and are about ½" wide.

Bloom Season: All year

Habitat/Range: Coastal strand, dunes, mangrove forests, salt marshes, and prairies from Lee and Martin Counties south into the Florida Keys (Monroe County)

Comments: *Capraria* means "nanny goat," but it is unclear how that name relates to this genus. Perhaps goats are fond of eating certain species. The name *biflora* relates to the paired flowers. It is used as a tea in the Caribbean to relieve high fever, colds, diarrhea, and vomiting and to cleanse the eyes and skin. On the Dutch island of Curaçao, a decoction of goatweed and *Heliotropium angiospermum* is given to infants but is now believed to contribute to throat and stomach cancer.

WEST INDIAN PINKROOT
Spigelia anthelmia L.
Strychnos family (Strychnaceae)

Description: Look for 4 opposite, prominently veined, nearly sessile leaves that reach up to 6" long and 3" wide, with 1 pair larger than the other. Terminal flower spikes bear tubular white flowers with pink, vertical lines. Each flower is about ⅜" long. The globose fruits are 2-lobed.

Bloom Season: March to November

Habitat/Range: Pinelands and coastal disturbed sites from Collier and Palm Beach Counties south to the Florida Keys

Comments: *Spigelia* honors Flemish anatomist and botanist Adriaan van den Spiegel (1578–1625), who latinized his name to Adrianus Spigelius. The name *anthelmia* means "to expel" and refers to its medicinal use to expel intestinal worms. The plant contains spigeline, which is effective against hookworms and tapeworms but is toxic if taken in quantity. The leaves can be fatal to grazing livestock. It is called worm-grass in the Caribbean.

FLORIDA PINKROOT
Spigelia loganioides (Torr. & A. Gray ex Endl. & Fenzl) A. DC.
Strychnos family (Strychnaceae)

Description: Florida pinkroot reaches 5"–10" tall with the oblanceolate lowermost leaves reaching about ⅜"–¾" long. The upper leaves are lanceolate to elliptic and measure 1¼"–1⅝" long and half as wide. The ⅜" white flowers have 5 triangular lobes, sometimes with pale violet lines.

Bloom Season: March to June

Habitat/Range: Endemic to seasonally wet forests of Hernando, Lake, Levy, Marion, Sumter, and Volusia Counties

Comments: The name *loganioides* alludes to the resemblance to a species of *Logania* (Loganiaceae). The type specimen of this state-listed endangered species was collected in Marion County in 1845. This plant family is most famous for members of the genus *Strychnos* that produce lethally poisonous strychnine and curare. Indigenous people of the tropical Americas use curare as a paralyzing arrow poison.

SOUTHERN BOG ASPHODEL

Tofieldia racemosa (Walter) Britton, et al.
False Asphodel family (Tofieldiaceae)

Description: A basal rosette of narrowly linear, lily-like leaves appear in spring and average about 10"–12" long. An erect scape reaches about 24" tall and is topped by a raceme of 6-petaled, ½" flowers.

Bloom Season: June to October

Habitat/Range: Pine savannas and bogs across the Florida panhandle from Escambia County east to Jefferson County; also Columbia, Baker, and Nassau Counties in northeastern Florida

Comments: *Tofieldia* was described as a genus in 1778 to honor British botanist Thomas Tofield (1730–1779), as does the family Tofieldiaceae. The name *racemosa* refers to the raceme of flowers. It is also called coastal false asphodel. British-American botanist Thomas Walter (1740–1789) first described this species as *Melanthium racemosum* in 1788, and it was placed in the Lily family (Liliaceae). A 2011 revision favors placing this species in the genus *Triantha*.

HEARTLEAF NETTLE

Urtica chamaedryoides Pursh
Nettle family (Urticaceae)

Description: The opposite, heart-shaped, coarsely toothed leaves measure 1"–3" long to ¾"–1¼" wide and are covered with stinging hairs (as are the stems). It typically reaches 6"–12" tall, with small white flowers clustered in the leaf axils.

Bloom Season: February to August

Habitat/Range: Deciduous woods from Jackson and Calhoun Counties east to Duval County and south to Lee, Polk, Osceola, and Brevard Counties

Comments: *Urtica* is the Latin name for stinging nettle. The name *chamaedryoides* refers to its resemblance to a species of *Chamaedrys* (Lamiaceae). All members of this genus have stinging hairs; some are so virulent they can cause death. It was stated in the *Journal of the Columbus Horticultural Society* that *Urtica urentissima* "stings so fearfully that the inflammation lasts a whole year." There are topical creams that will help alleviate the burning.

SOUTHERN FOGFRUIT

Lippia stoechadifolia (L.) Kunth
Verbena family (Verbenaceae)

Description: This species can reach 24" tall, with erect or arching stems lined with opposite, toothed, linear-lanceolate leaves that measure ¾"–2" long and to about ⅜" wide. Tiny white flowers turn pinkish violet with age and are arranged in a circle around a stalked, axillary head.

Bloom Season: All year

Habitat/Range: Freshwater wetlands of Collier, Broward, and Miami-Dade Counties

Comments: *Lippia* honors French-Italian naturalist and botanist Augustus Lippi (1678–1705), who was killed in Abyssinia. The name *stoechadifolia* is for the resemblance of the leaves to *Lavendula stoechos* (Lamiaceae). This is a larval host plant of the white peacock and phaeon crescent butterflies. The common name apparently refers to the plant's habit of growing in low, wet areas where fog settles, but the name is sometimes corrupted as "frogfruit." It is a state-listed endangered species.

CAPEWEED

Phyla nodiflora (L.) Greene
(Also *Lippia nodiflora* [L.] Michx.)
Verbena family (Verbenaceae)

Description: This mat-forming species has coarsely toothed, opposite leaves to 1" long and ⅜" wide. The flower head is rounded when young, becoming cylindrical with age. The flowers are ⅛" wide, opening white and turning pinkish violet.

Bloom Season: All year

Habitat/Range: A variety of habitats including lawns and roadsides throughout Florida

Comments: *Phyla* is Greek for "clan" or "tribe," alluding to the tight head of flowers. The name *nodiflora* means "knotted," also alluding to the flower head. The flowers are a popular nectar source for butterflies, and the leaves serve as larval food for the white peacock and phaon crescent butterflies. Although the species is regarded as a weed by those who like lawns, it makes an excellent substitute for lawn grasses. It is also called creeping charlie.

CAROLINA FALSE VERVAIN
Stylodon carneum (Medik.) Moldenke
(Also *Verbena carnea* Medik.)
Verbena family (Verbenaceae)

Description: Flowering plants of this species are often about 10"–14" tall but may reach 24"–36" in height. The square stems are covered with glandular hairs and are lined with opposite, lanceolate, sessile leaves that measure 1½"–3½" long, becoming smaller up the stem. The white, 5-lobed, ⅜" flowers have a pink corolla tube.

Bloom Season: March to July

Habitat/Range: Sandhills and dry, open forests south in Florida to Pasco, Polk, and Martin Counties

Comments: *Stylodon* is Greek for "pillar" and "tooth." The name *carneum* means "flesh-colored" and refers to the pink corolla tubes. German physician and botanist Friedrich Kasimir Medikus (1738–1808) described this species when he was the director of the University of Mannheim in Germany.

BOG WHITE VIOLET
Viola lanceolata L.
Violet family (Violaceae)

Description: The leaves of this violet are linear lanceolate and vary from 1"–6" long and ⅛"–⅜" wide. Flower stalks surpass the leaves and are topped by a solitary, ⅜" flower with conspicuous purple veins on the lower petal.

Bloom Season: December to August

Habitat/Range: Wet flatwoods, bogs, and marshes throughout mainland Florida

Comments: *Viola* is the classical Latin name for a violet. The name *lanceolata* refers to the lance-shaped leaves. Violets have been cultivated for their beauty and fragrance for more than 2,000 years and were once highly regarded as medicinal plants to cure gout, insomnia, epilepsy, pleurisy, and other maladies. The floral scent is "flirty" because when it is inhaled, compounds in the fragrance can temporarily keep it from being detected by the human nose again until the olfactory nerves recover. It is a larval host plant of the variegated fritillary butterfly.

PRIMROSELEAF VIOLET

Viola primulifolia L.
Violet family (Violaceae)

Description: The variable leaves of this species range from ovate to reniform (kidney-shaped) in outline, usually with distinct petioles, and average ¾"–1" wide. They also vary from glabrous to shaggy pubescent. The flower stalk usually surpasses the leaves and is topped by a single ⅜" flower.

Bloom Season: February to June

Habitat/Range: Wet flatwoods, bogs, and marshes throughout most of Florida south to Palm Beach and Collier Counties

Comments: The name *primulifolia* relates to the similarity of the leaves to those of a primrose (Primulaceae). This is an inhabitant of open, wet ground throughout central Florida. Although the flowers are similar to the previous species, the leaves are much different. Most botanists treat this as a distinct species, but some regard it as a fertile hybrid between *Viola lanceolata* and *Viola macloskeyi* (*Viola* x *primulifolia*).

CAROLINA YELLOWEYED GRASS

Xyris caroliniana Walter
Yelloweyed Grass family (Xyridaceae)

Description: The twisted, narrowly linear leaves are erect or ascending and measure 8"–20" long and ⅛"–¼" wide. The base of the sheath is chestnut brown. The flowering stems of this species are typically exceeded in height by the leaves. The flowers measure ½"–⅝" wide

Bloom Season: May to November

Habitat/Range: Flatwoods, sandhills, and scrub throughout Florida, including the Florida Keys

Comments: *Xyris* is Greek for "razor," in reference to the 2-edged leaves. The name *caroliniana* means "of Carolina." The petals of most species unfold in the morning, but those of this species open later in the day. This genus is taxonomically difficult, especially for novice wildflower enthusiasts, so pay close attention to leaf shapes and flower size. These species are seldom cultivated but would make interesting garden subjects.

GLOSSARY

Achene—a small, dry, one-seeded fruit.

Capsule—a dry, indehiscent fruit that releases seeds through splits or holes.

Column—the structure in the center of an orchid flower formed by the fusion of the stigma, style, and stamens.

Corm—the enlarged, fleshy base of a stem; tuber-like.

Deciduous—leafless at the end of the growing season.

Endemic—a native species restricted to a given area or region.

Epiphyte, epiphytic—growing on another plant as with many ferns, orchids, bromeliads, and mosses; not a parasite.

Hydroperiod—the length of time a habitat is flooded

Inflorescence—the flower cluster of a plant, or the disposition of the flowers on an axis.

Midrib—central leaf vein, often raised.

Neotropics—the region encompassing the West Indies (Bahamas), Mexico, Central America, and tropical South America.

Node—point of origin of leaves on a stem.

Pod—a dry fruit that splits open along the sides.

Pollinia—a sticky mass of pollen transported as a whole during pollination, especially in the Orchid family (Orchidaceae).

Pseudobulb—the thickened, aboveground stem of certain orchids.

Rachis—the primary axis of an inflorescence or a pinnately-compound leaf.

Revolute—having the edge curled under.

Rhizome—creeping, underground, horizontal stem.

Scape—a leafless flower stalk arising near ground level.

Spadix—a spike of flowers on a succulent axis enveloped by a spathe.

Spathe—a broad, sheath-like bract enveloping a spadix.

Stalk—as used here, the stem supporting the leaf or flower cluster.

Tepals—parts of a flower not clearly differentiated into petals and sepals, as in lilies.

Type—the specimen on which the description and name of a new species is based.

RESOURCES

To view native wildflowers in their natural habitats, the reader is encouraged to visit state and national parks, forests, and preserves throughout Florida. To learn more about wildflowers native to Florida, contact your local conservation organizations.

The Florida Native Plant Society has chapters throughout the state. These are diverse groups of amateur and professional plant enthusiasts organized to share information about the study, conservation, and propagation of plants native to their regions. For information about a chapter near you, visit fnps.org and join in on conferences, lectures, native-plant sales, raffles, newsletters, field trips, and more.

Other conservation organizations also host educational meetings and offer guided field trips. Rangers and naturalist volunteers offer guided field trips in many of Florida's parks and preserves.

AUDUBON OF FLORIDA
fl.audubon.org

FLORIDA DEPARTMENT OF ENVIRONMENTAL PROTECTION
dep.state.fl.us

FLORIDA STATE PARKS, FORESTS, AND PRESERVES
floridastateparks.org

FLORIDA TRAIL ASSOCIATION
floridatrail.org

FLORIDA WILDFLOWER FOUNDATION
flawildflowers.org

NATIONAL PARKS, FORESTS, AND PRESERVES
nps.gov/state/fl/index.htm

THE NATURE CONSERVANCY
nature.org

SIERRA CLUB OF FLORIDA
sierraclub.org/florida

INDEX

ABOUT THE AUTHOR

Roger L. Hammer is a professional naturalist and survivalist instructor for the Discovery Channel's reality television show *Naked and Afraid*. He grew up in Cocoa Beach and served in the US Army from 1965 to 1968 as a tank gunner and education specialist. He spent thirty-three years as the manager of the 120-acre Castellow Hammock Nature Center for the Miami-Dade County Parks Department. He received the first Marjory Stoneman Douglas Award presented by the Dade Chapter of the Florida Native Plant Society in 1982, the Tropical Audubon Society honored him with the prestigious Charles Brookfield Medal in 1996, and in 2003 he received the Green Palmetto Award in Education from the Florida Native Plant Society. He has given keynote speeches at Florida Native Plant Society state conferences, the 2008 World Orchid Conference, and the 2016 Florida Wildflower Foundation symposium. In 2012 he received an honorary Doctor of Science degree from Florida International University and a lifetime achievement award from the Florida Native Plant Society, Tropical Audubon Society, and the North American Butterfly Association.

Roger is an avid long-distance solo canoeist, kayak-fishing enthusiast, wildflower photographer, and connoisseur of expensive rums. He is also the author of *Florida Keys*

Wildflowers (Globe Pequot, 2004), *Florida Icons: 50 Classic Views of the Sunshine State* (Globe Pequot, 2011), *Everglades Wildflowers*, second edition (Rowman & Littlefield, 2014), *Exploring Everglades National Park and the Surrounding Area*, second edition (Rowman & Littlefield, 2015), *Central Florida Wildflowers* (Rowman & Littlefield, 2016) and *Attracting Hummingbirds and Butterflies in Tropical Florida* (University Press of Florida, 2015). He lives with his wife, Michelle, in Homestead, Florida.

For more information about the author, visit rogerlhammer.com